W9-BJN-554

FINANCIAL INSTITUTIONS

Financial institutions

Peter S. Rose
Donald R. Fraser

both of
Texas A&M University

1980

BUSINESS PUBLICATIONS, INC.
Dallas, Texas 75243

Irwin-Dorsey Limited
Georgetown, Ontario   L7G 4B3

ISBN 0-256-02205-4
Library of Congress Catalog Card No. 79–53968

Printed in the United States of America

1 2 3 4 5 6 7 8 9 0 MP 7 6 5 4 3 2 1 0

To Kandy, Lyn, Eleanor,
Jason, Michael, and Robbie

Preface

This book has been designed for use in undergraduate and beginning graduate courses dealing with the management of financial institutions. It may also be used as supplemental material in money and banking, money and capital markets, and financial markets courses. It has purposely been designed so that there are few necessary prerequisites for the student to be able to follow the discussion. The use of mathematical formulas is sparing, while numerous exhibits serve to reinforce major points covered in each chapter. Where needed, additional exposition of concepts underlying the discussion has been incorporated in explanatory footnotes. Questions suitable for discussion or testing follow each chapter and serve as a guide for reviewing the key points. In addition, problems for class discussion follow selected chapters.

The book has been written from the conviction that a student should not only be familiar with the framework of the financial system and the role that financial institutions play in that system but also should be able to view financial institutions from an internal, managerial perspective. All students play a role in the financial system and many pursue careers as managers of commercial banks, savings associations, insurance companies, and other financial intermediaries. In order to better understand the role of financial institutions in the economy of the nation, it is necessary to understand the principles which are relevant to the management of these institutions. Conversely, in order to effectively manage financial institutions it is necessary to understand their role in the economic and financial system. It is thus the conviction of the authors that a blend of internal and external perspectives is the appropriate approach to understanding financial institutions.

We have attempted to blend these perspectives in this book by first setting forth a general description of the objectives of financial institutions and the decision variables which management should concentrate upon in achieving its objectives. This general model is then applied to each major financial institution active in the U.S. economy. Moreover, Chapters 8–12 and 14–17 are followed by problems for class discussion, each of which incorporate a particular problem facing the management of the institution. The student should use the material in the chapters as the beginning point for the discussion of these problems.

Throughout the book we have attempted to emphasize the enormous changes which are taking place today in the nation's financial system and in the role of individual financial institutions. Chapters dealing with individual financial institutions contain a discussion of recent trends affecting that particular institution. The last two chapters of the book are devoted to the element of change in the regulation and operation of financial institutions and the financial system. While it is impossible to anticipate all significant developments, the student should be aware of these profound changes which are influencing career opportunities in the field and the role of the institutions themselves.

Acknowledgments

We are grateful to Ivan T. Call (Brigham Young University), Eugene F. Drzycimski (University of Wisconsin–Oshkosh), Morgan J. Lynge, Jr. (University of Illinois at Urbana), and Robert D. Mettlen (University of Texas–Austin) for their careful reading and numerous editorial suggestions on an earlier draft of the manuscript. Linda Hoelscher and Connie Cadenhead typed the final manuscript and helped greatly in making the many necessary last-minute corrections before the manuscript was ready for delivery. Naturally all errors that remain are the sole responsibility of the authors. Finally, we would like to express our deepest appreciation to our families for their understanding and encouragement during the many months in which this book was in preparation.

December 1979   Peter S. Rose
                                                    Donald R. Fraser

Contents

risk and return. Market risk. Aggresiveness of management. Other factors. Conclusions.

The purpose of capital. What is bank capital? *Capital trends.* Measures of capital adequacy. Evaluation of alternative means of raising capital.

section three
Nonbank financial institutions

The savings and loan association. The structure of the savings and loan industry. Sources and uses of funds for savings and loans: *Uses of funds. Sources of funds. Earnings, dividends, and expenses of savings and loans.* Regulation of savings and loans: *The future of the savings and loan industry.* Mutual savings banks. Structure of the industry. *Sources of funds. Uses of funds.* Growth of the industry: *Revenues, expenses, and taxes.* Conclusions.

The structure of the credit union industry: *Type of membership. Concentration of assets. Operating structure of credit unions.* Services provided by credit unions. Regulatory structure. Loan, investment, and deposit powers: *Deposit insurance.* Taxation of credit unions. Credit union portfolios: *Investments in securities and cash. Share capital and other funds sources. Revenues and expenses. Dividends and interest refunds.* Credit unions in the future.

Life insurance services. The investment process for life companies. Growth of life insurance companies: Principal sources of funds. Principal uses of funds: *Government securities. Corporate stock. Corporate debt securities. Mortgages. Other investments. Earnings and taxes.* Regulation. Structure of the industry. Conclusions.

Structure of the industry. Insurance services offered by property-casualty companies. Funds flows for property-casualty companies. *Allocation of funds by property-casualty insurers. Funds received by property-casualty insurers.* Regulation and taxation of property-casualty insurers. Recent developments in the industry.

Characteristics of pension funds. Factors which influence pension fund investment policies. Pension fund investments: *Private pension funds. State and local government pension funds. Federal government pension funds.* ERISA. Future trends.

section

I

Functions of financial intermediaries in the financial system

1

Role of financial intermediaries in the economy

This is a book about the behavior and characteristics of *financial intermediaries* in the American economy. These institutions are vitally important to the economic well-being and future growth of a market-oriented economy such as ours. As we will discuss in this and subsequent chapters, financial intermediaries receive approximately four fifths of all savings dollars generated each year in the U.S. financial system. The liabilities of financial intermediaries are the principal means for making payments for goods and services and their loans are the chief source of credit for all economic units in society—businesses, households, and governments. Moreover, the nature of individual financial institutions has been changing rapidly in recent years. For all of these reasons an understanding of the lending and borrowing activities, the portfolio behavior, the management policies, and the regulatory environment of financial intermediaries is essential for every serious student of the economic and financial system.

This book will acquaint the student with all the major types of financial intermediaries. We will focus in turn upon commercial banks, savings and loan associations, mutual savings banks, credit unions, finance companies, life insurance companies, property-casualty insurance companies, pension funds, investment companies, and other financial institutions. We will examine closely the role of these institutions in the financial markets and the contribution each makes to the proper functioning of the economic and financial system. Our perspective will be that of the manager seeking to understand the role of each financial institution in the nation's financial system and to understand the unique management problems faced by all financial institutions today.

THE NATURE OF FINANCIAL INTERMEDIATION

Financial intermediaries acquire the IOUs issued by borrowers—primary securities—and at the same time sell their own IOUs—secondary securities—to savers. A commercial bank, for example, is happy to accept your checking or savings account which, from your point of view, is a financial asset. To the banker it is debt—a secondary security—which can be used to make loans and investments by accepting primary securities (IOUs) from borrowers. The major types of financial intermediaries active in the United States are commercial banks, credit unions, mutual savings banks, savings and loan associations, life insurance companies, property and casualty insurance companies, investment companies, finance companies, pension funds, real estate investment trusts, leasing companies, and mortgage companies. All make heavy use of financial liabilities to attract savings and invest principally in financial assets in the form of borrower IOUs.

Financial intermediaries meet the financial needs of both savers and borrowers. (See Figure 1–1.) The majority of savers in the U.S. economy today have very limited financial resources and desire financial assets with very special characteristics. They desire *safety* (or minimal risk of borrower default) and *convenience*. Safety is promoted by strict regulation of financial institutions in the United States, especially regulation of the type and quality of loans made and the adequacy of equity capital invested in each institution. In the case of deposits in commercial banks, credit unions, savings and loan associations, and mutual savings banks the federal government insures the public against loss of its deposits up to $40,000 in the event the institution fails. Reflecting the desire of savers for convenience, many financial intermediaries have established branch offices in easy-to-reach locations, staying open long hours, and many also offer save-by-mail services. Savers, especially the smaller ones, also require financial assets that are *accessible*—that is, available in small denominations.[1] For example, the smallest denomination in which

---

[1] Another term frequently used in the finance literature to describe this feature is "divisibility." Middle- and low-income savers require financial instruments which are "divisible" into small denominations.

FIGURE 1-1
Nature of the financial intermediation process

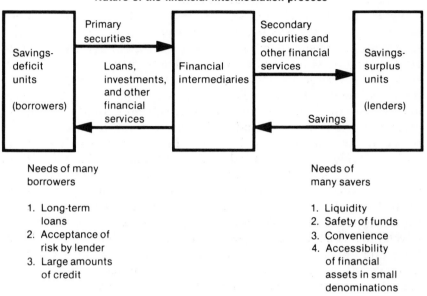

Needs of many
borrowers

1. Long-term
   loans
2. Acceptance of
   risk by lender
3. Large amounts
   of credit

Needs of
many savers

1. Liquidity
2. Safety of funds
3. Convenience
4. Accessibility
   of financial
   assets in small
   denominations

U.S. Treasury bills are sold today is $10,000, an amount beyond the reach of many savers. In contrast, a savings account may be opened at a commercial bank, savings and loan association, credit union, or mutual savings bank for as little as $5 or $10. Finally, many low- and middle-income savers look for *liquidity* in their savings. A financial asset is liquid if it can be converted into cash quickly with little or no loss in value. Certainly, savings accounts at commercial banks, savings and loan associations, credit unions, and mutual savings banks are liquid as are insurance policies which carry cash surrender values.

In contrast to the needs of savers, borrowers frequently issue liabilities with unique characteristics. They may require large amounts of funds for a long period of time (maturity). In addition, borrower IOUs may entail substantial risk of nonpayment (default). It is obvious that some of these features would be unacceptable to a saver interested in safety, convenience, accessibility, and liquidity. By issuing secondary securities to savers that are safe, convenient, liquid, and accessible, and at the same time accepting the primary securities of borrowers, financial intermediaries perform an indispensable function in the nation's economy. This intermediation process encourages saving, especially from those of limited means, and makes for a more optimal and efficient allocation of financial resources. It provides for the simultaneous satisfaction of businesses, households, and governmental units with fundamentally different interests by transforming the nature of financial claims available in the nation's money and capital markets.

Financial intermediaries actually perform several different kinds of intermediation. *Denomination intermediation* occurs when intermediaries accept small amounts of savings from individuals and others and pool these funds to make large loans, principally to corporations and governments. *Default-risk intermediation* refers to the willingness of financial intermediaries to make loans to risky borrowers and, at the same time, to issue relatively safe and liquid securities in order to attract loanable funds from savers. *Maturity intermediation* refers to the practice used by many intermediaries of borrowing comparatively short-term funds from savers and making long-term loans to borrowers who require a lengthy commitment of funds. *Information intermediation* refers to the process by which financial intermediaries substitute their skill in the marketplace for that of the saver who frequently has neither the time to stay abreast of market developments nor access to relevant information about market conditions and opportunities. Intermediaries also engage in *risk pooling* and take advantage of *economies of scale* in their activities. By investing in assets with a wide variety of risk-return characteristics, the benefits of financial diversification—greater stability in earnings and cash flow—are achieved, enhancing the safety of funds supplied by savers. As the intermediary increases in size, its operating costs per unit may decline which can lower the cost of financial services to customers.[2]

Financial intermediaries may be classified into different groups, depending upon the purposes of the analyst, policymaker, or researcher. One of the most important distinctions is between *depository intermediaries*, such as commercial banks, credit unions, mutual savings banks, and savings and loan associations and *contractual intermediaries*, including insurance companies and pension funds.[3] The former accept deposits from the public and are the principal repository of liquid savings in the economy. The timing and amount of savings placed with or withdrawn from a commercial bank, savings bank, or credit union is frequently not set by a rigid schedule or subject to elaborate contractual rules. Rather, the saver deposits or withdraws funds with little or no notice and in the amounts the saver chooses. In contrast, the amount and timing of saving through a contractual intermediary usually is specified in or by a contractual

---

[2] For a more complete discussion of these concepts see Kaufman [12], chap. 4; Van Horne [15], chap. 1; and Brill [3].

[3] See especially Brill [3] for a discussion of the distinctions between depository and contractual intermediaries.

agreement between the saver and the financial institution. This is particularly evident in the case of insurance companies where the policyholder (saver) must make periodic premium payments in order to keep a policy in force and provide adequate financial protection. Retirement income plans available through pension funds and life insurance companies also clearly are forms of saving by contract. Quite obviously, cash inflows and outflows of contractual intermediaries are more easily predicted, generally permitting these institutions to minimize short-term, liquid investments and reach for longer-term investment assets with higher yields.

ANALYZING THE BEHAVIOR OF FINANCIAL INTERMEDIARIES

Financial intermediaries are business firms organized and operated to achieve certain goals. A financial intermediary shares many basic characteristics common to all business firms. It uses inputs—land, labor, capital, and management skills—to produce units of output which customers demand. The intermediary, like any other business firm, contributes organization (or structure) to the production process, providing a location and a framework within which labor and capital can be combined with other resources to produce a product—financial services of various kinds.

Actually, the operation of a financial intermediary is more complex than for most business firms. As noted by Professor Haywood [11] in a recent research study, the intermediary possesses a *two-stage production process*. (See Figure 1–2.) Inputs in the form of land, labor, capital, and management skills are first applied to stage one—the sources-of-funds stage—where savings are attracted by offering interest-bearing deposits, insurance policies, safety deposit boxes, pension plans, and thousands of other financial services desired by the public. Then, once the intermediary puts aside a certain portion of its incoming funds in cash reserves to meet short-run demands for cash, the remaining funds (called "loanable funds") go into stage two of the institution's production process—the uses-of-funds stage—where the main activity is the making of loans and other kinds of investments. In order to provide financial services in a competitive environment and to earn a satisfactory return on invested capital, the intermediary applies land, labor, capital, and other resources to produce the maximum volume of output of financial services at the lowest possible cost.

Two fundamentally different questions must be dealt with by the management of a financial intermediary in these two stages of pro-

FIGURE 1–2
The financial intermediary as a firm

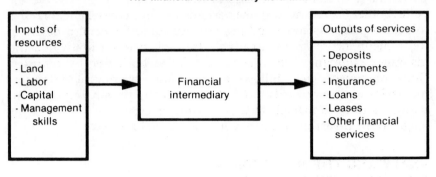

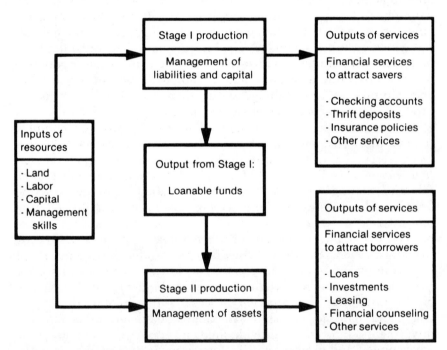

Source: Adapted from Charles F. Haywood, "Production of Consumer Financial Services," *Public Regulation of Financial Services, Costs and Benefits to Consumers,* phase I, interim report (Cambridge, Mass.: ABT Associates, Inc., 1977), vol. 1. This material is based upon research supported by the National Science Foundation under Contract No. NSF-C76-18548. Any opinions, findings, and conclusions or recommendations expressed in this publication are those of the author and do not necessarily reflect the views of the National Science Foundation.

duction. In stage one, the sources-of-funds stage, the problem is to raise funds from savers at the lowest possible cost—that is, by offering the lowest rates of return necessary to attract the public's funds. Management must decide what *mix* of funds sources will result in the lowest overall cost of funds raised. In stage two, the uses-of-funds stage, the problem is quite different. Management seeks that combination of loans and other assets resulting in the highest overall rate of return to the intermediary consistent with regulations and other goals of the institution. In this sense the principal objective of stage one is minimum cost and that of stage two, maximum return. Necessarily, though, these two stages are interrelated, and decisions made in one stage will affect decisions made in the other.

The goals of financial intermediaries are multidimensional. Some seek a larger share of the local market for savings, loans, and investments—that is, they try to be a bigger organization relative to their competitors. Others define their primary objectives as growth and service to the public. The more aggressive institutions emphasize maximization of the wealth of their shareholders or pursue the related goal of maximizing profits.

In pursuing its goals the management of a financial intermediary must consider five major areas of decision making (see Figure 1–3):

1. Management of assets (principally loans and securities).
2. Management of liabilities.
3. Management of capital (or net worth).
4. Expense control.
5. Marketing policy.

In the management of assets, liabilities, and capital, financial institutions must be especially conscious of the gap between the yields on their assets and the returns paid to savers for the loan of both debt and equity capital. While the intermediary will try to offer the lowest returns possible to savers and lend funds to borrowers at the highest possible interest rates, it will be limited in its ability to do so by *competition* from other financial institutions operating in the same markets for financial services. Indeed, competitive forces in conjunction with economic and financial conditions may temporarily result in a *negative* differential between yields earned by the intermediary on its assets and the returns it pays to savers. Under normal circumstances, however, yields earned by the intermediary on assets will exceed the rates paid savers to attract funds, resulting in a *positive* differential between revenues and costs. Indeed, such a positive differential must exist over the longer term for the financial institution to remain viable and keep its doors open. Management must be constantly alert to opportunities to increase the differential between

FIGURE 1–3
Areas for management decision making and the goals of a financial intermediary

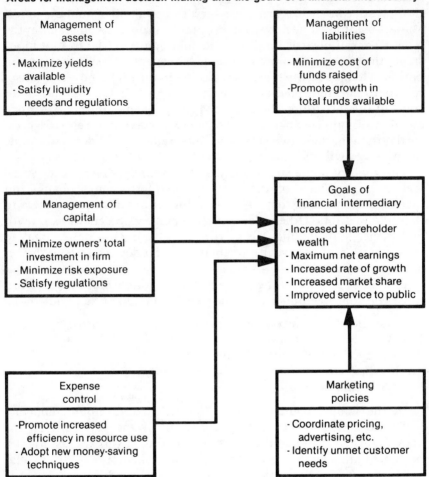

revenues and costs by reducing costs (such as by taking advantage of advances in technology, increasing the organization's size, or improving internal operating efficiency) and identifying new sources of revenue (such as by developing new services or penetrating new markets).

Management of assets, liabilities, and capital is also related to the degree of risk assumed by the individual institution. Indeed, the ability to appraise the relative return and risk characteristics of different financial instruments is essential to the successful management of a financial intermediary. There are two major kinds of risk of importance to a financial institution. One is the risk of a "cash-out"—of being illiquid when cash is needed. A financial institution is liquid if it can meet the demands for cash made upon it—principally from creditors and from good customers who need loans—precisely at the time cash is demanded. Different kinds of assets vary dramatically in their liquidity (or ability to be converted quickly into cash with little risk of loss). Moreover, the need for liquidity varies significantly among different financial institutions, depending primarily on the stability and predictability of their sources of funds.

The second major kind of risk which must be considered by the individual financial institution is the risk of insolvency, which is simply the inability to cover the intermediary's debts in the long run. If the market value of a financial institution's assets is less than the value of its aggregate liabilities, technically the institution is insolvent. Assets bearing greater default and market risk increase the probability that the institution will become insolvent. Similarly, liabilities whose amount and timing are more volatile and uncertain increase the risk that the institution's assets, when liquidated, will be inadequate to meet all legitimate demands for return of funds to the institution's creditors. There is a "trade-off" between the solvency and profitability of a financial institution. The highest-yielding assets generally carry the greatest risk of default, even though they also offer maximum expected earnings. Management must carefully steer a course which maximizes returns to the intermediary's owners, yet protects and preserves the fundamental solvency of the financial institution.

The risk of insolvency makes another area of financial institutions' management—the management of capital or net worth—especially important. In general, the institution's owners would prefer to keep net worth, which is an expensive source of capital, at minimal levels in order to permit maximum use of financial *leverage*. Leverage is the use of relatively fixed-cost sources of funds (principally debt) in order to increase returns to the firm's shareholders. While management desires to use maximum financial leverage, it must be careful that high levels of leverage, mainly through heavy use of debt as opposed to equity funds, does not so increase the institution's risk exposure as to substantially raise its cost of funds and increase the likelihood of its failure.

Control of expenses also is important to protecting or increasing the profitability of a financial intermediary. In fact, expense control is the most important discriminating factor between profitable and unprofitable financial institutions. Until the mid-1960s salaries and wages were generally the largest expense item for a financial institution, especially for commercial banks and nonbank thrift institutions which accept the public's deposits. At that point, however, competition across industry lines began to intensify as one type of financial intermediary increasingly came into direct competition with another. For example, commercial banks found themselves in direct competition with savings and loan associations and credit unions for deposits. Insurance companies, mutual funds, and pension funds found themselves in direct competition for the available supply of long-term savings. At the same time the public was becoming more and more financially sophisticated, demanding a greater rate of return on its savings, especially with the appearance of severe inflation during the 1960s and 1970s.

These forces combined to send the cost of raising funds to the highest levels in the 20th century. Indeed, so rapid was the escalation of interest rates during certain periods—especially 1966, 1969, and 1973–74—that these periods have been labeled "credit crunches" because of the sharply reduced availability of and high cost of loanable funds. In this kind of environment financial intermediaries were compelled to offer substantially higher yields in order to attract savings.[4] The result was that expenses associated with borrowed funds soon dominated all other costs.

Since interest costs are largely exogenous to the individual financial institution (i.e., are determined in the regional or national market for savings), management has been forced to find other ways of cutting down on expenses. Automation has entered the industry, principally through the use of computers to process financial data and store and retrieve information important to management. At the same time, as we shall see in later chapters, a consolidation movement toward larger, but smaller numbers of financial intermediaries is occurring. In several industries—savings and loan associations, credit unions, mutual savings banks, life and property-casualty insurance companies, finance companies, and others—the number of firms is declining through mergers and consolidations. Not surprisingly, the median size institution in each of these industries has been on the rise. To the extent that economies of scale exist in each instance, the unit production costs of providing important financial services has fallen as a partial offset to the growing cost of attracting funds from the public. Most experts argue that these trends toward financial

---

[4] Some financial institutions, especially the deposit type, were unable to offer adequate returns to savers during these periods, due either to the slow turnover of their assets or to legally imposed interest-rate ceilings or both. As a result, their more financially sophisticated customers simply withdrew their funds and bought securities available in the open market, generally earning higher yields. Commercial banks and savings and loan associations as a group lost billions of dollars in deposits due to such withdrawals. This phenomenon is usually called *disintermediation* since savings are withdrawn from the intermediation process, changing the direction (but not necessarily the magnitude) of credit flows in the economy.

institutions of larger and larger size will continue and that expense control will become one of the most critical aspects of financial institutions' management in the years ahead.[5]

The final area of importance to financial institutions' management concerns marketing policies, including the pricing of financial services offered to the public. Financial institutions are more marketing oriented today than at any time in their past history. There is a greater emphasis today on researching customer needs and targeting specific markets for the advertising of new financial services.[6] The use of marketing research tools imposes the discipline of the marketplace upon every aspect of a financial intermediary's operations, especially on the making of loans and attracting the public's savings. Advertising, customer relations, prices of financial services, and the location of office facilities all must be coordinated to reach customers and meet their needs conveniently and efficiently. A good marketing strategy demands that each financial institution state its goals in measurable terms, formulate short- and long-range plans, and continuously research the needs and requirements of its customers.[7]

Of course, in pursuing their goals, financial intermediaries are not completely free to behave as they choose. Acquisitions of loans, investments, and savings, management of capital, the territorial expansion of the institution, and sometimes both prices charged and interest rates paid are closely regulated by government. Financial intermediaries are thought to be of special importance to the welfare of society and to the health of the economy since they attract and hold the public's savings and are the principal source of its credit. An almost bewildering array of federal and state government laws and

---

[5] As we shall see later, the cost squeeze which financial intermediaries have endured in recent years also has stimulated management to *diversify* the package of financial services offered. For example, credit unions, which historically have dealt only in savings deposits and made relatively short-term loans to individuals and families, now find themselves in many cases offering check-type deposits and financial counseling, selling credit-related insurance, offering home mortgage credit, and assisting in the purchase of mutual funds shares. Similar types of diversification have entered the savings and loan, savings banking, and commercial banking industries. These changes represent an attempt by individual financial institutions to utilize existing management more efficiently and to open up new markets in order to increase revenues and offset rising costs.

[6] The spread of marketing techniques among financial intermediaries has been accelerated by the cost-earnings squeeze and the resulting reduction in profit margins discussed earlier. The growth of branching activity, the penetration of international markets by the largest intermediaries (especially commercial banks), and the spread of consumerism and social responsibility legislation also have contributed to an increased emphasis on marketing strategies.

[7] A goal of "increased growth," for example, is probably too vague for management planning purposes. To specify, however, that the institution wishes to increase its growth rate in total assets or sales from 8 percent to 10 percent a year gives management a target to shoot at and a way of measuring the institution's progress.

regulations have been built up over the years (especially during and after the Great Depression of the 1930s) in an attempt to ensure that intermediaries protect the public interest in their management decisions and operations.

A few examples of laws and regulations which restrict the activities of financial intermediaries may help to clarify the importance of the legal and regulatory factor in financial institutions' management. For example, savings and loan associations, in order to qualify for special federal tax concessions, must devote a majority of their assets to residential mortgage loans. Except for U.S. government securities and cash, savings and loans are granted few other outlets for their funds. Similarly, insurance companies and mutual savings banks in the management of their funds must follow the so-called *prudent man* rule. These intermediaries must confine their acquisitions of financial assets to those that a prudent investor would purchase (typically a security of BAA rating or higher). The influence of tax laws may be seen most dramatically in commercial bank purchases of state and local government securities (municipals). Commercial banks have dominated this market as buyers during the postwar period, principally because interest income from municipal securities is exempt from federal income taxation. Because commercial banks are subject to the same federal corporate income tax rates as are nonfinancial corporations, they find municipals an extremely attractive use of their funds. Therefore, to fully understand the management practices of financial institutions we need information concerning (1) the general principles of asset, liability, and capital management; (2) the sources and uses of funds received by each institution; (3) the level and nature of competition in each industry; (4) the current state of technology and the prospects for technological change; and (5) a knowledge of the laws and regulations which apply to individual financial institutions.

THE PLAN OF THIS BOOK

Before proceeding with our discussion of the vastly important role of financial institutions in the economy, it is appropriate to pause and look at a road map of where we are going. This text combines a substantial volume of descriptive material and analysis to give the reader as complete a picture as possible concerning the functions and behavior of all major kinds of financial institutions. However, the chapters emphasize not facts and figures, but the application of the principles of financial management to individual financial intermediaries. These principles, hopefully, will serve readers well as they deal with financial intermediaries in their daily life and, in some cases, become employees of financial institutions and build careers in this field. In short, the book attempts both to discuss the role of each major financial institution in the financial system and also to illustrate principles of financial management for individual institutions and their application to particular decision situations.

In order to accomplish these goals, however, a conceptual framework with which to analyze the functions of each major financial institution is needed. This is the basic purpose of Section I of the text. This section (which includes Chapters 1–5) examines the place of individual financial institutions within the financial system. The Flow of Funds Accounts of the Federal Reserve System are used to provide an overview of the sources and uses of funds at individual financial intermediaries as well as a brief explanation of why each intermediary possesses a unique mix of sources and uses of funds. Section I also includes a brief discussion of the major instruments of the money and capital markets that are important to financial institutions management and a discussion of how the yields (rates of interest) on money and capital market instruments are determined. The section concludes with an explanation of the role of government—specifically the Federal Reserve System and the U.S. Treasury—in the operation of the U.S. financial system.

Characteristics of the commercial banking industry and key problem areas in the financial management of financial intermediaries are discussed in Section II, while nonbank financial intermediaries— especially savings associations, insurance companies, finance companies, credit unions, mutual funds, and pension funds—are the focus of Section III. Most of the chapters in Sections II and III are followed by short problems for discussion in which the reader must unravel a typical problem in financial institutions' management. Thus, not only are readers introduced to the fundamental principles of financial institutions' management, but they are encouraged to *apply* those principles to specific problem situations.

Further understanding of the role of individual financial intermediaries is provided in Section IV (Chapters 20 and 21) which concentrates upon innovation and reform in the financial system. The emphasis in this section of the book is upon both developments external to the financial system—such as changes in legislation and regulation—and internal—such as the revolution now underway in the nation's payments mechanism.

We begin in the next chapter to build a conceptual framework for understanding the operations of our financial system and the special role of financial intermediaries within that system. The chapter focuses upon the Flow of Funds Accounts prepared regularly by the Federal Reserve System. These accounts provide comprehensive data on the flow of savings and the creation of financial assets in the American economy.

QUESTIONS

1–1. Define the following terms:
   a. Denomination intermediation.
   b. Default-risk intermediation.
   c. Maturity intermediation.
   d. Information intermediation.

1–2. In your opinion, does financial intermediation affect the growth of the economy and the nation's standard of living? Please explain.

1–3. What is disintermediation? Can you think of reasons why disintermediation may be less of a problem in future years than it was during the 1960s and 1970s?

1–4. What basic trade-offs are involved in the financial management of an intermediary? What are the different types of risk that financial intermediaries face?

1–5. Why is the proportion of liquid assets generally higher in a deposit-type intermediary, such as a commercial bank, rather than a contractual-type intermediary, such as an insurance company?

1–6. Financial intermediaries have a two-stage production process, involving the procuring of funds and the investing of those funds. Explain which of the five areas of financial institutions' management discussed in this chapter (Figure 1–3) apply to stage 1 of the production process and which to stage 2. Which management areas involve both stages of production?

REFERENCES

1. Harless, Doris E. *Nonbank Financial Institutions.* Federal Reserve Bank of Richmond, October 1975.
2. Board of Governors of the Federal Reserve System. *Flow of Funds Accounts, 1946–75.* Washington, D.C., 1976.
3. Brill, Daniel H. "The Role of Financial Intermediaries in U.S. Capital Markets." *Federal Reserve Bulletin*, January 1967.
4. Dougall, Herbert E. and Gaumnitz, Jack. *Capital Markets and Institutions.* Englewood Cliffs, N.J.: Prentice-Hall, 1976.
5. Goldsmith, Raymond W. *The Flow of Capital Funds in the Postwar Economy.* New York: National Bureau of Economic Research, 1965.

6. ———. *Financial Intermediaries in the American Economy since 1900.* Princeton, N.J.: Princeton University Press, 1958.

7. Gurley, John G., and Shaw, Edward S. "Financial Aspects of Economic Development." *American Economic Review,* September 1955.

8. ———. "Financial Intermediaries and the Saving-Investment Process." *Journal of Finance,* May 1956.

9. ———. "The Growth of Debt and Money in the United States, 1800–1950: A Suggested Interpretation." *Review of Economics and Statistics,* August 1957.

10. ———. *Money in a Theory of Finance.* Washington, D.C.: The Brookings Institution, 1960.

11. Haywood, Charles F. "Production of Consumer Financial Services." *Public Regulation of Financial Services, Costs and Benefits to Consumers,* phase I, interim report (Cambridge, Mass.: ABT Associates, Inc., 1977), vol. I, NSF/RANN Grant NSF-C76-18548.

12. Kaufman, George G. *Money, the Financial System, and the Economy.* New York: Rand McNally and Company, 1973.

13. Kuznets, Simon. *Capital in the American Economy: Its Formation and Financing.* Princeton: Princeton University Press, 1961.

14. Polakoff, Murray E., et al. *Financial Institutions and Markets.* Boston: Houghton Mifflin Co., 1970.

15. Van Horne, James C. *Financial Market Rates and Flows.* Englewood Cliffs, N.J.: Prentice-Hall, 1978.

2

Flow of funds analysis of the borrowing and lending behavior of financial intermediaries

In this chapter we examine the kinds of financial assets issued and acquired by the major types of financial intermediaries. We wish to trace the movement of savings through financial intermediaries into the hands of borrowers. This movement of funds through the financial marketplace, as we saw in the last chapter, gives rise to increased investment spending and to the creation of financial assets and liabilities. Our goal in this chapter is to examine in some detail one of the main sources of data on financial transactions in the U.S. economy. Developed during the 1950s, the Flow of Funds Accounts, published periodically by the Federal Reserve Board, provide a wealth of information on the financial behavior of intermediaries and other sectors of the economy.

THE FLOW OF FUNDS ACCOUNTS

The steps in preparing the Flow of Funds Accounts are relatively simple. First, the economy is separated into groups of decision-making units, called sectors, which have similar financial characteristics. Second, balance sheets are prepared for each sector for the beginning and end of the period examined. Third, a sources and uses of funds statement is constructed for each sector of the economy from the beginning and ending balance sheets. Finally, the sources and uses statements for each sector are merged into a flow of funds matrix representing all units in the economic system. The major sectors of the economy represented in the Flow of Funds Accounts include: (1) households, (2) businesses, (3) state and local governments, (4) the U.S. government, (5) federally sponsored credit agencies, (6) the monetary authorities, (7) commercial banks, (8) private nonbank financial institutions, and (9) the rest of the world. In addition, the Federal Reserve System provides data on the assets and liabilities of major groups of financial intermediaries.

After an appropriate number of sectors is selected, as we noted above, a balance sheet is constructed for each sector of the economy. Such a statement combines the assets, liabilities, and net worth for each individual and institution in that sector. Indeed, for each economic unit and for each secotr of the economy the basic balance sheet identity must hold:

$$\text{Total assets} = \text{Total liabilities} + \text{Net worth} \qquad (1)$$

The left-hand or asset side of each sector's balance sheet contains financial assets (i.e., money and near-money assets) and real assets (such as automobiles, buildings, equipment, and homes). The right-hand side of the balance sheet contains liabilities and net worth. Thus, the balance-sheet identity shown above may also be written:

$$\text{Financial assets} + \text{Real assets} = \text{Total liabilities} + \text{Net worth} \quad (2)$$

For the economy as a whole the total of all liabilities must equal the sum of all financial assets, whereas for any single unit or sector the amount of its liabilities need not equal the total of its financial assets. (A summary of relationships between assets, liabilities, and net worth for individual economic units or sectors and for the entire economic system is shown in Figure 2–1.) Similarly, for any single unit or sector, real assets do not necessarily equal net worth because financial assets do not necessarily equal liabilities. There is no particular reason why an individual business or household, for example, should hold an amount of financial assets exactly equal to its debts (liabilities) or hold real assets exactly equal to its accumulated savings (net worth). For the entire economic system, however, liabilities must equal the volume of financial assets, and therefore, real assets must equal net worth.

After beginning and ending balance sheets are constructed for each sector of the economy, sources and uses of funds statements must be drawn up. A balance sheet is a *stock* concept, indicating the volume of assets and liabilities held by a sector at the end of a specific time

FIGURE 2–1
Relationships within the financial system and the economy

Relationships applying to an individual unit or sector of the economy	Relationships applying to the entire financial system and economy
1. Financial assets + Real assets = Liabilities + Net worth	1. Financial assets + Real assets = Liabilities + Net Worth
2. Change in financial assets (lending) + Change in real assets (net investment) = Change in liabilities (borrowing) + Change in net worth (saving)	2. Change in financial assets (lending) + Change in real assets (net investment) = Change in liabilities (borrowing) + Change in net worth (saving)
3. Financial assets $\gtreqless$ Liabilities	3. Financial assets = Liabilities
4. Change in financial assets (lending) $\gtreqless$ Change in liabilities (borrowing)	4. Change in financial assets (lending) = Change in liabilities (borrowing)
5. Real assets $\gtreqless$ Net worth	5. Real assets = Net worth
6. Change in real assets (net investment) $\gtreqless$ Change in net worth (saving)	6. Change in real assets (net investment) = Change in net worth (saving)

period. We must transform these stocks into *flows* in order to trace the flow of funds within the financial system. *A sources and uses of funds statement is a statement of financial flows over time.* An example of such a statement is shown in Figure 2–2. Note that uses of funds are rep-

FIGURE 2–2
Sources and uses of funds statement

Uses of funds	Sources of funds
Change in financial assets	Change in liabilities
Change in real assets	Change in net worth
Total uses of funds	Total sources of funds

resented by *changes* in items on the asset side of the balance sheet; sources of funds are represented by *changes* in liability items and in net worth. Total uses of funds must always equal total sources of funds. Of course, to derive a sources and uses of funds statement for each sector of the economy we must sum the sources and uses of funds for each unit in that sector.

We may define the change in financial assets as net *lending;* and the change in real assets as net *investment.* [1] The change in liabilities rep-

---

[1] Frequently in discussions of funds-flow analysis, money is separated from other financial assets due to its unique properties as a perfectly liquid medium of exchange. Viewed in this context a rise in money holdings would be defined as *hoarding,* while a decline in money holdings would be labeled *dishoarding.* The hoarding of money

resents net *borrowing*, while the change in net worth reflects net *savings*. In addition to borrowing or saving, a sector or economic unit can raise funds by selling financial assets (including the spending down of money balances) or by selling real assets. Principal uses of funds include purchasing financial assets and real assets or paying off outstanding debt. In general, any increase in liabilities or any decrease in assets is a *source* of funds; any rise in assets or decline in liabilities represents a *use* of funds for an individual unit or sector of the economy.

One of the most important components of a sources and uses of funds statement is savings. How can we determine the amount of saving carried out by a sector during any given time period? Since the change in total assets must equal the change in total liabilities and capital on any unit or sector's balance sheet, it follows that:

$$
\begin{aligned}
\text{Change in net worth} &= \text{Change in total assets} - \text{Change} && (3)\\
&\quad \text{in total liabilities}\\
&= \text{Change in financial assets} +\\
&\quad \text{Change in real assets} - \text{Change in}\\
&\quad \text{total liabilities}
\end{aligned}
$$

This shift in net worth reflects *current saving*. We usually think of savings as a residual quantity. It is the spread between a unit of sector's receipts and its expenditures. When saving occurs, total assets may rise as a unit purchases stocks, bonds, notes, or other assets. Alternatively, the unit may pay off some of its IOUs, resulting in a decline in outstanding obligations. Some units will use their savings to simultaneously acquire assets and retire debt. Either way, current savings must match a unit's change in net worth. By analogy, the total amount of a unit or sector's net worth equals its accumulated savings from the current and all prior time periods. As Figure 2–1 shows, for any one business firm, household, unit of government, or sector of the economy, there is no reason for the change in the value of its real assets to match the change in its net worth or for the shift in financial assets and money holdings to match the shift in liabilities. An individual unit or sector may spend on investment more than it saves or borrow more than it lends and vice versa. The only equalities which must hold for each unit and sector are that total assets must equal total liabilities plus net

---

reduces the supply of loanable funds available for lending and investing, while dishoarding expands the quantity of loanable funds. In economic systems today it is becoming increasingly difficult to segregate money from other financial assets. For example, some money balances used to carry out transactions (such as NOW accounts and share drafts) bear interest. Moreover, virtually all forms of money in use today are the debt (liabilities) of some financial institution or unit and are matched by financial assets held somewhere within the financial system. Accordingly, in the discussion that follows we include money among holdings of financial assets.

worth on the balance sheet and total sources of funds must match total uses of funds on the sources and uses of funds statement.

When the economy has been divided into sectors and sources and uses of funds statements constructed for each sector, we may bring these statements together into a flow of funds matrix for the whole economic system. Changes in the assets, liabilities, and net worth of each sector will be represented in this matrix. It will show the total amount of saving and investment, the total volume of lending and borrowing, and the amount of money issued in the economy over a given time period (usually a quarter or a year).

An example of flow-of-funds construction

To more fully understand the method by which the flow of funds accounts are constructed, we present a simplified example. Suppose that we wish to construct a flow of funds matrix reflecting financial flows in the economy during the year 1980. Since we wish to construct the flow of funds accounts for the entire year, we need to prepare balance sheets for the beginning and ending of the year for each sector into which the economy is divided.

An example of balance sheets we might construct for the business sector is shown in Table 2–1. These financial statements show that the total assets of the business sector were 655 at year-end 1979, but increased to 900 by year-end 1980. This growth in total assets was led by an increase in real assets (mainly buildings, equipment, and inventories) from 400 to 600. At the same time the business sector's Net Worth account, reflecting principally savings in the form of retained earnings, rose from 340 at year-end 1979 to 500 year-end 1980. Liabilities outstanding rose from 315 to 400, indicating that current savings (the change in net worth) provided most of the funds for the business sector's growth in total assets, but additional borrowings (or external financing) also provided a substantial portion of the funds needed to support the purchase of assets during 1980. These changes in assets and liabilities between year-end 1979 and year-end 1980 are captured in the sources and uses of funds statement shown at the bottom of Table 2–1.

We would need to construct similar balance sheets and sources and uses of funds statements for the remaining sectors of the economy and enter each of these in a flow of funds matrix. The rows in the flow of funds matrix would reflect different sources and uses of funds drawn upon by each sector, while the columns would represent different sectors. Analysis of the economy's flow of funds matrix would show that some sectors are *savings-deficit* sectors—they save less than the amount of their net investment in real assets—while other sectors run

TABLE 2-1
Beginning and ending balance sheets for the business sector, 1980

Business Sector Balance Sheet
December 31, 1979

Assets		Liabilities and Net Worth	
Financial assets	255	Liabilities	315
Real assets	400	Net worth	340
		Total liabilities and net	
Total assets	655	worth	655

Business Sector Balance Sheet
December 31, 1980

Assets		Liabilities and Net Worth	
Financial assets	300	Liabilities	400
Real assets	600	Net worth	500
		Total liabilities and net	
Total assets	900	worth	900

Business Sector
Sources and Uses of Funds Statement
1980

Uses of funds		Sources of funds	
Change in financial assets	45	Change in liabilities	85
Change in real assets	200	Change in net worth	160
Total uses of funds	245	Total sources of funds	245

a corresponding *savings surplus* — the amount of their savings exceeds their net investment in real assets. In most economies, business firms constitute the chief savings-deficit sector. Table 2–1, for example, shows that business firms reported savings of 160, but made investments (net) totaling 200. Therefore, the business sector was forced to issue a substantial volume of liabilities (85, as shown in the sources and uses of funds statement) in order to cover its savings deficit.

The other major savings-deficit sector normally is government. Its investments typically are quite large since the government sector must build highways, bridges, public buildings, warships, airplanes, and thousands of other items demanded by its citizens. Both the business and government sectors typically are forced to make up their savings deficits by borrowing in substantial amounts and, therefore, significantly expanding their liabilities. In contrast, the household and financial institutions' sectors usually are savings-surplus sectors with current saving outstripping their net investment. These sectors usually dispose of their surplus savings by adding to their holdings of assets (including money balances) and retiring outstanding debt. The principal role of financial institutions is to attract the public's savings and to make loans.

The flow of funds matrix emphasizes several important equalities which must prevail in the financial system. These include:

1. For each sector and for the entire economic system, total uses of funds must always equal total sources of funds.
2. Aggregate saving must equal total net investment for the entire economy.
3. Financial assets must equal liabilities for the entire economic system.
4. The total volume of lending must be equal to the total volume of borrowing for the economy as a whole.
5. For all units, sectors, and the whole economy the sum of holdings of real assets and financial assets must equal the sum of liabilities plus net worth.

Actual flow of funds information for various sectors

In each issue of the *Federal Reserve Bulletin*, the Board of Governors of the Federal Reserve System presents flow of funds data for the entire economy. In addition, complete flow of funds data for all sectors is released quarterly on both a seasonally adjusted and unadjusted basis. Annually, the Federal Reserve Board revises historical flow of funds data, introducing new sources of information and refining current figures as well as those for previous years.[2] In compiling flow of funds data the Federal Reserve draws upon a wide variety of government and private industry sources, including the National Income and Product Accounts of the U.S. Department of Commerce, Census Bureau surveys, Federal Trade Commission financial reports from manufacturing, mining, and trade corporations, monthly statements of receipts and expenditures by the U.S. Treasury Department, business tax returns filed with the Internal Revenue Service, statistical reports from the Securities and Exchange Commission and the federal bank regulatory agencies, and regular surveys carried out by such industry trade associations as the National Association of Mutual Savings Banks, the Institute of Life Insurance, the National Association of REIT's, and the Investment Company Institute.[3]

Examples of the flow of funds reports provided regularly by the Federal Reserve Board are shown in Tables 2–2 and 2–3. To illustrate

---

[2] Examples of recent revisions in data are found in references [3], [4], and [5]. Historical data on a quarterly basis is available on computer tape from the Federal Reserve Board.

[3] For a more complete listing of the sources of financial data used in constructing the flow-of-funds accounts see especially [2, Table 8].

the kinds of important information contained in this data, we note that total funds raised in the financial markets by all sectors of the U.S. economy amounted to $399.4 billion during 1977, of which financial institutions accounted for $58.8 billion. Nonfinancial sectors (including nonfinancial corporations, households, and governments) raised $340.5 billion through borrowings and issuing stock. As expected, the total of $340.5 billion raised by nonfinancial units was exactly equal to the total funds advanced to these units by lenders in the economy. As Table 2–3 reveals, total funds advanced through the credit markets to nonfinancial sectors totaled $337.4 billion in 1977 and net issues of corporate equities (stock) totaled $3.1 billion for a total of $340.5 billion. However, sources and uses of funds in the flow of funds tables frequently do not balance and, in these situations, an additional item called a *statistical discrepancy* is added. As we have noted, the flow of funds accounts consist of a series of estimates, frequently based upon only partial data, so that small discrepancies are inevitable.

The U.S. Treasury borrowed net $57.6 billion during 1977 which was partially offset by net repayments and redemptions of securities by other U.S. government agencies amounting to $0.9 billion. In the nonfinancial sector, stock issued by corporations was dwarfed by the borrowings of these units—$3.1 billion in net equity issues compared to $280.6 billion in corporate debt instruments issued during 1977. If we consult the National Income Accounts for 1977, we can determine roughly where the bulk of the funds raised by corporate borrowings and stock issues were placed. Businessmen spent $190.4 billion during 1977 to acquire plant and equipment and purchased $15.6 in inventories of goods and raw materials. Expenditures of $91.9 billion were made to build residential structures in order to provide new housing for individuals and families. Clearly, the borrowings and stock issues recorded in the Flow of Funds Accounts assisted greatly in carrying out this massive volume of investment, but these externally raised funds were not enough. Massive saving (internally generated funds) by businesses and households also was necessary to carry out desired investment.

The Flow of Funds Accounts tell us the types of securities used to raise funds over an annual or quarterly period and who issued the securities. For example, line 13 in the top section of Table 2–2 indicates that a total of $29.2 billion in state and local government obligations were issued during 1977. The bulk of these "municipal" obligations were purchased by financial institutions. Private domestic nonfinancial investors, as shown in Table 2–3, line 34, purchased only $9.1 billion in state and local debt obligations.

Commercial banks led all other financial institutions in extending

TABLE 2-2
Summary of funds raised in credit markets ($billions)

SEASONALLY ADJUSTED ANNUAL RATES — CREDIT MARKET FUNDS RAISED BY NONFINANCIAL SECTORS

SUMMARY OF FUNDS RAISED IN CREDIT MARKETS — FUNDS RAISED BY NONFINANCIAL SECTORS

FUNDS RAISED IN CREDIT MARKETS — SEASONALLY ADJUSTED ANNUAL RATES

#	Item	1973	1974	1975	1976	1977	1977 I	1977 II	1977 III	1977 IV	1978 I	1978 II
1	TOTAL FUNDS RAISED BY NONFINANCIAL SECTORS	203.6	188.8	208.1	272.5	340.5	303.8	300.6	390.6	367.1	380.0	370.5
2	EXCLUDING EQUITIES	196.1	184.9	198.0	261.7	337.4	303.6	298.4	385.0	362.5	380.9	370.0
3	U.S. GOVERNMENT	8.3	11.8	85.4	69.0	56.8	47.3	37.8	80.1	61.9	66.1	28.5
4	TREASURY ISSUES	7.9	12.0	85.8	69.1	57.6	48.0	38.2	82.2	62.2	67.4	49.0
5	AGENCY ISSUES + MORTGAGES	.4	-.2	-.4	-.1	-.9	-.7	-.4	-2.1	-.3	-1.4	-.5
6	ALL OTHER NONFINANCIAL SECTORS	195.5	177.0	122.7	203.5	283.8	256.5	262.8	310.5	305.2	314.6	342.0
7	CORPORATE EQUITIES	7.9	3.8	10.1	10.8	3.1	.1	2.2	5.6	5.2	.5	.5
8	DEBT INSTRUMENTS	187.9	173.1	112.6	192.6	280.6	256.3	260.6	304.9	300.6	314.9	321.6
	PRIVATE DOMESTIC											
9	NONFINANCIAL SECTORS	189.3	161.6	109.5	182.8	271.4	250.4	253.8	288.5	292.9	301.4	300.0
10	CORPORATE EQUITIES	7.9	4.1	9.9	10.5	2.7	-.6	1.7	4.4	5.4	1.0	.7
11	DEBT INSTRUMENTS	181.4	157.5	99.6	172.3	268.7	251.0	251.1	284.1	287.5	300.4	299.3
12	DEBT CAPITAL INSTRUMENTS	105.0	98.0	97.8	146.8	161.1	144.8	181.9	198.4	199.3	171.7	188.5
13	ST.+LOC. OBLIGATIONS	14.7	16.5	15.6	19.0	29.2	20.5	38.2	33.0	25.0	22.3	35.8
14	CORPORATE BONDS	9.2	19.7	27.2	22.6	21.0	18.3	13.6	27.3	24.7	15.0	18.7
15	MORTGAGES	81.2	61.9	55.0	85.0	131.0	106.0	130.1	138.0	149.7	134.4	134.0
16	HOME MORTGAGES	46.4	34.8	39.5	63.7	96.4	79.1	97.1	103.9	104.6	92.4	89.7
17	MULTI-FAMILY RESID.	10.4	6.9	*	1.8	7.4	4.4	6.5	7.0	9.7	10.6	10.2
18	COMMERCIAL	18.9	15.1	11.0	13.4	18.4	13.9	14.4	18.6	26.6	21.9	24.4
19	FARM	5.5	5.0	4.6	6.1	8.8	8.6	9.2	8.6	8.8	9.5	9.7
20	OTHER DEBT INSTRUMENTS	76.4	59.6	1.8	45.5	87.6	106.2	70.2	85.7	88.2	128.7	110.8
21	CONSUMER CREDIT	23.8	10.2	9.4	35.0	35.0	33.2	38.3	32.0	36.2	38.0	51.0
22	BANK LOANS N.E.C.	39.8	29.0	-14.0	3.5	30.6	48.9	19.0	33.8	20.7	61.3	45.9
23	OPEN-MARKET PAPER	2.5	6.6	-2.6	4.0	2.9	1.7	5.3	5.3	4.2	5.3	5.1
24	OTHER	10.3	13.7	9.0	14.4	19.0	22.5	7.6	18.8	27.1	24.1	8.2
25	BY BORROWING SECTOR: ST.+LOC. GOVERNMENTS	189.3	161.6	109.5	182.8	271.4	250.4	253.8	288.5	292.9	301.4	300.0
26	ST.+LOC. GOVERNMENTS	13.2	15.5	13.2	16.5	25.9	19.6	34.8	34.8	23.2	20.9	24.4
27	HOUSEHOLDS	80.9	49.2	48.6	89.9	139.6	127.7	134.7	150.0	145.9	143.0	141.1
28	NONFINANCIAL BUSINESS	95.2	97.0	47.7	74.4	106.0	103.1	93.2	103.7	123.8	137.6	134.6
29	FARM	9.7	7.9	8.7	11.0	14.7	15.5	14.5	14.5	13.2	13.1	13.7
30	NONFARM NONCORPORATE	12.8	7.4	2.0	5.2	12.6	11.7	14.0	9.2	15.5	17.5	19.5
31	CORPORATE	72.7	81.8	37.0	58.2	78.7	75.9	63.7	80.1	95.2	107.0	101.3
32	DEBT INSTRUMENTS	64.8	77.7	27.1	47.7	76.0	76.6	62.0	75.7	89.8	106.0	100.6
33	EQUITIES	7.9	4.1	9.9	10.5	2.7	-.6	1.7	4.4	5.4	1.0	.7
34	FOREIGN	6.2	15.3	13.2	20.7	12.3	6.1	9.0	22.0	12.3	13.2	22.0
35	CORPORATE EQUITIES	-.2	-.2	.2	.3	.4	.8	.5	1.2	-.8	-1.3	-.3
36	DEBT INSTRUMENTS	6.4	15.6	13.0	20.4	11.9	5.3	8.5	20.8	13.1	14.5	22.2
37	BONDS	1.0	2.1	6.2	6.5	5.0	2.2	6.6	7.5	3.7	5.1	4.0
38	BANK LOANS N.E.C.	2.8	4.7	3.7	6.6	6.6	-3.9	-2.0	7.2	5.0	7.4	8.0
39	OPEN-MARKET PAPER	.9	7.3	.3	1.9	2.4	3.0	2.3	2.5	1.8	.9	6.1
40	U.S. GOVERNMENT LOANS	1.7	1.5	2.8	3.3	3.0	4.0	2.2	3.7	2.0	2.9	2.1

BILLIONS OF DOLLARS. II/78 BASED ON INCOMPLETE INFORMATION.

MEMO												
MEMO: U.S. GOVT. CASH BALANCE	-1.7	-4.6	2.9	3.2	1.1	-1.7	11.4	5.2	-10.6	-19.3	28.3	41
NET OF CHANGES IN U.S. GOVT. CASH BALANCES-- / TOTAL FUNDS RAISED BY U.S. GOVERNMENT	205.5	193.3	205.3	269.4	339.4	305.4	289.2	385.4	377.7	399.9	342.2	42
	9.9	16.4	82.5	65.9	55.7	49.0	26.4	74.8	72.5	85.3	20.2	43

CREDIT MARKET FUNDS RAISED BY FINANCIAL SECTORS

TOTAL FUNDS RAISED BY FINANCIAL SECTORS	57.6	36.4	11.7	29.2	58.8	57.6	65.4	41.3	71.1	111.1	94.3	1
U.S. GOVT. RELATED	19.9	23.1	13.5	18.6	26.3	27.4	22.6	25.4	29.7	38.8	39.8	2
SPONSORED CR. AG. SEC.	16.3	16.6	2.3	3.3	7.0	9.4	3.1	1.7	7.2	23.7	24.4	3
MORTGAGE POOL SECURITIES	3.6	5.8	10.3	15.7	20.5	22.6	13.1	23.7	22.5	15.1	15.3	4
LOANS FROM U.S. GOVERNMENT	-	.7	.9	-.4	-1.2	-4.7	-	-.7	-	-	-	5
PRIVATE FINANCIAL SECTORS	37.7	13.3	-1.9	10.6	32.6	30.2	42.8	15.9	41.4	72.0	54.5	6
CORPORATE EQUITIES	1.5	.3	.6	1.0	.6	-1.4	2.5	-1.4	2.8	1.2	1.7	7
DEBT INSTRUMENTS	36.2	13.0	-2.5	9.6	32.0	31.6	40.3	17.3	38.7	71.1	54.8	8
CORPORATE BONDS	3.5	2.1	2.3	5.8	10.1	7.3	13.4	8.5	11.7	10.3	2.6	9
MORTGAGES	-1.2	-1.3	2.3	2.1	3.1	2.7	3.8	3.1	2.8	2.6	1.6	10
BANK LOANS N.E.C.	.9	4.6	-3.0	-3.7	*	1.9	-.5	-.1	4.7	-.1	2.9	11
OPEN-MARKET PAPER + RP'S	17.8	.9	-.1	7.3	14.4	17.1	25.7	5.8	9.0	46.4	25.4	12
LOANS FROM FHLB'S	7.2	.7	-4.0	-2.0	4.3	2.6	-4.3	-.1	10.4	12.8	15.3	13
TOTAL, BY SECTOR	57.6	36.4	11.7	29.2	58.8	57.6	65.4	41.3	71.1	111.1	94.3	14
SPONSORED CREDIT AGENCIES	16.3	17.3	3.4	2.9	5.8	4.7	9.5	1.7	7.2	23.7	24.4	15
MORTGAGE POOLS	3.6	5.8	10.3	15.7	20.5	22.6	13.1	23.7	22.5	15.2	15.3	16
PRIVATE FINANCIAL SECTORS	37.7	13.3	-1.9	10.6	32.6	30.2	42.6	15.9	41.4	72.4	54.5	17
COMMERCIAL BANKS	14.1	-5.6	-1.4	7.5	4.8	10.0	10.0	2.5	-3.4	31.1	2.6	18
BANK AFFILIATES	2.2	3.5	.3	-.8	1.3	.4	.1	1.5	.3	3.6	6.0	19
SAVINGS + LOAN ASSNS.	6.0	6.3	-2.2	*	1.9	8.7	12.5	5.6	20.7	18.1	20.7	20
OTHER INSURANCE COMPANIES	.9	.9	1.0	.9	.9	.9	.9	.9	1.0	1.0	1.0	21
FINANCE COMPANIES	9.4	6.0	.6	6.4	16.9	15.1	19.8	11.1	21.6	14.0	16.9	22
REITS	6.5	.7	-1.4	-2.4	-2.4	-2.7	1.0	-2.6	-1.9	-1.9	-1.4	23
OPEN-END INVESTMENT COS.	-1.2	-.7	-.1	-1.0	-1.0	-2.6	1.0	-3.3	.9	*	*	24
MONEY MARKET FUNDS	-	2.4	1.3	*	.2	.3	-1.3	-.1	1.7	6.4	5.3	25

TOTAL CREDIT MARKET FUNDS RAISED, ALL SECTORS, BY TYPE

TOTAL FUNDS RAISED	261.4	225.1	219.8	301.7	399.4	301.3	306.0	431.8	438.2	491.7	404.8	1
INVESTMENT COMPANY SHARES	-1.2	-.7	-.1	-1.0	-1.0	-2.6	1.0	-3.3	*	*	.4	2
OTHER CORPORATE EQUITIES	10.4	4.8	10.8	12.9	4.8	1.3	3.7	7.5	6.5	.9	1.8	3
DEBT INSTRUMENTS	252.3	221.0	209.1	289.8	395.6	362.0	261.3	427.6	430.9	490.0	462.6	4
U.S. GOVERNMENT SECURITIES	28.3	34.3	96.2	88.1	84.3	79.5	60.6	105.0	91.7	105.0	88.4	5
STATE + LOCAL OBLIGATIONS	14.7	16.5	15.6	19.0	29.2	20.5	30.2	35.0	25.0	22.3	35.8	6
CORPORATE + FOREIGN BONDS	13.6	23.9	30.4	37.2	36.1	27.7	31.2	43.3	40.1	30.3	32.3	7
MORTGAGES	79.9	60.5	57.2	87.1	134.0	108.6	133.8	161.0	152.4	137.0	135.5	8
CONSUMER CREDIT	23.8	10.2	9.4	23.6	35.0	33.2	38.3	32.6	30.2	38.0	51.6	9
BANK LOANS N.E.C.	51.6	38.3	-13.9	6.4	32.2	40.9	4.9	40.9	30.9	67.6	50.6	10
OPEN-MARKET PAPER + RP'S	21.4	14.8	-2.4	15.3	19.8	-1.9	33.3	8.8	15.0	50.8	36.6	11
OTHER LOANS	19.1	22.6	8.7	15.3	25.1	24.4	14.0	22.4	39.6	39.9	25.6	12

Source: Board of Governors of the Federal Reserve System, *Flow of Funds Accounts, 2d Quarter 1978*, August 1978, p. 5.

TABLE 2-3
Direct and indirect sources of funds to credit markets ($billions)

AUGUST 30, 1978
CREDIT MARKET SUPPLY OF FUNDS

DIRECT AND INDIRECT SOURCES OF FUNDS TO CREDIT MARKETS

CREDIT MARKET SUPPLY OF FUNDS

	SEASONALLY ADJUSTED ANNUAL RATES						1977			1978		
	1973	1974	1975	1976	1977	I	II	III	IV	I	II	
1 TOTAL FUNDS ADVANCED IN CREDIT MARKETS TO NONFINANCIAL SECTORS	196.1	164.9	198.0	261.7	337.4	303.6	298.4	385.0	362.5	380.9	370.0	1
BY PUBLIC AGENCIES + FOREIGN												
2 TOTAL NET ADVANCES, BY TYPE	34.1	52.6	44.3	54.5	85.4	59.2	79.3	81.4	121.8	116.3	83.0	2
3 U.S. GOVERNMENT SECURITIES	9.5	11.9	22.5	26.8	40.2	14.8	39.7	40.8	65.6	48.7	33.9	3
4 RESIDENTIAL MORTGAGES	8.2	14.7	16.2	12.8	20.4	23.6	16.3	18.8	23.0	27.2	20.0	4
5 FHLB ADVANCES TO S+LS	7.2	6.7	-4.0	-2.0	4.3	2.6	4.2	-.1	10.4	12.8	15.3	5
6 OTHER LOANS + SECURITIES	9.2	19.4	9.5	10.9	20.5	18.2	19.1	21.9	22.8	27.5	13.8	6
TOTALS ADVANCED, BY SECTOR												
7 U.S. GOVERNMENT	2.8	9.7	15.1	8.9	11.8	10.3	1.8	17.4	17.8	28.7	8.5	7
8 GOVT-RELATED AG. + POOLS	21.4	25.6	14.5	20.6	26.9	28.4	24.9	25.7	28.7	39.9	43.6	8
9 MONETARY AUTHORITIES	9.2	6.2	8.5	9.8	7.1	-5.8	26.1	3.2	6.2	-4.1	30.7	9
10 FOREIGN	.6	11.2	6.1	15.2	39.5	26.2	26.5	36.2	69.2	51.8	.3	10
11 AGENCY BORROWING AND POOL SECURITY ISSUES NOT INCLUDED IN LINE 1	19.9	23.1	13.5	18.6	26.3	27.4	22.6	25.4	29.7	38.8	39.8	11
PRIVATE DOMESTIC FUNDS ADVANCED												
12 TOTAL NET ADVANCES	162.0	155.3	167.3	225.7	276.2	271.8	241.7	328.9	270.4	303.5	326.8	12
13 U.S. GOVERNMENT SECURITIES	16.8	22.4	75.7	61.3	44.1	64.7	20.9	64.8	26.1	56.3	54.5	13
14 STATE + LOCAL OBLIGATIONS	14.7	16.5	15.0	19.0	29.2	20.5	38.2	36.2	25.0	22.3	35.8	14
15 CORPORATE + FOREIGN BONDS	10.0	20.9	32.8	30.5	22.3	19.6	14.9	31.1	23.6	19.3	21.5	15
16 RESIDENTIAL MORTGAGES	48.4	26.8	23.4	52.7	83.2	59.9	90.0	92.0	91.2	79.8	79.8	16
17 OTHER MORTGAGES + LOANS	79.2	75.4	16.1	60.4	103.7	109.9	82.0	107.9	115.0	142.8	150.6	17
18 LESS: FHLB ADVANCES	7.2	6.7	-4.0	-2.0	4.3	2.6	4.3	-.1	10.4	12.8	15.3	18
PRIVATE FINANCIAL INTERMEDIATION												
19 CREDIT MARKET FUNDS ADVANCED BY PRIVATE FINANCIAL INSTS.	165.4	126.4	119.9	191.2	249.6	239.0	242.9	280.1	235.4	266.6	307.9	19
20 COMMERCIAL BANKING	86.5	64.5	27.6	58.0	85.8	85.0	77.1	103.1	77.9	114.2	130.8	20
21 SAVINGS INSTITUTIONS	30.9	20.9	52.0	71.4	84.8	85.5	85.1	89.1	79.6	79.1	81.6	21
22 INSURANCE + PENSION FUNDS	23.9	30.0	41.5	51.7	62.0	58.0	62.0	66.4	61.1	62.7	66.2	22
23 OTHER FINANCE	18.0	4.7	-1.1	10.1	16.9	10.2	18.7	22.0	16.8	10.6	23.3	23
24 SOURCES OF FUNDS	165.4	126.2	119.9	191.2	249.6	239.3	242.9	280.6	235.4	266.6	307.9	24
25 PRIVATE DOMESTIC DEPOSITS	86.0	69.4	90.0	121.5	136.0	140.3	113.7	165.4	124.5	112.3	124.0	25
26 CREDIT MARKET BORROWING	30.2	13.0	-2.5	9.6	32.0	31.6	40.3	17.3	38.7	71.1	52.8	26
27 OTHER SOURCES	42.5	43.8	31.9	60.1	81.6	67.3	89.0	97.9	72.3	83.2	131.1	27
28 FOREIGN FUNDS	5.8	16.8	-1.7	5.1	11.6	-7.6	9.1	20.4	24.4	-2.4	10.4	28
29 TREASURY BALANCES	-1.0	-5.1	1.5	1.4	4.3	4.3	-7.9	5.5	15.2	-14.1	10.3	29
30 INSURANCE + PENSION RES.	18.4	26.0	29.0	34.8	48.0	40.0	50.4	51.9	48.9	47.7	56.1	30
31 OTHER, NET	19.4	6.0	3.1	20.3	17.8	30.0	37.4	20.0	-16.2	52.0	54.3	31

PRIVATE DOMESTIC NONFINANCIAL INVESTORS

32	DIRECT LENDING IN CR. MARKETS	52.6	42.2	44.9	44.1	60.6	64.1	39.1	65.6	73.6	108.0	71.8
33	U.S. GOVERNMENT SECURITIES	19.2	17.5	23.0	19.6	24.6	34.3	-6.0	37.8	32.5	51.7	20.7
34	STATE + LOCAL OBLIGATIONS	5.4	4.7	8.3	6.8	9.1	2.1	14.2	7.3	12.9	4.4	9.6
35	CORPORATE + FOREIGN BONDS	1.3	2.4	-.8	2.1	1.1	.9		.5	.2	-3.5	-2.1
36	OPEN-MKT PAPER, ETC.	18.3			4.1	9.5	12.7	13.3	.5	11.5	37.2	22.0
37	OTHER	8.0	0.2	6.4	11.5	16.2	14.3	17.6	16.5	16.5	18.3	21.0
38	DEPOSITS + CURRENCY	90.6	75.7	90.8	128.8	144.3	146.9	116.3	162.2	129.7	123.2	133.9
39	TIME + SAVINGS ACCOUNTS	76.1	60.7	84.8	112.2	120.1	119.6	101.5	151.4	108.0	110.5	110.5
40	LARGE NEGOTIABLE CD'S	18.1	18.8	-14.1	-14.4	9.3	-13.5	4.8	13.1	32.7	5.4	19.8
41	OTHER AT COMMERCIAL BANKS	29.6	26.1	39.4	58.1	41.7	62.9	27.7	60.0	16.3	52.8	35.6
42	AT SAVINGS INSTITUTIONS	28.5	21.8	59.4	68.5	69.1	70.2	69.0	78.3	59.0	52.3	57.0
43	MONEY	14.4	8.9	12.0	16.0	24.2	27.3	16.8	30.8	21.7	12.7	23.5
44	DEMAND DEPOSITS	10.5	2.6	5.8	9.3	15.9	20.8	12.2	14.0	16.5	1.8	13.5
45	CURRENCY	3.9	6.3	6.2	7.3	8.3	6.6	4.6	16.8	5.2	11.0	9.9
46	TOTAL OF CREDIT MARKET INSTRU- MENTS, DEPOSITS + CURRENCY	143.4	117.8	141.6	172.9	204.9	211.1	157.3	247.8	203.3	231.3	205.7
47	PUBLIC HOLDINGS AS % OF TOTAL	17.4	28.5	22.4	20.8	25.3	19.5	26.6	21.1	33.6	30.5	22.4
48	PVT. FINAN. INTERMEDIATION (%)	90.9	81.3	71.7	84.7	69.7	88.0	100.5	85.3	87.1	87.8	94.2
49	TOTAL FOREIGN FUNDS	6.4	28.0	7.1	20.3	51.1	18.6	55.0	50.6	93.5	49.4	16.6

CORPORATE EQUITIES NOT INCLUDED ABOVE

1	TOTAL NET ISSUES	9.2	4.1	10.7	11.9	3.8	-1.3	4.7	4.2	7.4	.9	2.1
2	MUTUAL FUND SHARES	-1.2	-.7	-1.0	-1.0	-1.0	-2.6	1.0	-3.3	.9		.4
3	OTHER EQUITIES	10.4	4.8	9.7	12.9	4.8	1.3	3.7	7.5	6.5	.9	1.8
4	ACQ. BY FINANCIAL INSTITUTIONS	13.3	5.8	9.7	12.5	6.2	6.0	6.2	8.0	4.6	1.5	.4
5	OTHER NET PURCHASES	4.1	-1.6	1.0	-.7	2.4	-7.3	-1.5	-3.8	2.8	2.3	1.8

BILLIONS OF DOLLARS.   11/78 BASED ON INCOMPLETE INFORMATION.

Source: Board of Governors of the Federal Reserve System, *Flow of Funds Accounts, 2d Quarter 1978*, August 1978, p. 5.

credit to those demanding funds during 1977. Bank loans and investments during the year totaled $85.8 billion, as shown in Table 2–3. Savings institutions (including savings banks and credit unions) provided another $84.8 billion in loanable funds. The bulk of this lending (though not all) was supported by growth in deposits. Checking accounts or demand deposits held by private nonfinancial firms and individuals at banks and savings institutions rose $15.9 billion during 1977, while time and savings accounts (including large negotiable CDs) rose $120 billion, as indicated in lines 39 and 44 of Table 2–3. Insurance companies and pension funds supplied $62 billion in funds to the nation's credit markets. The remaining financial intermediaries provided an additional $16.9 billion in loanable funds during 1977.

These figures show quite clearly the critical role of financial intermediaries in providing loanable funds (credit) to other sectors of the economy. The degree of intermediation in the nation's financial markets has risen significantly during the postwar era as business, household, and governmental borrowers have turned increasingly to financial intermediaries for mortgages, instalment credit, commercial and industrial loans, and to support the issuance of corporate and government bonds. At the same time businesses, households, and governments have found deposits and other financial claims offered by intermediaries an increasingly attractive investment alternative to purchasing stocks, bonds, and other securities in the open market. Holdings of credit market instruments by intermediaries represented slightly less than 70 percent of all such instruments in the early 1950s but averaged well above 80 percent during the 1970s, as shown in line 48 of Table 2–3.

The potential uses of flow of funds data are numerous. The financial analyst can use the information to determine which sectors of the economy acquire certain kinds of financial assets and which sectors issue these assets. Movements of funds among the various sectors may be observed and some indication of the causes of major changes in interest rates determined. For example, by comparing the volume of securities issued in various periods of time, we can estimate trends in the demand for credit from various sectors and for the whole economy. If demand appears to be putting pressure on savings flows, interest rates would be expected to rise. When demand slackens, interest rates will tend to fall, other things equal.

The *net* volume of financial assets (or liabilities) issued and purchased in the economy also may be determined. For example, as we observed earlier, the U.S. Treasury raised a net $56.8 billion in credit-market funds during 1977 with $57.6 billion coming from issues of new securities minus a small amount ($0.9 billion) of federal agency securities and mortgages that were retired during the year. (See Table 2–2, lines 3, 4, and 5.) As shown in Table 2–3, government agencies and foreign investors purchased net $40.2 billion in various types of federal government securities, while private investors (including financial intermediaries) added $44.1 billion of these securities to their portfolios. Private domestic nonfinancial investors, excluding intermediaries, purchased $24.6 billion in Federal government securities, suggesting that financial intermediaries acquired about $19.5 billion of these securities during 1977. Some investors acquired outstanding U.S. government obligations as well as buying new government IOUs. These patterns in the demand and supply of various securities (financial assets) may be compared over time and estimates made for future periods. In some recent applications, econometric models have been constructed which attempt to explain security prices, interest rates, and the demand for and supply of credit on the basis of flow of funds data.

Assets and liabilities of various sectors of the economy

The Flow of Funds Accounts trace financial *flows* between points in time. The balance sheets of individual economic units and sectors from which the flow of funds data are derived, however, measure *stocks* of assets, liabilities, and net worth as of a single point in time. Of course, these stocks reflect the sum of current and past flows. For example, accumulated savings (which is captured by total net worth on a unit or sector's balance sheet) is a stock, whereas the amount of saving in the current period clearly is a *flow* of funds passing through the financial markets into the hands of borrowers. Similarly, the amount of total liabilities appearing on a sector's or unit's balance sheet is a stock, but borrowing in the current period is a flow of funds from lenders to borrowers.

Because of the interrelationships between stocks and flows, we can reconstruct the balance sheets—assets, liabilities, and net worth—of major sectors in the economy from flow of funds data. A recent example of such a reconstruction is shown in Table 2–4 which contains the financial assets and liabilities of the household sector. We note that households held a huge volume of financial assets by year-end 1977—more than $3 trillion. These assets far exceeded the debts (liabilities) of this sector which totaled slightly more than $1 trillion in 1977. Clearly, the dominant financial asset held by households is time and savings accounts at commercial banks and other savings institutions, totaling almost $992 billion at year-end 1977. Holdings of cor-

TABLE 2-4 Sector statements of financial assets and liabilities for the household sector, 1967–77 ($billions)

SECTOR STATEMENTS OF FINANCIAL ASSETS AND LIABILITIES

HOUSEHOLDS, PERSONAL TRUSTS, AND NONPROFIT ORGANIZATIONS

YEAR-END OUTSTANDINGS

Line		1967	1968	1969	1970	1971	1972	1973	1974	1975	1976	1977
1	TOTAL FINANCIAL ASSETS	1688.6	1914.2	1862.8	1926.9	2153.9	2389.0	2300.9	2198.2	2547.4	2928.9	3097.6
2	DEP. + CR. MKT. INSTR. (1)	641.4	698.3	743.6	797.3	874.1	972.9	1088.0	1192.8	1311.2	1447.2	1610.7
3	DEMAND DEPOSITS + CURRENCY	100.7	111.6	109.0	117.8	130.7	144.6	159.8	165.9	171.1	184.9	204.4
4	TIME + SAVINGS ACCOUNTS	342.9	373.9	383.1	426.7	494.6	569.2	633.4	690.6	775.4	883.5	991.9
5	AT COMMERCIAL BANKS	149.4	167.6	168.4	195.4	223.6	252.8	288.5	324.7	350.1	389.6	428.8
6	AT SAVINGS INSTITUTIONS	193.5	206.3	214.7	231.4	271.0	316.4	344.9	365.9	425.4	493.9	563.0
7	CREDIT MARKET INSTRUMENTS	197.8	212.9	251.5	252.8	248.8	259.1	294.7	336.3	364.7	378.8	414.4
8	U.S. GOVT. SECURITIES	91.3	97.6	113.5	107.2	97.1	96.4	113.2	128.6	143.1	148.3	152.4
9	TREASURY ISSUES	80.0	84.9	95.9	84.9	76.6	79.4	94.2	105.5	123.2	124.4	125.4
10	SAVINGS BONDS	51.2	51.9	51.8	52.1	54.4	57.7	60.4	63.3	67.4	72.0	76.8
11	OTHER TREASURY	28.8	33.0	44.1	32.8	22.2	21.7	33.8	42.1	55.8	52.4	48.7
12	AGENCY ISSUES	11.3	12.7	17.7	22.3	20.5	17.0	19.0	23.1	19.9	23.9	27.0
13	ST. + LOC. OBLIGATIONS	38.1	37.6	46.9	46.0	46.1	48.4	53.6	61.8	67.9	73.0	81.9
14	CORPORATE + FGN. BONDS	15.0	19.2	24.6	35.3	43.8	48.0	49.0	56.2	63.4	62.4	64.8
15	MORTGAGES	46.1	48.7	51.3	52.9	54.1	60.5	63.9	68.2	71.9	79.8	91.8
16	OPEN-MARKET PAPER	7.3	9.9	15.2	11.4	7.6	5.9	15.0	19.2	14.7	11.5	19.7
17	MONEY MARKET FUND SHRS.	—	—	—	—	—	—	—	2.4	3.7	3.7	3.9
18	CORPORATE EQUITIES	720.6	659.1	746.5	729.0	833.7	913.7	712.0	504.2	659.0	826.3	777.0
19	INVESTMENT COMPANY SHARES	44.7	52.7	48.3	47.6	56.7	59.8	46.5	34.1	42.2	47.0	42.8
20	OTHER CORPORATE EQUITIES	675.9	806.4	698.2	681.4	777.0	853.8	665.5	470.1	616.8	779.3	734.3
21	LIFE INSURANCE RESERVES	115.4	120.0	125.0	130.3	136.4	143.1	150.5	156.9	165.1	172.0	180.1
22	PENSION FUND RESERVES	186.4	208.1	218.7	239.6	276.2	323.0	311.4	303.6	367.2	431.2	469.8
23	SECURITY CREDIT	4.9	7.0	5.2	4.4	4.9	5.0	4.9	3.9	4.5	6.3	7.3
24	MISCELLANEOUS ASSETS	19.8	21.6	23.8	26.3	28.7	31.3	34.1	36.8	40.6	46.0	52.6
25	TOTAL LIABILITIES	405.3	441.6	473.5	497.6	546.9	616.8	693.7	742.6	793.8	891.0	1036.1
26	CREDIT MARKET INSTRUMENTS	385.0	417.6	451.9	476.8	522.5	586.8	667.1	716.1	764.7	854.9	994.6
27	HOME MORTGAGES	241.0	258.0	276.5	290.7	317.7	359.4	405.7	440.9	479.0	540.5	633.8
28	OTHER MORTGAGES	15.6	16.7	17.9	19.0	20.3	21.5	22.6	23.7	24.8	25.8	26.9
29	INSTALMENT CONS. CREDIT	79.4	87.7	97.1	102.0	112.7	126.6	148.2	157.5	165.0	185.5	216.6
30	OTHER CONSUMER CREDIT	21.4	23.0	24.0	25.1	27.4	30.5	32.9	33.8	35.7	38.7	42.7
31	BANK LOANS N.E.C.	14.3	16.3	18.3	19.1	22.1	23.6	31.5	30.8	28.8	30.9	39.1
32	OTHER LOANS	13.3	15.3	18.3	20.9	22.3	23.6	26.2	29.4	31.5	33.4	35.7
33	SECURITY CREDIT	12.7	15.6	12.2	10.4	13.1	17.6	13.2	11.4	12.1	17.2	20.3
34	TRADE CREDIT	3.7	4.1	4.7	5.3	5.8	6.5	7.1	8.0	9.1	10.5	11.8
35	DEFERRED AND UNPAID LIFE INSURANCE PREMIUMS	3.9	4.3	4.7	5.1	5.4	6.0	6.4	7.1	7.7	8.4	9.3

(1) EXCLUDES CORPORATE EQUITIES.

Source: Board of Governors of the Federal Reserve System, *Flow of Funds Accounts—Assets and Liabilities Outstanding, 1967–77*, August 1978.

porate stocks ran a distant second at $777 billion. The principal financial obligation of this sector is home mortgages, amounting to nearly $634 billion. Instalment debt taken on by households totaled $216.6 billion in 1977. A check of previous years shows that both household mortgage and instalment debt have risen rapidly in recent years, reflecting the combined effects of inflation, rising energy costs, and a greater willingness of consumers to take on debt to sustain their desired level of consumption.

The two financial statements—flow of funds and financial assets and liabilities—should be analyzed *together* for a complete understanding of long-run and short-run financial changes in the economy. One statement is incomplete without the other. The Flow of Funds Accounts—Tables 2–2 and 2–3—indicate *short-run* changes in financial assets and liabilities. In contrast, statements of financial assets and liabilities for the whole economy or for individual sectors, as in Table 2–4, reflect *long-run changes* (i.e., accumulated flows for past years) in balance sheets. Each statement contributes important and unique information not reflected in the other.

TYPES OF INSTRUMENTS TRADED BY FINANCIAL INTERMEDIARIES IN THE FINANCIAL MARKETS

In Chapter 1 we presented a framework for analyzing the behavior of financial intermediaries. We pointed out that intermediaries select which financial assets and liabilities to acquire on the basis of certain factors. Specifically, their portfolio choices depend upon: (1) the expected returns attached to various financial instruments which they are interested in acquiring or issuing; (2) the degree of default and market risk displayed by each financial instrument; (3) the probabilities of a cash-out (illiquidity) due to unexpected changes in inflows and outflows of funds; and (4) the character of law and regulation which limit the range of portfolio choices to those financial instruments deemed appropriate by society. In turn, the acquisition of financial assets (uses of funds) by an intermediary is heavily influenced by its choices of liabilities (sources of funds). Intermediaries which depend upon highly volatile, relatively risky funds sources usually seek assets which are liquid and readily marketable. Commercial banks are a good example of this kind of portfolio behavior. On the other hand, intermediaries with highly predictable and stable sources of funds typically find little need for substantial investments in liquid assets and usually remain almost fully invested in longer-term, higher-yielding assets, including bonds, mortgages, and stocks. Intermediaries with this kind of portfolio strategy include insurance companies and pension funds. Of course, the final portfolio choices made by an intermediary are also shaped by the goals of the organization. Clearly, a financial intermediary pursuing maximum earnings or maximization of the wealth position of its stockholders would make somewhat different portfolio selections than one interested solely in growth and public service.

In addition to giving us a glimpse of savings flows among various sectors of the economy, the Flow of Funds Accounts provide information on the actual portfolio choices made by financial intermediaries. Through these social accounts we can follow *changes* in the sources and uses of funds of each type of intermediary. The Flow of Funds Accounts also provide information on the stocks of assets and liabilities held by financial institutions at any given point in time. And, these accounts indicate flows of financial assets among the different kinds of intermediaries over a specific period of time and also show how the financial institutions' sector interacts with the remainder of the economic and financial system.

It is useful for us to examine in some detail the kinds of information on financial intermediaries available from the Flow of Funds Accounts. Stocks of financial assets and liabilities for each major kind of financial institution for the years 1967 to 1977 are shown in Tables 2–5 through 2–9. In the following sections we present a broad overview of the sources and uses of funds among the major classes of financial intermediaries.

1. Commercial banks and the monetary authorities

In many ways the commercial bank may be regarded as the most important financial intermediary. At year-end 1977, according to the flow of funds data in Table 2–5, total financial assets held by U.S. commercial banks (including their domestic affiliates, foreign banking agencies, and banks in U.S. possessions) totaled nearly $1.1 trillion, compared to $1.6 trillion for all nonbank financial intermediaries combined. Throughout the postwar period commercial banks have held slightly more than 40 percent of the assets of all U.S. financial institutions. The next most important type of financial institution — savings and loan associations — held $459 billion in financial assets, followed by life insurance companies with $341 billion. Equally significant, liabilities of the banking system represent about four fifths of the nation's money supply, while commercial banks are the principal conduit for government monetary policy.[4]

---

[4] The conventional definition of the money supply — the sum of currency in circulation and demand deposits at banks — emphasizes the role of money as a medium of exchange. This definition is usually designated M_1. A somewhat broader definition of money, known as M_2, includes M_1 plus time and savings deposits at commercial banks

As Table 2–5 suggests, commercial banks derive the majority of their funds from two sources—time and savings deposits (which totaled $550.7 billion in 1977) and demand deposits ($277.7 billion). On the uses-of-funds side commercial banks hold substantial quantities of liquid assets (principally cash and government securities), including cash reserves required by the regulatory authorities. Included in bank holdings of liquid assets at year-end 1977 was approximately $140 billion in U.S. government securities and $115 billion in state and local government obligations. Loans totaled $447.7 billion of which loans to consumers amounted to $118.7 billion. The remainder of the loan total included construction financing, short-term working capital loans, long-term credits to agriculture and non-farm businesses, and loans to other financial intermediaries.

An example of the effects of *disintermediation* may be seen in Table 2–5. Disintermediation occurs when funds are withdrawn from a financial institution by savers and invested in the open market through the purchase of securities. This phenomenon typically appears during periods of high and rising interest rates when intermediaries have difficulty adjusting the rates they offer savers quickly enough to keep up with interest rates available in the open market. We note, for example, in 1969 when interest rates were at record levels time and savings deposits held by commercial banks dropped nearly $10 billion, led by a decline of more than $12 billion in large ($100,000+) negotiable CDs. As a result, the financial assets of the banking system grew more slowly, especially loans and the purchase of securities. A similar pattern of disintermediation occurred in 1975 and to a lesser extent in 1978 and 1979.

The banking system, as defined by the Flow of Funds Accounts, also includes the financial accounts of the monetary authorities—the Federal Reserve System and the U.S. Treasury. The Federal Reserve banks hold the reserve deposits of member banks (which totaled $26.9 billion at year-end 1977) and the U.S. Treasury's checking accounts (which amounted to $7.5 billion). Through its monetary policy tools the Federal Reserve System changes the level of member-bank reserves and thereby affects the level of interest rates and the level

---

and stresses the role of money as a store of value. The distinction between M_1 and M_2 may well become less precise in the future, however, as individual depositors are permitted to have funds held in their savings accounts automatically shifted into their demand accounts to cover overdrafts. Effective November 1, 1978, the Federal Reserve Board and the Federal Deposit Insurance Corporation amended their regulations to permit insured member and nonmember banks to transfer funds from a customer's savings account to a checking account automatically whenever the customer's checking account balance drops below some agreed-upon minimum. The terms under which such transfers are permitted vary from bank to bank, depending upon the individual bank's marketing policies and competition in the local market area.

TABLE 2-5
Statements of financial assets and liabilities for the banking system, 1967-77
($billions)

YEAR-END OUTSTANDINGS

MONETARY AUTHORITIES

		1967	1968	1969	1970	1971	1972	1973	1974	1975	1976	1977
1	TOTAL FINANCIAL ASSETS	72.8	76.7	80.7	86.1	94.6	97.6	106.9	113.4	124.6	134.5	143.0
2	GOLD + FOREIGN EXCHANGE	13.5	12.4	12.3	10.9	10.1	10.5	11.5	11.6	11.7	11.7	11.7
3	TREASURY CURR. + SDR. CTFS.	6.6	6.8	6.8	7.5	8.0	8.7	9.1	9.7	10.6	12.0	12.6
4	F.R. FLOAT	2.5	3.5	3.4	4.3	4.3	4.0	3.1	2.0	3.7	2.6	3.8
5	F.R. LOANS TO DOMESTIC BANKS	.1	.2	.2	.3	*	2.0	1.3	.3	.2	*	.3
6	CREDIT MARKET INSTRUMENTS	49.3	53.0	57.2	62.2	71.1	71.3	80.6	86.7	95.3	105.1	112.2
7	U.S. GOVERNMENT SECURITIES	49.2	52.9	57.2	62.1	70.8	71.2	80.5	85.7	94.1	104.1	111.3
8	TREASURY ISSUES	49.1	52.9	57.2	62.1	70.2	69.9	78.5	80.5	87.9	97.0	102.8
9	AGENCY ISSUES	*	—	—	—	.6	1.3	2.0	5.2	6.2	7.1	8.5
10	ACCEPTANCES	.2	.1	.1	.1	.3	.1	.1	1.0	1.1	1.0	1.0
11	BANK LOANS N.E.C.	*	.1	.1	.1	—	—	—	—	—	—	—
12	MISCELLANEOUS ASSETS	.7	.9	.8	.9	1.1	1.1	1.4	3.2	3.2	3.0	2.4
13	TOTAL LIABILITIES	72.8	76.7	80.7	86.1	94.6	97.6	106.9	113.4	124.6	134.5	143.0
14	MEMBER BANK RESERVES	21.1	21.9	22.1	24.2	27.8	25.6	27.1	25.8	26.1	25.2	26.9
15	VAULT CASH OF COML. BANKS	5.9	7.2	7.3	7.0	7.5	8.7	10.7	11.7	12.3	12.1	13.9
16	DEMAND DEPOSITS + CURRENCY	44.1	45.6	48.9	52.0	56.4	60.4	65.0	71.9	82.5	93.1	98.0
17	DUE TO U.S. GOVERNMENT	2.5	1.4	2.0	1.6	2.0	2.2	2.9	3.3	7.8	10.9	7.5
18	DUE TO REST OF THE WORLD	.4	.5	.4	.3	.5	.4	.3	.5	.5	.6	.6
19	CURRENCY OUTSIDE BANKS	41.2	43.8	46.6	50.0	53.4	57.9	61.8	68.1	74.3	81.6	89.9
20	MISCELLANEOUS LIABILITIES	1.6	2.0	2.4	2.9	2.9	2.9	4.2	4.0	3.8	4.1	4.2
21	NET WORTH	—	—	—	—	—	—	—	—	—	—	—

COMMERCIAL BANKING (1)

		1967	1968	1969	1970	1971	1972	1973	1974	1975	1976	1977
1	TOTAL FINANCIAL ASSETS	404.8	450.2	471.6	513.3	574.2	655.3	760.7	848.0	880.9	961.8	1066.8
2	DEMAND DEPOSITS + CURRENCY	.2	.3	.4	.4	.5	.7	1.0	.8	.7	.7	1.3
3	TOTAL BANK CREDIT	365.0	405.1	422.4	459.5	510.3	585.6	669.0	731.4	761.1	826.3	912.7
4	CREDIT MARKET INSTRUMENTS	353.4	392.1	410.4	445.5	496.0	566.5	653.1	717.8	745.4	803.4	889.2
5	U.S. GOVT. SECURITIES	72.4	75.7	65.7	76.4	83.6	90.0	88.8	89.8	119.9	139.6	139.5
6	TREASURY ISSUES	63.3	65.3	55.6	62.5	65.6	68.0	59.2	56.6	85.4	103.6	102.7
7	AGENCY ISSUES	9.1	10.4	10.1	13.9	17.9	22.0	29.6	33.2	34.5	36.0	36.8
8	OTHER SECURITIES + MTGS.	111.2	126.6	131.7	145.4	169.0	194.6	220.5	240.1	247.6	265.2	301.9
9	ST. + LOC. OBLIGATIONS	50.3	58.9	59.5	70.2	82.8	90.0	95.7	101.2	102.8	105.9	115.1
10	CORPORATE BONDS	1.9	2.2	1.7	2.4	3.7	5.3	5.7	6.8	8.6	8.0	7.9
11	MORTGAGES	58.9	65.5	70.5	72.8	82.5	99.3	119.1	132.1	136.2	151.3	179.0

#	Item	1	2	3	4	5	6	7	8	9	10	11
12	OTHER CR. EXCL. SECURITY	169.8	189.8	213.0	223.6	243.4	281.9	343.8	387.9	377.8	398.5	447.7
13	CONSUMER CREDIT	40.8	46.3	51.0	53.9	61.3	72.1	83.7	87.3	90.2	101.7	118.7
14	BANK LOANS N.E.C.	123.2	138.1	155.4	161.6	173.7	201.5	253.1	291.4	277.3	282.9	314.7
15	OPEN-MARKET PAPER	5.8	5.4	6.7	8.2	8.5	8.3	7.0	9.2	10.3	14.0	14.3
16	HYPOTHECATED DEPOSITS	-	-	-	-	-	-	-	-	-	-	-
17	CORPORATE EQUITIES	.3	.4	.4	.5	.5	.6	.9	.9	1.2	1.2	1.2
18	SECURITY CREDIT	11.3	12.7	11.5	13.0	13.8	18.5	15.1	12.7	14.6	21.7	22.3
19	VAULT CASH	5.9	7.2	7.3	7.0	7.5	8.7	10.7	11.7	12.3	12.1	13.9
20	MEMBER BANK RESERVES	21.1	21.9	22.1	24.2	27.8	25.6	27.1	25.8	26.1	25.2	26.9
21	OTHER INTERBANK CLAIMS	2.0	2.8	4.5	6.3	9.6	11.9	23.0	33.0	26.9	31.8	32.3
22	MISCELLANEOUS ASSETS	10.5	13.0	15.0	16.4	18.4	22.8	29.9	45.4	53.7	65.7	79.8
23	TOTAL LIABILITIES	378.4	422.0	442.1	482.0	540.6	618.7	719.9	803.8	833.8	908.5	1008.1
24	DEMAND DEPOSITS, NET	162.5	175.8	180.5	189.8	202.9	223.3	236.6	236.6	241.8	254.0	277.7
25	U.S. GOVERNMENT	5.2	5.0	5.1	7.9	10.2	10.9	9.9	4.8	3.0	3.0	7.3
26	OTHER	157.3	170.8	175.4	181.8	192.7	212.4	226.3	232.0	238.7	250.9	270.3
27	TIME DEPOSITS	183.7	204.5	195.1	233.1	274.5	316.8	367.7	425.5	455.6	496.1	550.7
28	LARGE NEGOTIABLE CD'S	20.3	23.5	10.2	26.1	34.8	44.5	64.5	93.0	82.9	65.4	77.4
29	OTHER AT COMMERCIAL BANKS	162.8	180.2	183.2	205.6	238.0	271.1	301.4	330.5	370.2	428.8	471.6
30	AT FOREIGN BANKING AGS.	.6	.8	1.0	1.4	1.7	1.2	1.8	2.0	2.5	1.9	1.7
31	F.R. FLOAT	2.5	3.5	3.4	4.3	4.3	4.0	3.1	2.0	3.7	2.6	3.8
32	BORROWING AT F.R. BANKS	.1	.2	.2	.3	*	2.0	1.3	.3	.2	*	.3
33	OTHER INTERBANK CLAIMS	2.0	2.8	4.5	6.3	9.6	11.9	23.0	33.0	26.9	31.8	32.3
34	CREDIT MARKET DEBT	2.6	3.5	10.2	6.1	7.6	11.6	26.7	23.6	21.5	26.6	32.1
35	CORPORATE BONDS	2.0	2.2	2.0	2.1	3.0	4.1	4.1	4.3	4.5	5.2	5.7
36	OPEN-MARKET PAPER	.7	-	4.3	2.1	2.0	2.8	4.9	8.3	8.7	7.9	9.1
37	FEDERAL FUNDS AND RP'S	1.2	3.8	1.6	2.6	4.8	17.7	11.0	8.4	13.6	17.2	
38	PROFIT TAXES PAYABLE	.6	.5	.6	1.0	.9	.7	.8	.9	.6	.6	
39	MISCELLANEOUS LIABILITIES	24.2	31.3	47.6	41.2	40.8	48.5	61.2	81.7	83.4	96.7	110.7
40	LIAB. TO FGN. AFFILIATES	8.3	10.6	19.0	13.2	9.0	11.6	11.6	18.4	18.5	23.1	32.0
41	OTHER	15.9	20.6	28.6	28.0	31.8	36.9	49.6	63.2	64.9	73.6	78.7

(1) CONSISTS OF CHARTERED COMMERCIAL BANKS, THEIR DOMESTIC AFFILIATES, EDGE ACT CORPORATIONS, AGENCIES OF FOREIGN BANKS, AND BANKS IN U.S. POSSESSIONS. EDGE ACT CORPORATIONS AND AGENCIES OF FOREIGN BANKS APPEAR TOGETHER IN THESE TABLES AS "FOREIGN BANKING AGENCIES."

Source: Board of Governors of the Federal Reserve System, *Flow of Funds Accounts—Assets and Liabilities Outstanding, 1967–77*, August, 1978.

and growth of the nation's money supply.[5] The principal device used by the Fed to carry out its policies is open market operations—the buying and selling of securities in the money and capital markets. We note that the Fed held a substantial volume of securities for this purpose at year-end 1977, including $102.8 billion in U.S. Treasury obligations and $8.5 billion in the debt obligations of various federal agencies.

2. Savings and loan associations

Savings and loan associations (S&Ls)—often referred to as domestic building and loan associations—began in the 1830s for the express purpose of channeling the savings of members into the financing of homes. Similar to mutual savings banks (to be discussed below), these associations are principally mutual organizations in which savers are owners rather than creditors. It is clear from Table 2–6 that savings and loan associations derive the bulk of their funds from the savings deposits (shares) of individuals, trust funds, and other organizations. Other important sources of funds include bank loans, advances from the Federal Home Loan Banks (FHLB), reserves, and undivided profits.

The majority of savings and loan funds (typically at least 80 percent) are invested in residential mortgage loans and housing-related securities. In fact, savings and loans are the principal lending institution in the U.S. residential mortgage market. As Table 2–6 indicates, savings associations held $381 billion in mortgages by year-end 1977. In contrast, S&Ls hold small amounts of cash (in the form of demand deposits and currency) and other liquid investments, such as time deposits and U.S. government securities. Because savings deposits are a relatively stable source of funds, the savings and loan industry has relatively minimal liquidity needs.

3. Mutual savings banks

Mutual savings banks are similar to savings and loan associations in both their sources and uses of funds. Founded in Scotland in the early 19th century, mutual savings banks operate mainly along the East Coast of the United States. The principal focus of savings bank activity is attracting and channeling the savings of small- and middle-income households and organizations into mortgages, corpo-

---

[5] The principal monetary policy tools of the Federal Reserve include: (1) setting member-bank reserve requirements; (2) setting the discount rate on loans to member banks made through its discount window; and (3) buying and selling securities in the open market. These policy tools are discussed at length in Chapter 5.

rate bonds, U.S. government and federal agency securities, and corporate stock. The Flow of Funds Accounts indicate that savings deposits placed in mutuals totaled $134 billion in 1977. (See Table 2–6.) Historically, about 90 percent of the industry's funds have come from savings deposits. Borrowings from banks and other intermediaries and various equity reserves account for the remainder of funds available to mutuals.

With relatively stable deposits, mutuals have only a limited need for liquidity. Their holdings of U.S. government securities (including federal agency obligations) totaled only $17.6 billion in 1977, or about 20 percent of their mortgage holdings. Cash assets in the form of demand and time deposits and currency represented less that 2 percent of the industry's total resources. Clearly, the principal investment of mutuals is mortgages which represented about three fifths of their total financial assets at year-end 1977. Industry holdings of corporate bonds ran a distant second to mortgages, accounting for approximately 15 percent of all financial assets.

4. Credit unions

Credit unions are cooperative associations whose membership consists of individuals with some common relationship—usually the same employer or group of employers, labor union, church, fraternal society, or residential location. In return for their savings deposits, members receive shares in the association and are eligible to borrow, subject to certain rules. As revealed by the flow of funds data in Table 2–6, the bulk of credit union funds come from member savings deposits (shares) and are loaned out to members (consumer credit). However, small amounts of funds are obtained also from commercial bank loans and reserves.

As of year-end 1977, U.S. credit unions held $37 billion in consumer loans, representing about 70 percent of their total financial assets. Because their liquidity needs are modest, credit unions hold relatively small amounts of liquid assets. At year-end 1977, for example, the industry held $5.2 billion in U.S. government securities— about 10 percent of its total financial assets. Holdings of share accounts at savings and loan associations, commercial bank deposits, and currency and coin amounted to $6.5 billion, or about 13 percent of total assets. In some states credit unions are allowed to acquire high-quality corporate and municipal bonds and real estate mortgages. Beginning in 1977 credit unions chartered by the federal government were given permission to make certain types of long-term residential mortgage loans.

TABLE 2-6

Statements of financial assets and liabilities for nonbank thrift institutions,
1967–1977 ($billions)

YEAR-END OUTSTANDINGS

SAVINGS AND LOAN ASSOCIATIONS

	1967	1968	1969	1970	1971	1972	1973	1974	1975	1976	1977	
TOTAL FINANCIAL ASSETS	143.5	152.9	162.1	176.2	206.0	243.1	271.9	295.5	338.2	391.9	459.3	1
MORTGAGES	121.7	130.6	140.0	149.8	174.3	206.2	231.7	249.3	278.6	323.0	381.2	2
CONSUMER CREDIT	1.5	1.6	1.8	2.1	2.9	3.8	4.9	5.6	6.5	7.5	8.7	3
OTHER ASSETS	20.4	20.7	20.3	24.3	28.8	33.1	35.3	40.7	53.1	61.4	69.4	4
DEMAND DEPOSITS + CURR.	2.0	1.6	1.4	1.2	.9	1.2	1.0	1.0	1.3	1.5	1.4	5
TIME DEPOSITS	.2	.2	.2	.6	2.2	3.2	2.5	2.9	7.4	6.8	6.7	6
U.S. TREASURY SECURITIES	9.3	9.6	8.1	6.8	6.2	5.7	4.0	4.0	5.3	9.1	7.8	7
U.S.G. AGENCY SEC.	1.0	1.1	2.3	4.1	7.2	9.6	11.9	13.1	17.2	17.9	22.8	8
STATE + LOCAL GOVT. SEC.	–	.1	.1	.1	.2	.2	.2	.5	1.1	1.2	1.3	9
OPEN-MARKET PAPER	–	.1	.3	1.8	2.8	3.3	2.0	1.8	2.7	2.6	2.6	10
FEDERAL FUNDS + RP'S	–	–	–	–	.5	.9	2.2	4.0	2.6	4.8	7.4	11
MISCELLANEOUS ASSETS	7.9	8.0	7.8	9.5	8.9	9.1	11.4	13.3	15.5	17.6	19.5	12
TOTAL LIABILITIES	134.0	142.6	150.9	164.2	192.4	227.9	254.8	277.1	318.5	369.9	434.1	13
SAVINGS SHARES	124.5	131.6	135.5	146.4	174.2	206.8	227.0	243.0	285.7	335.9	386.9	14
CREDIT MARKET INSTRUMENTS	7.0	8.2	12.3	14.1	14.1	16.0	22.0	28.3	26.1	26.1	38.0	15
CORPORATE BONDS	–	–	–	–	–	–	–	–	.1	.1	1.3	16
MORTGAGE LOANS IN PROCESS	2.3	2.4	2.5	3.1	5.0	6.2	4.7	3.2	5.1	6.8	9.9	17
BANK LOANS N.E.C.	.4	.5	.5	.4	1.1	1.5	1.9	1.5	1.2	1.4	3.8	18
FHLB ADVANCES	4.4	5.3	9.3	10.6	7.9	8.0	15.1	21.8	17.8	15.9	20.2	19
SECURITY RP'S	–	–	–	–	–	–	.3	1.8	1.9	1.8	2.8	20
PROFIT TAXES PAYABLE	.1	.1	.1	.1	.2	.2	.2	.3	.4	.6	.9	21
MISCELLANEOUS LIABILITIES	2.4	2.7	3.0	3.6	4.0	4.9	5.6	5.5	6.2	7.3	8.4	22
MEMO: TOTAL CR. MKT. ASSETS	133.4	143.1	152.7	164.9	194.0	229.6	257.0	278.3	314.0	366.0	431.7	23

MUTUAL SAVINGS BANKS

1	TOTAL FINANCIAL ASSETS	67.2	71.6	74.5	79.3	90.1	101.5	106.8	109.1	121.1	134.8	147.3
2	DEMAND DEPOSITS + CURRENCY	.8	.8	.9	1.0	.9	1.0	1.1	1.1	1.2	1.3	2.1
3	TIME DEPOSITS	.2	.2	.1	.3	.5	.6	.8	1.0	1.1	1.1	.3
4	CORPORATE EQUITIES	2.5	2.4	2.5	2.8	3.5	4.5	4.2	3.7	4.4	4.4	4.8
5	CREDIT MARKET INSTRUMENTS	62.7	67.1	70.1	73.9	83.5	93.2	98.3	100.6	111.2	124.5	136.2
6	U.S. TREASURY SECURITIES	4.3	3.8	3.2	3.2	3.3	3.5	3.0	2.6	4.7	5.8	5.9
7	U.S.G. AGENCY SEC.	1.2	1.6	1.8	2.2	3.0	4.2	4.2	4.4	6.1	9.1	11.7
8	STATE + LOCAL OBLIGATIONS	.2	.2	.2	.2	.4	.9	.9	.9	1.5	2.4	2.8
9	CORPORATE BONDS	5.3	6.6	6.9	8.1	12.0	14.2	13.1	14.0	17.5	20.3	21.5
10	MORTGAGES	50.5	53.5	56.1	57.9	62.0	67.6	73.2	74.9	77.2	81.6	88.1
11	CONSUMER CREDIT	.7	.9	1.0	1.1	1.2	1.3	1.6	1.7	1.9	2.2	2.5
12	COMMERCIAL PAPER	.5	.4	.5	.7	1.0	.9	.8	.9	1.0	1.5	1.6
13	SECURITY RP'S	—	.1	.3	.4	.7	.8	1.5	1.2	1.1	1.5	2.1
14	MISCELLANEOUS ASSETS	1.0	1.1	1.0	1.3	1.7	2.1	2.4	2.6	3.2	3.6	3.9
15	TOTAL LIABILITIES	61.4	65.9	68.7	73.3	83.3	93.6	99.0	101.6	112.6	125.8	137.3
16	SAVINGS DEPOSITS	60.1	64.5	67.1	71.6	81.4	91.6	96.3	98.7	109.9	122.9	134.0
17	MISCELLANEOUS LIABILITIES	1.3	1.4	1.6	1.7	1.8	2.0	2.6	2.9	2.8	2.9	3.3

CREDIT UNIONS

1	TOTAL FINANCIAL ASSETS	13.2	14.5	16.1	18.0	21.1	24.6	27.8	31.1	36.9	43.2	51.5
2	DEMAND DEPOSITS + CURRENCY	.7	.7	.6	.8	.9	1.0	1.1	1.2	1.3	1.2	1.3
3	TIME DEPOSITS	—	—	—	—	—	—	.2	.2	.6	.4	.5
4	SAVINGS + LOAN SHARES	2.3	2.1	1.7	2.1	3.0	3.6	2.9	3.3	3.3	3.9	4.7
5	CREDIT MARKET INSTRUMENTS	10.2	11.7	13.8	15.2	17.2	20.1	23.7	26.4	31.7	37.8	45.1
6	U.S. GOVERNMENT SECURITIES	.5	.7	1.0	1.4	1.6	2.1	2.6	3.0	4.1	4.7	5.2
7	HOME MORTGAGES	.7	.7	.7	.8	.8	1.0	1.4	1.5	2.0	2.5	2.9
8	CONSUMER CREDIT	9.0	10.3	12.0	13.0	14.8	17.0	19.6	21.9	25.7	30.5	37.0
9	CREDIT UNION SHARES	11.1	12.3	13.7	15.5	18.4	21.6	24.5	27.5	33.0	39.0	46.8

Source: Board of Governors of the Federal Reserve System, *Flow of Funds Accounts—Assets and Liabilities Outstanding, 1967–77*, August 1978.

5. Life insurance companies

Life insurance companies provide both an outlet for savings and protection against financial losses and reduced income associated with death and old age. Collection of insurance premiums and the investment strategy pursued by life companies is based upon the principle that the number of policyholders in each age group who will die each year is highly predictable. The predictability in the total amount of benefit payments that will be required means that life companies have very small liquidity needs. The bulk of their policy reserves accumulated from premiums paid by the public tend to be invested in longer-term, higher-yielding assets, such as corporate bonds, stocks, and mortgages.

As Table 2–7 shows, total financial assets of life companies amounted to $340.5 billion in 1977. The largest single category of assets was corporate bonds (about 40 percent of the total) followed by mortgages (making up another 30 percent of total financial assets). Holdings of U.S. government securities were small (less than 2 percent of assets) and have been relatively stable as a percentage of assets during the past decade. Further reflecting the industry's minimal liquidity needs, holdings of cash (demand deposits and currency) totaled only $2.1 billion, or less than 1 percent of total financial assets in 1977.

6. Property-casualty insurance companies

Similar to life insurance companies, property-casualty insurers protect their policyholders against risk—in this instance, the risk of damage to property or health from accidents, disease, fire, and other sources of harm. While some property-casualty insurers offer only specialized kinds of policies, most offer a broad range of protection against property damage as well as liability coverage and health insurance. Benefit claims against property-casualty insurers, however, are considerably less predictable than policyholder claims against life insurance companies. As a result, property-casualty companies must hold substantially larger liquid reserves than life companies and also more marketable long-term assets.

As Table 2–7 suggests, financial assets held by nonlife ("other") insurance companies are concentrated principally in state and local government obligations (municipals), corporate stocks, and corporate bonds. Holdings of cash assets (demand deposits and currency) accounted for only about 2 percent of total resources, but investments in U.S. government securities (including U.S. Treasury issues and federal agency obligations)—the principal source of liquidity—

TABLE 2-7
Statements of financial assets and liabilities for insurance companies, 1967–1977

YEAR-END OUTSTANDINGS

LIFE INSURANCE COMPANIES

		1967	1968	1969	1970	1971	1972	1973	1974	1975	1976	1977
1	TOTAL FINANCIAL ASSETS	172.6	183.1	191.3	200.9	215.2	232.4	244.8	255.0	279.7	311.1	340.5
2	DEMAND DEPOSITS + CURRENCY	1.6	1.7	1.6	1.8	1.8	2.0	2.1	2.0	1.9	2.0	2.1
3	CORPORATE EQUITIES	10.9	13.2	13.7	15.4	20.6	26.8	25.9	21.9	28.1	34.3	32.9
4	CREDIT MARKET INSTRUMENTS	153.3	160.7	167.6	174.6	182.8	192.5	204.8	217.7	234.6	258.3	286.5
5	TREASURY ISSUES	4.7	4.5	4.1	4.0	3.8	3.8	3.4	3.4	4.7	5.4	5.7
6	AGENCY ISSUES	.2	.3	.4	.8	.7	.7	.7	1.1	1.4	2.3	3.9
7	STATE + LOCAL OBLIGATIONS	3.1	3.2	3.2	3.3	3.4	3.4	3.4	3.7	4.5	5.6	6.0
8	CORPORATE BONDS	67.2	70.9	72.7	74.1	79.6	86.6	92.5	96.4	105.5	122.4	140.7
9	MORTGAGES	67.5	70.0	72.0	74.4	75.5	76.9	81.4	86.2	89.2	91.6	96.8
10	OPEN-MARKET PAPER	.5	.5	1.4	2.1	2.8	3.0	3.0	4.1	4.8	5.2	5.9
11	POLICY LOANS	10.1	11.3	13.8	16.1	17.1	18.0	20.2	22.9	24.5	25.8	27.5
12	MISCELLANEOUS ASSETS	6.9	7.5	8.3	9.2	10.1	11.1	12.0	13.4	15.0	16.5	19.0
13	TOTAL LIABILITIES	159.0	168.1	177.5	187.7	201.0	216.3	230.1	243.9	267.0	296.1	324.8
14	LIFE INSURANCE RESERVES	106.2	112.9	117.8	122.9	129.0	135.5	142.7	149.1	157.1	163.8	171.7
15	PENSION FUND RESERVES	32.1	35.0	37.9	41.2	46.4	52.3	56.1	60.8	71.7	88.4	101.0
16	PROFIT TAXES PAYABLE	.5	.6	.7	.8	.8	.8	.8	.8	.7	.9	1.3
17	MISCELLANEOUS LIABILITIES	18.2	19.7	21.1	22.8	24.9	27.7	30.5	33.2	37.5	43.0	50.8

OTHER INSURANCE COMPANIES

		1967	1968	1969	1970	1971	1972	1973	1974	1975	1976	1977
1	TOTAL FINANCIAL ASSETS	40.9	44.9	45.6	49.9	57.4	67.5	69.5	67.8	77.3	93.9	108.8
2	DEMAND DEPOSITS + CURRENCY	1.3	1.4	1.3	1.4	1.5	1.5	1.5	1.6	1.7	1.9	2.2
3	CORPORATE EQUITIES	13.0	14.6	13.3	13.2	16.6	21.8	19.7	12.8	14.2	16.9	17.1
4	CREDIT MARKET INSTRUMENTS	23.5	25.4	27.0	30.9	34.6	38.3	41.8	46.4	53.7	66.2	79.6
5	TREASURY ISSUES	4.3	3.9	3.4	3.4	3.2	3.2	2.8	2.9	4.7	7.3	9.8
6	AGENCY ISSUES	1.2	1.4	1.6	1.6	1.9	2.3	2.3	2.7	3.3	3.9	4.4
7	STATE + LOCAL OBLIGATIONS	13.5	14.4	15.5	17.0	20.5	24.8	28.5	30.7	33.3	38.7	48.2
8	CORPORATE BONDS	4.3	5.5	6.3	8.6	8.9	8.1	8.0	10.0	12.2	16.1	16.9
9	COMMERCIAL MORTGAGES	.2	.2	.2	.2	.2	.2	.2	.2	.2	.3	.4
10	TRADE CREDIT	3.2	3.5	3.9	4.4	4.7	5.8	6.5	7.0	7.7	8.9	10.0
11	TOTAL LIABILITIES	25.1	27.5	30.9	34.4	38.0	42.9	47.7	52.6	58.8	69.2	80.3
12	PROFIT TAXES PAYABLE	.0	.1	.1	.2	.2	.3	.3	.3	.3	.4	.5
13	POLICY PAYABLES	25.0	27.5	30.8	34.2	37.8	42.6	47.4	52.3	58.5	68.8	79.8

Source: Board of Governors of the Federal Reserve System, *Flow of Funds Accounts—Assets and Liabilities Outstanding, 1967–77*, August 1978.

represented slightly over 13 percent of industry assets in 1977. Property-casualty companies have been making sizeable additions to their holdings of corporate and municipal bonds in recent years, reflecting the need for higher after-tax yields and greater stability in funds sources. Their holdings of corporate stocks have fluctuated widely, reaching a high point in the early 1970s and then falling significantly. More recently, investments in corporate stocks have been on the rise as the industry struggles to keep pace with the effects on inflation on property repair costs and health care.

7. Private pensions funds

Private pension funds have been the fastest growing major financial intermediary in the postwar period. In 1977 total financial assets held by private pension funds amounted to $185.5 billion compared to only $89.0 billion in 1967. Because liquidity requirements for pension funds are virtually nil since cash outflows are easily predicted, pension funds can remain almost fully invested in corporate stocks and bonds. The rising cost of pension fund operations has created a demand for common stock as a hedge against inflation with corporate bonds a distant second, as indicated in Table 2–8. Reflecting the extremely low liquidity needs of pension funds, cash holdings and investments in time deposits and U.S government securities combined represented only about 14 percent of total industry assets.

The future growth of private pension funds in the United States is somewhat uncertain. Positive factors include the strong drive by labor unions and other groups for greater financial security, the rapid development during the 1970s of pension programs for self-employed individuals, and expected increases in per capita income. Limiting factors on the future growth of pension funds appear to center on competition from life insurance companies in the form of annuity policies, the rising cost to employers of pension programs, and new funding standards imposed by federal and state governments which further increase costs. Most authorities expect the growth of private pension plans to slow in the 1980s compared to their spectacular performance during the 1960s and 1970s.

8. Government pension funds

While not growing as fast as private pension funds, public (or government) pension funds also have displayed very rapid development during the postwar period. This growth, like that of private funds, reflects rising per capita incomes and the drive of Americans for increased financial security. As indicated in Table 2–8, total

TABLE 2-8
Statements of financial assets and liabilities for private and state and local government pension funds ($billions)

	1967	1968	1969	1970	1971	1972	1973	1974	1975	1976	1977	1978		
PRIVATE PENSION FUNDS														
TOTAL FINANCIAL ASSETS	89.4	101.5	102.4	110.6	130.5	156.7	135.2	116.6	148.9	175.5	185.5		TOTAL FINANCIAL ASSETS	1
DEMAND DEPOSITS + CURRENCY	.9	1.0	1.0	1.1	1.3	1.6	1.4	1.3	1.5	1.6	1.7		DEMAND DEPOSITS + CURRENCY	2
TIME DEPOSITS	.4	.6	.6	.7	.3	.3	1.1	3.7	2.4	2.3	4.8		TIME DEPOSITS	3
CORPORATE EQUITIES	51.1	61.5	61.4	67.1	88.7	115.2	90.5	63.3	88.6	109.7	101.9		CORPORATE EQUITIES	4
CREDIT MARKET INSTRUMENTS	32.8	33.8	34.6	36.9	35.4	34.6	37.1	42.9	51.0	56.2	68.5		CREDIT MARKET INSTRUMENTS	5
TREASURY ISSUES	2.0	2.4	2.2	2.1	2.1	3.0	3.1	3.0	7.4	11.1	15.9		TREASURY ISSUES	6
AGENCY ISSUES	.3	.4	.6	.9	.6	.7	1.3	2.0	3.3	3.6	4.2		AGENCY ISSUES	7
CORPORATE BONDS	26.4	27.0	27.6	29.7	29.0	28.2	30.3	35.0	37.8	39.1	45.6		CORPORATE BONDS	8
MORTGAGES	4.1	4.1	4.2	4.2	3.7	2.7	2.4	2.4	2.4	2.4	2.7		MORTGAGES	9
MISCELLANEOUS ASSETS	4.2	4.6	4.7	4.9	4.8	5.0	5.1	5.3	5.5	5.7	8.7		MISCELLANEOUS ASSETS	10
STATE AND LOCAL GOVERNMENT EMPLOYEE RETIREMENT FUNDS														
TOTAL FINANCIAL ASSETS	42.6	48.0	53.2	60.3	69.0	80.6	84.7	88.0	104.7	120.8	130.5		TOTAL FINANCIAL ASSETS	1
DEMAND DEPOSITS + CURRENCY	.5	.6	.5	.6	.7	1.0	1.3	1.8	1.4	1.4	1.8		DEMAND DEPOSITS + CURRENCY	2
CORPORATE EQUITIES	3.9	5.8	7.3	10.1	15.4	22.2	20.2	16.4	24.3	30.1	30.0		CORPORATE EQUITIES	3
CREDIT MARKET INSTRUMENTS	38.3	41.6	45.5	49.6	52.9	57.4	63.1	69.8	79.0	89.3	98.7		CREDIT MARKET INSTRUMENTS	4
U.S. GOVERNMENT SECURITIES	7.0	7.3	7.0	6.6	5.4	5.7	5.5	5.5	7.6	9.2	12.6		U.S. GOVERNMENT SECURITIES	5
TREASURY ISSUES	6.2	5.9	5.4	5.1	3.9	3.6	2.5	1.6	2.5	4.1	6.4		TREASURY ISSUES	6
AGENCY ISSUES	.8	1.4	1.6	1.5	1.5	2.1	3.0	3.9	5.1	5.2	6.2		AGENCY ISSUES	7
STATE + LOCAL OBLIGATIONS	2.4	2.4	2.3	2.0	2.2	2.0	1.7	1.0	1.9	3.4	3.6		STATE + LOCAL OBLIGATIONS	8
CORPORATE BONDS	23.9	26.6	30.6	35.1	39.0	43.2	48.8	55.6	61.9	68.9	74.3		CORPORATE BONDS	9
MORTGAGES	5.0	5.4	5.6	5.9	6.3	6.5	7.1	7.7	7.5	7.7	8.2		MORTGAGES	10

Source: Board of Governors of the Federal Reserve System, *Flow of Funds Accounts—Assets and Liabilities Outstanding, 1967–77*, August 1978.

financial assets of state and local government employee retirement funds rose from $42.6 billion in 1967 to nearly $131 billion in 1977.

Corporate bonds are the most important asset held by this financial intermediary, representing about three fifths of its total financial resources in 1977. The next most important asset was corporate stock, representing 23 percent of the total, while holdings of mortgages were only about 6 percent of the whole industry portfolio. The rapid growth of investments in common stock in recent years is closely correlated with increases in the rate of inflation. The high yields available on good quality corporate bonds also have attracted considerable interest on the part of fund trustees for both private and public pension funds.

Public pension funds are similar to private funds in their extremely limited liquidity needs. With cash outflows easily predicted it is not surprising to find only negligible investments by government pensions in cash and riskless U.S. government securities. Table 2–8 indicates that cash holdings (demand deposits and currency) were little more than 1 percent of total financial assets in 1977, while investments in U.S. government securities represented less than 10 percent of the total. Holdings of state and local government bonds were relatively unimportant.

9. Finance companies

Automobiles, home appliances, industrial equipment, building and home repairs, business inventories, mobile homes, and numerous other commercial and consumer goods are financed today by finance companies. These intermediaries raise their funds principally by issuing money market securities and bonds or by borrowing from banks. In turn, the funds rasied are invested in consumer and business loans and, less frequently, in mortgages.

As shown in Table 2–9, total financial assets held by U.S. finance companies more than doubled between 1967 and 1977, rising to $125 billion in the latter year. Loans extended to consumers totaled $55.2 billion at year-end 1977 and were roughly equal to business credits (excluding mortgages). However, there is a trend in the industry today toward more emphasis upon business lending, especially leasing, and less emphasis upon consumer loans. Mortgages granted by finance companies ran a distant third as a use of funds, accounting for less than 10 percent of the industry's total assets. Finance companies stay fully invested and have only modest liquidity needs. At year-end 1977, for example, demand deposits and currency held by these intermediaries represented only about 3 percent of their total assets.

10.   Real estate investment trusts

Created by act of Congress in the early 1960s real estate investment trusts (REITs) were set up to expand the flow of funds into the mortgage market and, hopefully, to improve the availability of funds for the construction of multifamily and single-family residences. The industry grew rapidly in the late 1960s and early 1970s due to a heavy demand for mortgage credit. The high point was reached in 1974 when REITs held total financial assets of $17.5 billion. Unfortunately, numerous bad loans were made, especially for commercial and apartment construction projects, and the market value of industry assets declined precipitously in 1975, 1976, and 1977. Many REITs are affiliated with banks and bank holding companies. These affiliations coupled with more careful portfolio management practices should help the industry stabilize its financial affairs in future years.

11.   Investment companies

One of the simplest and most direct illustrations of the financial intermediation process is the operation of investment companies (more commonly called mutual funds).[6] These intermediaries attract funds from thousands of small savers and reinvest those dollars in financial assets, principally corporate stock. The investment company pools the savings of many investors in order to acquire a diversified portfolio of securities at reasonable cost. Dividends and interest received on investments and capital gains earned on sales of securities are paid to shareholders as a return on their investment, less, of course, portfolio management fees and other costs. Presumably, most, investors are unable diversify their portfolios sufficiently in order to reduce risk to acceptable levels and may not possess the skills and market contacts necessary to invest wisely in the open market.

Common stock mutual funds have lost a substantial amount of prestige in recent years. Recent downturns in the stock market have resulted in significant losses. At the same time the investment goals of certain funds proved to be unrealistic in the competitive and volatile atmosphere that prevailed in the market during the 1960s and 1970s. As Table 2–9 indicates, total financial assets held by open-end investment companies declined from a high of $59.8 billion in 1972 to

---

[6] Strictly speaking, mutual funds are only one kind of investment company—an open-end company. Open-end companies stand ready at all times to repurchase their shares of stock and to issue any number of new shares in response to public demand. In contrast, closed-end companies issue a fixed number of shares so that new investors desiring to buy into the company must acquire existing shares from other investors. Open-end companies typically issue only common stock, while closed-end companies also may issue preferred stock and bonds.

TABLE 2-9
Statements of financial assets and liabilities for miscellaneous types of financial intermediaries ($billions)

YEAR-END OUTSTANDINGS

	1967	1968	1969	1970	1971	1972	1973	1974	1975	1976	1977		
FINANCE COMPANIES													
TOTAL FINANCIAL ASSETS	47.7	52.9	61.6	64.0	69.4	79.1	90.8	96.1	97.7	106.7	125.0	TOTAL FINANCIAL ASSETS	1
DEMAND DEPOSITS + CURRENCY	2.2	2.3	2.4	2.7	2.9	3.2	3.5	3.7	3.9	4.1	4.3	DEMAND DEPOSITS + CURRENCY	2
CREDIT MARKET INSTRUMENTS	45.5	50.6	59.2	61.3	66.5	75.9	87.4	92.4	93.8	102.6	120.7	CREDIT MARKET INSTRUMENTS	3
MORTGAGES	4.3	4.9	5.7	7.4	8.9	10.6	12.5	10.6	9.3	9.0	10.5	MORTGAGES	4
CONSUMER CREDIT	26.9	29.2	32.0	32.1	34.4	37.9	42.6	44.6	45.2	48.9	55.2	CONSUMER CREDIT	5
OTHER LOANS (TO BUSINESS)	14.3	16.5	21.5	21.8	23.2	27.4	32.3	37.2	39.3	44.7	55.1	OTHER LOANS (TO BUSINESS)	6
TOTAL LIABILITIES	43.9	49.1	58.5	62.4	67.1	76.3	88.0	93.5	94.8	103.0	120.8	TOTAL LIABILITIES	7
CREDIT MARKET INSTRUMENTS	36.9	40.8	49.0	51.7	54.3	61.1	70.5	76.2	76.8	83.4	100.1	CREDIT MARKET INSTRUMENTS	8
CORPORATE BONDS	14.0	14.2	15.1	17.2	19.7	23.3	26.2	28.0	30.7	36.0	44.5	CORPORATE BONDS	9
BANK LOANS N.E.C.	8.3	9.7	11.0	10.9	11.5	15.9	20.5	20.7	18.0	16.1	16.0	BANK LOANS N.E.C.	10
OPEN-MARKET PAPER	14.1	16.9	23.0	23.6	23.1	21.9	23.8	27.4	28.0	31.3	39.6	OPEN-MARKET PAPER	11
PROFIT TAXES PAYABLE	.2	.2	.2	.3	.3	.3	.3	.3	.3	.3	.3	PROFIT TAXES PAYABLE	12
MISCELLANEOUS LIABILITIES	6.9	8.2	9.2	10.5	12.5	14.9	17.2	17.1	17.7	19.3	20.4	MISCELLANEOUS LIABILITIES	13
REAL ESTATE INVESTMENT TRUSTS													
PHYSICAL ASSETS	—	.4	.7	.9	1.4	2.5	3.2	4.3	7.3	8.9	8.6	PHYSICAL ASSETS	1
MULTI-FAMILY STRUCTURES	—	.1	.2	.3	.4	.8	1.1	1.4	2.4	3.0	2.8	MULTI-FAMILY STRUCTURES	2
NONRESIDENTIAL STRUCTURES	—	.2	.5	.6	.9	1.7	2.2	2.9	4.9	6.0	5.7	NONRESIDENTIAL STRUCTURES	3
TOTAL FINANCIAL ASSETS	—	.8	2.0	3.9	6.4	11.4	17.0	17.5	14.0	9.8	7.2	TOTAL FINANCIAL ASSETS	4
HOME MORTGAGES	—	*	.2	.6	.8	1.2	1.9	1.7	1.4	1.1	.9	HOME MORTGAGES	5
COMMERCIAL MORTGAGES	—	.7	1.3	2.0	3.2	5.0	7.5	7.7	7.0	5.2	3.8	COMMERCIAL MORTGAGES	6
MULTI-FAMILY MORTGAGES	—	.1	.5	1.3	2.2	4.2	6.6	6.8	4.8	3.1	2.3	MULTI-FAMILY MORTGAGES	7
MISCELLANEOUS ASSETS	—	—	—	—	.2	1.0	1.0	1.4	.8	.5	.2	MISCELLANEOUS ASSETS	8

Open-end investment companies — liabilities (lines 9–17):

Item												Line
TOTAL LIABILITIES	—	.8	1.5	2.2	4.1	8.8	14.4	16.6	17.8	16.0	13.0	9
CREDIT MARKET INSTRUMENTS	—	.8	1.5	2.2	4.1	8.8	14.4	15.8	15.7	13.8	11.3	10
MORTGAGES	—	.2	.4	.5	.7	1.2	1.5	1.6	2.0	2.4	2.4	11
MULTI-FAMILY RESIDENTIAL	—	.1	.1	.2	.2	.4	.5	.5	.7	.8	.8	12
COMMERCIAL	—	.1	.3	.4	.5	.8	1.0	1.1	1.4	1.6	1.6	13
CORPORATE BONDS	—	—	.1	.6	1.0	1.4	1.9	2.1	2.1	1.9	1.8	14
BANK LOANS N.E.C.	—	.6	1.0	1.0	1.6	3.0	7.0	11.4	10.8	8.9	6.5	15
OPEN-MARKET PAPER	—	—	—	—	.8	3.2	4.0	.7	.8	.6	.5	16
MISCELLANEOUS LIABILITIES	—	—	—	—	1.4	1.4	2.6	.8	2.1	2.3	1.8	17

OPEN-END INVESTMENT COMPANIES

Item												Line
TOTAL FINANCIAL ASSETS	44.7	52.7	48.3	47.6	56.7	59.8	46.5	34.1	42.2	47.0	42.8	1
DEMAND DEPOSITS + CURRENCY	.7	.8	.7	.7	.9	.9	.7	.5	.6	.7	.7	2
CORPORATE EQUITIES	39.2	46.1	40.9	39.7	48.6	51.7	38.3	26.3	33.7	37.0	31.7	3
CREDIT MARKET INSTRUMENTS	4.8	5.8	6.7	7.2	7.2	7.2	7.5	7.2	7.9	9.0	10.4	4
U.S. GOVERNMENT SECURITIES	.9	1.1	.7	.9	.6	.7	.7	1.1	1.1	1.1	1.8	5
CORPORATE BONDS	3.0	3.4	3.6	4.3	4.9	5.1	4.2	3.8	4.8	7.0	6.5	6
OPEN-MARKET PAPER	1.0	1.2	2.4	2.1	1.7	1.4	2.6	2.3	2.0	.9	2.1	7

MONEY MARKET FUNDS

Item												Line
TOTAL ASSETS	—	—	—	—	—	—	2.4	3.7	3.7	3.7	3.9	1
DEMAND DEPOSITS + CURRENCY	—	—	—	—	—	—	—	*	*	*	*	2
TIME DEPOSITS	—	—	—	—	—	—	1.6	2.1	1.5	1.8	1.8	3
CREDIT MARKET INSTRUMENTS	—	—	—	—	—	—	.8	1.5	2.1	1.9	1.9	4
U.S. GOVERNMENT SECURITIES	—	—	—	—	—	—	.1	.9	1.1	.9	.9	5
OPEN-MARKET PAPER	—	—	—	—	—	—	.6	.5	.9	1.1	1.1	6
MISCELLANEOUS	—	—	—	—	—	—	*	.1	.1	.1	.1	7
SHARES OUTSTANDING	—	—	—	—	—	—	2.4	3.7	3.7	3.7	3.9	8

Source: Board of Governors of the Federal Reserve System, Flow of Funds Accounts—Assets and Liabilities Outstanding, 1967–77, August 1978.

$42.8 billion in 1977. Net redemptions of shares by individual investors fluctuated between $700 million and nearly $2 billion per year during the 1970s, resulting in a sharp drop in industry assets.

In recent years the industry has tried to recoup some of its losses through the development of specialty funds. Historically, the most common type of investment company is the "stock fund" in which all assets not needed for liquidity are channeled into common stock. Today, however, new types of funds, centered on corporate and municipal bonds and money market securities, are attracting considerable investor interest. The sudden appearance and rapid growth of money market funds, which specialize in short-term liquid investments, is a good example of the innovation and specialization now underway in the investment company field.

A CONCLUDING NOTE

In this chapter we have examined the construction of the Flow of Funds Accounts prepared by the Federal Reserve System. We have observed how this system of social accounting can provide us with important information concerning savings flows in the American economy and the lending and investing activities of major financial intermediaries.

The Flow of Funds Accounts show clearly that different financial intermediaries draw upon different sources of funds. Some, such as commercial banks, savings and loan associations, mutual savings banks, and credit unions, receive deposits from the public. Others receive payments from savers in return for risk protection, as in the case of insurance companies and pension funds, or portfolio management services, as in the case of investment companies. Different financial intermediaries also hold unique kinds of financial assets, influenced largely by the types of claims held by savers against their assets, by laws and regulations imposed by state and federal authorities, and by the relative yields (rates of return) available on different financial assets. In the next chapter we look more closely at the factors which determine the yields on different financial instruments. Then, in the succeeding chapter, we will take a detailed look at the characteristics of financial instruments most frequently acquired by financial intermediaries.

QUESTIONS

2–1. How might the Flow of Funds Accounts be used to determine such things as:

a. Future interest rates.
b. The general state of the economy?

2–2. Outline the steps involved in the construction of the Flow of Funds Accounts.

2–3. Define the following terms:
   a. Lending.
   b. Net investment.
   c. Borrowing.
   d. Saving.
   Explain how these concepts are related to each other within the framework of the financial system.

2–4. What is a savings-deficit sector? How does it differ from a savings-surplus sector? Give examples of each.

2–5. Make a list of the kinds of information contained in the Federal Reserve Board's Flow of Funds Accounts for each sector of the economy. From where is this information derived?

2–6. Discuss the basis differences in terms of types of assets held and basic functions or services of:
   a. Commercial banks.
   b. Savings and loan associations.
   c. Life insurance companies.
   d. Private and government pension funds.
   e. Mutual savings banks.
   f. Credit unions.
   g. Property-casualty insurance companies.
   h. Finance companies.
   i. Real estate investment trusts.
   j. Investment companies.

2–7. What factors appear to determine the kinds of financial assets and liabilities acquired by a financial intermediary? Can you explain the differences in asset portfolios held by life insurance companies versus property-casualty insurers? Commercial banks versus savings and loan associations? Pension funds versus credit unions?

REFERENCES

1. Bain, A. D., "Surveys in Applied Economics: Flow of Funds Analysis." *Economic Journal*, December 1973, pp. 1055–93.

2. Board of Governors of the Federal Reserve System. *Introduction to Flow of Funds*. Washington, D.C., February 1975.

3. _____. *Flow of Funds Accounts, 1946–75*. Washington, D.C., December 1976.

4. _____. *Flow of Funds Accounts, Assets and Liabilities Outstanding, 1965–76.* Washington, D.C., December 1977.

5. _____. *Flow of funds Accounts,* 2d quarter 1978. Washington, D.C., August 1978.

6. Cohen, Jacob. "Copeland's Moneyflows after 25 Years." *Journal of Economic Literature,* 10, no. 1 (March 1972).

7. Copeland, M. A. *A Study of Moneyflows in the United States.* New York: National Bureau of Economic Research, 1952.

8. Freund, William C., and Sinborg, Edward D. "Application of Flow of Funds to Interest-Rate Forecasting. "*Journal of Finance,* vol. 18 (May 1963).

9. National Bureau of Economic Research. *The Flow-of-Funds Approach to Social Accounting.* New York: Princeton University Press, 1962.

10. Powelson, John P. *National Income and Flow-of-Funds Analysis.* New York: McGraw-Hill Book Co., 1960.

11. Ritter, Lawrence S. "The Flow of Funds Accounts: A Framework for Financial Analysis." Chapter in *Financial Institutions and Markets,* by Murray E. Polakoff et al. Boston: Houghton Mifflin Co., 1970.

12. Van Horne, James C. *Financial Market Rates and Flows.* Englewood Cliffs, N.J.: Prentice-Hall, 1978.

3

Determination of interest rate levels

This chapter deals with the factors which determine the levels of interest rates over time (as opposed to the relative structure of rates at a point in time). The concept of "the" interest rate is, of course, an abstraction since there are literally thousands of interest rates on different financial contracts. Yet "the" interest rate is an extremely important concept especially for financial institutions.

Existing levels of interest rates affect both the inflow and outflow of funds at intermediaries. Of course, the major source of revenue for most intermediaries is the interest return on their loans and investments; and the major expense category, at least for the depository intermediaries, is interest payments for borrowed funds (including deposits). Even intermediaries such as investment companies (mutual funds) and pension trusts which have investments concentrated in equity securities (common and preferred stocks) are influenced significantly by the level of short- and long-term interest rates. Indeed some observers have argued that in recent years the level of stock prices has been substantially affected by changes in the general level of interest rates.[1]

Changes in interest rates and interest rate expectations also affect the income and expenses of financial intermediaries. Rising rates typically squeeze the earnings of intermediaries, especially those (such as savings and loan associations) who borrow short-term funds and make long-term loans. This happens because short-term interest rates tend to rise more rapidly than long-term rates during periods of economic expansion. Interest rate expectations also influence the earnings and the volume and composition of intermediary portfolios. Unanticipated movements in interest rates often create an unusually profitable or especially unsuccessful year for a financial intermediary. Indeed, sharp and unexpected increases in interest rates may destroy the viability of a financial intermediary. For all of these reasons, it is important that the management of financial intermediaries understand the determinants of interest rate levels and movements in interest rates and be familiar with the major approaches used for forecasting interest rate pressures in various segments of the financial markets.

While there are many alternative approaches to understanding changes in interest rate levels, one widely used by industry practitioners in explaining and forecasting changes in interest rates and the one that we concentrate on in this text is based upon the *loanable funds theory*. This method, which is short run in concept, concentrates on the magnitudes of financial flows from various sectors of the economy. It seeks to explain changes in interest rates by examining the combined demands for funds of the business, household, and government sectors. Major emphasis is placed on shifts in the needs of business firms for funds due to changes in inventory holdings, capital expenditures, or other factors. In addition, since government, especially the federal government, is frequently a deficit unit, emphasis is often placed on this sector (especially during periods of recession and heavy deficit financing) as a net demander of funds.

Turning to the other side of the supply-demand nexus, the supply of funds represents the combined supply of the household, business, and government sectors. Since the principal net surplus-spending sector in the U.S. economy is the household sector, changes in the supply of

---

[1] The basis for this hypothesized relationship is fairly simple. Common stock prices should reflect the present value of all anticipated dividends payable during the life of the firm, including a liquidating dividend at the termination of the life of the business. As interest rates generally increase, the discount rate used to determine the present value of that expected stream of dividends is raised and the present value of that stream (i.e., the current market price per share of the stock) is reduced. Conversely, as interest rates fall the discount rate is reduced and the present value of the cash flow (market price of the stock) is increased.

loanable funds must take into account the behavior patterns of consumers. However, there is one very important complicating feature. The supply of funds is not only a function of the volume of saving carried out by different sectors of the economy but also includes money created by the banking system. Since money creation is the result of actions by the commercial banking system in acquiring primary securities—and since the process is strongly affected by the Federal Reserve's monetary policy—there is substantial attention devoted to both commercial banks and the Federal Reserve in this approach. And a further complication is that not all new money created is necessarily available in the loanable funds market. Part or all of the new money created may be held as idle balances by the public (i.e., hoarded); therefore, the supply of loanable funds must take into account the volume of saving and desires by the public to hoard as compared to the stock of money available.

DEMAND FOR LOANABLE FUNDS

The demand for loanable funds is composed of several parts and emanates from all sectors of the economy—businesses, households, and governments. Each of these sectors has a demand for loanable funds which derives from a different motivation. It is, therefore, important to explore separately these basic behavioral factors in seeking to understand the reasons for shifts in the overall demand for loanable funds. However, in the interest of simplicity, this section concentrates on the business and government sectors which are usually net demanders of funds and views the household sector from a net position, as a net supplier of funds.[2]

Business demand

An understanding of the motives for demanding loanable funds by *business firms* is especially important because the business sector is the principal borrower in most years. Moreover, and perhaps of greater significance for understanding changes in interest rates, business demand for loanable funds is highly unstable from year to year. Hence, changes in interest rates are to a considerable extent associated with changes in business demand for funds. This is especially true of changes in short-term (money market) interest rates.

---

[2] This does not, of course, imply that households are not very important in affecting the demand for loanable funds and that business firms through internally generated funds are not significant in affecting the supply of loanable funds. It merely simplifies by concentrating on the fact that, taking each economic sector as a whole, the household sector is a net supplier of funds and businesses are a net demander of funds.

Demands for loanable funds by business firms arise principally from a desire by firms to acquire real assets—plant and equipment and inventories. This act of investment is, in turn, assumed to be a function of the *expected* rate of return from making the investment (in a capital budgeting sense, the internal rate of return) and of the cost of obtaining the necessary funds (the rate of interest or, in a capital budgeting sense, the weighted average cost of capital). It is important to note that the return that is relevant is the profitability that business managers *expect* to obtain in the future from the commitment of funds today (as opposed to the actual return currently realized on investments or past rates of return). This return, therefore, is affected to some extent by psychological factors. Hence, the state of "business confidence" may be of considerable significance in affecting the total volume of investment carried out by the business sector.

For any given investment demand schedule, the higher the cost of funds the lower the quantity of investment. If management were contemplating an investment in a plant to produce a particular consumer good and that plant was expected to yield a rate of return of 10 percent, it would be financially desirable to make the investment only if the cost of funds was less than 10 percent, where the cost of funds is the "true" cost and represents the combined cost of debt and equity. However, if the cost of funds were to increase to 14 percent (or to any level above 10 percent), the project would not be financially attractive. Therefore, the higher the cost of funds the more projects will be eliminated as potentially unprofitable. The relationship between the cost of funds and the amount of investment spending is thus thought to be a negative one.[3]

A second important aspect of the relationship between interest rates and the volume of investment spending is the degree of responsiveness of investment to changes in the cost of funds. It is one thing if small changes in interest rates produce large movements in investment. It is an entirely different matter if large changes in interest rates produce small changes in investment. While there is some disagreement about this relationship, it appears that the degree of responsiveness of business investment demand for funds to changes in interest rates is quite small. Economically, this relationship implies that business investment spending and thereby the demand for loanable funds by business cannot be affected to any considerable degree by public policy measures such as monetary policy which focuses upon changes in the rate of interest. This suggests that business in-

---

[3] It should be pointed out, of course, that the demand for loanable funds by the business sector is dependent upon other factors as well as the volume of investment. In particular, the demand for loanable funds from external sources is affected by the amount of internal funds available after the payment of cash dividends.

vestment spending may be much more affected by the availability of funds—credit rationing, for example—than by its cost.

A third important feature of the business investment demand function is its volatility or shiftability. Since the investment demand function is affected by the state of business confidence (essentially psychological in nature), it may be subject to sudden changes. At the time when public policy is seeking to increase interest rates in order to curtail investment spending, the investment demand function may shift to the right due to optimism about the future. As a result, despite the higher interest rates, the total volume of investment may rise instead of decline. Similarly, in periods when public policy is attempting to increase investment demand through lowering interest rates, business confidence may sag and the investment demand function may shift to the left, resulting in less total investment spending at every possible rate of interest.

Business investment demand is composed of two basic parts: the volume of inventory accumulation (changes in the quantity of inventory held) and the amount of investment in fixed assets. These different components of investment behave quite differently. For example, changes from quarter to quarter and year to year in inventory accumulation appear to derive primarily from differences between anticipated sales and realized sales. If actual sales fall short of expected sales, business firms are left with undesired amounts of inventory. In contrast, if actual sales exceed expected sales, these firms may have inventory levels which are lower than desired. While these changes in inventory levels are usually small compared with the total volume of sales, they may be and indeed frequently are large when compared with the amount of original inventory levels. As a result inventory fluctuations often are significant in affecting the business demand for loanable funds.[4] Since accumulations of inventory are financed generally through short-term borrowings (usually at commercial banks), substantial changes in the volume of these inventories often cause much larger fluctuations in business demand for short-term funds and, thus, in short-term interest rates. Moreover, the rate of interest appears to be relatively unimportant in influencing changes in inventory levels.

The largest component of business demand for loanable funds is associated with spending for plant and equipment. These expenditures are more clearly determined by the joint influence of the expected profitability from the planned investment and by the cost of funds since they usually result from careful deliberation by manage-

---

[4] These inventory fluctuations also may have substantial effects on the entire economy. Indeed, most post–World War II recessions in the United States have been associated with inventory adjustments.

ment over a substantial period. While this type of spending should be influenced by interest rates, the variation in total investment spending as a result of changes in interest rates appears to be relatively slight. Hurdle rates established by many firms for investment projects appear in practice to be sufficiently above the cost of funds so that small changes in interest rates have limited effects on investment plans. Moreover, investment projects which are replacement in nature appear to be little affected by interest rate levels.

Changes in the demand for loanable funds as the result of shifts in plans for the purchase of plant and equipment appear to be less variable than shifts in the demand for loanable funds as the result of changes in inventories. Since plant and equipment expenditures generally are financed with long-term funds, the demand for *long-term* loanable funds tends to be less variable than the demand for *short-term* loanable funds. This tends to create greater stability in rates in the long-term sector of the financial markets than in the short-term area.

Government demand

The other major sector which is frequently a net demander of funds in the financial markets is government—both state and local governments and the federal government. State and local government demands for loanable funds are principally for the purpose of constructing facilities for providing education and other governmental services. This demand is determined primarily by the growth rate in population, changes in the geographic location and age structure of the population, and the willingness of citizens to bear taxes in order to obtain desired services. It is commonly accepted that this demand for loanable funds is affected to only a minor degree by changes in interest rates.[5] While there is some responsiveness of state and local government borrowing to changes in interest rates, it would be expected that the effect of variations in interest rates on this borrowing should be considerably less than in the case of business demand for loanable funds.

Federal government demand for loanable funds arises primarily from federal fiscal policy (i.e., tax and expenditure policy). The size of the federal budget is determined as the result of decisions concerning tax rates, federal expenditures for goods and services, and transfer

---

[5] There is some evidence that the timing of the demand for loanable funds by state and local governments is influenced to some degree by periods of extremely high interest rates. It appears that these governmental units reduce their borrowing during such periods but that—due to the long lag between borrowing and capital expenditures—this postponement of borrowing has a minimal effect on real capital spending.

payments. There are few reasons to believe that these decisions should be affected by changes in interest rates. Rather it would be more reasonable to argue that federal fiscal policy is a determining factor in shaping the level and pattern of interest rates. It may be argued, therefore, that the demand for loanable funds by the federal government is completely unrelated to interest rate levels (i.e., completely inelastic).

In summary, the principal net demanders of loanable funds in the financial markets are business firms, state and local governments, and the federal government. The demand for loanable funds by business firms appears to be somewhat but not greatly responsive to interest rates. The quantity of funds demanded by state and local governments is slightly responsive to changes in interest rates. In contrast, the quantity of funds demanded by the federal government is almost completely unresponsive to interest rate changes. The total demand for funds then by all of these sectors is the sum of the demands by businesses, state and local governments, and the federal government. This total demand for funds can be illustrated by Figure 3–1.

FIGURE 3–1

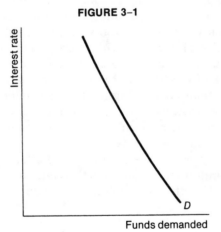

THE SUPPLY OF LOANABLE FUNDS

The supply of loanable funds is the result of a number of separate factors: the volume of saving, the amount of money existing, and desires by the public to hold or dispose of all or a portion of the quantity of money available.[6] Since the only sector which consis-

---

[6] The volume of hoarding (or dishoarding) could be treated conceptually either as a reduction in the supply of loanable funds or an increase in the demand for loanable funds.

tently has a net surplus is the household sector, our discussion of the volume of saving and its influence will concentrate on examining the motives for household saving. As discussed above, we are viewing the household sector as a *net* supplier of funds after allowance is made for household demand for funds. In addition, since the amount of money is considerably affected by the Federal Reserve, it is necessary to include in the discussion a treatment of the monetary policy actions of the Fed. Finally, since any money created may be unavailable to the market due to hoarding (holding idle money balances), it is important to discuss the reasons for holding money.

Saving

Saving refers to the postponement of current consumption. Saving is the act of abstaining from using current income for the purposes of acquiring goods and services. It is important to note the act of saving and the act of investing in assets are different actions motivated by different factors. Saving is important because it releases resources that can be used to expand the productive capacity of the economy. Those resources not used to produce goods for current consumption can then be employed to produce investment goods.

The volume of saving by individual consumers is a function of a number of factors, including the amount of current and expected income, the stock of wealth held by the individual, the level of interest rates, expectations concerning the future rate of inflation, as well as other variables. However, the most important determinant of the amount of personal saving (and thereby personal consumption expenditures) appears to be the level of income. In contrast, the interest rate level—while it may have a substantial effect on the particular disposition of funds made available through saving—is thought to have little impact on the total volume of saving.

Money

An important addition to the potential flow of loanable funds from saving comes from the money stock. The volume of money is affected both by the commercial banking system and the Federal Reserve System. Commercial banks transform a given quantity of reserves into money through the process of making loans and investments. The banking system creates a multiple volume of money out of a given reserve base because only fractional reserves are required to support each dollar of deposits. However, the ability of commercial banks to make loans and investments and thereby create money is limited by the amount of these reserves, while the quantity of reserves within the entire banking system is determined by the Federal Reserve System in its role of conducting monetary policy.

The Federal Reserve uses its techniques of monetary control—open market operations, changes in reserve requirements,and changes in the discount rate—in order to influence the volume of bank reserves and deposits. If the Federal Reserve wishes to accelerate the growth rate of the economy, it can provide ample reserves to the banking system through purchasing securities in the open market, lowering reserve requirements, or reducing the discount rate. In contrast, should the Federal Reserve wish to reduce the growth rate of the economy, it can curtail the volume of reserves in the banking system through selling securities, increasing required reserves, and increasing the discount rate.

The quantity of money outstanding during a give period then is essentially controlled by the Federal Reserve through its influence over the volume of bank reserves. There is no reason to expect that the volume of money is very sensitive to interest rate changes, although there may be some influence of interest rates on the money stock since the commercial banking system would be expected to use bank reserves more efficiently in a high rather than in a low interest rate environment.

Hoarding

The supply of loanable funds is also affected by the volume of hoarding desired by the public. It is quite possible, for example, that during a given period a substantial volume of new money is created and yet there is no increase in the volume of loanable funds. This would occur if all the new money created was hoarded (i.e., held as idle balances). In order to understand the influence of hoarding on the amount of loanable funds, it is important to understand the motives for holding money. The demand for money can be viewed as a combination of three different motives: the first motive, the *transactions* demand for money, is that amount of money required to conduct day-to-day transactions in goods and services. Individuals and business firms do, of course, need funds for purchasing goods and services. Additional funds also are needed because of uncertainties in the volume and timing of cash inflows and outflows. Funds held for this purpose are referred to as *precautionary* balances. Finally, the *speculative* demand for money refers to the holding of idle balances for the purpose of speculating on changes in the prices of financial assets. For example, an individual or business may hold funds in a checking account rather than hold an interest-bearing asset (bond) if the expectation is that the price of these interest-earning assets will fall in the future.

The transactions demand for funds is thought to be principally determined by the volume of transactions in the economy and therefore by the level of income. In contrast, the demand for money for transactions purposes appears to be little affected by the level of interest rates. The precautionary demand for money should also be primarily influenced by the volume of transactions in the economy and, therefore, depend principally upon the level of income. Again, the amount of money held in order to reduce uncertainty should not be influenced substantially by changes in interest rate levels.

The speculative motive for holding money is much more complicated than either transactions or precautionary demands. It perhaps may best be explained by the use of a simple example. Suppose that an individual investor has $1 million in a checking account. Further suppose that the only alternative place in which that investor could invest is in long-term government securities. If the investor wished to speculate, the individual could compare present interest rate levels with expectations of future interest rates. If the investor believed that future interest rates would be lower than current interest rates, then there would be a speculative incentive to move from money to bonds. If the interest rate expectation were realized (i.e., a fall in interest rates), the price of bonds would increase and a speculative gain would be realized. In contrast, if the investor believed that future interest rate levels would be higher than current interest rates, there would be an incentive to remain in cash. If this interest rate expectation were realized, the price of bonds would fall and the holder of these bonds would suffer a capital loss.

If interest rates are high currently by historical standards, it seems reasonable for market participants to expect that rates will be lower in the future. Therefore, at high interest rate levels, it would be expected that the speculative demand for money would be low. Conversely, if interest rates are low by historical standards, it seems reasonable to expect higher rates in the future and a high speculative demand for money.

The total demand for money is thus a combined function of the transactions, precautionary, and speculative demands. The first two demand motives are influenced principally by the level of income. However, the third motive seems to be substantially affected by interest rates. The total demand for money to hold then appears to be somewhat sensitive to interest rate levels.

Hoarding and the supply of loanable funds

The supply of money and the demand for money to hold as idle balances interact to produce a supply of loanable funds which may be larger or smaller than the supply of savings coming from the various sectors of the economy.[7] For example, if the demand for money to hold at a particular interest rate exceeds the quantity outstanding, then the supply of loanable funds will be less than the volume of saving. Conversely, if the demand for money to hold is less than the existing stock of money at some interest rate level, the volume of loanable funds will exceed the volume of savings. Since the demand for money to hold is related (inversely) to the level of interest rates, the amount of desired hoarding or desired dishoarding will also be affected by the interest rate.

Interest rates and the supply of loanable funds

The relationship between the interest rate and the supply of loanable funds can thus be summarized as follows: the basic determinant of the supply of loanable funds is the volume of saving. In addition, however, the supply of loanable funds is influenced by the amount of the money stock as compared to the demand for money to hold. At high interest rates (such as n_1), the quantity supplied of loanable funds is likely to exceed the volume of saving (due to dishoarding); while at low interest rates (such as n_2), the quantity supplied of loanable funds may be less than the amount of saving (due to hoarding). (See Figure 3–2.)

In summary, the interest rate is determined by the interaction of the supply and demand for loanable funds. The supply of loanable

FIGURE 3–2

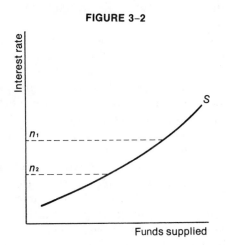

Funds supplied

---

[7] For a more complete exploration, see Polakoff [8], chap. 3.

funds is determined by the volume of new saving, the amount of new money creation, and the volume of hoarding. The demand for loanable funds is determined principally by business demand for funds for expansion of plant capacity and inventory accumulation as well as by the amount of funds necessary to finance deficit spending by governmental units at both the federal and the state and local levels. Graphically, the interaction of the supply and demand for loanable funds is illustrated in Figure 3–3.

FIGURE 3–3

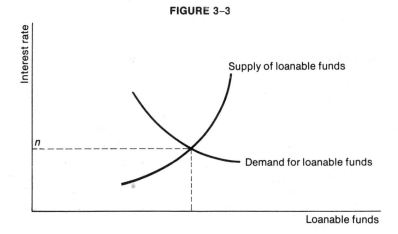

An illustration

An understanding of the manner in which the supply and demand for loanable funds affects interest rate levels can perhaps best be obtained through the use of a simple example. In interpreting this illustration, though, the reader should recognize that other factors besides those discussed which influence the level of interest rates are implicitly held constant. Suppose that the economy is entering a period of slack business activity. It would be expected that the demand for loanable funds would fall. This decline in the demand for funds (shift in the demand schedule) might occur due to a reduction in inventory levels at business firms or for other reasons. As the recession intensifies, it might be expected that the amount of capital spending by businesses would fall as optimism concerning the future profitability of capital outlays is reduced. Both of these factors would shift the demand for funds to the left, indicating that at each rate of interest the quantity of loanable funds demanded is reduced. In contrast, the supply of loanable funds might increase during this period. Consumers may react to the recession by increasing their saving, perhaps by accelerating the repayment of their debt obligations or deferring the

taking on of any new debts.[8] More importantly, perhaps, it would be
expected that the Federal Reserve System would increase the quantity of bank reserves and that the commercial banking system would
use these reserves to make new loans and investments, thereby expanding the nation's money stock. The increase in the supply of loanable funds coupled with a decline in the demand for loanable funds
would be expected to lower the equilibrium interest rate. Moreover,
it would probably lower interest rates to a greater extent in the
money then in the capital market, due to the combined effect of the
sharp reduction in the demand for short-term inventory financing
and the expansion in funds available through the commercial banking system which is principally a short-term lender and investor.
These relationships are illustrated in Figure 3–4.

FIGURE 3–4

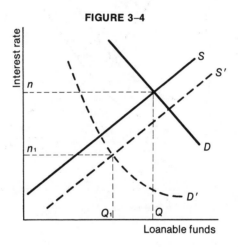

The original level of interest rates was at n, while the original
quantity of loanable funds bought and sold was at Q. Responding to
the increase in the supply and the reduction in the demand for loanable funds, interest rates fall from n to n_1. It is important to note that
the quantity of loanable funds traded is also reduced. Moreover, these
changes will, in turn, set in motion longer-term changes in income,
government borrowing, and other responses in the economy.

As another example of the use of the loanable funds explanation of
interest rate changes, let us suppose that there was a sharp upsurge in
the economy which stimulated inflationary price movements. The
demand for loanable funds should expand as businesses desire to

---

[8] The repayment of debt is merely one way in which the consumer may dispose of
saving.

accumulate inventory and add to capital outlays. At the same time, the supply of loanable funds should contract due to efforts by the Federal Reserve System to restrict the availability of bank reserves. Interest rates should therefore increase, reflecting both the increase in the demand for loanable funds and the decrease in the supply of loanable funds. Again we might expect short-term interest rates to increase to a greater extent than long-term rates. This scenario is illustrated in Figure 3–5 where n represents the original level of

FIGURE 3–5

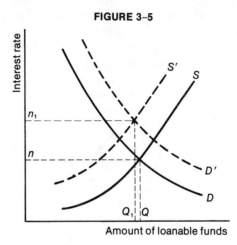

Amount of loanable funds

interest rates and n_1 is the higher level following shifts in the supply and demand for loanable funds.

An alternative explanation

To this point the discussion has centered on the supply and demand for loanable funds. However, there is an alternative explanation of interest rate determination to that which stresses the flow of funds and which is the mirror image of the loanable funds market: this is the supply and demand for securities. In every transaction in which loanable funds are transferred from surplus spending units to deficit units, securities are transferred from savings deficit units to the savings surplus units. These securities may be primary securities (the obligation of ultimate deficit units) or secondary securities (the obligation of financial intermediaries). Moreover, the securities may be moved to surplus units either directly (without intermediation) or indirectly (through financial intermediaries). Regardless, the common element of these translations is that surplus units who have funds to invest create a demand for securities. Other economic units—either the ultimate deficit units or financial intermediaries—wish to obtain funds and thereby offer to supply securities. The interaction of the supply and demand for securities then determines the price of securities and the price of the securities determines the return (interest rate) to the investor, just as the supply and demand for loanable funds determines the interest rate in the loanable funds market.

To illustrate how interest rates are determined through the interaction of the supply and demand for securities, assume that the security in question is a corporate bond. For this bond (indeed any debt obligation) the issuer promises in exchange for the loanable funds being provided today to pay a fixed interest return to the investor during the life of the bond and to return the principal amount at maturity. For example, assume that the bond has a principal value of $1,000, matures in 1990, and has a coupon rate of 6 percent. The borrower thus promises to pay the lender $60 per year (6 percent of $1,000) for each year until 1990 and $1,000 at maturity in return for the receipt of a fixed amount of dollars today. The cost to the borrower and the return to the investor vary with the amount paid (market price) for the bond. The higher the value of that promise to pay (i.e., the higher the price of the bond), the lower the cost to the issuing firm and, of course, the lower the return to the investor. Conversely, the lower the price of the bond, the higher the cost to the issuing firm, and the higher the return to the investor. In summary, *bond prices and effective rates of interest move inversely.* Higher bond prices mean lower effective interest rates, while lower bond prices mean higher effective interest rates.

The relationship between the quantity of bonds supplied and demanded and bond prices would be as illustrated in Figure 3–6.

FIGURE 3–6

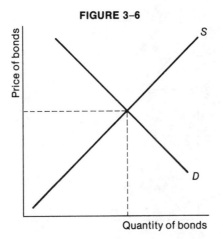

As bond prices increase, the quantity of bonds supplied should expand since the cost of the funds to the issuing firm would be reduced. In terms of the previous discussion, at higher bond prices and lower interest rates the quantity demanded of loanable funds by business (supply of bonds) would be increased. In contrast, with higher prices for bonds, the yield to the investor would be reduced and the amount of bonds demanded by investors would fall. Again in terms of the previous discussion, at higher bond prices and lower interest rates investors would be willing to supply a smaller quantity of loanable funds to the market.

This approach can be used in a similar fashion to the supply and demand for loanable funds in order to explain changes in interest rates and is, of course, applicable both to short- and long-term securities. For example, suppose that there was a sharp increase in business activity associated with an expansion in fixed capital investment by business firms and a substantial volume of inventory accumulation. Business firms could finance this spending by selling bonds. At each level of interest rates, then, the supply of bonds would be larger than before (S'). As a result, other things equal, the price of bonds would fall (P'). A fall in the price of bonds would mean a rise in interest rates. In terms of the earlier (loanable funds) explanation, the business firms which supplied bonds demanded loanable funds and this increased interest rates. At the same time, as explained earlier, it might be expected that the volume of savings and new money creation would diminish. Hence, there would be a reduction in the demand for bonds (supply of loanable funds) which would accompany the increase in the supply of bonds (demand for loanable funds). Both of these factors would contribute to an increase in the level of interest rates. These developments are illustrated in Figure 3–7.

FIGURE 3–7

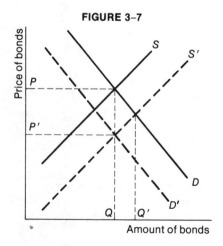

Explaining recent interest rate fluctuations

The loanable funds explanation of interest rate movements can be used as a framework to explain the recent sharp fluctuations in interest rate levels. For example, in 1969, there was a substantial rise in interest rates with many yields reaching the highest levels in the 20th century. This development had a number of causes. First, business firms sharply increased their demand for loanable funds, reflecting the persistence of a buoyant economic climate and a rapid rate of inflation. Business expenditures for plant and equipment and for the accumlation of inventory exceeded internal savings (profit after taxes plus depreciation minus cash dividends) by roughly $23 billion, necessitating substantial external financing and thereby demands upon the market for loanable funds. In contrast, during the previous year, business capital expenditures exceeded internally generated funds by only $14 billion. As a result of the greater external need for funds, business relied upon the financial markets for $39 billion, an amount $8 billion more than in the previous year. Sales of new stock were $3 billion greater than in 1968. Borrowings from banks expanded by $2.0 billion, commercial paper sales were $1.0 billion more than in the previous year, and loans from finance companies increased $2.5 billion.[9]

Despite a sharp increase in the demand for funds by businesses, saving by households was curtailed. The difference between gross saving by the houshold sector and expenditures on fixed assets (the surplus of the household sector) declined from $33 billion in 1968 to $31 billion in 1969. But perhaps the most striking change occurred in the nation's money supply. Responding to intense pressure applied to bank reserves by the Federal Reserve System, demand deposits at commercial banks (the principal component of the money supply) grew at a much reduced rate. Total demand deposits had increased $12.3 billion in 1968. But in 1969 total demand deposits expanded by a much less $4.6 billion. Responding to the sharp increase in the demand for loanable funds but a decline in the potential supply, interest rates moved upward sharply.

In contrast to 1969 when rates accelerated dramatically, the year 1975 presents an instance in which the loanable funds explanation of interest rate changes can be used to understand a period of sharp reductions in both short- and long-term interest rates. That year was marked by the sharpest decline in economic activity since the Great Depression of the 1930s. For the first time in memory expenditures by business for capital assets fell below gross internal savings. For example, capital expenditures by corporate nonfinancial businesses were

---

[9] All these data are from the Federal Reserve's Flow of Funds Accounts.

$132.8 billion in 1975, while gross saving by this sector amounted to a slightly larger $139.0 billion, In contrast, in the previous year, capital expenditures by business exceeded gross saving by $54 billion. Most of the change in the deficit/surplus position of the business sector was concentrated in the inventory position of these firms. Business accumulated inventories of $9.7 billion in 1974, while liquidating inventories by $14.2 billion in 1975—a net change in inventory investment of $23.9 billion. In contrast, fixed investment by business remained virtually unchanged between 1974 and 1975 in terms of nominal dollars.[10]

Reflecting the substantial shift in the deficit-surplus position of this vitally important sector, business demands for loanable funds declined appreciably. Total credit market borrowings amounted to $33.9 billion in 1975, less than one half of the $88.0 billion in demands on the loanable funds market in 1974. As expected, given the nature of the change in business investment (reductions in inventory holdings), most of the decline in the demand for funds was centered in the area of short-term borrowings. For example, bank loans fell by $13.4 billion in 1975, after increasing by $29.8 billion the previous year.

The slack demand for loanable funds by business firms in 1975 was offset to a considerable extent by the borrowing activities of the federal government. Reflecting conscious changes in expenditures and taxes associated with discretionary fiscal policy, as well as declines in receipts due to the faltering economy, the federal deficit expanded from $15 billion in 1974 to $77 billion in 1975. As a result, the federal government's demand for loanable funds increased sharply, especially the demand for short-term funds.

There also was a substantial increase in the flow of loanable funds from the household sector in 1975. Gross saving of the household sector increased $25 billion in 1975 over its 1974 level. In contrast, the capital expenditures (most of which are associated with home ownership) of this sector expanded only $3 billion. Most of this surplus was channeled into the depository financial institutions (especially commercial banks and savings and loan associations). Total time and savings accounts at commercial banks and savings and loan associations expanded by $22.2 billion more than in the previous year.

Somewhat surprisingly, the volume of new money created in 1975 did not expand sharply over its rate of growth in 1974. This apparently did not reflect the lack of willingness by the Federal Reserve System to expand the quantity of money. Indeed, total bank reserves grew much more rapidly in 1975 than in 1974. Due to a number of

---

[10] Many of these figures are distorted to a considerable extent by the rapid inflation which occurred during the period, especially in 1974.

factors, however, the reserves were used to support additional time and savings deposits rather than demand deposits.

To summarize the developments in 1975, the traditional deficit sector—corporate nonfinancial business—reduced its demands on the credit markets by a massive amount, especially in the short-term area. Part of this demand for loanable funds, however, was replaced by borrowings of the federal government. On the supply side the major development was a substantial increase in the surplus of the household sector. Reflecting a slackening demand for funds and a substantial increase in the supply of loanable funds, interest rates fell during 1975. The decline was especially sharp in the short-term sector of the loanable funds market as both curtailment in the demand for and increases in the supply of loanable funds were concentrated in this area.

Interest rate forecasts

The loanable funds concept is frequently combined with flow of funds data in order to project future changes in interest rate levels. These projections not only include estimates of interest rate movements generally in the money and capital markets (short- versus long-term rates) but also in particular markets. For example, emphasis might be placed on the relative supply and demand pressure in the mortgage market or in the municipal market. Such published interest rate forecasts are made by Salomon Brothers, Bankers Trust Company of New York, and the Life Insurance Company Institute of America as well as other organizations. The particular approach used by Salomon Brothers is explained below.[11]

The Salomon Brothers approach to forecasting interest rates concentrates on the supply and demand for loanable funds. Separate estimates are made of the supply of credit provided by the major nonbank financial intermediaries such as savings and loan associations, the supply of credit from commercial banks, and the supply of credit from other organizations such as finance companies, business corporations, state and local governments, and foreigners. The demand for credit is separated into the demand for long-term credit by nonfederal borrowers (including state and local government borrowing), the demand for short-term financing by business and consumers, and the demand for credit by the federal government (including both U.S. Treasury debt and federal agency debt).

The relative balance of these demand and supply factors is of sub-

---

[11] The accuracy of forecasters in projecting interest rate movements is not especially impressive. See Fraser [4].

TABLE 3-1

Summary of supply and demand for credit ($billions)

	See Table	Annual net increases in amounts outstanding							Amounts outstanding 12/31/74e
		1969	1970	1971	1972	1973	1974e	1975p	
Net demand									
Privately held mortgages	II	22.7	20.2	41.7	59.0	60.0	35.4	33.5	614.9
Corporate bonds	III	13.8	22.8	23.7	19.1	12.7	24.7	31.3	273.4
State and local securities	IV	7.1	14.7	21.3	12.5	14.5	15.5	15.0	208.3
Domestically held foreign bonds	V	1.0	0.9	0.9	1.0	1.0	2.2	3.1	18.8
Subtotal long-term non-federal		44.6	58.6	87.6	91.6	88.2	77.8	82.9	1,115.4
Business loans	IX	18.4	2.5	7.7	24.8	38.4	34.3	12.1	248.8
Consumer loans	IX	10.4	6.0	11.2	19.2	22.9	9.9	3.5	190.4
All other bank loans	IX	2.0	2.0	7.3	10.1	7.8	2.2	4.5	72.2
Open market paper	VIII	12.4	2.1	-0.1	1.6	8.4	16.9	9.6	66.9
Subtotal short-term private		43.2	12.6	26.1	55.7	77.5	63.3	29.7	578.3
Privately held treasury debt	VI	-5.8	5.7	18.9	15.1	-2.1	10.7	41.0	268.9
Privately held federal agency debt	VII	8.1	9.0	2.8	9.2	21.5	20.0	9.7	101.8
Subtotal federal		2.3	14.7	21.7	24.3	19.4	30.7	50.7	370.7
Total net demand for credit		90.1	85.9	135.4	171.6	185.1	171.8	163.3	2,064.4

*Net supply**

Mutual savings banks	X	2.5	3.8	9.0	8.9	5.3	2.7	6.6	99.1
Savings and loan associations	X	10.1	11.9	30.5	37.4	29.3	23.3	26.5	285.6
Credit unions	X	1.5	1.5	2.6	3.1	2.9	3.2	3.5	26.4
Life insurance companies	X	4.4	4.7	7.2	8.8	9.6	10.9	12.5	194.9
Fire and casualty companies	X	1.6	3.8	3.7	3.8	3.5	3.7	2.9	44.9
Private noninsured pension funds	X	1.0	2.5	-1.8	-0.5	2.1	5.4	5.0	43.0
State and local retirement funds	X	3.7	3.8	3.7	3.7	3.7	5.7	6.7	65.2
Open-end mutual funds	X	0.9	0.5	0.0	0.0	-0.2	0.9	-0.2	7.9
Real estate investment trusts	X	0.9	2.1	2.5	4.9	4.5	1.2	0.2	16.2
Total non bank investing institutions		26.6	34.6	57.4	70.1	60.7	57.0	63.7	738.2
Commercial banks†	X	15.6	33.7	51.0	73.3	77.6	53.6	65.0	704.4
Finance companies	X	8.1	0.7	4.2	10.7	10.2	4.9	1.4	89.8
Business corporations	XI	7.4	0.8	5.2	1.3	5.4	8.0	5.7	76.6
State and local governments	XI	3.4	-0.5	-1.5	4.1	4.5	2.4	-3.0	30.1
Foreigners	XI	-0.9	10.3	26.4	9.1	2.0	7.0	10.5	71.7
Subtotal		60.2	79.6	142.7	168.6	160.4	132.9	143.3	1,755.8
Residual: Individuals and miscellaneous	XII	29.9	6.3	-7.3	3.0	24.7	38.9	20.0	308.6
Total net supply of credit		90.1	85.9	135.4	171.6	185.1	171.8	163.3	2,064.4

* Excludes funds for equities, cash, and miscellaneous demands not tabulated above.
† Includes nonoperating holding and other bank related companies.
Source: Salomon Brothers, *The Supply and Demand for Credit in 1975*, p. 2.

stantial significance in explaining interest rate movements. The difference between the net demand and the net supply of funds is the amount that individuals and miscellaneous investors must absorb. Since individuals generally place most of their surplus funds with financial intermediaries, it would be expected that increases in interest rates would be necessary in order to induce these individuals to provide a substantial amount of credit directly to the marketplace. Conversely, if the gap between the net demand for credit and the net supply of credit is relatively slight, the amount of securities that individuals must absorb is small and interest rates might be expected to fall.

This approach to interest rate forecasts can perhaps best be explained by the Salomon Brothers' interest rate outlook for 1975 (a period of exceptional changes in the flow of funds) as contained in its publication, *The Supply and Demand for Credit in 1975*. Consistent with our previous explanation of the supply and demand for loanable funds in periods of economic decline, the Salomon Brothers forecast (prepared in the fall of 1974) estimated a decline in the net demand for credit and an increase in the net supply of credit. As a result, the supply of credit that would have to be provided by individuals was expected to fall sharply, placing downward pressure on interest rates. The total net demand for credit was forecasted to fall from $171.8 billion in 1974 to $163.3 billion in 1975. Similarly, the net supply of credit was expected to increase from $132.9 in 1974 to $143.3 billion in 1975. As a result, the residual supply necessary from individuals was expected to fall from $38.9 billion in 1974 to $20.0 billion in 1975. These data are contained in Table 3–1.

It is interesting to observe the various areas in which substantial changes in the supply and demand for credit were expected in 1975. The major expected demand changes were in the volume of business loans—down from $34.3 billion in 1974 to a projected $12.1 billion in 1975—and an increase in privately held Treasurey debt—from $10.7 billion in 1974 to $41.0 billion in 1975. Both of these changes essentially represent shifts in the demand for short-term credit. In contrast, the demand for long-term credit was not expected to fall and indeed was projected to expand somewhat. These expected developments are consistent with the observation made earlier that the demand for short-term funds is much more volatile than the demand for long-term funds.

On the supply side, perhaps the most striking expected change in the supply of credit was in that provided by commercial banks. Again, this is quite consistent with the discussion earlier on the loanable funds theory of interest. Reflecting easier monetary policy, the supply of credit provided by the commercial banks was projected to expand $65.0 billion, up substantially from the $52.6 billion gain in 1974. In contrast, the supply of funds from nonbank financial institutions was expected to increase only slightly. Hence further evidence of the greater volatility of the supply of short-term credit is provided. Commercial bank credit is principally in the short-term area while nonbank financial institution credit is primarily in the long-term area. As a result of these developments, it was expected that there would be reduced pressures on the credit markets in 1975, but that these reduced pressures would be most striking in the short-term area of the market.

The Salomon Brothers estimate of the supply and demand for credit is useful not only in explaining general movements in the pressures on credit markets but also in focusing on particular segments of these markets. For example, estimates are made of the supply of mortgages—classified by type of mortgage—in order to estimate the pressures on the socially important mortgage market, and the supply and demand for municipal securities is estimated.

SUMMARY

This chapter has discussed the importance of interest rate movements on the behavior of individual financial institutions. Financial institutions are both affected by interest rate changes and are one of the principal factors in the determinants of interest rates. Major emphasis was placed upon the loanable funds explanation of interest rate movements and on the basic sectors of the economy—business, government, and households—which are net suppliers and net demanders of funds. An understanding of the role of each of these sectors is crucially important to understanding interest rate developments and also changes in the financial position of individual financial institutions. Finally, an illustration of how the loanable funds concept may be used to explain recent financial developments as well as to forecast future financial changes was provided.

QUESTIONS

3–1.   What are the major elements of the demand and supply curves of the loanable funds theory? Examine how interest rates are affected by the supply and demand for loanable funds in the (a) business sector, (b) government sector, and (c) household sector. What are some of the determinants that influence the levels of supply and demand for loanable funds in these sectors?

3–2.   What are the three motives for holding money?

3–3. How does the demand for loanable funds, the creation of new money, and the phenomenon of hoarding affect the interest rate?

3–4. Examine the relationship between bond prices and effective interest rates.

3–5. What were the economic conditions which precipitated the rise of interest rates in 1969 and their decline in 1975? Using the same logic explain the rise in interest rates in 1978 and 1979. What effects did these conditions cause in short- and long-term debt financing?

3–6. Discuss the similarities between interest rate theory and the general economic theory of supply and demand.

REFERENCES

1. Conard, Joseph W. *An Introduction to the Theory of Interest.* Berkeley: University of California Press, 1959.
2. Culbertson, John. *Money and Banking.* New York: McGraw-Hill, 1972.
3. Fisher, Irving. *The Theory of Interest.* New York: Macmillan, 1930.
4. Fraser, Donald R. "On the Accuracy and Usefulness of Interest Rate Forecasts." *Business Economics,* Fall 1977.
5. Homer, Sidney. *A History of Interest Rates.* New Brunswick, N.J.: Rutgers University Press, 1963.
6. Keynes, John Maynard. *The General Theory of Employment, Interest and Money.* New York: Harcourt Brace Jovanovich, 1936.
7. Lutz, Frederick A. *The Theory of Interest.* Dordrecht, Holland: D. Reidel Publishing Co., 1967.
8. Polakoff, Murray, et al. *Financial Institutions and Markets.* Boston: Houghton Mifflin Co. 1970.

4

Money and capital markets: Instruments and yield relationships

Managers of financial intermediaries are heavily involved in transactions using financial instruments. Indeed, as pointed out earlier, the distinguishing feature of financial intermediaries is that their principal assets are financial in nature. It is, therefore, important for management to be knowledgeable about the various characteristics of these financial instruments—short- and long-term, debt and equity. Moreover, it is important for the managers of financial intermediaries to understand the factors which affect the price and yield relationships among different kinds of financial assets. The present chapter seeks to provide a brief discussion of the major instruments traded in the financial markets and of the factors which affect the relative yields on financial instruments. Necessarily the treatment of each financial instrument is quite general in nature. While money market instruments are discussed in some detail, discussion of capital market instruments is limited to the general factors which influence the pattern or structure of yields. For more specific information the reader should refer to the references listed at the end of the chapter.

The term *money market* refers to the market for short-term financial instruments with a time to maturity of one year or less. The term *capital mar-*

ket refers to the market for long-term financial assets having actual maturities of more than one year. Distinctions between short and long are somewhat arbitrary although one year is the most common dividing point. Both of these markets perform important services in the financial system. The focus of the money market is on providing a means by which individuals and business firms are able to rapidly adjust their actual liquidity position to the amount desired. The money market is the medium through which holders of temporary cash surpluses meet those with temporary cash deficits. Hence, an individual with a temporary excess of investable funds is able to use the money market as a place where these funds may be "stored" for a short period of time at some positive rate of interest. Similarly, the individual or business firm with a temporary shortfall of liquidity can obtain funds in the money market for a short period of time. The money market then becomes important because of the lack of synchronization among inflows and outflows of cash at individual economic units. In both cases, the economic unit is using the money market—either as a supplier or demander of funds—as a means by which to adjust its liquidity.[1]

The capital market also plays a significant role in the financial system. Given the fact that saving and investment are vital for the growth of the economy, and also that, in an advanced economy, the economic units which save are different from the economic units which invest, the capital market provides a bridge by which the saving of surplus units may be transformed into the investments of deficit units.[2] In this process, the capital market contributes to economic stability by matching saving and investment and to economic growth by expanding the total amount of saving and investment. In short, an efficient capital market contributes to a rising standard of living.

COMPARISON OF THE ROLES OF THE MONEY AND CAPITAL MARKETS

While both the money and capital markets are significant in the financial system, it is important to recognize that these markets differ in a number of respects. As pointed out above, the money market primarily exists as a means of liquidity adjustment. In contrast, the

---

[1] It is also important to observe that the holding of cash forces economic units to carry a significant opportunity cost since cash deposits earn no explicit rate of return. The money market serves to reduce the opportunity cost from holding liquid assets. This is especially important in periods of high and rising interest rates and during periods of severe inflation when the opportunity cost associated with idle cash balances increases.

[2] Saving here refers to the postponement of current consumption while investment refers to the purchase of real capital assets such as new buildings and equipment.

capital market's principal function is to serve as a link between the ultimate surplus and deficit sectors (i.e., a conduit for saving and investment) and thereby to play an important role in the process by which "real" saving is transformed into "real" investment.[3]

The money and capital markets also differ in a number of other important respects. Many money market instruments but not all have strong *secondary markets;* that is, can be sold to another investor prior to the maturity of the instrument. For example, the Treasury bill market is frequently referred to as one of the best secondary markets in the world. The relatively strong secondary market plus the short maturity of instruments and the low *default risk* provide substantial liquidity for these money market instruments. In contrast, many capital market instruments have a relatively weak secondary market.[4] For example, the market for home mortgages has traditionally been a relatively poor secondary market. The relatively weak secondary market plus the long period to maturity and (frequently) substantial default risk make capital market instruments generally unsatisfactory holdings for liquidity purposes.

The money and capital markets also differ in terms of the volume of transactions. The total volume of transactions in the money market is extremely large when compared to the amount of capital market transactions. This reflects, to a substantial degree, the differences in the financial functions performed by these two markets. Since the money market principally serves as a vehicle for the adjustment of the liquidity position of economic units to expected and unexpected changes in cash flows, it is to a considerable extent a secondary market in which existing instruments are bought and sold. In contrast, since the capital market is principally a mechanism by which ultimate surplus units with excess funds are able to "lock-up" investments for long periods of time this market is essentially a *primary* one—that is, a market for newly issued securities. This statement is, of course, much more correct for the mortgage and bond (both corporate and municipal) markets than for the equity market. But in general it is not too inaccurate to assert that money market instruments are bought to be sold as soon as cash is needed, while capital market securities are bought to be held as long-term investments. The rate of interest (yield) is the primary factor which motivates savers to part with their funds in the capital market, while the safety and liquidity

---

[3] This does not, of course, mean that surplus units are only suppliers of funds in the money and capital markets and that deficit units are only demanders of funds in these markets. Indeed, surplus units may have to make very large (but temporary) demands on the money and capital markets for funds. Similarly, deficit units may provide very large (but temporary) supplies of funds to the money and capital markets.

[4] One obvious exception to this statement is the market for frequently traded stock such as the New York Stock Exchange.

of the financial instrument is at least as important as its rate of return or yield in the money market.[5]

Money and capital market instruments also differ greatly in terms of risk. Money market instruments generally carry low default and low market risk. As a general rule, only instruments issued by economic units of the highest standing qualify for entry into the money market. The very short maturity of money market securities and their good secondary market reduces the impact on price of changes in interest rates. In contrast, both default and market risk in the capital market are often substantial. Capital market instruments include both debt and equity. Equity issues represent claims on the earnings and assets of an individual firm which are inferior to those of debt instruments; necessarily these equity issues carry more risk than debt instruments of the same firm. Moreover, debt quality ranges from U.S. government securities and highly rated corporate issues with limited default risk to unrated bonds of small and new business ventures and to other securities with more substantial default risk. In addition, capital market instruments are long term in nature, with the result that interest rate changes have a substantial impact on the prices of these instruments.

The money market is dominated by one set of financial institutions—the commercial banks and the Federal Reserve System. The commercial banking system is by far the largest group of financial institutions in the nation. Moreover, because of the nature of their deposit liabilities and the regulations they face, commercial banks are heavily concentrated in short- and medium-term loans and investments. In addition, one of the major liabilities of the commercial bank—the large business ($100,00 and over) certificate of deposit (CD)—is the second most important instrument by dollar volume in the money market. The behavior of the commercial bank is, in turn, affected and indeed controlled to a considerable extent by the Federal Reserve System. The Federal Reserve System supplies or withdraws reserves from the commercial banking system through its techniques of monetary control. It is, therefore, necessary for management to understand current monetary policy actions by the Federal Reserve in order to anticipate movements in interest rates and in the prices of financial assets. To a considerable extent, expecially in the short run, money market rates are principally what the Federal Reserve wishes them to be.

External influences on capital market rates and the prices of capital market instruments are much more complex. No single financial institution dominates the capital market. While individual financial institutions (such as the savings and loan association) may dominate

---

[5] The yield on a financial instrument does, of course, incorporate the safety and marketability of the instrument as well as other factors.

certain subsectors of the capital market—such as the single-family residential mortgage market—no one financial institution can be said to dominate the capital market in the way that the commercial bank and the Federal Reserve influence the money market. As a result, the level of yields and the pattern of yields among different financial instruments is much more complex. Certainly monetary policy influences are transmitted to the capital market. However, changes in inflationary expectations, corporate profits and liquidity, business spending for inventories and plant and equipment, and the relative inflows of funds into the major financial institutions are also of substantial importance.

Finally, the capital market is dominant in terms of the *volume* of securities outstanding at any one time. This dominance reflects the differing maturities of the financial instruments traded in these markets. The money market instrument is, of course, short term in nature. Its maturity is generally measured in days, weeks, or months. In contrast, capital market instruments are long term in nature; their maturity usually is measured in terms of years. Moreover, common stock and most preferred stock—theoretically at least—have no maturity, though many corporations plan to retire their preferred stock issues when conditions are favorable.

It is important for the management of financial institutions to be knowledgeable about the specific financial characteristics of both money and capital market instruments as well as to understand the functions of the money and capital markets within the financial system. Financial institutions—whether bank or nonbank—participate actively in the money and capital markets. Commercial banks are active primarily in the money market, while nonbank financial institutions are active principally in the capital market. However, there is a considerable degree of overlap in the functions of different financial institutions. For example, while commercial banks are primarily short-term lenders, they also make a considerable volume of so-called term loans to businesses with maturities of five years or more. Moreover, commercial banks invest heavily in relatively long-term municipal securities. Similarly, while savings and loan associations are principally long-term lenders, they also make a large amount of short-term construction loans for homes and other related purposes. Furthermore, while the major nonbank financial institutions are primarily long-term lenders, they all have a need for participation to a limited degree in the money market in order to adjust their liquidity positions. Certainly it should be kept in mind that financial institutions operate on both sides of the market—borrowing and lending—and frequently do so simultaneously. In addition, with the striking changes in the sources and use of funds at the major financial institutions in recent years—and the expectation of greater changes in the future—the degree of overlap among these financial institutions will undoubtedly increase in the future.

MONEY AND CAPITAL MARKET INSTRUMENTS

Table 4–1 provides information on the volume of of the major money and capital market instruments outstanding in the U.S. financial sys-

TABLE 4–1
Money and capital market instruments outstanding as of December 31, 1977 ($billions)

Instrument of the money market	Volume outstanding
U.S. government securities	$ 151.0
Securities issued by agencies of the U.S. government	141.4
Municipal securities	18.5
Commercial paper	62.0
Bankers acceptances	27.5
Large, negotiable certificates of deposit	77.4
	$ 477.8
Instrument of the capital market	
U.S. government securities	123.0
Mortgages	1023.5
Municipal securities	240.1
Corporate equities	996.7
Corporate bonds	298.1
	$2,681.4

Source: Board of Governors of the Federal Reserve System, Flow of Funds Accounts.

tem as of year-end 1977. As mentioned earlier, the volume of capital market instruments—particularly corporate equities ($996.7 billion) and mortgages ($1,023.5 billion)—far exceeds the volume of money market securities outstanding.[6] It is interesting to note that securities issued by governmental units do not dominate the U.S. capital market. Rather private debt securities—principally corporate equities and mortgages—are the most important financial instrument by volume in the U.S. capital market. In contrast, the securities of the U.S. government and its agencies clearly dominate the money market. This reflects the enormous amount of deficit spending carried out by the U.S. government as well as the decision to finance this deficit principally with short-term securities.

---

[6] Some distortion is introduced into these data since the volume of equity securities is measured at market rather than book value.

MONEY MARKET INSTRUMENTS

U.S. Treasury securities

Securities issued by the U.S. Treasury are important in both the money and capital markets. As pointed out in Table 4–1, however, these securities are especially significant in the money market; indeed, Treasury securities (including agency securities) have historically played a dominating role in the U.S. money market. Moreover, the average maturity of the Treasury's debt has fallen considerably in recent years, further increasing the role of these securities as money market instruments. U.S. Treasury securities are the major liquid asset held by a number of financial institutions.

Treasury securities (or "governments" as they are usually called) may be classified in a number of ways. One approach is to classify these instruments by their original maturity. By this method, governments may be divided into bills (with an original maturity of one year or less), notes (with an original maturity of one to ten years), and bonds (with an original maturity of more than ten years). All Treasury bills are money market instruments. Moreover, notes and bonds may be money market instruments if their maturity has become sufficiently short. However, short-term notes and bonds generally do not have the strong secondary market liquidity of bills. Moreover, there also appears to be some difference in the bill market with regard to liquidity. Bills with a maturity of six months or less appear to have greater liquidity for secondary market trading than bills with a maturity of more than six months.

Treasury bills differ from other government securities not only in terms of their original maturity but also by their return to investors. Treasury bills are discount instruments; that is, the return to the investor is derived from the difference between the original purchase price (at a discount from par) and the par value of the instrument. For example, an investor pays $9,500 for a bill but will obtain $10,000 for that bill (its par value) at maturity. The $500 increase in the value of the bill (taxable as ordinary income not as capital gains) would constitute the return to the investor. In contrast, all other Treasury securities (except Series E savings bonds) pay an explicit rate of interest in which the investor receives separate payment of interest.

Since Treasury bills are discount instruments, their yields cannot be compared directly with the returns on Treasury notes and bonds or on some other money market instruments. Bill yields are calculated on a "bank discount basis" which produces an estimate of the return to the investor that is different from and lower than the yield to maturity. For example, in the situation discussed above, (the purchase of a one-year bill at $9,500), the investor receives a total dollar return of $500. To calculate the rate of return, the investor would divide the absolute return (or discount), D, by the par value, P, and multiply by 360 divided by the number of days held (up to a maximum of 360 days). In symbols,

$$DR = \frac{D}{P} \times \frac{360}{H}$$

where DR equals the discount or interest rate return to the investor, D equals the amount of the discount in dollars; P is the par value of the security; and H is the number of days remaining until maturity. In the example given, the discount yield to the investor is:

$$DR = \frac{\$\ 500}{\$\ 10,000} \times \frac{360}{360} = 5\%$$

This 5 percent return calculated on the bank discount basis is different from and lower than the true yield on a security for the following reasons. First, the absolute amount of the discount is divided by par rather than by the purchase price of the instrument. Yet the investor only had to commit the amount of the purchase price (neglecting transactions costs), and it is this figure rather than par which is really relevant in determining the investor's return. Second, the return is calculated on a 360-day rather than a 365-day year. For all of these reasons the discount yield is lower than the true yield to maturity. As a rough rule of thumb it is sometimes argued that the true yield may be approximated by adding 30 to 40 basis points to the bank discount yield. However, there is a more precise method for determining the yield to maturity of Treasury bills which permits the investor to compare directly bill yields with the returns on all other taxable securities. In order to convert the bill's (or indeed any other discount instruments) yield from the bank discount yield to a bond equivalent or yield to maturity we may use the following formula:

$$\text{Investment return} = \frac{365 \times \text{Discount basis}}{360 - (\text{Discount basis} \times \text{Days to maturity})}$$

In the example cited above, the bank discount yield was 5 percent. The investment return or true yield was:[7]

$$\text{Investment return} = \frac{365 \times 0.05}{360 - (0.05 \times 360)}$$

$$= \frac{18.25}{342}$$

$$= 5.336\%$$

---

[7] For a useful discussion of yield computations on Treasury bills, see *Securities of the United States Government and Federal Agencies*, 26th ed. 1974, First Boston Corporation.

Treasury bills are important not only because of their quantitative significance but also due to their use by a diverse group of financial and nonfinancial firms, as well as by the Federal Reserve System in its conduct of monetary policy. Treasury bills have been the traditional means for liquidity adjustment by commercial banks. Also, Treasury bills have appeared frequently in the portfolio of manufacturing and other nonfinancial firms, as these firms have relied upon bills as a known storehouse of funds to pay dividends, taxes, and other short-term obligations. Also, of major significance, the Federal Reserve System conducts open market operations primarily in Treasury bills. For all of these reasons, an understanding of the role of Treasury securities in general and the Treasury bill, in particular, is important.

A more detailed view of the distribution of ownership of Treasury securities is presented in Tables 4–2 through 4–4. While private in-

TABLE 4–2
Ownership of federal interest-bearing debt securities,
September 1978 (in $millions)

	Total outstanding
Held by U.S. government accounts	$167,973
Public issues held by Federal Reserve	114,764
Held by private investors	484,234
	$766,971

Source: U.S. Treasury Bulletin.

vestors (financial and nonfinancial) are the largest single holder of Treasury securities (Table 4–2) the U.S. government itself and its agencies also are a major force in the demand for Treasury securities. The Federal Reserve and various U.S. employee retirement funds have accumulated large amounts of Treasury issues. Indeed, in recent years federally related investment demand has resulted in a growing internalization of the Treasury debt within the government. Table 4–3 shows the very short-term nature of the public debt. The average maturity of the Treasury debt is roughly two years, while about two thirds of the debt matures within five years. Such short maturities may have inflationay potential, and certainly lead to frequent refundings and some interference with monetary policy. Within the private sector, individuals, commercial banks, and foreign investors are the dominant investors (Table 4–4). Perhaps the most significant development has been the enormous accumulation of U.S. Treasury securities by the oil surplus countries in recent years.

TABLE 4–3
Interest-bearing marketable government debt classified by type and maturity, September 30, 1978 (in $millions)

By type of security	Total outstanding
Treasury bills	$160,936
Treasury notes	267,865
Treasury bonds	56,355
	$485,155
By final maturity	
Within 1 year	$225,396
1–5 years	168,474
5–10 years	49,273
10–15 years	14,316
15–20 years	2,258
20 years and over	25,439
	$485,155

Source: U.S. Treasury Bulletin.

TABLE 4–4
Ownership of public debt securities by private investors, September 1978 (in $billions)

Held by	Total outstanding
Commercial banks	$ 95.3
Individuals	109.3
Insurance companies	15.1
Mutual savings banks	5.4
Corporations	21.5
State and local governments	67.8
Foreign and international	121.0
Other	52.9
	$488.3

Source: U.S. Treasury Bulletin.

Federal funds

Another important subdivision of the money market is the market for federal funds. It is significant from a variety of perspectives and to a number of different economic units. To commercial banks, the federal funds market is an inexpensive and efficient way to obtain or dispose of extra reserves. Indeed for very short-term purposes (i.e., one or two days) the federal funds market has become the dominant means of adjusting bank reserves. Moreover the federal funds market has become increasingly a source of permanent funds for larger banks and a means for permanent disposal of funds for smaller banks. The federal funds market has become significant in terms both of the implementation of monetary policy and in the interpretation by investors of monetary policy changes by the Federal Reserve System.

The term *federal funds* is a shorthand abbreviation for Federal Reserve funds, which are reserve balances held by member commercial banks at the Federal Reserve banks. Federal Reserve funds are a financial asset and a liability, appearing on the balance sheets of two economic units. They appear on the books of the Federal Reserve banks in an account called "Deposits of Member Banks," which is a liability of the Federal Reserve banks owed to member banks in their district. Federal funds are an asset to the member banks who carry them on their balance sheet as "Deposits at the Federal Reserve." Since the member banks own these reserve balances, they may be used to make loans or to purchase assets (such as currency and coin), much like individuals and businesses use checking accounts to carry out transactions.

Transactions in federal funds then refer to the buying and selling of the deposits of member banks at the Federal Reserve—either originated by the owning bank itself for its own purposes or by another party. These purchases and sales are generally for a one-day period but may be longer if desired. A loan made in federal funds is immediately available to the lending institution until repayment is made. This occurs because the transaction is carried out by wire and/or telephone communication between the banks involved and the Federal Reserve, and the funds are transferred by a simple bookkeeping entry from the account of one bank to the account of another. Contrast this with payment by check where the recipient of funds normally does not have use of the money until the check passes through the check clearing mechanism. If the writer of the check and the recipient are a considerable distance apart, funds transferred by check (usually referred to a clearinghouse funds) may take several days to reach their destination. The shortest time for a check to clear through most clearinghouse systems is one day, but even that is too long for banks, security dealers, and other institutions who trade daily in the financial markets since each day that the transfer of funds is delayed is a day's interest income lost.

The federal funds market began in the 1920s and was confined almost exclusively to short (overnight) loans between major U.S. banks. In recent years, however, the number of institutions (both financial and nonfinancial) which use this market has expanded sharply, and commercial banks—especially large ones—have begun to employ the federal funds market for more permanent transfers of funds.

Commercial banks have used the federal funds market for many years as a temporary means for liquidity adjustment. Those banks with short-term surplus funds available have frequently found that the return from disposing of these funds in the federal funds market has exceeded the net return (after transactions costs) from investments in Treasury bills or other money market instruments. Moreover, the federal funds market has provided an attractive source of funds when the reserve position of banks is strained. The attractiveness of the federal funds market as a source of funds relative to attracting deposits (especially large certificates of deposit) was especially important in periods of tight money in the middle and late 1960s since there is no legal limit on the rate a bank may pay to obtain federal funds while there were and still are some limits on the amount banks can pay to obtain funds through the sale of deposits.[8]

In recent years, however, the federal funds market has been used by commercial banks of widely varying size as both a more permanent source and use of funds. Large money center banks have arranged to acquire a given amount of federal funds from their correspondent banks on a daily basis. Through this means, the larger bank is able to acquire funds beyond its local deposit potential and to expand its earning assets (especially loans) beyond the volume that could be supported only through deposits. In some periods the cost of these funds is less than the cost of funds raised through deposits. For the smaller bank, the arrangement represents an assured use of funds that may be employed without "spoiling" the local loan market.

The number of nonbank participants in the federal funds market has broadened considerably in recent years. Many savings and loan associations, for example, now use the federal funds market as a means for meeting their liquidity needs, accomplishing these transactions through their correspondent banks. Moreover, U.S. government security dealers and many nonfinancial firms now use the federal funds market for a number of purposes, particularly through the device of repurchase agreements on U.S. government securities payable in federal funds.

The federal funds market has become especially important as an indicator of the current posture of monetary policy. In recent years the Federal Reserve has announced specific growth rate targets for

---

[8] The attractiveness of federal funds transactions versus large CD operations has been reduced since the Regulation Q ceilings on the maximum rates payable to obtain funds has been eliminated for large CDs. Ceiling limits continue, however, on the smaller denomination certificates.

the amount of money in circulation.[9] Through its open market operations the Fed has then sought to increase or decrease the growth rate of the nation's money supply through altering the availability and cost of bank reserves. For example, should the Federal Reserve wish to expand the monetary growth rate, it may purchase securities in the open market, thereby increasing the availability of bank reserves and reducing the federal funds rate. Conversely, should the Fed wish to reduce the growth rate of money in circulation, it could sell government securities from its portfolio, thereby reducing the availability of reserves and increasing the federal funds rate. The Federal Reserve then establishes a target federal funds rate which it believes is consistent with its desired money supply growth rates. Since the Fed does not announce its policies until well after the fact, observers of monetary policy and Federal Reserve actions pay especially careful attention to day-to-day and week-to-week movements in the federal funds rate as published in major business and financial periodicals as signals of changes in monetary policy. Such movements have substantial implications for the loan and investment policies of all financial institutions and especially for commercial banks.

Certificates of deposit

One of the newest and most important money market instruments is the large ($100,000 or over) certificate of deposit. These obligations of commercial banks are relatively new as a money market instrument—in fact, less than 20 years old. Credit for the creation of the large certificate of deposit as a money market instrument is generally given to First National City Bank of New York (Citibank), the second largest bank in the United States and considered by many to be the most innovative bank in the nation.

The large New York banks have traditionally been wholesale institutions, obtaining funds from demand deposits of businesses and concentrating their credit-granting activities in the field of commercial lending. They have not historically relied upon the small accounts of consumers. But since World War II with a period of relatively high interest rates, the large corporate depositors of these banks have found it profitable to shift idle balances into interest-bearing assets and out of demand deposits. When this happened, the shift did, of course, affect the growth rates of deposits at all banks, but especially at the large New York banks which had relied so heavily on business demand deposits.

---

[9] See Chapter 5 for a discussion of alternative definitions of the money stock and the Federal Reserve's monetary growth targets.

To compete effectively with the open market for funds and to pre-vent continued erosion of the importance of the banking system in the flow of funds, it was necessary for commercial banks to develop an instrument which had characteristics similar to other open market financial instruments and yet would bring funds directly into the bank. The instrument would have to be short term in nature, of very low credit risk, and have a good secondary market. When First National City Bank began to offer the large CDs in 1961 and when major dealers agreed to create a secondary market, a financial instrument with these desirable characteristics was created. The CDs have met with enormous success, so that by year-end 1978, there were almost $100 billion of these money market instruments outstanding, making them the second most important money market instrument by dollar volume behind Treasury bills.

The certificates of deposit which are considered money market instruments are negotiable and have a minimum denomination of $100,000, although a $1,000,000 CD is a more standard denomination (a normal round lot for trading purposes is $1,000,000). The original maturity of the large CDs ranges from a minimum of 30 days to a maximum of over one year, although most have original maturities of less than one year. There is a good secondary market, especially for the instruments of the largest banks. CDs are generally classified as prime and nonprime. Prime CDs are those issued by a few banks which are generally very large and experienced in the CD market. Nonprime CDs are those issued by all other banks, generally at a higher interest rate.

It is important to understand both the reasons for the sale of large CDs by major banks and also the reasons for the purchase of these money market instruments by investors. To understand why banks sell CDs, it is important to refer back to the traditional way in which banks managed their assets and to the development of liability management techniques in the early postwar period. Historically, management has concentrated upon the control of assets and has regarded deposits as essentially determined by external factors outside the bank's control. Management decision making concentrated on the selection of specific assets in which to invest available funds. With the growth of large certificates of deposit and indeed with the development of the federal funds market, banks do not need to rely completely on assets for providing liquidity nor do they need to view their deposits as totally beyond the control of management. With the development of CDs banks could obtain funds not only by liquidation of their assets (such as by selling Treasury bills) but also by selling certificates of deposit. In the latter case the bank is using liability management to at least partially control its rate of growth and meet short-term reserve needs. Not only can banks use liability management to obtain relatively short-term funds, but they can also use the CD market for longer term purposes; that is, they can raise funds through the CD market in order to expand their asset base. Moreover, the success of the CD encouraged major banks to develop new sources of funds subject to management decision making, such as Eurodollars and commercial paper.

Large CDs are purchased primarily by major business firms who wish to place temporarily available funds in a relatively safe instrument but would like a return which exceeds that available on Treasury bills. Risk involved in the investment in CDs is higher than with Treasury bills, as revealed by the failure of U.S. National Bank of San Diego and Franklin National Bank, both of which had substantial amounts of CDs outstanding at the time of their collapse. In addition, the secondary market for large CDs is inferior to that of Treasury bills. For these reasons, market yields available to the investor on large CDs are slightly higher than those available on Treasury bills. As a general rule, the highest quality negotiable certificates of deposit offer a return of 50 to 100 basis points above those available on comparable maturity Treasury bills, although the differential varies widely over time as supply and demand forces shift in each market.

Commercial paper

Commercial paper consists of short-term promissory notes issued by large, established business firms with strong credit ratings. These firms include both financially oriented and nonfinancial enterprises, and in fact, in recent years the commercial paper market has been used extensively by commercial banks as a source of loanable funds. Commercial paper notes are unsecured. They are issued for periods of no more than 270 days since the Securities and Exchange Commission has ruled that longer term paper must be registered. Commercial paper is sold at a discount, as are Treasury bills, and their yield is determined by the bank discount method. In contrast to Treasury bills and large CDs most commercial paper has no important secondary market, thereby reducing its liquidity. However, many borrowers have attached an informal buy-back arrangement, whereby the issuer will repurchase the paper if the buyer wishes to sell it prior to maturity. It is understood, though, that the buyer will use the informal buy-back arrangement only when there is a real need for funds and not merely to suit the investor's convenience.

There are two basic varieties of commercial paper. One form is sold by the very largest finance companies in the United States—such as General Motors Acceptance Corporation and CIT Financial. The paper issued by these firms is frequently referred to as "finance company" paper. It is sold directly to ultimate buyers of the financial instrument without the use of brokers or dealers. The issuers of this type of commercial paper are in the market almost continuously and have developed dependable sources of funds. The issuers usually post rates and stand ready to accommodate investors willing to accept the posted rates and maturities. In contrast, the second form of commercial paper is brought to the market by smaller, less well known firms and businesses usually on an irregular basis. These firms include many industrial companies, a large number of electric and gas utilities, the smaller finance companies, and some banks through their holding companies. This form of commercial paper typically is sold through brokers or dealers. The rate offered to the market for this "dealer-placed" paper is usually higher than for finance company paper, both because the dealers must be compensated for their services and because the issuers of the dealer-placed paper are perceived as somewhat more risky, perhaps because of their smaller size.

Commercial paper carries a number of significant advantages for both borrowers and lenders in this market. These advantages help to explain why the commercial paper market has been one of the fastest growing parts of the money and capital markets during the postwar era. One obvious reason for the use of commercial paper by many business firms is its cost. It is generally cheaper to finance short-term cash needs with commercial paper than by borrowing from a commercial bank. The commercial paper rate typically is lower than the prime rate on business loans at commercial banks. In addition, the cost of commercial paper is further enhanced compared to bank borrowing at large commercial banks by the absence of compensating balance requirements which adds to the effective cost of the bank loan. The only mitigating element that reduces this cost spread between commercial paper and bank loans is the frequent requirement that issuers of commercial paper have a standing line of credit at a commercial bank. There are other reasons, though, for the use of commercial paper by those firms which do have the option to issue it (i.e., the larger firms). One important justification is that a firm may be able to obtain a larger total volume of credit. If a business mixes both bank credit and commercial paper as sources of funds it may be able to obtain a larger total volume of short-term funds than if it used exclusively either commercial credit or bank credit. This, of course, assumes that the credit markets are imperfect.[10] Another advantage of commercial paper for the issuer is the added bargaining power it brings when dealing with banks. If the borrowing firm has an alterna-

---

[10] This is consistent with the fact that commercial banks are limited by their capital in the size of unsecured loans to a single customer.

tive source of credit it is less likely to be placed in a position of taking whatever deal the bank offers. Finally, there may be a certain element of prestige involved in selling commercial paper since it has generally been sold only by the largest and most highly rated firms in the nation.

From the buyers' perspective, the two principal advantages of commercial paper compared with Treasury bills are yield and maturity. Commercial paper generally carries a higher yield than Treasury bills due to its greater credit risk and reduced liquidity. In addition, the maturity of commercial paper may be tailored precisely to the needs of the investor while Treasury bills come in fixed maturities which may be less convenient to the lender.

As with other money market instruments, the commercial paper market is a wholesale market with a normal round lot of $1 million, although paper is often available in smaller denominations. Most commercial paper is purchased by nonfinancial firms. As a result, it is frequently argued that commercial paper is a financial device by which business firms finance other business firms and bypass the commercial banking system. The growth of the commercial paper market necessarily reduces the share of the total flow of credit which is captured by the commercial banking system. Indeed some observers believe the commercial paper market has grown very rapidly in recent years due to basic inadequacies of the domestic banking system in meeting the credit needs of major corporations, especially during periods of tight money and high interest rates. Most industrialized nations today are served by a few very large banks operating hundreds of branch offices and possessing enormous credit-granting potential. In contrast, the U.S. banking system is composed of thousands of small and moderate size banks, many of which simply cannot accommodate the credit needs of large and rapidly growing corporations.[11]

Bankers acceptances

One of the oldest and yet one of the smallest money market instruments by volume is the bankers acceptance. The bankers acceptance is a draft or order to pay (a bill of exchange) a specified amount at a specified time. It is drawn on an individual commercial bank by a business firm and becomes a bankers acceptance when the bank stamps "accepted" on the face of the draft. Bankers acceptances are known as "two-name paper" since they have the names of both the drawer and the drawee on their face. They are used primarily to finance the shipment of goods between different countries of the

---

[11] See Chapter 7 for a description of the structure of U.S. banking.

world. In addition to providing financing for foreign trade, however, bankers acceptances also are used to finance the domestic shipment of goods, the domestic or foreign storage of readily marketable staples, and the provision of dollar exchange credit to banks in designated countries.

The workings of the bankers acceptance as a tool of international commerce may best be explained by an example. Suppose that an American importer wished to purchase shoes from a Brazilian exporter. He could obtain an irrevocable letter of credit in favor of the Brazilian exporter. This letter of credit would allow the Brazilian exporter to draw a draft on the American bank. This draft would be an order to pay the Brazilian exporter a specified amount at a specified time in the future (a time draft as opposed to a sight draft). The Brazilian exporter—probably acting through its bank—would then send the draft to the American bank. This draft would be stamped "accepted" by the American bank, indicating its liability for payment at the maturity date of the draft. The acceptance may then either be returned to the Brazilian bank (in which case the Brazilian bank is the true source of credit for the transaction), held by the American bank (financing is then done by the American bank), or sold to an acceptance dealer (financing then is provided by the acceptance dealer).

The bankers acceptance market provides a number of important functions. Perhaps most importantly it is an efficient means for the financing of international trade. In domestic commerce, where information on the credit worthiness of the buyer is readily available, trade credit (open account) provides the means for financing of the flow of goods. In international commerce, where information about the buyer is much less readily available, the bankers acceptance has provided an attractive financing device. Indeed, it is the only way to finance some international commerce. Moreover, it is a relatively low-cost means of financing. The interest rate on bankers acceptances is generally only slightly higher than the rate on Treasury bills.[12] Finally, the bankers acceptance offers a number of advantages to the accepting banks. If the bank chooses to dispose of the acceptance, it still is able to accommodate the credit needs of one of its customers and yet not use up any of its credit-creating capacity. On the other hand, if the accepting bank chooses to hold the acceptance and thereby provides the financing, it holds a highly liquid money market instrument.

The bankers acceptance has an excellent secondary market. There

---

[12] The fee charged by the bank for creating the acceptance (usually 1.5 percentage points) must, of course, be added to the bankers acceptance rate in order to measure the true cost of financing with bankers acceptances.

are a number of dealers who regularly hold sizable inventories of acceptances. Moreover, the Federal Reserve was instrumental in developing the bankers acceptance market and has authority to buy and sell acceptances as part of its open market operations. Other than the acceptances held by dealers in their market-making capacity, most bankers acceptances are held by the Federal Reserve, foreign central banks, and domestic bank investors (most of whom hold "own bills").

YIELD RELATIONSHIPS AMONG CAPITAL
MARKET INSTRUMENTS

Turning our attention from short- to long-term financing, the capital market plays a vital role in the process of transferring saving from surplus sectors to deficit sectors in the economy. In this process, both direct and indirect securities are created. As revealed in Table 4–1, the volume of securities outstanding in the capital market is enormous. As of December 31, 1977, the total volume of capital market instruments was over $2 trillion. Of this total, the volume of mortgages and corporate equities were especially significant. These mortgages would, of course, include claims on single-family residences, multifamily residences (apartment houses), and commercial buildings. The amount of mortgages outstanding is large not only because of the great amount of real estate activity in the post-World War II era but also due to the large amount of financial leverage which has been traditionally employed in financing construction.

While the outstanding volume of mortgages and corporate equities is quite similar in size, the rate of growth of these capital market instruments has been very different. The volume of corporate equities outstanding has grown very little in recent years for a variety of reasons. Perhaps most importantly, American business firms have found that the cost of raising funds through debt has been substantially less than obtaining funds with external equity. This difference in relative cost has—to a considerable extent—been the result of the fact that interest payments on debt are a tax deductible expense while dividend payments on preferred and common stock are not deductible for tax purposes. Moreover, many firms have decided to add to their equity base only through the retention of earnings. In addition, the greater use of debt may also reflect the improved stability of the U.S. economy in the post-World War II period. With greater stability, it would be expected that the optimal amount of debt for a firm would increase.

In contrast to the enormous volume of mortgages and corporate equities, it is interesting to note that the amounts of U.S. government securities and municipal obligations outstanding are relatively modest. As previously discussed, the maturity of the debt of the U.S. government has shortened considerably in recent years. The maturity has indeed been reduced to the point where U.S. government securities may be considered to be more of a money rather than a capital market instrument. In contrast, municipal debt, while small compared to the amount of mortgages and corporate equities outstanding, has grown very rapidly in recent years. The substantial geographic shifts in population coupled with an expansion in the role of state and local governments has created an enormous expansion in the volume of municipal securities outstanding. Moreover, with substantial demands for services coupled with resistance to tax increases, there has been a tendency for state and local governments to finance through borrowings rather than increased taxes, both through the sale of general obligation bonds and also especially through the marketing of revenue bonds for specific revenue-producing functions.

Yields on capital market instruments are affected by a number of different factors. These include, to name the major ones, maturity, credit risk, purchasing power risk, marketability, callability, and taxability. A brief analysis of each of these factors follows. It is important for the manager of a financial intermediary to be aware of how these factors affect the price and yields on financial assets. Such knowledge may not only be used to reduce the possible loss on investments (a defensive strategy) but may also be useful in reaching for higher yields (an offensive strategy) and therefore greater earnings for the institution.

Time to maturity

One of the most pervasive influences on the yield of capital market instruments is time to maturity. As the time to maturity increases, the yield available on financial instruments usually rises, and of course, the cost of raising funds through issuing capital market instruments increases. Conversely, as the time to maturity shortens, the yield available on capital market instruments usually falls, and of course, the cost of raising funds through issuing capital market instruments declines. The relationship between yield to maturity and time to maturity of a financial instrument is referred to as the "yield curve" or the term structure of interest rates. For the investor a "normal" yield curve indicates that a higher return on the investment may be obtained by seeking investments of longer maturity. Notice, however, that seeking investments of longer maturity means accepting greater market risk.[13] Of course, the issuer of securities must pay a

---

[13] Since, for a given charge in interest rates, the price of longer term securities fluctuates more than the price of shorter term issues.

higher cost in order to obtain the increased liquidity that goes with longer-term liabilities.

Yield curves may and do take a variety of shapes over the course of the business cycle. The "normal" yield curve is upward sloping. Occasionally, however, the yield curve is downward sloping, especially at or near peak levels of interest rates during periods of tight money. Moreover, during some periods of tight money the yield curve often takes on a hump in the middle. Each of these possibilities is illustrated in Figure 4–1.

There are a number of explanations for the yield-maturity relationship. Perhaps the most widely accepted view is the expectations hypothesis. This hypothesis argues that the current relationship between short- and long-term interest rates is determined by the expectations of market participants regarding future short-term interest rates. For example, if investors feel that future interest rates will be higher than current interest rates, the yield curve would tend to have an upward slope. Conversely, if investors felt that future interest rates would be lower than current interest rates, the yield curve would tend to be downward sloping. Finally, if market participants expect that future interest rates would be the same as current interest rates, the yield curve should be flat or horizontal.

One difficulty with the so-called pure expectations explanation of the yield curve is that it does not explain satisfactorily the fact that the yield curve normally displays an upward slope. It would seem that there should be equal periods of upward and downward sloping yield curves unless investors are nearly always expecting increases in interest rates. To reconcile this problem some have argued—in the so-called modified expectations hypothesis—that investors have a preference for liquidity and are willing to accept a lower rate of return in order to obtain greater liquidity in their investments. Therefore, investors are willing to accept lower rates of return for shorter-term as opposed to longer-term securities because the former tend to be more liquid. Thus, even if the expectation is for unchanged interest rates in the future, the yield curve today should be upward sloping.

The expectations hypothesis relies heavily upon profit-maximizing behavior on the part of both lenders and borrowers, modifying financial decisions as expectations of future interest rates change. It assumes that lenders and borrowers are indifferent with regard to the maturity of their assets (lenders) or liabilities (borrowers). It does not, however, take into account the institutional rigidities that exist in the financial system in which most primary securities are purchased by financial institutions who are subject to significant legal and other restrictions on their investment behavior, nor of the desire by borrowers to issue securities of different maturities. This limitation of the

FIGURE 4–1

A. Upward sloping yield curve

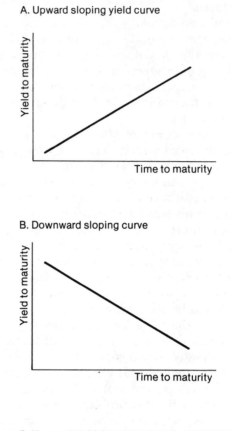

B. Downward sloping curve

C. Humped yield curve

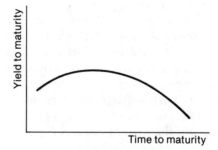

expectations hypothesis has resulted in the development of the segmented markets or hedging explanation of the yield curve.

The segmented markets explanation of the yield curve is based upon the argument that financial institutions as investors and business firms as borrowers tend to specialize in the maturity of their investments.[14] Commercial banks, for example, are purchasers principally of relatively short-term financial assets (money market instruments). In contrast, life insurance companies are involved primarily in long-term financial instruments of the capital market (principally corporate bonds and mortgages). Similarly, it is good financial management practice for business firms which are temporarily building inventory to finance using short-term sources of funds and for business firms which are expanding their fixed assets to finance with long-term sources of funds.

The segmented markets explanation of the term structure would then explain a downward-sloping yield curve as the result of a scarcity in the supply of funds from commercial banks (perhaps because of a tight money policy on the part of the Federal Reserve System) and a high demand for short-term funds (perhaps due to heavy inventory accumulation by business firms). Similarly, an upward-sloping yield curve may be explained by an easy monetary policy and slack business conditions.

The yield curve has a number of uses for financial managers. For those who accept the expectations hypothesis, or some variant of it, the yield curve may be used as a device to forecast future interest rates. For example, an upward-sloping yield curve suggests a rise in short-term interest rates. In addition the yield curve may be useful in order to determine the best maturity of a security issue for the borrower and the best maturity for the lender. For example, a humped yield curve would indicate that, while there is a substantial interest rate penalty for extending the maturity of an issue up to the peak of the hump, there is little or no penalty to the borrower for further extensions. This may suggest that the borrower should increase the maturity of a planned issue. Conversely, the existence of a humped yield curve might suggest to the investor that a purchase be kept near the short-term end of the maturity spectrum. As a third possible use of the yield curve, it may be possible (assuming some inefficiencies in the market) to find overpriced and underpriced securities through the use of the yield curve.

---

[14] For example, one of the largest private economic and financial forecasting groups explain their approach to forecasting interest rates in the following fashion: "the money and capital markets are viewed as segmented, with demand and supply factors interacting in each segment to determine the level of interest rates." *The Data Resources Review*, April 1977, Data Resources Inc., Lexington, Mass., p. 172.

Default risk

There are many other factors in addition to time to maturity which might be expected to affect the yield to maturity on a capital market instrument. One of the most important of these is default or credit risk—the possibility that the principal and/or interest payments on a debt security will not be made in a timely fashion. It would be expected that the larger the default risk involved in the commitment of funds to a security, the higher must be the expected yield to maturity. The influence of default risk on relative yields is illustrated by the yields to maturity offered in the market for fixed-income securities. U.S. government securities—thought to carry no default risk—have the lowest return to the investor. In the corporate category, Aaa-rated securities have the lowest default risk and also lowest rate of return. Similarly, default risk and yield increase as the rating diminishes through Aa, A, and down to lower grade issues. This relationship is known as the risk structure of interest rates.

The risk structure of interest rates appears to vary over the business cycle and especially so for corporate bonds. In periods of prosperity and stability in the nation's financial markets the yield differential between high-rated and low-rated bond issues usually narrows. In contrast, in periods of recession or depression, the yield differential between corporate debt obligations of varying credit risk widens appreciably. This suggests that financial markets underprice risk in periods of economic buoyancy and overprice risk in periods of economic decline and suggests that astute financial management of a bond portfolio could produce substantial gains. In contrast, there appears to be a much smaller change in the risk structure of interest rates for municipal obligations over the course of the business cycle.

Inflation

The rate of inflation has accelerated dramatically in recent years. As a result, current and expected inflation rates have been one of the major influences on yields of fixed-income securities. While there is some disagreement on the manner in which inflation affects interest rates, the dominant view appears to be that the nominal interest rate (or rate as reported in the financial press) at a given time is composed of two factors—the "real" interest rate (determined by the underlying factors of thrift and productivity) and the inflation premium (a premium for the *expected* rate of inflation over the time period of the debt obligation). In a world of no inflation, the investor should be able to obtain the real rate of interest on a commitment with no credit risk (the real rate is thought to be around 2 to 3 percent). However, since inflation reduces the purchasing power of any fixed amount of funds promised in the future, the investor would expect protection in the form of an inflation premium for the amount of inflation which could be expected over the time of this commitment. As an example, suppose that the real rate of interest was 3 percent. If an investor expected an annual rate of inflation of 8 percent to prevail over the duration of an investment, a nominal rate of 11 percent would be required as compensation. Any rate less than this would reduce the return after adjustment for inflation to less than 3 percent. In contrast, if the investor expected the inflation rate to be 4 percent over the period of the commitment, the investor would demand a nominal return of 7 percent in order to obtain a real return of 3 percent. There is some question as to whether the market adjusts fully for changes in the expected rate of inflation (i.e., whether an increase of 1 percentage point in the expected rate of inflation brings about an increase of 1 percentage point in the interest rate) and how long is the adjustment process, but there appears to be general agreement that the inflation rate is important in influencing interest rates on financial assets.

Marketability

Another variable which does affect the yield to maturity on capital market securities is marketability. While investments in capital market securities are generally planned for a considerable period in advance, it may be that due to unforeseen circumstances, the holder would want to liquidate the securities prior to maturity. In that case, the ability to eliminate the security from the portfolio quickly and with little impact on market price is an important factor to the investor. Among fixed-income securities, U.S. Treasury securities stand out as having the best secondary market. In contrast, municipal securities and corporate bond issues generally have a limited secondary market. At the extreme, investments in mortgages are generally quite illiquid. Among equity securities, the marketability of the issue varies widely. Equity investments in closely held corporations are often difficult to liquidate. In contrast, shares in a relatively stable security listed on the New York Stock Exchange are generally easier to liquidate, although the market price may be unsatisfactory due to variations in general market conditions.

Callability

Callability is another factor that may have some influence on market yields. Callability is defined as the ability of a borrower to retire a capital market instrument prior to maturity. The borrower may "call" the security at a previously specified price, thereby forcing holders of the security to exchange it for cash. Callability is an especially important feature for long-term investors. Not only does the call of a security disturb the portfolio of the investor but it also usually will reduce the yield in the portfolio. Most corporate bonds are callable. In contrast, most U.S. government securities and many municipals are not callable.

Since the call feature is undesirable to the investor (but desirable to the issuer), it would be expected that securities which are immediately callable would carry a higher yield than securities which are not callable or in which the call feature has been postponed or deferred for some period. However, the investor would demand a call premium only if there was some real possibility that the issue would, in fact, be called. Such a call would be most likely to occur when interest rates have fallen from higher levels when the security was issued. In fact, studies have shown that the market requires a substantial call premium only in periods when interest rates are unusually high and are expected to fall.

Taxability

A final factor is taxability. Taxability refers to the tax status of the return from the security. The most publicized impact of the taxability feature occurs for municipal securities. The interest return on all issues of state governments and any instrumentality of the states such as cities, counties, school districts, and other local governmental units are exempt from the federal income tax. Moreover, the returns on these issues usually are exempt from the income tax of the area which has issued the security. For example, securities issued by the State of New York would be exempt from the New York State income tax. As a result of this tax exemption, municipal securities carry substantially lower yields in the market than corporate obligations. Capital gains realized on municipal securities, however, are taxable. As a result, municipal securities on which part of the investment return occurs in the form of capital gains must carry a higher yield than comparable securities in which the total return is in the form of interest. As a final and little noted feature, the interest income from U.S. government issues is exempt from state and local taxes.

CONCLUSIONS

Some of the more important relationships among the money and capital markets which stem from the features discussed in this chapter are illustrated in Table 4–5. This table presents the market yield on selected money and capital market instruments for 1975, 1976, 1977, and 1978. A number of important observations can be made based upon the information presented in this table. First, all three

TABLE 4–5
Interest rates on selected money and capital market instruments (percent)

	1975	1976	1977	1978
3-month Treasury bills	5.80	4.98	5.27	7.19
Large CDs	6.43	5.26	5.58	8.20
90–119 day commercial paper	6.26	5.24	5.54	7.94
20-year U.S. government bonds	8.19	7.86	7.67	8.48
AAA municipal bonds	6.42	5.66	5.20	5.52
AAA corporate bonds	8.83	8.43	8.02	8.73

Source: Federal Reserve Bulletin, various issues.

money market rates—rates on Treasury bills, large CDs and commercial paper—tend to cluster together reflecting the substitutability of these instruments in the investors portfolio. Second, yields on Treasury bills are lower than yields on other money market instruments, reflecting both the lower default risk on Treasury issues and their superior marketability. Third, the yield curve is upward sloping for each time period presented in the table. For example, in 1977 the yield on 3-month Treasury bills was 5.27 percent while the yield on 20-year U.S. government bonds was 7.67 percent. In the capital market, the structure of relative yields also reflects many of the factors discussed above. Yields on municipal bonds are below yields on either U.S. government or corporate issues due to the taxability feature. Also, yields on U.S. government bonds are below yields on corporate bonds in response to the reduced default risk on U.S. government issues and their greater marketability.

Given the significance of money and capital market instruments both to the sources and uses of funds at financial institutions, it is important for the management of financial institutions to develop an appreciation for the different kinds of instruments and for the factors which produce differences in yields among the instruments. While this chapter could do no more than highlight these considerations and point out some of the major factors which influence these markets, it is hoped that the reader will delve more deeply into the subject through additional readings.

QUESTIONS

4–1. Compare and contrast the differences between the money market and the capital market in terms of (*a*) purpose, (*b*) secondary market, (*c*) volume of transactions, (*d*) risk, (*e*) importance of different financial institutions, and (*f*) volume of financial instruments outstanding.

4–2. What are the characteristic financial instruments of the respective money market and capital market?

4–3. Note the different characteristics of U.S. Treasury bills, Treasury notes, and Treasury bonds. How are they different in terms of maturity?

4–4. What is a discount instrument? Which of the Treasury instruments are discount instruments?

4–5. A U.S. Treasury bill is purchased for $9,350. It has a maturity of one year. What is its (a) bank discount yield, (b) bond equivalent or true yield?

4–6. Differentiate between prime and nonprime certificates of deposit. How should this distinction affect the yield on these certificates?

4–7. What is the difference between a bearer certificate and a registered certificate?

4–8. What is the expectations hypothesis? the modified expectations hypothesis? the segmented markets or hedging explanation of the yield curve?

4–9. Examine how the following factors may affect the yield of a security:
   a. Maturity.
   b. Credit risk.
   c. Purchasing power risk.
   d. Marketability.
   e. Callability.
   f. Taxability.

REFERENCES

1. Federal Reserve Bank of Richmond. *Instruments of the Money Market,* 1975.
2. Henning, Charles; Pigott, William; and Scott, Robert. *Financial Markets and the Economy.* 2d ed. Englewood Cliffs, N.J.: Prentice-Hall, 1978.
3. Homer, Sidney, and Leibowitz, Martin L. *Inside the Yield Book.* Englewood Cliffs, N.J.: Prentice-Hall, 1972.
4. Lendow, W. *Inside the Money Market.* New York: Random House, 1972.
5. Robinson, Roland, and Wrightsman, Dwayne. *Financial Markets.* New York: McGraw-Hill Book Co., 1974.
6. Van Horne, J. C. *Financial Market Rates and Flows.* Englewood Cliffs, N.J.: Prentice-Hall, 1978.
7. Woodworth, G. W. *The Money Market and Monetary Management.* New York: Harper & Row, 1972.

5

Monetary policy, debt management, and the financial system

Financial markets are affected both by the monetary policy actions of the Federal Reserve (the Fed) and by the U.S. Treasury through the management of the public debt. Changes in financial markets in response to monetary policy and debt management policy may have important influences on the behavior of financial institutions. As discussed earlier, changes in interest rates in the money and capital markets influence the prices which financial institutions must pay to obtain funds and also the returns which these institutions can earn on their loans and investments. Moreover, the volume of funds flowing into financial institutions and the demand for these funds varies substantially over the business cycle. In periods of intense monetary restraint, the flow of funds into financial institutions, especially depository financial institutions, is curtailed to a considerable extent (referred to earlier as disintermediation). Conversely, in periods of low interest rates and monetary ease, financial institutions frequently have excessively large inflows of funds and find difficulties in investing these funds at reasonable rates of return. Since the Federal Reserve and the Treasury affect interest rate levels and the flow of funds to such a large extent, it is important for managers of financial institutions to understand the role of these institutions in the

105

marketplace. Necessarily, the impact of government financial policy falls most directly, although not necessarily more powerfully, on bank as opposed to nonbank financial institutions.

INFLUENCE OF THE FEDERAL RESERVE SYSTEM

The Federal Reserve System is the principal organization in the United States for controlling the quantity and cost of money. It is the nation's central bank, analogous in that role to the Bank of England and other central banks around the world. Created by the United States Congress in 1913 to play a defensive role in eliminating "money panics," the Federal Reserve now plays a more aggressive role in seeking to achieve broad economic objectives such as full employment, stable prices, economic growth, and balance in the international accounts of the United States. As a result of the more aggressive role of the Fed in carrying out these objectives, and its substantial influence on interest rates and funds flows, the day-to-day behavior of the Federal Reserve System is watched intently by the management of financial institutions and by other participants in the financial markets. In fact, many large financial institutions have a number of professional staff members whose principal function is to anticipate changes in monetary policy and to evaluate the implications of current and future policy for the investment strategy of their institution.

Organization of the Federal Reserve

In order to understand the particular organizational framework of the Federal Reserve (which is quite different than that of other major central banks around the world), it is necessary to remember that the central bank of the United States was established as an independent, politically neutral organization. It was the intent of the founders of the Federal Reserve System to isolate to a substantial extent the making of monetary policy from the political process. As a result, members of the Board of Governors—the chief administration unit within the Federal Reserve System—are appointed for long, overlapping terms of 14 years. Moreover, the Federal Reserve was established as a system composed of a variety of different components with a substantial degree of geographic diversification in order to prevent the centralization of power, especially on Wall Street. In addition, funds for operating the Fed were to come from its earnings and not from appropriations by the United States Congress.[1]

---

[1] Moreover, the Federal Reserve System's expenditures are not subject to audit by the General Accounting Office although in recent years there has been increasing pressure to bring the Fed's expenditures under the scrutiny of this arm of Congress.

The Board of Governors

The Federal Reserve System is composed of a large variety of important groups. These include the Board of Governors, 12 Federal Reserve banks, and the Federal Open Market Committee. The Board of Governors (located in Washington, D.C.) is composed of seven members appointed for 14-year terms by the president of the United States and confirmed by the United States Senate. The long terms (longer than the term allowed by law for any president) and the overlapping of terms for individual governors was designed to insulate the board from the influence of the president and the political process generally. This intent was strengthened by the feature that, while the president has the power to appoint board members, the president does not have the authority to remove those members prior to the expiration of their terms. However, in practice, the political independence of the Federal Reserve System should not be overestimated. The chairman of the Board of Governors participates, usually actively, in the formulation of the economic policy of the current administration and is a regular member of major economic advisory committees within the administration. Moreover, it is unlikely that the Fed could stray too far from the desires of Congress. It is frequently said that the Federal Reserve System is independent within the government, but not of the government.

The Board of Governors and its staff is primarily concerned with the formulation and implementation of monetary policy. Relying upon a large staff of professional economists, the board continually monitors current and forecasted developments in the financial and nonfinancial sectors of the economy. Current interest rate movements in the money and capital markets are of great significance to the board; however of even greater significance is the outlook for future interest rates since interest rates, as we have seen, are closely linked to the volume of saving and investment in the economy and, therefore, the general level of employment and prices. Careful analysis is made of trends in production, prices, employment, and other important economic variables. Based upon an analysis of these economic data, the board participates as a part of the Federal Reserve System in the conduct of monetary policy, and in the case of some specific techniques of monetary policy, the board is vested legally with total control. Of the major instruments of monetary policy, the board alone can determine the appropriate level of reserve requirements for member banks. It "reviews and determines" the discount rate established by the individual reserve banks. The board also has a majority vote in the Federal Open Market Committee, the chief policymaking body of the system. It generally plays a particularly visible role in informing the economic and financial community about current Federal Reserve policy. In recent years the power of the board within the Federal Reserve System has grown at the expense of other components of that system.

The reserve banks

Congress wanted originally to create a decentralized system for conducting monetary policy, realizing that the central bank would possess great power and influence. Accordingly, 12 reserve banks were chartered stretching from Boston to San Francisco as well as over 20 branch offices. Each bank was to be responsible for keeping track of economic and financial conditions in its own specific region of the country and for regulating member banks in that area. Originally each reserve bank was relatively autonomous and possessed the authority to set its own rate on discount loans to member banks without board approval. Over time, however, especially during the Great Depression of the 1930s, authority within the system became more centralized in the Board of Governors in Washington, D.C.

Today the 12 reserve banks are concerned greatly with service functions such as the clearing of checks, providing currency and coin to member banks, and handling wire transfer of funds among member banks. In addition, the individual reserve bank serves as a useful conduit of information from all regions of the nation to the Board of Governors and its staff. Moreover, the reserve banks increasingly have become active in the development of electronic funds transfer systems.

The reserve banks also play a significant role in the implementation of monetary policy. The individual reserve bank presidents are members of the Federal Open Market Committee, perhaps the most important organization operating within the Federal Reserve System. Moreover, concurrence of the reserve bank presidents is frequently sought by the Board of Governors prior to major changes in monetary policy.

The Federal Open Market Committee

The Federal Open Market Committee (FOMC) has become the focal point of Federal Reserve deliberation in recent years and its concerns include all aspects of monetary policy and every technique available to the Federal Reserve. The Federal Open Market Committee is composed of the 7 members of the Board of Governors and 5 reserve bank presidents—a total of 12 voting members. The chairman of the Board of Governors is the chairman of the Federal Open Market Committee.

The president of the Federal Reserve Bank of New York is always a voting member of the FOMC and serves as its vice chairman. The other four positions for the reserve bank presidents are rotated on a yearly basis. While five of the reserve bank presidents are voting members of the FOMC at any one time, all of the reserve bank presidents (along with representatives of their staffs) are present at each of the meetings and participate fully in the discussion.

The FOMC meets roughly every month at the offices of the Board of Governors in Washington. At each meeting FOMC members hear presentations from the board's staff on the outlook for the economy and the financial markets during the next few months as well as an evaluation of recent developments. Based upon its assessment of these economic and financial developments, the FOMC formulates a strategy to guide the trading desk of the New York Fed in the period until the next meeting of the committee. This strategy is embodied in a directive which reviews current and prospective economic and financial conditions, and instructs the manager of the System Open Market Account, an official of the Federal Reserve Bank of New York, on the conduct of open market operations.

While the Federal Open Market Committee has direct control only over the purchases and sales of securities for the System Open Market Account, the meeting of the committee is concerned with the whole range of monetary policy tools. Any changes in the discount rate or in reserve requirements are likely to be discussed at the FOMC prior to the decision by the Board of Governors to change any of these policy tools. The FOMC thus has become the heart of the policymaking function of the Federal Reserve System.

TECHNIQUES OF MONETARY CONTROL

Reserve requirements[2]

Reserve requirement changes are an infrequently used but powerful tool of monetary policy. Every member bank is required to maintain a specified percentage of its deposits in the form of reserves, either as cash in the bank's vault or as deposits with the Fed (see Table 5–1). Changes in the percentage of reserves required of member banks by the Federal Reserve can have a substantial impact on the lending ability of the individual bank and indeed on the total credit creating power of the entire banking system. For example, the Federal Reserve could increase the reserve requirement ratio for either time or demand deposits if it wished to reduce the ability of the banking

---

[2] For a more complete explanation of these techniques, see Luckett [7].

TABLE 5–1
Reserve requirement in effect January 31, 1979

	Percent
Type of deposit and deposit *internal ($millions)—Net demand*	
0–2	7.00
2–10	9.50
10–100	11.75
100–400	12.75
Over 400	16.25
Savings	3.00
Time 0–5, maturing in	
30–179 days	3.00
180 days to 4 years	2.50
4 years or more	1.00
Over 5, maturing in	
30–179 days	6.00
180 days to 4 years	2.50
4 years or more	1.00

Source: *Federal Reserve Bulletin*, February 1979.

system to expand credit. If commercial banks held excess reserves prior to the reserve requirement increase and thereby have unused lending capacity, the Federal Reserve could eliminate the excess reserves and prevent any further expansion of bank credit. For example, with deposits of $1,000, actual reserves of $100, and a reserve requirement ratio of 5 percent, the banking system has $50 of excess reserves and can expand the amount of loans and investments by a multiple of the $50 of excess reserves. However, should the Fed increase the reserve requirement ratio to 10 percent it would eliminate the excess reserves, and should it further increase the ratio to 15 percent it would cause a contraction in the amount of potential loans and investments.

Similarly, if the Federal Reserve wished to expand the availability of credit it could lower reserve requirements. If banks had no excess reserves prior to the reduction in reserve requirements, the change in required reserves would place the individual bank in a position to expand its loans and investments (i.e., bank credit) and would allow the banking system to increase the total amount of bank credit by a multiple of the change in reserve requirements. Similarly, if the banking system did have excess reserves prior to the reduction in reserve requirements, the change in reserve requirements would allow further increases in bank credit extension.

There is one very important difference between lowering and increasing reserve requirements. An increase in reserve requirements can always have the desired result of lowering the volume of bank credit if that reserve requirement increase is sufficiently large. By increasing the amount of reserves required behind every dollar of deposits, the Federal Reserve can always *force* the management of commercial banks to curtail the growth of loans and investments. However, the impact of a reduction in reserve requirements may be quite different. The Federal Reserve by supplying reserves gives the banking system the capacity of expanding the quantity of bank credit. However, the increase in bank credit will occur only if the commercial banking system does not leave those reserves idle but instead makes loans and investments. The productive use of bank reserves depends upon many factors including: (1) the strength of the demand for loans; (2) interest rate levels on loans and investments; (3) the need for liquidity; and (4) the risk involved in making loans and purchasing securities. It has been argued, for example, that commercial banks did not respond to the availability of reserves provided by the Federal Reserve during the Great Depression of the 1930s because of a lack of loan demand and also because, with the wave of bank failures, management was concerned especially about maintaining satisfactory levels of liquidity. In that instance, reserves which were excess from a legal perspective were not really excess from the viewpoint of bank management.

Reserve requirement changes are infrequently used both because of their excessive strength and because of their potentially uneven impact on individual member banks. Moreover, reserve requirements have been lowered more frequently than raised during the postwar period; the secular trend clearly has been toward a reduction in reserve requirements, especially on time and savings deposits. Part of the explanation for this trend lies in the need to provide more usable reserves to the banking system in order to support a growing economy without adding further to the already large U.S. government security holdings of the Fed. Another important factor is the Federal Reserve membership problem. In recent years, substantial numbers of banks have withdrawn from the Federal Reserve due principally to the large amounts of assets required by the Fed to be held in noninterest-earning form.[3] The Fed has responded to this change by gradually reducing the level of the required reserve ratio.

Discount rate

Another important technique used by the Federal Reserve in the conduct of monetary policy is the manipulation of the discount rate.

---

[3] See Chapter 7 for a discussion of the Fed membership problem.

The discount rate refers to the interest rate charged by the Federal Reserve to member commercial banks when those banks borrow from the Fed. Such borrowing is viewed by the Federal Reserve as a privilege of membership, rather than a right, and the loans are usually quite short term (15 days or less). The discount rate (or the rediscount rate as it is often called) is established by the individual reserve banks subject to "review and determination" by the Board of Governors. In practice, the board has effective control over the discount rate.

When the Fed reduces its discount rate, investors in the marketplace usually interpret this as a move toward easier credit conditions. Such a change provides an incentive to commercial banks to obtain additional reserves and thereby may create additional lending capacity for these financial institutions. Conversely, should the Fed wish to curtail the pace of economic expansion, it could increase the discount rate. An increase in the discount rate might discourage any increase in reserve availability by raising the cost of reserves and might also serve as a signal to outside observers that the Fed wished to reduce the expansion rate of the nation's economy.

Not all changes in the discount rate reflect the Fed's desire to bring about a change in policy. Many such changes represent reactions to other financial developments, some of which may be associated with the implementation of monetary policy by the use of one or more of the other techniques under the control of the Fed. For example, the Federal Reserve may have already used an increase in reserve requirements to curtail the quantity of bank reserves. This increase in reserve requirements and reduced availability of bank reserves would be expected to result in an increase in interest rates. As the cost of alternative sources of funds to the individual commercial bank increases relative to the discount rate, it would be expected that more banks would turn to the discount window. This change in the relative cost of funds might then create intense pressure on the Federal Reserve's discount window by individual commercial banks. If the Fed were to meet that demand and provide the reserves (even though only for a short period), this action might negate the credit tightening sought through an increase in reserve requirements. Moreover, the discount window would not be serving its principal function as a "lender of last resort." Bank borrowing would be stimulated by profitability rather than need. Hence, the Federal Reserve would raise the discount rate and seek to restore the more normal relationship between the discount rate and other interest rates in the market. Such a move, though, would not necessarily mean a change in monetary policy; rather the Federal Reserve in its announcement of the discount rate change might state, as it frequently has in the past, that the change was made "for the purpose of bringing the discount rate into alignment with other open market rates."

The discount rate is one of the weakest monetary tools under control of the Federal Reserve. The discount rate does not affect the amount of required reserves at all, nor does it directly affect the total quantity of reserves. Of course, when a bank uses the discount window the quantity of reserves does change; however the control is with the individual commercial bank, in its decision to borrow, rather than with the Federal Reserve. Moreover, as pointed out above, while there may be an announcement effect associated with discount rate changes, the importance of this aspect of the technique is muted by the fact that changes in the discount rate may reflect adjustments to money market rates as well as other factors.

Open market operations

By far the most important tool for the implementation of monetary policy is open market operations. Open market operations refer to the purchase and sale of securities (usually U.S. government securities) by the Federal Reserve in the open market. These transactions are implemented by the trading desk of the Federal Reserve Bank of New York for the entire Federal Reserve System. Such purchases and sales add to or subtract from a single account, referred to as the System Open Market Account. The trading desk of the New York Fed acts under the direction of the Federal Open Market Committee. In order to understand the mechanics and impact of open market operations it is useful to examine how open market transactions are carried out and the role of the Federal Open Market Committee.

The Federal Reserve System acting through the trading desk of the New York Fed will generally purchase securities if it wishes to expand the volume of bank credit (see Table 5–2). For example (refer to Figure 5–1), the trading desk of the New York Fed might place an order for $500 million of Treasury securities with the government security

TABLE 5–2
Government security holdings of Federal Reserve,
January 31, 1979

U.S. government issues	$millions
Bills	33,959
Notes	54,855
Bonds	12,465
Total	101,279
Federal agency obligations	7,507

Source: *Federal Reserve Bulletin*, February 1979.

FIGURE 5–1
Purchase of $500 million of U.S. government securities

Federal Reserve Banks ($000,000)		Commercial Bank ($000,000)	
Government secur- ities + $500	Deposits of mem- ber banks + $500	Reserves at Fed + $500 Government secur- ities − $500	

Note: This illustration assumes that the government security dealer is a commercial bank.

dealers with which it transacts business. The purchase of these securities by the Fed would expand the volume of bank reserves by an equal amount. Following the transaction, the Federal Reserve would have added $500 million in government securities to its portfolio. Some dealer in government securities (either a large bank or a securities trader) would have $500 million less in government securities. This is simple and direct. But here is the important and less simple part of the transaction: the dealer's bank will receive credit on behalf of its customer (the dealer) for the U.S. government securities sold by a credit to the bank's reserve account at the Federal Reserve. This credit would appear on the books of the commercial bank as an asset (reserves at the Federal Reserve) and on the books of the Federal Reserve as a liability (deposits of member commercial banks). This item is sometimes referred to as high-powered money since $1 of bank reserves can create—due to the fractional reserve banking system— more than $1 of bank credit and money (deposits).

Where did the Federal Reserve get the money to pay for the government securities? *It created the money.* The Federal Reserve through buying and selling securities or, indeed, through any expansion or contraction of its assets creates high-powered money (i.e., reserves). In that instance, the Federal Reserve bought securities and thereby created high-powered money. However, if the Fed had wished to curtail the volume of bank credit it might have sold securities. The impact of the sale of securities on the banking system is illustrated in Figure 5–2. In this case, the transfer of securities is from the Federal Reserve (its holdings fall by $500 million) to the dealer (its holdings increase by $500 million). Payment for the securities is again made by adjusting the reserve account of the dealer's bank at the Federal Reserve. The dealer's bank, in effect, writes a check payable to the Federal Reserve. Clearing of the check, which is instantaneous, then results in a $500 million decrease in bank reserves. This transaction appears on the books of the Fed as a $500 million reduction in the deposits of member commercial banks and on the books of

FIGURE 5–2
Sale of $500 million in U.S. government securities

Federal Reserve Banks ($000,000)		Commercial Bank ($000,000)	
Government secur- ities – $500	Deposits of mem- ber banks – $500	Reserves at Fed – $500 U.S. government securities + $500	

Note: This illustration assumes that the government security dealer is a commercial bank.

the dealer's bank as a $500 million decrease in reserves at the Fed. The importance of the transaction is that reserves of the commercial banking system are reduced by $500 million (i.e., high-powered money is reduced by $500 million) and the credit- and deposit-creating ability of the banking system will decline by more than $500 million.

In viewing open market operations it is important to distinguish two distinct categories: dynamic and defensive transactions. This distinction is based upon the Fed's motivation in conducting open market operations. *Dynamic* open market operations refer to the purchase or sale of securities in the open market for the purpose of implementing monetary policy objectives. In contrast, *defensive* open market operations refer to the purchase or sale of securities for the purpose of preventing some external factor—such as a seasonal swing in currency demand by households and/or business firms—from having an undesired effect on the availability and cost of credit. For example, if the Fed desired to expand the economy's growth rate and lower the amount of unemployment, the FOMC might issue a directive to the trading desk of the New York Federal Reserve Bank which would result in the purchase of securities. These purchases would represent dynamic monetary policy—an attempt to change the status quo. In contrast, defensive operations attempt to preserve the status quo. For example, around the Christmas-New Year's period there is usually a substantial outflow of cash from commercial banks and other financial institutions. These outflows reduce (dollar for dollar) the amount of bank reserves and thereby curtail by a multiple amount the ability of the banking system to create credit. The Federal Reserve would usually buy securities during this period in order to negate the impact of this important seasonal factor on monetary policy. Such purchases would represent defensive open market operations and would be unrelated to any monetary policy actions.

Since purchases and sales of securities in the open market by the

Federal Reserve may be either for defensive or dynamic purposes, it is not possible to interpret precisely the goal of monetary policy from examining the buying or selling behavior of the Fed. For example, in a period in which seasonal factors were draining reserves, the Fed might be tightening credit and yet also be buying securities. In this instance, of course, it would be buying a smaller amount of securities than the Fed would normally purchase if it wished to fully counteract seasonal factors draining bank reserves. For this reason as well as others Federal Reserve policy is often difficult to interpret for those outside the system. Yet understanding the current thrust of monetary policy is highly important to financial institutions as interest rates and financial flows are closely correlated with the activities of the Federal Reserve System.

The major advantages and disadvantages of open market operations and the other two policy techniques are summarized in Figure 5–3. The flexibility of open market operations and the adaptability of this technique to "fine-tuning" market conditions is especially notable. In contrast, for short-term psychological purposes, the discount rate is quite useful, especially for dealing with international financial disturbances. The use of the discount rate to "defend the dollar" in late 1978 and also in late 1979 are excellent examples of the use of this policy tool for international purposes.

Other policy tools

Two other techniques of monetary policy are worthy of mention: Regulation Q and moral suasion. Federal Reserve regulations governing the activities of member commercial banks are listed according to the letters of the alphabet—A to Z. Regulation Q governs the payment of interest on deposit accounts. By law, commercial banks can pay no explicit interest on demand deposits; banks do, of course, implicitly pay interest on demand deposits through offering "free" checking accounts or some other type of bonus for the maintenance of checking balances. Moreover, the ability of commercial banks to offer automatic transfer from savings to checking accounts beginning in late 1978 creates further latitude for banks to indirectly pay interest on demand deposits, and the spread of negotiable order of withdrawal (N.O.W.) accounts is a further innovation allowing banks to pay interest on "transactions" accounts. Banks and other depository financial institutions do pay interest on time and savings deposits, but the rate of interest is limited by the regulatory authorities. The maximum rate payable on time and savings deposits for member commercial banks is specified by Regulation Q. More generally, Regulation Q is

FIGURE 5–3
Principal policy tools of the Federal Reserve System

Item	Reserve requirements	Discount rate	Open market operations
Purpose	Change level and growth of bank reserves (i.e., liquidity of banking system), availability, and cost of credit	Same	Same
Method	Raise or lower percent of demand and time deposits which must be held in cash or on deposit within limits set by Congress	Raise or lower discount rate charged member banks on short-term loans (up to 15 days)	Buy or sell securities through dealers
Advantages	Affects entire system (nondiscriminatory) at once; works quickly; useful for major changes in policy	Useful for international capital flow problems; safety valve for Fed operations; aids banks in trouble	Flexible, changed quickly; suitable for fine tuning of market conditions; defensive versus dynamic
Disadvantages	Too powerful and clumsy for fine tuning credit and market conditions	Fed has only partial control over bank borrowing; negative psychological effects	Unable to effect massive changes in short period; some negative psychological effects

frequently used to mean the maximum rates payable by all financial institutions on their deposit liabilities.

Regulation Q was used in the mid-1960s and early 1970s as a policy tool in periods of credit restraint. For example, if the Federal Reserve wished to place downward pressure on the lending ability of commercial banks, it could fail to increase Regulation Q ceilings at a time when other interest rates were increasing. With rising market yields but limited ceiling rates for time and savings deposits, investors would be expected to shift funds away from commercial banks. As a result, the lending ability of those banks which lost deposits would be reduced.

It is likely that Regulation Q will diminish considerably in importance in the near future as a monetary policy tool. Indeed, the Federal Reserve has already eliminated the Q ceiling for negotiable time certificates of deposit of over $100,000 and has become much more flexible in adjusting other Q ceilings in line with market rates. Furthermore, the recent ability of commercial banks and savings and loan associations to offer short-term certificates of deposit of relatively small denomination ($10,000 and up) at a rate tied to the Treasury bill rate further reduces the significance of Regulation Q.

There are numerous complaints that Regulation Q ceilings discriminate against the small saver, forcing the saver to accept below-market rates of return. Moreover, there is considerable evidence that the Q ceilings are ineffective as a monetary policy tool; that is, that the Q ceilings affect the allocation of credit but not its total amount. The financial markets seem to be quite innovative in devising new techniques to avoid artificial restraints such as Regulation Q, and many academic studies of the monetary policy process have opposed the use of Regulation Q on other than a standby basis.

Moral suasion refers to the public and/or private acts of officials of the Federal Reserve System which are taken with the purpose of achieving some particular monetary policy purpose. Moral suasion would encompass speeches given by the members of the Board of Governors or the reserve bank presidents, telephone calls from Federal Reserve officials to bank officers and others, and letters from the Federal Reserve to commercial banks concerning monetary policy goals. An excellent example of the use of moral suasion occurred in August 1966. In that period, the Federal Reserve was attempting through the use of a number of different policy techniques to reduce inflation associated with the Vietnam War. Commercial banks were facing intense pressure for loans and sold municipal securities in order to raise funds to satisfy that loan demand. As a result, the municipal market was in turmoil and many banks were finding it extremely difficult to obtain the liquidity they needed. The Federal

Reserve responded by sending a letter to each member bank stating, in effect, that if the bank would curtail its liquidation of municipal securities and practice moderation in satisfying its loan demand, loans from the Fed's discount window would be available on a more liberal basis and borrowing could be made for longer periods of time.

Moral suasion is an especially important tool of monetary control in other industrialized countries. For example, in England, the Bank of England is able to exercise considerable influence through using moral suasion. However, in England there are only a few banks and direct, personal communication is relatively simple. In the United States, however, there are over 14,000 commercial banks, and the use of moral suasion is a much more complicated process.

MONETARY POLICY TARGETS

As pointed out above, open market operations represent a particularly important technique of monetary policy. But the Fed has other less significant weapons under its control such as changes in reserve requirements, changes in the discount rate, Regulation Q, and moral suasion. The tools of policy are used to move the nation closer to its goals—relative price stability, full employment, economic growth, and balance of payments stability. However, in implementing its policy and in seeking to achieve these objectives, the Fed must observe and react to changes in a number of variables which are intermediate between the ultimate objectives and the techniques. These variables are often referred to as intermediate targets. They are especially important to the management of financial institutions as they provide some evidence of the thrust of current monetary policy.[4]

An intermediate target should have a number of desirable characteristics. It should be closely associated with the ultimate goal; that is, the intermediate target and GNP, the unemployment rate, and other economic goal variables should move together. In addition, the target should be a variable which is closely controlled and significantly influenced by monetary policy. It would, of course, be of little significance if there was some variable which was closely correlated with the ultimate target but over which the Federal Reserve has little control. It is also necessary that the target variable be one that can be measured often. Even if there was some variable which was closely correlated with the gross national product and also was one which the Fed could control within reasonable limits, it would not be a good target if the Fed did not know the value of the variable except with some considerable lag. In addition, there must be a minimum feed-

---

[4] See Saving [10].

back from the *ultimate* target to the intermediate target. For example, while changes in the target should affect the gross national product (GNP), changes in the GNP should not affect the target. Otherwise, there would be no way to know if the movement in the monetary variable is the result of changes in policy or the effect of feedback from the ultimate goal. Conceptually this problem is quite severe since many, perhaps most, variables are associated with movements in the GNP, the most widely used goal variable. This problem is widely known as the "reverse causation" or "feedback problem."

There are a number of monetary variables which, to one degree or another, have been suggested as meeting the criteria of a monetary target. These include measures of money market conditions such as interest rates and marginal bank reserve positions (various measures of the difference between actual and required reserves, such as the net free reserve position), aggregate reserve measures such as the monetary base and reserves available for private deposits, and monetary aggregates such as the money supply (variously defined) or total bank credit. Some of the more widely used targets are:

1. Money market conditions and marginal reserve measures:
   a. The free reserve position of member banks—total reserves less required reserves and borrowings from the Federal Reserve.
   b. Borrowings from the Federal Reserve by member banks.
   c. The three-month (or some other maturity) Treasury bill rate.
   d. The interest rate on federal funds.
2. Aggregate reserve measures:
   a. Total reserves of member banks.
   b. The monetary base—defined as the total of member bank balances at the Federal Reserve banks and the amount of currency in circulation, and in bank vaults.
   c. Reserves available for private deposits (RPDs). Total member bank reserves minus the reserves required against U.S. government deposits and against net interbank deposits.
3. Monetary aggregates:
   a. The money supply narrowly defined (M_1)—demand deposits plus currency in circulation.[5]
   b. The money supply broadly defined (M_2)—M_1 plus time and savings deposits at commercial banks except the large ($100,000 and over) certificates of deposit.

[5] In late 1978, following the implementation of automatic transfer from saving to checking accounts, the Federal Reserve adopted M_1^+ and M_2^+ which added to the conventional definitions those time accounts at bank, savings and loans, and mutual savings banks which are subject to withdrawal by third party payment devices such as negotiable orders of withdrawal.

$c.$ The money supply more broadly defined $(M_3)-M_2$ plus deposits at savings and loan associations and credit unions.

$d.$ Total bank credit—total loans plus total investments at all commercial banks.

Monetary policy: An illustration

A more complete understanding of the influence of the Federal Reserve on the cost and availability of funds at financial institutions and upon the demand for credit could perhaps be supplied by tracing through the steps involved in the monetary policy transmission process—both the decision-making and implementation aspects of a particular policy. Suppose that it appears that a substantial inflationary environment is developing within the economy. This event may be the result, for example, of an acceleration in defense spending at a time when the economy is already fully employed (the classic demand-pull inflation). How might the Federal Reserve react to such a development and how might its actions affect the cost and availability of funds at financial institutions? The Fed might increase the discount rate and/or increase reserve requirements. Moreover, the Fed might not increase Regulation Q ceilings on interest rates paid by commercial banks, and the Board of Governors would be expected to caution commercial bankers to proceed carefully in granting loan requests. However, since the primary focus of attention would be upon open market operations, let us proceed with a detailed discussion of the formulation and implementation of open market policy.

As discussed above, the Federal Open Market Committee has the authority to formulate general policy and guidelines for the trading desk of the New York Federal Reserve Bank. While this group generally meets once a month, extraordinary circumstances might prompt an emergency meeting either in Washington or by telephone conference call. Prior to the regular monthly meeting the individual members of the Board of Governors and the reserve bank presidents carefully review current and prospective economic and financial developments with the assistance of their staffs. The staffs of both the board and the reserve banks have amassed detailed evaluation of current and prospective developments, frequently including econometric forecasts of the gross national product and its components, as well as anticipated movements in short- and long-term interest rates. Moreover, the staff of the Board of Governors writes and makes available to all those concerned within the system a review of economic and financial developments.

Following a careful review of these and related sources of information, the members of the Federal Open Market Committee meet at the board's offices in Washington, D.C. Members present their views on the outlook for the economy and for the financial markets and make recommendations on the proper course of open market operations until the time of the next meeting of the committee. The staff of the board has usually provided two or more alternative policy choices and their anticipated implications for the financial markets. A vote is then taken on these policy guidelines and the one adopted (referred to as the directive) becomes the operating framework for the trading desk of the New York Fed.

For example, the domestic policy directive issued by the FOMC to the Federal Reserve Bank of New York following its July 1978 meeting reads as follows:

> In light of the foregoing developments, it is the policy of Federal Open Market Committee to foster monetary and financial conditions that will resist inflationary pressures while encouraging continued moderate economic expansion and contributing to a sustainable pattern of international transactions. At its meeting on July 18, 1978, the Committee agreed that these objectives would be furthered by growth of M_1, M_2, and M_3 from the second quarter of 1978 to the second quarter of 1979 at rates with ranges of 4 to 6½ percent, 6½ to 9 percent, and 7½ to 10 percent, respectively. The associated range for bank credit is 8½ to 11½ percent. These ranges are subject to reconsideration at any time as conditions warrant.[6]

It is, of course, necessary to operationalize these general guidelines. Over the recent past, this has been done in a number of ways. In the early postwar period and through the 1960s, the variables which the Federal Reserve observed most directly and used to guide open market operations were those involving money market conditions, especially the level of free reserves (i.e., excess reserves less borrowings from the Federal Reserve). If, for example, the level of free reserves was higher than desired, the Fed would generally sell securities to reduce the amount of actual reserves and thereby the level of free reserves. Conversely, if the level of free reserves was lower than desired, the Fed might buy securities. However, careful study has discredited the hypothesis that the amount of free reserves bears a close correlation with changes in the ultimate target variables such as the gross national product.[7] Moreover, emphasis on the quantity of free reserves and other money market variables ignores the substantial evidence developed by economists concerning the importance of the money supply in affecting the economy. Hence, in recent years the Federal Reserve has focused on two separate variables: the federal

---

[6] *Federal Reserve Bulletin*, November 1978, pp. 855–56.

[7] For an excellent discussion and critique of money market conditions as a useful variable for Federal Reserve policy, see [9].

funds rate and the money supply (variously defined) as an intermediate variable. The Fed would generally seek to specify that rate on federal funds which would, over the period until the next meeting of the FOMC, create the desired change in the money supply.[8]

In this instance, the FOMC might specify a higher federal funds rate in order to create "moderate" growth in the money supply in an inflationary environment. As a result, it might be expected that the trading desk would be a net seller of Treasury securities (apart from seasonal factors). The resultant increase in interest rates and the reduction in bank reserves should have a number of important effects. The cost of credit to consumers and businesses should increase. While this might discourage borrowing to only a minor extent if the interest elasticity of the demand for borrowed funds is relatively low, there might be an even more important impact on the availability of credit. With smaller available reserves, the banking system would not be able to extend as much credit as it was able to do previously. As a result, the availability of credit to both consumers and business firms might be reduced. This rise in the cost and reduction in the availability of funds would be expected to reduce the spending of each sector of the economy (especially the private sector) and thereby reduce the inflationary pressures caused by excess demand.

It is also important to understand the implications of a tightening of monetary policy from the perspective of the management of an individual financial institution. It would be expected that the change in monetary policy along with the economic conditions that produced that change would significantly affect the financial position of the individual financial institution in a number of ways. First, the reduced availability of reserves and the slowdown in new money creation at the macro level should be reflected at the level of the individual financial institution in a reduction in the inflow of funds. From the viewpoint of the deposit-type financial institutions, the growth rate of deposits would slow. From the viewpoint of non-depository financial institutions such as life insurance companies and pension funds, the inflows of funds might also be reduced although the impact on these "contractual" financial institutions would generally be smaller. Moreover, this reduction in funds inflows should be further accentuated by the increasingly unattractive comparison between the rates offered by financial institutions and the rates available in the market. Just as the inflow of funds to financial institutions

---

[8] This has not been very successful. While the Fed has generally kept the federal funds rate at or near the desired level, it has not been successful in controlling the money supply as desired. This may reflect substantial feedback effects from the economy itself or an unstable relationship between the federal funds rate and the various measures of the money supply.

was reduced by the tightening monetary policy, the demand for funds would be expected to rise. This increase should be especially pronounced for the commercial bank where inventory accumulation loans should be large. The increase would be less at savings and loan associations and other real estate lenders, since the demand for mortgages varies less with the business cycle than the demand for inventory loans. In summary, the availability of funds at the individual financial institution would be reduced but the demand for credit should be substantial. For some time, perhaps, financial institutions could meet the additional loan demand by liquidating securities and borrowing in the open market. At some point, however, these alternatives no longer become viable (the cost of funds sources becomes prohibitive) and financial institutions must curtail credit availability. Clearly, it is important for the management of the individual financial institution to be aware of and anticipate these changes in monetary policy which may have such a profound effect on the welfare of their institution.

INFLUENCE OF THE TREASURY: DEBT MANAGEMENT

Treasury debt management refers to the conscious management of the maturity structure of the federal debt in order to achieve certain desired economic goals. Debt management is closely related to both fiscal and monetary policy, but less important than either. Fiscal policy is concerned with the impact of government spending and taxation on the level of employment, income, and other macroeconomic variables. Debt management, on the other hand, is concerned with the financial consequences of current and past fiscal policy actions. The decision by the federal government to run a budget deficit is a fiscal policy decision. However, that deficit must be financed by selling Treasury securities to the bank and nonbank public. Therefore, the current level of the federal debt, (i.e., the total amount of Treasury securities outstanding) is the combined result of all past fiscal policy decisions. The Treasury in selling new debt to finance the current budget deficit or in selling new debt to refund existing debt created by past budget deficits must make a number of important choices, which we collectively refer to as the debt management decision. Probably the most important choice the Treasury must make with each security offering is what maturity of securities to offer — bills, bonds, or notes. This decision affects the maturity structure of the whole federal debt. It is this choice which is at the center of Treasury debt management. In essence, in conducting debt management operations the Treasury is performing a central banking function.

The outstanding debt of the U.S. government is enormous (see Chapter 4 for details). Moreover, as pointed out earlier, government debt is extremely short in maturity; the average maturity of the debt is approximately two years while a substantial fraction of the debt is in the form of Treasury bills which have an original maturity of less than one year. In addition, in recent years the U.S. government has had substantial budget deficits (over $50 billion in some years), requiring a large volume of new debt financing. For all these reasons—to refinance the large volume of existing securities and to finance the current budget deficit requirements—the U.S. Treasury is often in the financial markets selling securities and raising new funds. As a general rule, bills are offered each week, while notes and bonds usually are sold quarterly.

In the process of financing the U.S. government the Treasury has a number of important influences on the financial system. One important influence is upon the Federal Reserve in its conduct of monetary policy. During the sale of a new issue of securities (excluding the regular marketing of Treasury bills), the Federal Reserve is under pressure to follow an "even-keel" policy. With even-keel, the Fed does not make any major changes in monetary policy during the period of the Treasury financing. During periods of large budget deficits when the Treasury is constantly in the market offering new debt, the flexibility of the Federal Reserve may be reduced to a considerable extent.

It is possible, however, to view the Treasury financing in a positive fashion. The Treasury can affect the total liquidity of the economy to a degree through the careful selection of the maturity of its newly issued debt. In a period of economic expansion, the Treasury should finance its need for funds with long-term securities. This action would shift the securities portfolio of the public and financial institution portfolios to longer-term assets, thereby reducing its liquidity and discouraging both consumption and investment spending. The great difficulty with this policy prescription from the perspective of the Treasury, however, is that this period would likely be one of high interest rates, and the Treasury would thereby commit itself to high interest payments for a considerable period of time. Moreover, there are legal restraints on the volume of long-term securities which the Treasury can sell. Except for a fixed amount authorized by Congress, the Treasury cannot sell bonds with an interest rate above 4.25 percent. Conversely, in periods of economic slack, proper debt management policy would emphasize the sale of short-term securities. By selling short-term securities the Treasury would add to the quantity of liquid assets held by the public and thereby encourage spending. However, in this period interest rates are likely to be low and there is some pressure for the Treasury to "lock-in" the lower long-term yields by selling bonds. There is a fundamental conflict between the goal of the Treasury to minimize the cost of the public debt (i.e., reducing interest payments as low as possible) and its goal of using the maturity of the debt as an instrument of economic stabilization. In the recent past with few exceptions the Treasury has emphasized financing the public debt at the least cost. Debt management policy has atrophied as an active tool of economic stabilization.

QUESTIONS

5–1. What are the functions of the different components of the Federal Reserve System? What is the Fed's most important policymaking unit?

5–2. What are the different methods available to the Federal Reserve for influencing the availability and cost of money and how do they function? Discuss the strengths and weaknesses of each of the following policy tools:

  a. Reserve requirements.
  b. Discount rate.
  c. Open market operations.
  d. Regulation Q.
  e. Moral suasion.

5–3. What is the relationship between "high-powered money" and the fractional reserve banking system?

5–4. In open market operations, what is the distinction between dynamic as opposed to defensive transactions? Give an example of each.

5–5. What is debt management? Why has it fallen into disuse?

REFERENCES

1. Ascheim, Joseph. *Techniques of Monetary Control.* Baltimore: Johns Hopkins, 1961.

2. Blinder, Alan S., and Goldfeld, Steven M. "New Measures of Fiscal and Monetary Policy, 1958–1973." *The American Economic Review,* December 1976, pp. 780–96.

3. *Controlling Monetary Aggregate II: The Implementation.* Boston: Federal Reserve Bank of Boston, September 1972.

4. Davis, Richard G. "Implementing Open Market Policy with Monetary Aggregate Objectives." *Monthly Review,* Federal Reserve Bank of New York, July 1973, pp. 170–82.

5. Gaines, Tilford C. *Techniques of Federal Debt Management.* New York: Free Press, 1962.

6. Holmes, Alan R. "A Day at the Trading Desk." *Monthly Review,* Federal Reserve Bank of New York, October 1970, pp. 234–38.

7. Luckett, Dudley G. *Money and Banking.* New York: McGraw-Hill Book Co., 1976, chap. 15.

8. Mayer, Thomas. *Monetary Policy in the United States.* New York: Random House, 1968.

9. Meigs, A. James. *Free Reserves and the Money Supply.* Chicago: University of Chicago Press, 1962.

10. Saving, Thomas R. "Monetary Targets and Indicators." *Journal of Political Economy,* August 1967.

11. Van Horne, James E., and Bowers, David A. "Liquidity Impact of Debt Management." *Southern Economic Journal,* April 1968, pp. 526–27.

Commercial banking
and problem areas of
financial institutions
management

6

Role of commercial banks in the economy

As we noted in Chapter 2, the most important financial intermediary in the U.S economy is the commercial bank. Banks hold a little more than 40 percent of the total assets of all financial intermediaries combined. The reserves of the banking system are the vehicle used by the nation's money manager—the Federal Reserve System—to regulate money and credit conditions in the economy. Of the approximately $310 billion making up the U.S money supply (currency plus demand deposits) at year-end 1978 about $270 billion, or 73 percent, was in the form of checking accounts held at commercial banks. Banks are a principal source of short-term business credit and are a dominant influence in the markets for state and local government securities (municipals), U.S. government securities, consumer credit, foreign exchange, and Eurocurrencies. Moreover, commercial banks through their trust departments are a major force in the equity and corporate bond markets.

This chapter discusses the most important services offered by commercial banks to the public. In addition, recent trends in the sources and uses of funds of the commercial banking industry are discussed.

SERVICES OFFERED BY COMMERCIAL BANKS

Commercial banks display all of the basic characteristics of financial intermediaries. Similar to insurance companies, savings and loan associations, credit unions, and savings banks, they attract funds from savings-surplus units by issuing attractive financial assets (secondary securities) and lend those funds to borrowers or savings-deficit units. Still, commercial banks are unique financial intermediaries in one key respect: their capacity to create money in the guise of new deposits by granting credit to borrowers. Other financial intermediaries cannot create a larger volume of funds than they receive from their depositors or from their owners. Commercial banks, however, can create a multiple amount of funds from any injection of new reserves into the banking system.

Individual banks receive deposits from a wide variety of sources. Households deposit their paychecks and other receipts in both demand (checking) accounts and time and savings deposits. Businesses, too, deposit their sales receipts, income from investments, and other funds in demand accounts and in time deposits. Both the federal government and state and local governments deposit tax collections and income from fees, fines, sales of securities, and other revenues received from the private sector. These deposits from businesses, households, and governments represent so-called *primary deposits* since they arise at the discretion of a bank's customers and the bank must place cash reserves behind these deposits as required by the regulatory authorities. In contrast to merely receiving primary deposits from their customers, commercial banks also have the unique capacity to create *secondary deposits*, which arise when they make loans and investments.[1] When a bank makes a loan to an individual or a business firm, for example, it merely creates a deposit on its books in favor of the borrower. Similarly, when a bank buys U.S. Treasury bills or other securities for its portfolio, deposits are created on behalf of the seller of those securities. Secondary deposits are, like all bank deposits, the IOU of the bank that creates them. However, an important difference between a bank's IOU and that of other borrowers is that the bank's IOU is generally accepted as money—a medium of exchange that may be used to purchase goods and services.

Commercial banks provide an outlet for savings set aside by the public out of current income by offering financial assets with attractive rates of return. Time and savings deposits of commercial banks represent more than half of all thrift deposits held at depository in-

---

[1] Secondary deposits are sometimes referred to as *derivative deposits*. For a good discussion of the process of money creation by banks see Hutchinson [4] or Board of Governors of the Federal Reserve System [1] in the references at the conclusion of this chapter.

termediaries (commercial banks, credit unions, mutual savings banks, and savings and loan associations). Like the thrift deposits offered by credit unions, savings and loans, and savings banks, commercial bank time and savings deposits are regarded as a nearly riskless outlet for the public's savings which can be cashed in almost immediately if funds are needed to meet an emergency. Federal insurance of bank thrift deposits (up to $40,000) has further enhanced the desirability of these deposits, particularly to the small saver.

Demand deposits (checking accounts) offered by banks serve as the principal medium of exchange with which to purchase goods and services. Until recently, banks had a clear field in the competition for demand deposits. No other financial institution offered an instrument with the unrestricted capacity to make payments to third parties immediately upon demand. Only in bidding for time and savings deposits did banks face stiff competition from nonbank financial institutions. However, state and federal laws and regulations governing the activities of savings banks and credit unions were liberalized during the late 1960s and early 1970s, especially in New England. Today many nonbank thrift institutions throughout the nation offer third-party payments services which compete directly with commercial bank demand deposit accounts. Most prominent among these new services are NOW (negotiable order of withdrawal) accounts offered by commercial banks and savings banks in New England and share drafts offered by many federal credit unions throughout the nation. We will examine these new payments devices more closely in Chapter 21.

Commercial banks are central to the process of paying for purchases of goods and services in a modern economy. Funds flow freely across state and national boundaries only because individual banks are willing to honor immediately any drafts made against them. A seller of goods in Cleveland, Ohio, is willing to accept a check from a buyer in San Diego, California, because the seller knows that the bank will accept that check for deposit, route it through the banking system to the buyer's bank in San Diego, and receive payment within a very short space of time (typically two to three days). The whole system rests upon public confidence and a willingness to accept bank demand deposits (checking accounts) as a medium of exchange in payment for goods and services.

The payments system of the United States is presently in a period of transition. The volume of checks written in the U.S. has expanded more than sixfold during the postwar period. However, with the exception of some fairly minor advances, our present check collection system is similar to that established more than 60 years ago. Many analysts, including Federal Reserve officials, are concerned with the increasing congestion of paper represented by checks and other cash items used to transfer funds. Moreover, the costs of handling the enormous volume of checks written each year in the United States have increased rapidly and are now in the range of $7 to $8 billion a year. The most promising remedies for this growing problem involve the computer and various electronic processing systems. We will discuss the new techniques for electronic transfer of funds (EFTS) and their associated benefits and costs in Chapter 21.

A banking role of growing importance in the nation's financial system is providing trust or fiduciary services to businesses, individuals, and community organizations. The trust function consists of managing the accumulated assets and financial affairs of an individual or institution for the benefit of that particular customer. It requires the careful administration of the customer's financial affairs, continuing expert analysis of the customer's financial position, allocating funds for the customer's benefit, and protecting the customer's property. Modern bank trust departments rely upon the skills of economists, lawyers, and financial analysts to make decisions involving property that are of maximum benefit to their customers.

Bank trust departments in the United States administer the largest pool of investment funds of any financial institution.[2] Bank trust assets stood at $404 billion in 1972, compared to only $283 billion in 1968—an increase of more than 40 percent in four years. Personal trusts and estates accounted for nearly half of the total; another third were represented by employee benefit trusts and the remainder by employee benefit agencies and other miscellaneous agencies. Employee benefit plans generally have grown the fastest of all trust assets.

THE SOCIAL RESPONSIBILITIES OF BANKING

In managing a financial institution, perhaps more than in any other industry, the stockholders, board of directors, and officers must chart a course that balances social goals and responsibilities with private interests. This is an especially difficult problem for commercial banks. As we have seen in the preceding sections, banks provide services that profoundly influence the nation's economic and financial well-being. Recognizing this, banks are chartered by both federal and state authorities to serve the convenience and needs of the public and are closely regulated in virtually all of their activities. They are expected to cooperate with the monetary authorities to ensure that the

---

[2] See Green and Schuelke [2] for a description of bank trust services and an analysis of their recent growth.

growth of money and credit is consistent with national goals of full employment, sustainable economic growth, reasonable price stability, and equilibrium in the nation's balance of payments. Their lending, investing, and other business activities must be conducted in a reasonable and prudent manner that does not risk unduly the safety of depositor funds or reduce public confidence in the stability of the nation's financial system.

POSTWAR TRENDS IN COMMERCIAL BANKING

Now that we have looked at the basic services offered by commercial banks today, it is useful to examine how the composition of banking industry assets, liabilities, capital, sources of revenue, and expenses have changed in recent years and why these changes have occurred. Our source of information is the aggregate of all financial statements that insured commercial banks must file with the Federal Deposit Insurance Corporation in Washington, D.C. each year.

In many ways the American banking system is passing through a financial and organizational revolution. Larger banks are emerging through the growth of branches, mergers, and holding company activity. New financial services continually appear as banks try to open up new markets and compete more aggressively with other financial institutions. Automation and increased use of the computer have helped to reduce costs and open up new possibilities for serving the customer. And, American banks, more than those of any other nation, have reached across international borders to attract new sources of funds and increase their revenues.

Not surprisingly, all of these changes have significantly altered the industry's balance sheet, earnings, and expenses. One of the most noticeable changes during the postwar period is the gradual shift toward less liquid assets, particularly loans, and away from cash and investments in securities. (See Figures 6–1 and 6–2.) For example, the percentage of cash assets has declined during the postwar period from more than 20 percent of total industry assets to less than 15 percent. In 1950 holdings of marketable securities represented about 45 percent of total bank assets; by 1960 the percentage was close to 30 percent. In the most recent year security investments accounted for less than 25 percent of the assets of all insured U.S. banks. Factors which have contributed to this declining trend include rising interest rates that have increased the opportunity cost of holding cash and more liquid securities and rapid growth in the demand for bank credit, especially from consumers, corporations, and state and local governments. Then, too during the late 1960s and 1970s several periods of tight monetary policy drove interest rates to record or near-

FIGURE 6–1
Principal assets of commercial banks (call report dates, 1926–1947; seasonally adjusted, end of quarter, 1948–   )

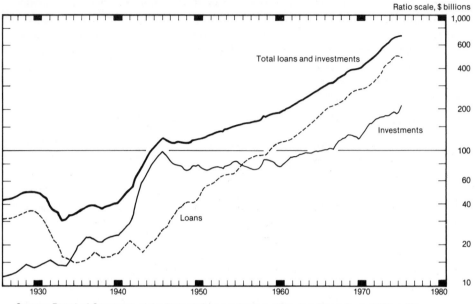

Source: Board of Governors of the Federal Reserve System, *Historical Chart Book, 1975,* p. 78.

FIGURE 6–2
Balance sheet ratios for all commercial banks (semiannual call report dates)

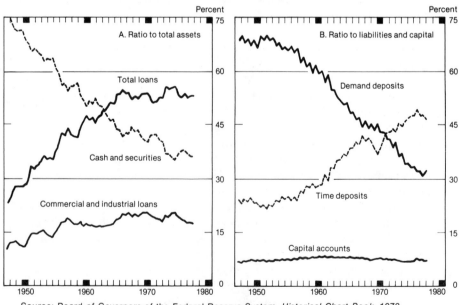

Source: Board of Governors of the Federal Reserve System, *Historical Chart Book, 1978.*

record levels, encouraging banks to become more efficient in the use of their funds. Also, there has been an increase in the ratio of more stable deposits (principally time and savings deposits) to less stable deposits (especially demand deposits), reducing the industry's need for cash and other liquid assets. Finally, the development of techniques to borrow liquidity (known as liability management) has enabled individual banks to reduce their reliance upon cash assets and securities as a source of liquid funds.

Within the securities portfolio there also have been dramatic changes. The most important include a decline in holdings of U.S. government securities and an increase in bank holdings of state and local government obligations (municipals) and federal agency securities. (See Figure 6–3.) Municipals have nearly tripled as a percentage of total bank assets, while securities issued by federal agencies also have become substantially more important. Many factors explain why U.S. government securities generally have declined in importance and state and local government securities have risen in bank portfolios. Since commercial banks are subject to the full corporate income tax, municipals offer an investment whose after-tax yield compares favorably with loans. In addition, the supply of state and local government debt available for bank purchase has grown very

FIGURE 6–3
Principal classes of investments for all commercial banks (semiannual call report dates)

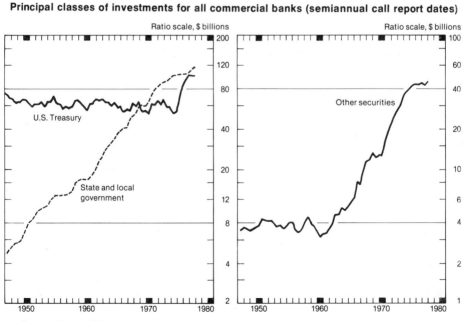

Source: Board of Governors of the Federal Reserve System, *Historical Chart Book, 1978.*

rapidly in the postwar period due to population increases and citizens demanding more services from their local governments. Many banks also have felt constrained to purchase the securities of municipal governments in their area as tangible evidence of support for their local communities. The supply of federal agency debt has increased dramatically, improving its marketability and yield and stimulating heavy commercial bank purchases of these securities. In a sense commercial banks in recent years have been partners with the federal government in redirecting the flow of credit to so-called disadvantaged sectors (especially agriculture, small businesses, and home buyers). Most commercial banks today hold at least some securities issued by such federal agencies as the Federal Land Banks, the Farmers Home Administration, the Federal Home Loan Banks, the Federal National Mortgage Association, the Banks for Cooperatives, the Federal Intermediate Credit Banks, and the Export-Import Bank.

The decline in security holdings and in cash assets has made room for more loans in bank portfolios. The ratio of total commercial bank loans to assets rose from about 30 percent in 1950 to nearly 50 percent in 1960. Loan-asset ratios during the 1970s generally fluctuated between 50 and 60 percent of total U.S. bank assets, though larger banks in metropolitan areas frequently pushed their ratios even higher. Numerous factors have contributed to the rapid growth of bank loans. Among the most important are a willingness of bankers to accept more risk, increased economic stability during the postwar period, higher bank costs and increasing pressure on banks to find assets with higher yields, and more intense competition from other financial institutions, especially in mortgage and consumer lending. Which categories of loans have grown the most rapidly? Actually the composition of bank loans has been fairly stable during the postwar period when adjustments are made for changes in reporting procedures. On balance, however, loans secured by real estate and loans to individual families and businesses appear to have gained somewhat, while the growth of agricultural and security loans has lagged.

Turning to the liability side of the industry's balance sheet, the most marked change has been in the relative proportions of demand and time deposits. Demand deposits dropped from about three fifths of total liabilities and capital in 1950 to around a third today. In contrast, time and savings deposits increased from less than 30 percent to about 50 percent of total funds raised over the same period. The rapid growth of time and savings deposits is the result of several forces. Among the most important is the desire of banks to retain corporate deposits, which in the late 1950s and early 1960s threatened to be withdrawn in pursuit of higher-yielding investments in the money market. Coupled with this is the willingness of bankers to accept smaller profit margins and higher costs in order to secure the funds necessary to meet loan demand. Increased competition from nonbank financial intermediaries, especially savings and loan associations and credit unions, also has been important. In addition, bankers have felt the need for greater control over their sources of reserves, particularly during periods when available funds are scarce.

Bankers generally avoided competing aggressively for time deposits in the early postwar years because of fear that there would be little net gain in total deposits (i.e., deposits would be switched from demand to time deposits but the total volume of deposits would not change significantly). In addition, it was obvious that bank costs would rise as more funds were derived from interest-bearing accounts. The result would be a squeeze on profit margins. However, competition for funds soon became so intense and loan demand so heavy that most large banks overcame their reluctance to issue large denomination thrift deposits. During the early 1960s the negotiable certificate of deposit (CD) was developed in order to attract large corporate, individual, and government deposits.

Since then, nondeposit sources of funds have become increasingly important. These include short-term borrowings from such sources as the federal funds market, mortgage debt, Eurodollars, borrowings from the Federal Reserve banks, and borrowings from correspondent banks. These sources, unlike deposits, are exempt from interest-rate ceilings. Moreover, funds frequently have been more readily available from these sources than from time and savings deposits in periods of tight money. The growing importance of nondeposit funds sources is indicated by the fact that miscellaneous (nondeposit) liabilities of banks provided only 1 percent of the total bank funds in 1950, between 2 and 3 percent in 1960, and over 10 percent in the most recent period.

One particularly interesting development has been the increased use of capital notes and debentures in order to expand bank capital. A 1963 ruling by the Comptroller of the Currency allowed national banks to count these debentures as part of their capital accounts. Many states followed suit on behalf of state-chartered banks. With the rapid expansion of loans and deposits in the postwar period the need for bank capital has increased sharply. Many banks have been hesitant to simply issue more stock in these situations due to the high cost of equity financing, the potential dilution of ownership, and the lack of an adequate market for the stock of some (especially smaller) banks. Capital debentures aid in the resolution of some of these problems. Generally, their cost is below the cost of issuing new stock, and ownership dilution is avoided.

Total bank capital generally has declined relative to assets in the postwar period. This development concerns bank regulators and depositors, because one of the prime functions of capital is to serve as a cushion against a fall in the value of a bank's assets. In the short run, capital acts as a "sponge" to absorb losses until management can make adjustments in the bank's policies to correct the situation. Some authorities feel, however, that banks may actually "need" less capital today because their deposits are more stable and severe recessions are less likely than in the past. Then, too, there are many different avenues through which banks today find the funds they need to make loans and investments.

Just as the mix of sources and uses of funds has changed in postwar U.S. banking, so have the banking system's sources of revenue and expenses. (See Figure 6–4.) Throughout the postwar period loans

FIGURE 6–4
Member bank income and expenses (annually)

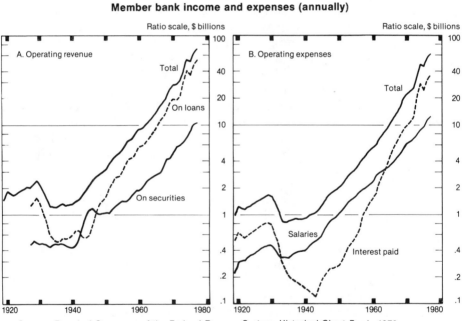

Source: Board of Governors of the Federal Reserve System, *Historical Chart Book, 1978.*

have been the number one revenue source. In the early postwar years income from U.S. government securities was in second place as a source of bank revenues. By the late 1960s and early 1970s, however, "other" securities (mainly municipals) had surpassed U.S. government securities as a source of industry revenue. At the same time, as we have seen, the distribution of expenses shifted away from salaries and wages as the key expense item toward interest on time and savings deposits and nondeposit borrowings.

In this chapter we have taken a broad overview of the commercial bank as a firm and also of recent financial trends in the industry. In subsequent chapters we look closely at the most important areas of bank and nonbank financial institutions management. These include liquidity management, liability management, loan management, and capital adequacy. Before proceeding to these important topics, however, we pause next to look at the structure or organization of the banking industry. Here, too, dramatic changes are underway with significant effects on service to the public and the long-run viability of individual banks.

QUESTIONS

6– 1. What is unique about a commercial bank in terms of its ability to furnish credit? How do banks differ from other financial institutions in this regard?

6– 2. Discuss the following services offered by commercial banks:
a. Credit.
b. Deposit.
c. Clearing of checks.
d. Fiduciary.
Explain why each is important to the functioning of a modern economy.

6– 3. What major changes have occurred in commercial bank assets in recent years? In sources of bank funds? In revenues and expenses? Explain why these changes have occurred. Would you expect these trends to continue in future years? Why or why not?

REFERENCES

1. Board of Governors of the Federal Reserve System. *The Federal Reserve System: Its Purposes and Functions.* Washington, D.C., 1972.
2. Green, Donald S., and Schuelke, Mary. *The Trust Activities of the Banking Industry.* Chicago: Trustees of the Banking Research Fund, Association of Reserve City Bankers, 1975.
3. Hempel, George, H., and Yawitz, Jess B. *Financial Management of Financial Institutions.* Englewood Cliffs, N.J.: Prentice-Hall, 1977.
4. Hutchinson, Harry D. *Money, Banking, and the United States Economy.* 2d ed. New York: Appleton-Century-Crofts, 1971.
5. Nadler, Paul. *Commercial Banking in the Economy.* New York: Random House, 1968.

7

Structure of the commercial banking industry

The structure of the American banking system (i.e., the number and relative sizes of banks across the nation) is one of the most unusual to be found anywhere in the world. There were more than 14,700 commercial banks in the United States in 1977. In contrast, the majority of other nations in the world rely upon only a handful of very large commercial banking institutions operating a vast network of branches to provide needed banking services to the public. Frequently in foreign countries the government owns and operates all or part of the banking system. The United States, however, relies upon thousands of independent banks varying widely in size, the majority of which (nearly 8,700) operate no full-service branch offices.

American banks typically are very small by world standards. Fully a quarter of all U.S. banks hold less than $10 million in assets each and more than 90 percent hold assets of less than $100 million, while most banks in industrialized nations are many times larger. However, U.S. banks are far from homogeneous in size since they also include some of the world's largest. For example, six of the 10 largest commercial banks in the world are located in the United States, including the three largest. And, these few very large banking institutions control a major proportion of U.S. banking resources.

The 100 largest U.S. banks, for example, hold close to half of the nation's commercial bank deposits. The ten largest commercial banks hold nearly a fourth of U.S. bank deposits. And so, while the U.S. banking system is dominated numerically by small banks, there is also a heavy concentration of market power in the hands of only a few institutions, not only at the national level but also at many local levels. Countless small towns outside the nation's major metropolitan areas contain only one, two, or three banks.

The U.S. banking structure has been changing in recent years at a rapid pace, reflecting forces operating within the industry and external developments. A gradual consolidation of resources into fewer, but larger banking organizations seems to be underway with these larger units offering a wider and wider array of financial services. Competition between banks themselves and between bank and nonbank financial institutions has intensified. In this chapter we examine in some detail recent changes in the U.S. banking structure and some of the reasons behind them.

THE IMPORTANCE OF BANKING STRUCTURE

As we begin our study of the structure of U.S. banking, it is important to understand precisely what the structure of an industry refers to and why it is important. Economists use the word *structure* in at least two different ways—the structure of a market and the structure of an industry. Either way, the term *structure* refers to the number of firms present in an industry or market area, their relative sizes, particular geographic locations, and mix of services offered from each location.

For example, if we wished to describe the structure of the market for banking services in your community, we would need to gather data on how many banks there are and how they compare in size with each other. We would be interested in how far apart the banks are and how close or near to potential customers each one is. Another important piece of structural data would be the types of services offered by each bank from its offices and whether these services are convenient to the customers who use them. Finally, in assessing the structure of the local banking market we would inquire about the number of and services offered by financial institutions closely related to the banking business, such as credit unions, savings and loan associations, mutual savings banks, and finance companies. To what extent do these institutions compete actively with banks for deposits and loans?

Why is this kind of information important? The answer is found in the almost universal belief among economists and the regulatory authorities that the structure of firms in a market area influences the degree of *competition* that prevails. In our society the ideal is to approach "perfect competition" as closely as possible. However, in any practical situation this is virtually impossible to achieve since perfect competition requires: (1) completely free entry of new firms in response to profitable opportunities; (2) free exit of inefficient firms or of those who refuse to compete; and (3) complete absence of collusion among existing firms which might result in price fixing or a division of the market. As a practical matter, we strive through law and regulation to promote as much competition as possible among banks and other financial institutions consistent with other social goals. Beginning in the late 19th century the federal government and then the states enacted laws forbidding monopolies and restraint of trade. Today, these rules of the competitive game are enforced by the U.S. Department of Justice and the Federal Trade Commission for virtually all industries. In banking, federal and state regulatory agencies must give heavy weight to competition in deciding upon applications for new bank charters or new branch offices, mergers among existing banks, or the formation of bank holding companies. In general, mergers or other combinations among existing firms cannot be approved if they would adversely affect competition.[1]

Why is competition so important? Economic theory suggests that the answer lies in the performance of banks and other financial institutions (i.e., their behavior in the marketplace). Competitive markets, it is believed, generally yield lower prices for the consumer, a larger quantity and better quality of goods and services produced, greater efficiency in the use of scarce resources, and lower profits for individual firms. On the other hand, when one (monopoly) or only a few banks or other institutions (oligopoly) serve the local market, competition may be reduced or eliminated, resulting in higher prices for the consumer and less adequate service. In brief, theory suggests that *structure affects competition and competition influences the performance of firms in serving the customer.*

If competition is so desirable, why don't we charter a large number of banks and other financial institutions to serve each market and completely forbid any mergers or other combinations among these? There are two principal reasons—one related to economic factors and the other to social goals. In most industries, including financial institutions, there is one particular size firm which is optimal in terms of producing its goods or services at the lowest possible operating

---

[1] The exceptions to this rule center upon the convenience and needs of the public and the so-called failing firm doctrine. If a proposed merger, for example, would result in significantly improved service to the public or save a firm whose collapse would endanger the economic vitality of the local community, it may be approved even if the level of competition would be reduced.

cost per unit. Firms smaller or larger than optimal size produce at higher unit costs and thereby waste resources. Such *economies of scale* (size) have been found to exist in commercial banking, savings and loan associations, and insurance companies and probably exist elsewhere in the financial institutions' sector. In the long run, individual firms tend to approach optimal size or exit from the industry.

The U.S. Department of Justice and most regulatory agencies in recent years have followed a relatively simple philosophy in dealing with economies of scale. The very largest banks and other financial institutions frequently are denied mergers with other firms in the same industry or market to discourage these companies from growing significantly beyond the lowest-cost (optimal) size. In contrast, smaller institutions which presumably are below optimal size may be encouraged to grow larger through favorable rulings on mergers, branch office applications, or the entering of new markets. At the same time these firms may be protected from the entry of new competitors by regulatory barriers since the chartering of additional firms would make it more difficult for any one firm to approach optimal size. The purpose of such a policy, of course, is to reduce costs to the consumer and thereby lower prices while at the same time improve the quantity and quality of output. Public policy attempts to reach a compromise in most industries so that effective competition prevails, but is not so strong as to prevent individual banks and other financial intermediaries from producing and selling their services at the lowest possible cost.

The second reason why restraints are placed upon competition among financial institutions centers upon the issue of safety or soundness. A number of laws have been passed in the United States to restrict competition among banks and other financial institutions in order to reduce the probability of failure. These laws include requirements that, before a new bank or other deposit-type intermediary can be chartered, the proponents of the charter application must prove the new institution will be profitable in a short period of time (usually two to three years), that there is a need for a new financial institution in the community, and that existing financial institutions will not be unduly harmed. Interest rates offered on deposits and rates on loans frequently carry legal ceilings to reduce the likelihood of "destructive" price competition. Extensive restrictions are applied at both federal and state levels on the kinds of loans and securities that may be acquired by commercial banks, credit unions, savings banks, insurance companies, and pension funds. These laws and regulations are grounded in the belief that too much competition would increase the risk of a significant number of failures among intermediaries and threaten public confidence in the nation's financial system. Thus, competition is tempered by regulation to protect the safety of individual financial institutions and by the desire for maximum economic efficiency in the production of financial services.

REGULATION OF COMMERCIAL BANKS

Commercial banks are among the most heavily regulated of all financial intermediaries. Regulations exist at both federal and state government levels to cover: (1) the chartering of new banks; (2) the establishment of branch offices and exercise of trust powers; (3) the formation of holding companies and mergers; (4) the offering of new financial services; (5) the adequacy of bank capital; (6) the quantity and quality of loans and investments; (7) the level of cash reserves; (8) maximum rates payable on deposits; and in some areas, (9) maximum rates that can be charged on loans. As we will see in Chapter 9, new federal laws and regulations dealing with consumer protection and civil rights have appeared during the 1970s affecting the advertising of bank credit services, the types of information which can be requested of credit customers, the methods for reporting financial charges on loans, and the procedures for handling billing disputes between credit customers and their banks.

Why do we impose such extensive regulatory controls over bank behavior? Several arguments have been advanced over the years to justify these regulations. Commercial banks, as we have seen, are the principal source of the nation's money supply which is closely linked to the growth and stability of the economy. Banks hold the public's savings and imprudent practices might jeopardize those funds, adversely affecting the financial position of many businesses, families, and individuals. Access to bank credit directly affects the financial well-being and standard of living of many individuals and institutions, especially consumers, small businesses, and state and local governments. Finally, commercial banks, because of their unique combination of services, possess great financial power. The failure of a major bank in a local community can have disastrous consequences. And, if bankers get together and illegally agree not to compete on prices, rates, or services offered, the resulting damage to consumers of financial services could be tremendous. Throughout U.S. history there has been considerable fear at both state and federal levels that concentrated financial power would have dire consequences for the businessman and the consumer who must rely on banks for essential services. This widespread fear of financial power and influence accounts for much of the law and regulation today governing branch banking, bank holding companies, and bank mergers.

Banks and other financial intermediaries in the United States face a *dual regulatory system,* with controls operating at both federal and state levels. There are three principal federal bank regulatory agencies—the Federal Reserve System, the Federal Deposit Insurance Corporation, and the Comptroller of the Currency (or Administrator of National Banks). Each of the 50 states, in turn, has a banking commission or department with powers generally paralleling those possessed by one or more of the three federal regulatory agencies. With so many agencies overseeing the same industry it is not surprising that there is considerable overlapping of regulatory powers, occasional conflicts among the agencies, and even competition from time to time.

The *Federal Reserve System* (the Fed) is one of the most important and powerful regulatory agencies in the federal government. As we saw in Chapter 5, its principal function is to carry out monetary policy—control over interest rates and bank reserves in order to achieve national economic goals. However, the Fed also possesses important supervisory powers over individual bank operations. It must approve or disapprove applications of holding companies to acquire bank and nonbank businesses and ensure that holding company organizations do not endanger the solvency or stability of the banks they acquire. The Fed supervises those commercial banks electing to join its system (so-called member banks), which include all national banks and more than 1,000 state-chartered banks. It generally confines its detailed examinations of banking practices to state-chartered members of its system and secures examination reports on national banks from the Comptroller of the Currency. The Fed sets maximum permissible rates payable on deposits for member banks through its Regulation Q. (The other regulatory agencies keep their maximum permissible deposit rates in close conformity with the Fed's Regulation Q.) Finally, the Fed oversees member bank compliance with recent social responsibility laws and regulations, including truth in lending and equal credit opportunity rules.

The *Federal Deposit Insurance Corporation* insures the deposits of approximately 98 percent of all U.S. commercial banks. Depositors who keep their funds in FDIC-insured banks are protected up to a maximum of $40,000—an amount which is satisfactory for most individuals and families but is of little help for major corporate depositors. The FDIC is responsible for the disposition of all failures among insured banks, paying off depositors up to the legal $40,000 maximum where necessary. While the FDIC is legally empowered to regularly examine all insured banks, it limits its examinations to insured banks not members of the Federal Reserve System. Generally, these examinations are conducted jointly with the state banking agencies to minimize the burden upon both the banks and the supervisory agencies. Insured commercial banks must submit financial statements to the FDIC containing a detailed breakdown of their assets, liabilities, capital, revenues, and expenses.

The oldest of the federal bank regulatory agencies is the *Office of the Comptroller of the Currency*, created by Congress in 1863. The Comptroller's Office is empowered to issue federal charters for new national banks provided there is a demonstrable public need, management appears qualified, and the proposed bank is adequately capitalized and has reasonable prospects for success. This agency has direct responsibility for the examination of national banks, which are examined at least once a year on the quality of their loans, adequacy of capital, and competence of management. Since there are about 4,700 national banks, including most of the largest banks in the United States, this is a formidable task. To aid in the chartering, supervisory, and examination functions of the Comptroller's Office that agency has set up several offices across the country staffed with attorneys, economists, and examiners. Each office is responsible for a different region of the nation.

Finally, the individual *state banking commissions* supervise and examine all state-chartered commercial banks in the United States. These state agencies must pass on applications for charters to establish new banks, reviewing basically the same factors which the Comptroller's Office considers in deciding whether to issue federal charters for national banks. Each state also maintains a staff of examiners who regularly review the operations of state-chartered banks operating within that state's borders. In addition, most of the state commissions must approve or at least be notified of any mergers or holding company acquisitions involving banks they charter and supervise. One of the most important of all banking powers possessed by the states is control over branching activities. Federal law dictates that even national banks must conform to state rules regarding the establishment of branch offices and the permissible range of services which may be offered through those branches. As we shall soon see, most states have elected to restrict or prohibit branching activity by a single bank, though there is a trend toward broader and broader branch banking powers.

In summary, federal and state regulations have greatly expanded over the years, especially during and since the Great Depression of the 1930s, to achieve multiple and often conflicting goals in the banking field—competition, safety, public convenience, efficiency, and equity. Today nearly all aspects of bank operations are covered by federal or state regulations administered by the Federal Reserve System, the Federal Deposit Insurance Corporation, the Comptroller of the Currency, and banking commissions in each of the 50 states. In the following sections we look more closely at recent changes in the structure and regulation of the commercial banking industry and at their implications for competition and for the safety and soundness of individual banks.

BRANCH BANKING

Growth of branch banking

The dominant trend in postwar U.S. banking is the spread of branch banking. Unit banks (which operate out of only one office) were clearly dominant in the United States at the end of the World War II and throughout all prior U.S. banking history. Totaling more than 13,000 at the end of 1945, they outnumbered branch banking offices (including head offices) more than two to one. By the end of the 1960s, however, more than 3,000 unit banks had disappeared, most of them caught up in a massive postwar merger movement. The majority of these merged unit banks were converted into branch offices of larger banking organizations. While branch offices totaled only about 5,000 in late 1945, the number had climbed to more than 33,000 by 1977. (See Figure 7–1 and Table 7–1). About four fifths of

FIGURE 7–1
Commercial banks in the United States (number, by class)

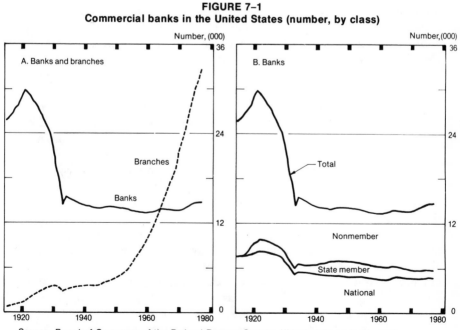

Source: Board of Governors of the Federal Reserve System, *Historical Chart Book, 1978.*

TABLE 7–1
Growth of commercial banks and bank deposits in the United States in selected years (year-end figures)

Year	Number of commercial banks	Branch offices	Total volume of bank deposits ($billions)
1960	13,471	10,483	$ 229.8
1962	13,426	12,345	262.1
1964	13,760	14,601	307.1
1966	13,769	16,908	353.5
1968	13,679	18,777	435.2
1970	13,688	21,424	481.7
1972	13,928	24,850	616.6
1974	14,465	29,775	786.5
1976	14,697	31,403	841.9
1977	14,740	33,088	1,116.5

Source: Board of Governors of the Federal Reserve System, *Federal Reserve Bulletin;* and Federal Deposit Insurance Corporation, *Annual Report,* selected issues.

this increase in branches resulted from the creation of new branch offices; the rest was due to mergers in which smaller banks were absorbed.

On balance, the total number of banking corporations gradually declined until the early 1960s when an uptrend began. For example, the total number of separately incorporated commercial banks stood at 14,142 in 1945, but had dropped to less than 13,500 by 1960. (See Table 7–1). This slow downward drift in bank numbers was accounted for by extensive merger and branching activity which more than offset the growth in new banks. Since the mid-1960s, however, a definite uptrend has been in progress so that by 1973 there were more commercial banks in the United States than at the end of World War II. Between 1960 and 1977 the number of insured commercial banks in the nation increased by nearly 1,300—from 13,471 to 14,740. During this same period, as we have seen, branch offices approximately tripled in number, far outstripping the growth in banks. Deposits and assets of all U.S. banks, as might be expected, kept pace with the growth of branch offices, more than quadrupling during the same time period.

Several factors have brought about these changes. Among the most important are growing demands for financial services, the rising cost of bank operations, and a steady decline in the industry's gross profit margin during the postwar era. Rapid growth in personal income and total population have dramatically raised the demand for expanded banking facilities, particularly in the form of consumer banking services such as checking accounts and instalment loans. Many metropolitan-based commercial banks have been forced to keep up with their customers by moving to suburbia and opening branch office systems or merging with smaller banks situated in more desirable locations. Rapid industrial growth also has intensified pressures on banks to expand in order to provide more credit, increase the stability of deposits, and secure more efficient management control. Branch banking has offered a way for the banking industry to grow rapidly in areas where the market appears most promising.

Other factors explaining the growth of branch banking include rising operating costs and a squeeze on profit margins. Both factors have put commercial banks under pressure to expand their size, diversify, and seek new sources of revenue. As we saw in Chapter 6, interest-bearing sources of funds have increased relative to cheaper demand deposits, and more costly services (such as leasing, factoring, trust operations, and financial counseling) have been demanded by businesses and households. The result has been a major shift in bank policies in recent years away from the traditional position of being a short-term lender to business to a more aggressive, marketing-oriented banking operation, utilizing new techniques for attracting funds and placing greater emphasis upon consumer loans, leasing, mortgages, and nonfunds-using financial services. These developments have accelerated the need for larger and more diversified banking organizations in the form of branch systems.

The effects of branch banking

Over the years there has been intense research interest in the impact of branch banking activity upon how and where individual banks provide their services to the public. State laws vary enormously on the type of branching activity permitted commercial banks within the borders of each state. About 40 percent of the states permit branching statewide subject only to minimal capital requirements and public necessity. These include such major states as Arizona, California, Connecticut, Maryland, New York, North Carolina, Oregon, Virginia, and Washington. Roughly another third restrict branching activity to cities or counties. These typically are referred to as "limited branching" states and include such states as Alabama, Georgia, Indiana, Massachusetts, Michigan, Ohio, Pennsylvania, and Wisconsin. The remaining group of states—usually labeled "unit banking" areas—require that the business of banking be carried on in only one location, though remote drive-in or other limited-service facilities may be permitted. Important states in this category include Colorado, Iowa, Minnesota, Missouri, Oklahoma, and Texas.

There is a definite geographic pattern in branch banking laws. Unit banking states are prominent in the Midwest and South, while in the Far West statewide branching predominates. In areas east of the Mississippi River, limited branching and statewide branch banking are especially important. A few states have changed their position on branching since World War II. Florida, Kentucky, Maine, New Hampshire, New Jersey, New York, and Virginia, for example, have liberalized their branching laws to permit banks to establish branch offices over wider areas. The State of Michigan, on the other hand, switched from statewide to limited branch banking. Proponents of branch banking claim that unrestricted entry into new markets through branching encourages competition and promotes efficiency in providing financial services. Since branching fosters larger and fewer banks, allegedly the consumer benefits by receiving financial services at lower cost due to economies of scale and greater productive efficiency. Opponents of branching, on the other hand, maintain that it results in greater concentration of resources and increased market power for the largest banks. Potentially at least, the customer may have fewer real alternatives under a branch banking regime, and therefore, prices charged for financial services may be higher. To some extent, acceptance of branch banking by the public may require a trade-off between competition (which may call for a market composed of many banks, each of only moderate size) and efficiency (which may necessitate fewer and larger banks serving the public).

A number of recent studies have examined the impact of branching on bank operating efficiency, the availability of banking services, prices, credit policies, mobility of funds, and market structure. Unfortunately, the results of these studies are much less than conclusive. For example, Horvitz and Shull [10] find that branching results in more branch offices in rural areas, but fewer separately incorporated banks in metropolitan areas compared with unit banking. Branching seems to result in more services, though research studies conflict as to whether these are offered at higher or lower prices.[2] Branch banks do seem to make more credit available in local communities, especially to consumers. However, Edwards [8] finds some evidence that interest paid on time and savings deposits is lower and rates on many types of loans are higher at branch banks than at unit banks. Also, there is limited evidence of discrimination against small businesses in credit availability and the pricing of loans under branch banking. Branching leads to fewer but larger commercial banks in a state, but frequently more total branch offices in metropolitan areas and in smaller communities, resulting in greater public convenience.[3] Finally, there is virtually no concrete evidence that the character of a state's branch banking laws affects income levels or rates of economic growth in local communities. We are still very much in the dark on

[2] See, for example, Horvitz and Shull [10] and Weintraub and Jessup [29].

[3] See especially Edwards [8] and Jacobs [11].

the real long-run benefits of having a branch banking or a unit banking structure.

BANK HOLDING COMPANIES

Characteristics and growth

In addition to the growing dominance of branch banking, the other major structural movement reshaping the U.S. banking industry today is the spread of holding companies. A bank holding company is a corporation or other business firm that holds stock in one or more banks. Today bank holding companies hold stock in commercial banks representing more than 70 percent of all U.S. bank deposits and about half of all bank offices. (See Table 7–2.) These proportions contrast sharply with the situation as recently as 1970 when only 16 percent of all U.S. bank deposits and 12 percent of bank offices were affiliated with holding companies.[4]

TABLE 7–2
Expansion of registered U.S. bank holding companies, 1960–1977

	Year-end figures					
	1960	1970	1971*	1974*	1976*	1977*
Number of companies......	47	121	1,567	1,752	1,913	2,027
Affiliated banks	426	895	2,420	3,462	3,793	3,903
Affiliated banks as a percent of all U.S. banks	3.2%	6.5%	17.7%	23.9%	25.9%	26.5%
Offices of affiliated banks	1,463	4,155	13,252	20,593	22,995	25,126
Affiliated bank offices as a percent of all U.S. bank offices	6.1%	11.8%	36.1%	47.6%	49.9%	52.4%
Deposits of affiliated banks ($ billions)	18.2	78.0	341.0	509.7	553.7	814.3
Deposits of affiliated banks as a percent of all U.S. bank deposits	7.9	16.2	55.1	67.9	65.5	72.9

* Figures beginning with 1971 include one-bank holding companies which were first required to register with the Federal Reserve Board in that year as well as multibank organizations which were required to register as early as 1957.
Source: Board of Governors of the Federal Reserve System; and Federal Deposit Insurance Corporation.

---

[4] The growth of bank holding companies in recent years reflects both growth within the sector and a change in federal reporting requirements. Beginning in 1971 one-bank holding companies were required to register with the Federal Reserve Board. The 1970 figure and those for earlier years back to 1957 include only holding companies with investments in two or more banks which were required to register with the Federal Reserve Board under the provisions of the Bank Holding Company Act of 1956.

The reasons behind the growth of bank holding companies are generally agreed upon by authorities in the field. The bank holding company has been employed as a vehicle to: (1) circumvent state laws and regulations prohibiting or restricting branch banking; (2) allow banking organizations to diversify by entering new markets and offering new services; and (3) gain easier access to sources of capital. There is also evidence that holding companies realize economies of organization through centralized management and service facilities, especially in the fields of portfolio management, data processing, and liability management.

Chase and Mingo [5] in a recent study contend that holding company activity may result in important social benefits. By further pooling the risks of lending, these organizations may make the intermediation process more efficient. In general, holding companies are capable of greater portfolio diversification than single, independent commercial banks. Because these organizations typically are quite large, they may have an advantage in attracting highly qualified management personnel, resulting in more efficient operations and perhaps improved returns to their stockholders. On the negative side, however, bank holding company activity may lead to a greater concentration of financial resources and raise the probability that individual banks will fail. Only limited research evidence exists today concerning the potential benefits and costs of bank holding company activity, and the results of that research are mixed and frequently contradictory.

Most holding company acquisitions of banks have occurred in the Midwest and South where unit banking and limited branching laws dominate. In fact, a recent study by Rose [20] indicates that nearly half of holding company acquisitions of banks during the early 1970's were concentrated primarily in the states of Florida, Missouri, Michigan, Ohio, and Texas. Three of these states have prohibited branch banking through most of their history, though Florida converted recently from unit banking to countywide branching. Michigan and Ohio, on the other hand, restrict branching to local areas. Moreover, holding companies generally have preferred banks in larger metropolitan areas where population and personal income are growing rapidly. Presumably, these dynamic market areas offer holding company organizations higher expected returns on their investments and the opportunity to attract a greater volume of deposits. The result in the long run may be larger dividends to shareholders and an increase in overall firm size and share of the available market for financial services.[5]

---

[5] Holding company investments in banks have not always resulted in higher returns to shareholders. For example, Piper [17] examined 146 holding company acquisitions of

Bank holding company laws

Bank holding companies have been regulated by the federal government since the 1930s. Under the Banking Act of 1933, the Board of Governors of the Federal Reserve System was given limited powers to regulate some holding company activities. It was empowered, for example, to examine holding companies and their subsidiaries, to supervise their financial practices, and to set reserve requirements. But, the Federal Reserve Board was not able to exercise effective control over the formation and expansion of bank holding companies or to prevent acquisitions that might adversely affect competition. Effective power to regulate the postwar expansion of holding companies was granted to the Fed with passage of the Bank Holding Company Act of 1956. Under this act, a holding company which controlled either as much as a fourth of the voting stock of two or more banks or the election of a majority of the directors of two or more banks was required to register with the Federal Reserve Board. Having thus become a "registered" holding company, the firm was required to divest itself of the control of corporations with interest not related to banking, submit to Federal Reserve regulation and examination, and secure Fed permission before acquiring more than 5 percent of the stock of another bank. In considering an application to form a bank holding company, the board was required to consider the solvency of the company, its management and prospects for earnings, any benefits to the public that might result from the transaction, and the possibility that the local banking market might become too concentrated.[6]

Ten years later, in 1966, the Bank Holding Company Act was amended to clarify the relative importance of public convenience and competition as matters to be examined by regulators in approving or denying holding company acquisitions. The 1966 amendments permitted the Federal Reserve Board to approve holding company acquisitions that might lessen competition provided this effect was clearly outweighed by benefits to the public. However, the amendments did not require holding companies controlling only one bank to

---

banks during the 1960s. He found that only about half were profitable. Excessive premiums paid for bank stock adversely affected the returns from many individual acquisitions. However, a recent study by Varvel [28] finds that holding companies experienced lower earnings during the initial period of reorganization and acquisition, but in later years, earnings grew at a more rapid pace for the holding company than would have been true if the holding company had not been formed.

[6] It was expressly left to the states, however, to regulate holding company activity within their own borders if they so chose. A few states, such as Oklahoma and Louisiana, have moved to restrict or prohibit the formation of holding companies. Others, such as New Jersey, have increased the potential for holding company growth by changing their laws to permit statewide expansion. See especially Rose and Fraser [19].

register. As a result of this loophole in the law, the number of one-bank holding companies grew rapidly during the late 1960s and included some of the largest banks in the United States. These companies sought to diversify into new product lines and new geographic markets by acquiring a variety of nonbank businesses—mortgage companies, leasing firms, finance companies, data processing firms, and many others. Fearing that holding company penetration into areas other than banking would break down the traditional separation between banking and commerce, Congress passed the 1970 amendments to the Bank Holding Company Act.[7]

The 1970 amendments had three main goals, each of which will significantly influence the future growth of U.S. bank holding companies. First, one-bank holding companies were no longer excluded from registration requirements. Now one-bank as well as multi-bank companies must register with the Federal Reserve Board and secure approval for any acquisitions of bank or nonbank businesses. Second, the definition of holding company "control" over individual banks was expanded. If a company was found to exercise a "controlling influence" over a bank, it might be required to register with the Federal Reserve Board as a bank holding company regardless of what proportion of bank stock the company held. Finally, the nonbanking activities which a company can pursue were restricted to include only those "so closely related to banking or managing or controlling banks as to be a proper incident thereto. . . ." In addition to this so-called closely related test, the 1970 amendments imposed a public benefits test on all future bank holding company acquisitions of nonbank firms. Only those nonbank acquisitions which "can reasonably be expected to produce benefits to the public, such as greater convenience, increased competition, or gains in efficiency, that outweigh possible adverse effects, such as undue concentration of resources, decreased or unfair competition, conflicts of interest, or unsound banking practices" may be approved.[8]

The provision of the 1970 amendments applying to nonbanking activities confined holding company acquisitions to business activities functionally related to banking. Beginning in 1971 the Federal Reserve Board conducted hearings on various nonbanking activities

---

[7] Public policy in the United States since the 19th century has aimed at minimizing the interconnections between commercial banking and the industrial and manufacturing sectors. The fear that if banks and their corporate customers were linked by common ownership, this would represent a formidable and undesirable concentration of economic and financial power is reflected in a host of federal and state banking regulations. Probably the most notable is the historic prohibition against commercial banks investing in common stock or underwriting new stock issues.

[8] Bank Holding Company Act, Section 4(c)(8) as amended by the Bank Holding Company Act Amendments of 1970.

which holding companies were then seeking to acquire. Since then, the board has added a substantial number of permissible nonbank activities to its approved list, including mortgage banking, leasing, armored car services, finance companies, credit life insurance, credit card companies, data processing companies, insurance agencies, and real estate investment trusts. However, the addition of new nonbank activities has slowed significantly in recent years due to financial problems experienced by many banks and bank holding companies, a more conservative regulatory stance at federal and state levels, and the lack of sufficient numbers of skilled management personnel in the holding company field.

CHAIN BANKING

Bank offices may be linked together through banking chains as well as through holding companies. *Chain banking* refers to the control of more than one bank by an individual or informal group of individuals. Due to the informal nature of most chain relationships the extent of chain banking is extremely difficult to determine. However, substantial chain banking activity is known to exist in certain sections of the United States, especially where there are large numbers of relatively small unit banks and branch banks.

A survey was carried out in the early 1960s by the Federal Reserve Board for evidence on the extent of chain banking in the United States.[9] A summary of the survey's results by Darnell [7] revealed that 19 percent of all member banks were then parts of chains having common ownership ties. In addition, an estimated 1,150 nonmember banks were operating in chains, bringing the total for all chain banks to about 2,300 institutions representing nearly 18 percent of all U.S. insured commercial banks. These 2,300 banks held nearly $53 billion in assets, or close to 20 percent of the assets of all U.S. banks with insured deposits. A bank was defined as a member of a chain if it had a major stockholder (with 5 percent or more of total shares outstanding), director, or officer in common with one or more other banks.

Since the Bank Holding Company Act forces a company holding as much as 25 percent of the stock of at least one bank to register with the Federal Reserve, many companies have held their ownership interests in banks to slightly less than 25 percent of the outstanding shares, thus escaping federal registration requirements. Where control was required, these firms would bring together informal groups of stockholders who, collectively, would hold a controlling interest in the bank. Many large chain banking organizations today consist of

---

[9] The full report on the Federal Reserve survey is contained in [26].

large metropolitan-based commercial banks with minority stock holdings in smaller affiliated banks in surrounding areas.[10] A number of holding company bank acquisitions approved in recent years have been designed merely to bring under a corporate umbrella what had previously been accomplished through chain banking organizations. Indeed, a significant proportion of the future growth of bank holding companies probably will reflect acquisitions of commercial banks formerly parts of chain banking arrangements, principally in states in the Midwest and South where chain banking is still very important.

BANK MERGERS

One of the most important vehicles for change in the banking structure during the postwar period has been the merger. Mergers have absorbed more than 3,000 separately incorporated U.S. banks since World War II. The pace of bank merger activity has slowed in recent years, however, due to tougher regulatory and antitrust restrictions, liberalization of branch banking laws in many states, the growth of bank holding companies, and difficulties in the stock market. Nevertheless, mergers still continue to be an important avenue for structural change in U.S. banking.

In the early years after World War II, bank mergers were regulated primarily by the states—a fact that contributed to the rapid increase in mergers, particularly in the mid-1950s. But with the passage of the Bank Merger Act of 1960, Congress required that all mergers involving insured banks have the prior approval of their principal federal supervisory agency—the Comptroller of the Currency, the Board of Governors of the Federal Reserve System, or the Federal Deposit Insurance Corporation. The Bank Merger Act also enunciated the factors regulatory agencies must consider in approving a merger, such as its effect on competition and the convenience and needs of the public.

It was widely thought until the mid-1960s that as part of a regulated industry, commercial banks were exempt from the antitrust laws. This belief was dispelled in 1963 and 1964, however, when in the Philadelphia National Bank and First National Bank of Lexington cases, the Supreme Court held that the impact on *competition* was the

---

[10] Early in 1978 the three federal banking agencies carried out a study of the number and amount of loans made by each bank to executive officers, major stockholders, and directors of other U.S. banks. A total of 6,721 commercial banks, or about 48 percent of all U.S. banks, reported having such loans outstanding as of September 30, 1977. Similarly, 902 banks reported loans secured primarily by the stock of other banks or bank holding companies totaling $2.7 billion. Thus, chain banking still appears to be a substantial factor in U.S. banking. See, in particular, reference [27].

controlling factor in determining the legality of a bank merger and that the antitrust laws were fully applicable to commercial banking.[11] Congress responded to these court decisions by passing the 1966 amendments to the Bank Merger Act. These amendments permit the regulatory authorities to approve a merger if its anticompetitive effects are clearly outweighed by a probable improvement in the convenience and needs of the public. The courts and bank regulatory agencies, however, continue to emphasize the competitive aspects of any proposed merger.

The rapid pace of postwar U.S. bank mergers has raised a number of important public policy questions. For example, who benefits (if anyone does) from the merger of two or more banks: the public? bank management? bank employees? the stockholders? Moreover, there is a great deal of conflict in the existing research evidence concerning the real impact of mergers upon the behavior of individual banks. Some recent studies suggest that bank mergers have improved the quality of services offered, lowered prices charged, and resulted in greater public convenience. For example, Kohn [14] examined data for all commercial banks in New York State which had merged at least once during the 1950s. He found that the public generally was charged lower rates on loans and reduced service charges on deposits in the wake of a merger transaction. On the negative side, however, compensating balances required on loans to small business firms and rates on new car loans tended to be higher as did service charges on special demand deposits. Horvitz and Shull [10] looked further into the issues raised by Kohn, studying the behavior of unit banks converted into branch offices after merger. They found that the policies of banks acquired by merger were soon made to coincide with those of the acquiring institutions. Higher interest rates on thrift deposits and lower rates on instalment loans, mortgages, and business loans generally were the result. Credit policies regarding permissible loan maturities and down payments generally were liberalized in favor of the customer.

Not all studies of bank mergers come to such positive conclusions, however. For example, Cohen and Reid [6] observed that overall bank size rose, which contributed to the prestige of management but did little for stockholders or the public. Another study by Bacon [1] reviewed the effects of 15 bank mergers in Marion County, Indiana. Stockholders of these banks were given substantial premiums on their stock, while management salaries and fringe benefits improved. Finally, a study by Smith [24] found very few changes of any kind

---

[11] See *United States* v. *Philadelphia National Bank et al.,* 210 F. Supp. 348 (1962); 835 Ct. 1715 (1963); and *United States* v. *First National Bank and Trust Co. of Lexington et al.,* 208 F. Supp. 456 (1962); 84 S. Ct. 1033 (1964).

flowing from the merger of two or more banks. Total revenues increased following consummation of the merger transaction, but expenses climbed as well. As a result, bank earnings were generally unaffected by merger. Thus, the true effects of mergers among commercial banks are in dispute and remain an open question awaiting further research.

MEMBERSHIP IN THE FEDERAL RESERVE SYSTEM

Another major structural change in U.S. banking in recent years has been the withdrawal of member banks from the Federal Reserve System. This exodus from the Fed has resulted in a decline in both the total number of member banks and in the volume of bank assets and deposits subject to direct Fed regulation. For example, in 1960 there were 6,174 member banks out of a total of 13,471 commercial banks, or 46 percent of the total. These member institutions held 84 percent of all U.S. bank deposits. By 1978, however, only 38 percent of all U.S. banks were Fed members, and the percentage of deposits controlled by member banks had fallen to only 71 percent. Moreover, the speed of withdrawal seems to have increased during the past decade.[12] (See Table 7–3).

TABLE 7–3
The trend of bank membership in the Federal Reserve System

Year	Number of member banks	Percent of all U.S. deposits held by member banks
1945	6,884	86.3
1950	6,873	85.7
1955	6,543	85.2
1960	6,174	84.0
1965	6,221	82.9
1970	5,767	80.1
1975	5,787	75.1
1976	5,758	73.8
1977	5,664	71.8
1978	5,593	70.8

Source: Board of Governors of the Federal Reserve System.

The principal reason banks appear to be leaving the Fed is the higher reserve requirements levied against deposits by the Fed as compared to most states. Reserve requirements for nonmember

---

[12] See especially the comprehensive summary of recent trends in system membership prepared by J. T. Rose [18].

banks are set by the state where each bank is headquartered. These state-imposed requirements vary significantly from state to state, and seven states actually impose lower *percentage* reserve requirements than the Federal Reserve.[13] However, in about half the states percentage reserve requirements imposed on demand deposits are about the same as those called for by the Fed, and 15 states actually levy higher percentage requirements than does the Federal Reserve. The critical distinction between Federal Reserve and state required reserves is not in the percentages required, but in the *definition* of those assets eligible to be counted as "legal reserves."

As we pointed out in Chapter 5, legal reserves are simply those assets held by a commercial bank which the regulatory authorities permit it to count in meeting reserve requirements called for by law. For banks that are members of the Federal Reserve System, only vault cash held on bank premises and deposits with the Federal Reserve bank in the region qualify as legal reserves. In contrast, individual state laws differ greatly in the assets which may be counted as legal reserves. Like the Fed, nearly every state counts vault cash in meeting reserve requirements, but most states also allow "due from" balances held with correspondent banks. These deposits are not just idle cash as are Federal Reserve deposits. For example, the larger metropolitan banks provide important services to their smaller bank customers, such as check clearing and portfolio management, in return for receiving these correspondent deposits. Some correspondent accounts may be held in the form of a time deposit which earns interest. Thus, there is both an implicit and an explicit return on "due from" balances which generally exceeds the implicit return on balances held with the Federal Reserve banks.[14] A few states add to the return on legal reserves by allowing their banks to count investments in interest-bearing U.S. government and municipal securities as meeting reserve requirements.

Does the trend of commercial banks away from the Fed have any serious consequences? The Federal Reserve Board argues in the affirmative. Allegedly, the growth of the nonmember bank sector has reduced the Fed's control over the nation's supply of money and credit.

---

[13] The most conspicuous example is the state of Illinois which levies no statutory reserve requirement on any category of deposits. Connecticut does not require reserves behind savings deposits, while Louisiana, Massachusetts, and Rhode Island do not levy required reserves against time and savings deposits. See Knight [13].

[14] Membership in the Federal Reserve System entitles a bank to the free shipment of currency and coin, clearing of checks, and wire transfer of funds. In addition, member banks may borrow reserves on a short-term, temporary basis from the Fed's discount window. These services represent an implicit rate of return to member banks since, in their absence, a member institution would be forced to purchase such services from other sources.

In recent testimony before the House Banking Committee, G. William Miller, Chairman of the Federal Reserve Board, stated:

> It is essential that the Federal Reserve maintain adequate control over the monetary aggregates if the nation is to succeed in its efforts to curb inflation, sustain economic growth, and maintain the value of the dollar in international exchange markets. The attrition in deposits subject to reserve requirements set by the Federal Reserve weakens the linkage between member bank reserves and the monetary aggregates.[15]

In July 1975 the Fed introduced the Reserve Requirements Act in the U.S. Senate which would have imposed common reserve requirements on both member and nonmember bank demand deposits (including NOW accounts) for all but the very smallest banks. The proposed act immediately ran into stiff opposition in Congress from organizations representing state-chartered nonmember banks and state bank supervisors. These groups believe strongly in preserving the dual banking system, in which both federal and state regulatory authorities exist side by side. The failure of Congress to pass the original reserve requirements act resulted in the introduction in 1978 of the Federal Reserve Membership Act (H.R. 12706), the Federal Reserve Requirements Act (H.R. 13476), and the Interest on Reserves Act (H.R. 13477). These bills call for payment of interest on member-bank reserve balances, universal reserve requirements for all deposit-type financial institutions, and specific fees for Federal Reserve services now provided without charge to member banks. Additional bills were introduced early in 1979 by members of the House and Senate with varying proposed reserve requirements and exemptions for small banks. Reflecting the strength of groups opposing additional federal reserve requirements, no bill dealing with the Fed withdrawal problem had been enacted by Congress at the time this book was going to press in the summer of 1979.

Many students of the banking industry disagree with the Fed's analysis of the nonmember bank problem and its alleged consequences. For example, economists point out that reserve requirements are not used very often as a tool of monetary policy, principally because their impact on the banking system is too powerful and difficult to control. Moreover, monetary policy in the United States is carried out mainly through open market operations conducted at the trading desk of the Federal Reserve Bank of New York. Open market operations do not depend for their effectiveness on the level or distribution of bank deposits. However, the powerful opposition to uni-

---

[15] Statement by G. William Miller, Chairman of the Federal Reserve Board, before the Banking Committee, U.S. House of Representatives, January 24, 1979.

form Federal Reserve requirements points to a key issue in the Fed membership controversy—the question of *regulatory equity*. Is it fair to impose strict regulatory restraints upon one type of financial intermediary and not on another when both compete in essentially the same market? This issue is much broader than just commercial banking since many nonbank thrift institutions, principally savings and loan associations and mutual savings banks, carry much lower average reserve requirements than commercial banks. Yet, bank and nonbank depository intermediaries compete aggressively with each other for consumer loans, real estate credit, and savings deposits. Lower reserve requirements grant nonmember banks as well as nonbank thrift institutions more flexibility in managing their assets and perhaps greater earnings than possessed by member banks of the Federal Reserve System.

Several research studies have appeared in recent years trying to measure the impact of Federal Reserve membership on bank operating performance. Unfortunately, the studies do not always agree on the costs and benefits of belonging to the Fed. For example, a study of Illinois banks by Mayne [15] indicates that cash assets held by member banks were significantly higher than those held by nonmembers of comparable size and location. As a result, nonmember banks in that state reported higher average returns on their capital and total assets. However, member banks in Illinois are at an extreme disadvantage relative to nonmembers since that state imposes no reserve requirements. In most other states differences in regulations applying to member and nonmember institutions are much narrower, and therefore, studies focusing upon other states have generally found only marginal differences in the earnings of member versus nonmember banks.

How do bankers feel about the benefits and costs of belonging to the Federal Reserve System? A handful of studies have surveyed the banking community on that issue and most have found a decided adverse reaction to the burdens of Fed membership. For example, Mayne [15] found that, in the minds of most Illinois bankers, membership depressed bank earnings and that free Fed services provided member banks were also available to nonmembers through correspondents or were of considerably less importance than the lost earnings due to higher Fed reserve requirements. Rose [21] carried out a nationwide survey of the advantages and disadvantages of Fed membership among a sample of 600 member and nonmember banks. He found that the key *advantages* of system membership as viewed by both member and nonmember banks were: (1) access to the discount window; (2) use of the Fed's wire transfer network; (3) prestige; (4) the availability of free shipments of currency and coin; (5) the statutory

6% dividend on Federal Reserve stock paid to member banks; and (6) the provision of relevant statistical information by the Federal Reserve Board and regional Federal Reserve banks. Among the most important *disadvantages* listed were: (1) federal reserve requirements; (2) burdensome capital requirements; (3) the required purchase of Fed stock; (4) nonmember bank access to Fed services; (5) restrictions on employee behavior; and (6) the provision of similar services by correspondent banks. Among banks withdrawing from the system, reserve requirements were listed by two out of every three respondents as the main disadvantage of belonging to the Fed. Moreover, a majority of withdrawing banks claimed that their withdrawal goals—principally improvement in earnings—were attained once they pulled out of the system.

The adverse reactions of bankers toward Fed reserve requirements and their relative lack of enthusiasm regarding most Federal Reserve services suggests a continuing erosion of system membership in the absence of new legislation. This possibility is of some concern since the long-run *supervisory* influence of the Federal Reserve over the nation's banking system is at stake. Moreover, if system membership continues to erode, it is not clear that monetary policy would be as effective or as swift if member banks were a minority in terms of both numbers and resources. In addition, the equity of having two sets of reserve requirements—one for member and another for nonmember banks—remains an open question. This form of legal discrimination is likely to be viewed by bankers as a growing burden, especially as more and more nonbank thrift institutions which are not under Federal Reserve regulations come to offer services comparable to those offered by commercial banks.

INTERNATIONAL BANKING ACTIVITIES

U.S. banks play a vital role in providing funds for international commerce and investment. They have led in the growth and development of multinational banking facilities to serve foreign governments, agencies, and multinational corporations, especially corporations based in the United States. Until the mid-1970s the foreign banking activities of U.S. banks were centered mainly in their overseas offices due to federal government controls. Beginning in 1963 the federal government restricted foreign lending from domestic banking offices in order to reduce the outflow of capital from the United States and strengthen the American balance of payments position. However, in 1974 the Nixon Administration relaxed government controls on foreign loans. The result has been an aggressive expansion of international banking services provided by the domestic offices of American banks as well as by their foreign offices and subsidiaries.

U.S. bankers have developed a number of different organizational forms to aid them in overseas operations. The larger American banks typically operate branch offices in major financial centers and establish "representative offices" to ferret out business contacts in smaller market areas. In regions where risks appear to be greater or other, competing banks have established a strong foothold consortiums, correspondent arrangements, joint ventures, and minority acquisitions of existing firms may be used. Smaller U.S. banks frequently carry on international operations principally through their domestic offices. However, most experts feel that successful international banking requires a bank to have both offices and highly competent personnel present in foreign markets to maintain close personal contact with customers. The largest U.S. banks moved abroad with office facilities early in the postwar period. However, the overseas movement really gathered momentum after 1960 due to high foreign credit demands and relatively high interest rates available in foreign financial markets. When the U.S. economy began to grow rapidly after 1965, American banks found they needed a substantial volume of new deposits to keep pace with loan demand. However, tight credit policies of the Federal Reserve System, aimed at cooling off domestic inflation, severely limited the growth of domestic deposits. U.S. bankers began to look elsewhere for additional funds. The most attractive outside source proved to be the Eurodollar market, where foreign-bank deposits denominated in U.S. dollars are actively traded on a thin margin of profit. The supply of these funds was ample due to huge U.S. balance of payments deficits and there were no interest rate ceilings (such as Regulation Q) to inhibit the acquisition of Eurodollar funds. The volume of Eurodollar borrowings by U.S. banks rose sharply in the late 1960s and early 1970s, especially during those periods when domestic interest rates climbed above legal rate ceilings.

Data on U.S. foreign bank operations is difficult to obtain because many overseas activities are unregulated. According to data prepared by the Federal Reserve, the assets held by foreign branches of U.S. banks totaled more than $150 billion in 1975 compared to only about $9 billion a decade earlier. While only 13 U.S. banks had established foreign branches in 1965, the number had jumped to 125 by year-end 1975. Earlier estimates indicate that the total assets of U.S. bank foreign branches expanded eight times between 1965 and 1972 and doubled once more between 1972 and 1975. As reflected in Table 7–4, most branch offices are located in Latin America followed closely by

TABLE 7-4
Overseas branches of U.S. member banks, 1965–1975 (as of January 1)

Country of location	1965	1966	1967	1968	1969	1970	1971	1972	1973	1974	1975
Belgium-Luxembourg	2	4	6	8	9	11	11	8	8	15	15
France	4	4	4	6	7	11	12	15	17	15	17
Germany	3	6	8	9	14	17	21	22	27	30	30
Greece	1	1	1	2	5	8	9	13	14	16	18
Italy	1	1	3	2	2	3	4	6	7	8	10
The Netherlands	3	3	3	3	5	7	7	7	6	6	6
Switzerland	1	1	2	3	3	6	7	8	8	9	9
United Kingdom	17	21	21	24	32	37	41	45	49	52	55
Total Europe*	32	43	48	59	80	103	116	128	142	157	167
Bahamas	2	3	3	3	8	32	60	73	94	91	80
Cayman Islands	—	—	—	—	—	—	—	—	2	32	44
Total Caribbean†	5	9	9	10	22	53	89	107	131	164	164
Argentina	16	17	17	25	33	38	38	38	38	38	37
Brazil	15	15	15	15	15	15	16	19	21	21	19
Colombia	5	6	6	8	17	23	26	28	28	32	36
Panama	10	12	15	19	21	26	29	29	32	33	33
Total Latin America‡	72	79	93	123	155	182	191	195	190	195	198

Taiwan	—	2	2	2	2	2	2	2	3	5	7
Hong Kong	6	6	8	10	12	13	13	15	19	23	24
India	5	6	8	8	11	11	11	11	11	11	11
Indonesia	—	—	—	—	4	6	6	6	6	6	6
Japan	13	14	14	14	14	15	15	17	21	25	31
Lebanon	3	3	3	3	3	3	3	3	3	3	3
Persian Gulf§	2	2	8	8	8	9	8	11	10	10	11
Singapore	—	8	8	8	8	9	11	11	11	14	18
Total Asia‖	45	55	63	69	78	83	91	98	112	126	143
Total Africa#	3	2	2	3	3	1	2	2	2	2	5
Overseas areas of U.S.	23	23	29	31	35	38	43	47	50	55	55
Grand total	180	211	244	295	373	460	532	577	627	699	732
U.S. member banks with overseas branches**	11	13	13	15	26	53	79	91	107	125	125

* Also includes Austria, Ireland, Monaco, and Romania.
† Also includes Barbados, Haiti, Jamaica, Netherlands Antilles, Trinidad-Tobago, British Virgin Islands, and other West Indies.
‡ Also includes Bolivia, Chile, Dominican Republic, Ecuador, El Salvador, Guatemala, Guyana, Honduras, Mexico, Nicaragua, Paraguay, Peru, Uruguay, and Venezuela.
§ Includes Bahrain, Qatar, Saudi Arabia, and United Arab Emirates.
‖ Also includes Brunei, Fiji Islands, Israel, Jordan, Korea, Malaysia, Pakistan, Philippines, Thailand, and Vietnam.
Includes Liberia, Kenya, Mauritius, and Nigeria.
** No resident U.S. branches as of January 1, 1975.
Source: Federal Reserve Bank of Chicago, *Business Conditions*, September 1975, p. 5.

the Carribean area. Branch offices in the latter region are used principally to funnel Eurodollars to U.S. shores and supply capital for offshore investments. Most of the recent growth in branch offices has been concentrated in the United Kingdom (principally London), West Germany, the Caymen Islands, Colombia, Japan, Singapore, and the Middle East. Not included in these branch office statistics are foreign facilities of U.S. banks which engage in commercial and consumer financing, investment banking, leasing, and trading in the money market.

A number of the largest U.S. money-center banks today receive close to half their net income from foreign operations. Frequently the restrictions on their activities are more lenient overseas and the opportunities for return greater. However, this differential character of foreign versus domestic banking regulations has created problems for bank regulatory authorities, especially the Federal Reserve System. The Federal Reserve under the law must supervise foreign activities of member banks. Any member bank which wishes to set up a foreign branch or invest in foreign firms must receive the approval of the Federal Reserve Board in Washington, D.C. Nonmember banks, on the other hand, must follow the regulations of their own state banking commission, though most states have not exerted effective control over international banking operations.

One major problem the Federal Reserve System must deal with in supervising international operations of domestic banks is the more lenient regulations abroad. Foreign banks typically are allowed to purchase the stock of other business firms and to underwrite equities. In contrast, U.S. banks have been forbidden to engage in investment banking for corporate securities since passage of the Glass-Steagall Act in 1934. The Federal Reserve Board, therefore, typically allows U.S. banks to offer a greater variety of services in foreign markets than at home. The Fed seems to favor the principle of *mutual nondiscrimination* with respect to permissible international banking activities—foreign banks should be allowed to operate under the same regulations and be able to offer the same range of services as domestic banks. This regulatory philosophy is nondiscriminatory and eliminates the necessity for establishing a different set of rules for domestic banks and foreign banks.

FOREIGN BANKS IN THE UNITED STATES

Paralleling the rapid expansion of U.S. banks overseas, foreign banks have entered the United States in increasing numbers in recent years. A survey carried out by the Federal Reserve Board in 1976 revealed that foreign bank installations chartered and licensed within the continental United States numbered about 180 with total resources exceeding $60 billion. (See Table 7–5.) The latter figure, representing more than 6 percent of all U.S. bank assets, has grown rapidly; in fact, total assets of foreign banks have roughly tripled since 1972. British banks have set up full-service banking facilities on the American continent mainly by establishing branches and acquiring domestically chartered banks. Canadian banks have used at least three different devices to carry on their operations in the United States: (1) trust companies to provide for the safekeeping of valuables and the processing of security payments; (2) agencies; and (3) wholesale-retail affiliates. Banks in Switzerland and Germany have established branch offices and securities affiliates operating in the U.S. money market. Japanese banks have established wholesale banking affiliates, retail banking outlets, and agency offices which deal in securities and the financing of international trade and commerce.

Canadian banks were among the first to enter the United States, establishing affiliate and agency facilities before the turn of the century. The American money market today aids the larger chartered banks in Canada in meeting their liquidity needs. In addition, the chartered banks frequently make loans to U.S. security brokers and dealers and hold substantial deposits with major U.S. money-center banks. During the 1920s a number of foreign branches opened in the western part of the United States and in the state of Illinois. However, many states reacted negatively to this invasion by foreign banks into local banking markets. Several enacted laws forbidding branching by foreign-owned banks. Only in recent years has the notion that international banking is mutually beneficial to all regions become widely accepted. A few states have moved to lift their restrictions against foreign bank entry.[16]

Foreign banks have entered the United States for a wide variety of reasons. Two dominant factors stand out—the rapid expansion of international commerce and the huge size of the U.S. market. Then, too, many foreign banks have followed their own corporate customers to U.S. shores. Once they had gained a foothold in the United States, however, foreign banks grew rapidly by attracting deposit and loan business from both foreign and domestic corporations. Moreover, the U.S. economy in recent years has been more stable and prosperous than in many other countries with milder recessions and less severe inflation.

Despite the rapid growth of foreign banking activities in the

---

[16] For an in-depth analysis of the scope and growth of foreign bank operations in the United States see Edwards [8] and Klopstock [12].

TABLE 7-5

Assets and liabilities of U.S. offices of foreign banks, August 1976 ($millions)

Item:	All reporters	Agencies	Branches	Commercial banks	New York investment companies
Assets					
Total	61,921	25,868	21,221	13,245	1,586
Standard banking assets	44,125	16,925	14,467	11,448	1,285
Loans and credits	23,806	10,276	6,157	6,798	575
Commercial and industrial	19,608	9,755	5,645	3,783	425
U.S.	14,976	7,990	3,444	3,243	299
Foreign	4,632	1,765	2,201	540	126
Other loans	4,198	521	512	3,015	150
Money market assets	11,851	3,374	7,209	975	293
Interbank loans and deposits	11,161	3,018	6,977	874	293
U.S.	7,270	2,383	4,048	738	100
Foreign	3,892	634	2,929	136	193
Loans for purchasing or carrying securities	690	357	232	101	1
Securities	3,729	659	456	2,436	179
Miscellaneous	4,738	2,616	646	1,239	237
Clearing balances	4,902	1,059	2,342	1,354	148
Due from directly related institutions	12,894	7,884	4,412	443	154
U.S.	5,384	4,451	758	121	54
Foreign	7,510	3,433	3,655	323	100

Liabilities

Total	61,921	25,868	21,221	13,245	1,586
Standard banking liabilities	35,782	12,567	11,274	11,097	845
Liabilities to nonbanks	20,356	2,082	8,001	9,732	541
Demand deposits and credit balances	4,652	498	961	3,030	163
U.S.	3,591	272	474	2,784	61
Foreign	1,062	226	487	246	102
Time and savings deposits and other borrowings	15,704	1,584	7,040	6,702	378
U.S.	9,407	458	2,918	6,008	22
Foreign	6,298	1,126	4,122	694	356
Interbank	11,210	7,871	2,643	593	102
U.S.	10,268	7,769	1,877	525	97
Foreign	942	101	767	68	6
Miscellaneous	4,216	2,614	629	771	202
Clearing liabilities	3,196	1,107	1,323	454	312
Due to directly related institutions	20,942	11,872	8,458	348	264
U.S.	5,771	3,040	2,499	212	19
Foreign	15,172	8,832	5,960	135	244
Capital accounts and reserves	2,001	322	166	1,347	166

Note: Details may not add to totals due to rounding.
Source: Board of Governors of the Federal Reserve System, *Federal Reserve Bulletin*, October 1976, p. 824.

United States, their investments in this country are still very small compared to U.S. bank investments overseas. For example, in the London money market, American banks outnumber British banking institutions and account for the majority of Eurodollar loans. It has been estimated that London branches of U.S. banks hold at least 10 percent of all bank loans in pounds sterling extended to residents of Great Britain. Foreign branches of U.S. banks hold approximately four times the assets of all branches and affiliates of foreign banks active in the United States. In addition, the equity holdings of U.S. banks in financial institutions abroad—particularly commercial banks, finance and leasing companies, and merchant banks—are substantial. Clearly, U.S. commercial banks play a larger and more substantial role in foreign markets than do foreign banks active in the continental United States.

Nevertheless, reflecting the concern of domestic banking organizations and the regulatory authorities, Congress passed and the president signed the International Banking Act into law on September 17, 1978. Under this new law foreign banks operating agencies, branches, or commercial lending companies within U.S. borders are subject to federal regulation and supervision. Federal branches and agencies of foreign banks with total worldwide consolidated bank assets exceeding $1 billion are subject to federal reserve requirements and Regulation Q interest rate ceilings. The act also authorizes the Federal Reserve Board to levy reserve requirements and impose rate ceilings on state agencies and branches of foreign banks in cooperation with state bank supervisory authorities. Moreover, no foreign bank may establish a federal branch office which accepts deposits of less than $100,000 without securing federal deposit insurance. (In those states requiring deposit insurance for the banks they charter, state-authorized branches of foreign banks which accept deposits of less than $100,000 also must be insured.) Foreign banks that maintain U.S. offices other than branches or agencies must register with the Secretary of the Treasury upon the establishment of such an office. Finally, any foreign bank operating an agency, branch, or commercial lending company in the United States is subject to the Bank Holding Company Act and must register with the Federal Reserve Board.

While the new International Banking Act appears to apply strict regulations to foreign banking activities, this is not really the case. Instead, the act places foreign banks on essentially the same regulatory footing as domestic banks. It is an extension of the principle of mutual nondiscrimination used widely around the globe in the regulation of foreign banks. Moreover, for the first time non-U.S. citizens are permitted to serve as directors of Edge Act Corporations, and foreign banks can acquire majority ownership in these corporations which aid in carrying out international transactions.

BANK FAILURES

Commercial banks in the United States are private corporations organized to provide maximum, or at least satisfactory, profits for their shareholders. Not all banks are successful, however, and a few are forced to close their doors each year. Indeed, in the absence of effective regulations to protect the public, substantial numbers of banks probably would fail each year. For example, prior to the imposition of federal and state controls over the chartering and operations of commercial banks, a massive number of U.S. banks collapsed during the 1920s and 1930s. Succumbing to the deepest economic recession in American history the number of U.S. banks dropped from about 30,000 in 1920 to little more than 14,000 by 1940. In the wake of that calamity Congress created a system of deposit insurance under the administration of the Federal Deposit Insurance Corporation (FDIC). Banks were forbidden to underwrite corporate stocks and maximum permissible rates were imposed on all categories of deposits, to mention only a few of the more important regulations.

Due to more stringent federal and state regulations and prosperous economic conditions, the number of failures in the postwar period has been relatively small—only about 1 percent of the total U.S. banking population. Between 1946 and 1977 only 187 U.S. commercial and savings banks failed, an average of just 5.8 bank failures each year. (See Table 7–6.) The relative sizes of these bankrupt institutions varied markedly. The largest bank to fail in U.S. history was Franklin National Bank in New York City which closed in 1974 with $1.4 billion in total deposits. Franklin's failure occurred less than a year after U.S. National Bank in San Diego closed its doors with over $930 million in deposits, ranking second in size on the FDIC's list of biggest bank failures. However, two banks with less than $50,000 in deposits also were closed during the postwar period. Both the number of bank failures and the mean-size failed bank seem to have increased during the 1970s. For example, between 1969 and 1977, 64 U.S. banks failed—about 8 per year. Moreover, of the ten largest bank failures in U.S. history all but one has occurred since 1970.

Reports issued by the bank regulatory agencies generally imply that the principal causes of bank failures are: (1) self-serving loans to bank management or to the bank's owners; (2) general mismanagement of loans, defalcations, or embezzlements; and (3) miscellaneous manip-

TABLE 7–6
Number of U.S. failed banks, 1946–1977

Year	Insured	Non-insured	Total	Year	Insured	Non-insured	Total
1946	1	1	2	1962	1	2	3
1947	5	1	6	1963	2	0	2
1948	3	0	3	1964	7	1	8
1949	5	4	9	1965	5	4	9
1950	4	1	5	1966	7	1	8
1951	2	3	5	1967	4	0	4
1952	3	1	4	1968	3	0	3
1953	4	1	5	1969	9	0	9
1954	2	2	4	1970	7	1	8
1955	5	0	5	1971	6	0	6
1956	2	1	3	1972	1	2	3
1957	2	1	3	1973	6	0	6
1958	4	5	9	1974	4	0	4
1959	3	0	3	1975	13	1	14
1960	1	1	2	1976	16	1	17
1961	5	4	9	1977	6	0	6

Source: Federal Deposit Insurance Corporation, *Annual Report*, various issues.

ulations of bank funds.[17] General economic conditions are not usually assigned a major role in causing recent bank failures. However, the number of U.S. bank failures has been slightly higher, on average, in periods of recession than in periods of prosperity since World War II. Another factor closely related to failures is the size of individual banks. The large majority of closings have occurred among relatively small banks. Close to 60 percent of U.S. banks collapsing during the postwar years held $2 million or less in total deposits. Clearly, smaller banks are more vulnerable to failure than larger institutions. The asset portfolios of the smaller institutions are not as well diversified, exposing them to more risk.

Few efforts have been made until recently to predict bank failures. One of the more successful studies by Meyer and Pifer [16] used regression analysis in an attempt to discriminate between banks about to fail and paired sound banks operating in the same economic area. These researchers were successful in identifying the majority of failing institutions on the basis of a limited set of operating ratios. However, few financial ratios were able to forecast financial collapse more than a year or two before the event. Later, Sinkey and Walker [23] studied the behavior of banks identified by federal examiners as problem institutions. Statistical comparisons with sound banks revealed that the problem institutions had lower liquidity and were less efficient in controlling expenses. Examiners' ratings of individual

---

[17] See especially Barnett [2], Benston [3] and [4], and Rose and Scott [22].

banks also were the subject of a study by Stuhr and Van Wicklen [25]. The ratings are an overall index of each bank's financial condition based upon information contained in bank examination reports. Variables used to sort banks into high- and low-rated categories included measures of the mix of assets, adequacy of capital, the competency of management, bank size, and organizational structure. The discriminant functions were quite satisfactory, correctly classifying more than 95 percent of all banks studied. These results seem promising as a possible forerunner of an "early warning" system for bank problems. However, the authors point out that more work needs to be done to determine if the results will still hold for other banks in other time periods. Finally, a recent study by Rose and Scott [22] compared 69 U.S. commercial banks failing during the years 1965–75 with comparable-size solvent banks serving the same countywide banking markets. Failing institutions were found to display greater risk exposure and lower proportions of liquid assets to total assets than solvent institutions. The failing banks also appear to have been beset by serious expense control problems which served to reduce their earnings significantly below industry norms for an extended time period. The authors concluded that the failing institutions were vulnerable over a considerable length of time before financial and other problems over-powered their weak defenses.

In brief, the question of whether bank failures and banks in financial trouble can be detected in advance and, presumably, helped is an interesting and unresolved issue. Limited evidence suggests that selected financial ratios—particularly those linked to earnings, efficiency, and liquidity—are able to distinguish between "normal" institutions and those with financial problems. Generally, however, there is not much advance warning—perhaps two to three years— before a bank is in serious trouble and in need of closer supervision by the regulatory authorities. Fortunately, large numbers of bank failures appear unlikely today due to federal and state regulations and the determination of government to prevent major economic downturns. As in the past, the number of bank failures in future years will depend primarily on the competency and honesty of management.

CONCLUSIONS

The structure of the American banking system has a profound impact upon the performance of individual commercial banks that operate within that system. The number and relative sizes of competitors that each commercial bank faces influence the makeup of its balance sheet, earnings, expenses, and growth. And, as we have seen, state and federal laws are a major determinant of the competitive environment faced by individual banks. Indeed, we can confidently make the same statement regarding *all* major financial intermediaries active today in the U.S. economy: *state and federal regulation is one of the most important elements in determining the structure of financial intermediation and, through structure, the degree of competition faced by individual financial institutions.*

We must not overemphasize the role of structure, however. Within the constraints imposed by law and structure there is still great latitude for the management of individual financial institutions, including commercial banks, to shape their performance. Whether a bank, savings and loan association, insurance company, or other financial institution is profitable, fast growing, or public-service oriented depends upon the quality and dedication of its management. More specifically, the success of the individual financial institution depends upon management's ability to solve key problems related to that institution's liquidity, capital adequacy, the composition of its assets and liabilities, and organizational makeup. In the ensuing chapters we examine closely these problem areas faced by the management of all financial intermediaries.

QUESTIONS

7–1. Explain the meaning of the word *structure*. Of what importance is structure to the consumer of financial services?

7–2. Why has branch banking grown rapidly in importance during the postwar period in the United States? How has the trend toward increased branching affected the structure of the industry? the quantity and quality of service to the public?

7–3. What is a bank holding company? Explain why bank holding companies have grown so rapidly in recent years, particularly since 1970. What are the major potential advantages and disadvantages to the public of holding company expansion?

7–4. Give a brief history of U.S. bank holding company legislation. Can you explain why this legislation appears to be necessary?

7–5. Explain what is meant by the term *chain banking*. In what parts of the United States is chain banking most important and why?

7–6. Why have so many member banks withdrawn from the Federal Reserve System in recent years? Explain what the consequences of this withdrawal trend might be for effective control of the nation's money supply. Can you suggest a way to reverse the present exodus from the Fed?

7–7. List the major reasons behind the spread of U.S. banks into international markets. What problems does U.S. bank expansion overseas pose for the regulatory authorities? What is the principal of mutual nondiscrimination?

7–8. Why have so many foreign banks entered the United States in recent years? List the major provisions of the International Banking Act. Why did Congress pass this law?

7–9. Explain why bank failures are of such concern to the public and the regulatory authorities. According to the regulatory agencies why do most banks fail? Is there any evidence suggesting that impending bank failures might be predicted? Are there reasons for suggesting the proportion of bank failures might increase in the future?

REFERENCES

1. Bacon, Peter W. *A Study of Bank Mergers in Marion County, Indiana, 1945–66.* Unpublished doctoral dissertation, Indiana University, 1967.

2. Barnett, Robert A. "Anatomy of a Bank Failure." *The Magazine of Bank Administration*, April 1972, pp. 20–24, 43.

3. Benston, George. "Bank Examination." *The Bulletin*, New York University, nos. 89–90 (May 1973).

4. Benston, George J. "How Can We Learn from Past Bank Failures." *The Bankers Magazine*, vol. 158, no. 1 (Winter 1975), pp. 19–25.

5. Chase, Samuel B., and Mingo, John J. "The Regulation of Bank Holding Companies." *Journal of Finance*, vol. 30, no. 2 (May 1975), pp. 281–92.

6. Cohen, Kalmen, and Reid, Samuel R. "Effects of Regulation, Branching, and Mergers on Banking Structure and Performance." *The Southern Economic Journal*, October 1967, pp. 231–49.

7. Darnell, Jerome C. "Chain Banking." *National Banking Review*, vol. 3, no. 3 (1966), pp. 307–31.

8. Edwards, Franklin. "The Banking Competition Controversy." *National Banking Review*, vol. 3, September 1965, pp. 1–34.

9. ———. *Regulation of Foreign Banking in the United States: International Reciprocity and Federal-State Conflicts*, Columbia University Graduate School of Business, research paper no. 64. New York: Columbia University, 1974.

10. Horvitz, Paul M., and Shull, Bernard. "The Impact of Branch Banking on Bank Performance." *National Banking Review*, vol. 2, no. 2 (December 1964), pp. 143–89.

11. Jacobs, Donald P. *Business Loan Costs and Bank Market Structure: An Empirical Estimate of Their Relations.* New York: National Bureau of Economic Research, 1971, occasional paper 115.

12. Klopstock, Fred H. "Foreign Banks in the United States: Scope and Growth of Operations." *Monthly Review,* Federal Reserve Bank of New York, vol. 55, no. 6 (1973), pp. 140–54.

13. Knight, Robert E. "Reserve Requirements—Part I: Comparative Reserve Requirements at Member and Nonmember Banks." *Monthly Review,* Federal Reserve Bank of Kansas City, April 1974, pp. 3–20.

14. Kohn, Ernest. *Branch Banking, Bank Mergers and the Public Interest.* New York State Banking Department, 1964.

15. Mayne, Lucille S. *The Effect of Federal Reserve System Membership on the Profitability of Illinois Banks, 1961–63.* University Park: Pennsylvania State University, 1967.

16. Meyer, Paul A., and Pifer, Howard W. "Predictions of Bank Failures." *Journal of Finance,* September 1970, pp. 853–68.

17. Piper, Thomas R. *The Economics of Bank Acquisitions by Registered Bank Holding Companies.* Federal Reserve Bank of Boston, research report no. 48, March 1971.

18. Rose, John T. *An Analysis of Federal Reserve System Attrition since 1960.* Board of Governors of the Federal Reserve System, staff economic study no. 93.

19. Rose, Peter S., and Fraser, Donald R. "State Regulation of Bank Holding Companies." *The Bankers Magazine,* Winter 1974, pp. 42–48.

20. ———. "The Pattern of Bank Holding Company Acquisitions." *Journal of Bank Research,* vol. 7, no. 3 (Autumn 1976), pp. 236–40.

21. ———. "Banker Attitudes toward the Federal Reserve System: Survey Results." *Journal of Bank Research,* vol. 8, no. 2 (Summer 1977), pp. 77–84.

22. Rose, Peter S., and Scott, William L. "Risk in Commercial Banking: Evidence from Postwar Failures." *The Southern Economic Journal,* June 1978.

23. Sinkey, Joseph F., Jr., and Walker, David A. "Problem Banks: Identification and Characteristics." *Journal of Bank Research,* Spring 1975, pp. 208–17.

24. Smith, David L. "The Performance of Merging Banks." *Journal of Business,* April 1971, pp. 184–92.

25. Stuhr, David P., and Van Wicklen, Robert. "Rating the Financial Condition of Banks: A Statistical Approach to Aid Bank Supervision." *Monthly Review,* Federal Reserve Bank of New York, September 1974.

26. U.S. Congress, House Committee on Banking and Currency, Subcommittee on Domestic Finance. *Twenty Largest Stockholders of Record in Member Banks of the Federal Reserve System.* 88th Congress, 2d sess. Washington, D.C.: U.S. Government Printing Office, 1964.

27. U.S. Congress, Senate Committee on Banking, Housing and Urban Affairs. *Special Survey of Bank Stock Loans, Loans to Officials, and Major Stockholders of Other Banks, Insider Loans and Overdrafts.* U.S. Senate, March 16, 1978.

28. Varvel, Walter A. "A Valuation Approach to Bank Holding Company Acquisitions." *Economic Review*, Federal Reserve Bank of Richmond, July–August 1975, pp. 9–15.

29. Weintraub, Robert, and Jessup, Paul. *A Study of Selected Banking Services by Bank Size, Structure, and Location.* Subcommittee on Domestic Finance of the House Committee on Banking and Currency. Washington, D.C.: U.S. Government Printing Office, 1964.

30. U.S. Congress, House Committee on Banking, Currency and Housing. *Financial Institutions and the Nation's Economy.* Discussion principles, House of Representatives, 94th Cong., 1st sess., Title VI (1975).

8

Liquidity management

The management of liquidity is an important aspect of the financial management of every financial intermediary. In terms of the model presented in Chapter 1, liquidity management is a central part of Stage II production—the management of assets. Since all financial institutions engage in maturity intermediation—borrowing short and lending long—they are necessarily placed in a potentially illiquid position. Such potential illiquidity must be planned for, the amount of needed liquidity estimated, and a strategy developed for providing the liquidity in the amount required and at the necessary time. The basic concepts involved in liquidity are common to all financial institutions—bank and nonbank, depository and nondepository, contractual and noncontractual—although the degree of the problem and hence its concern to management will vary markedly among different institutions. The discussion of liquidity management below is in terms of the commercial bank, but only minor modifications will need to be made to extend the analysis to most other financial institutions. Indeed, the needed modifications to this analysis for other financial institutions should diminish over time as nonbank financial institutions attain the legal authority to offer third-party payments services and become more like commercial banks in other ways also.

LIQUIDITY OF AN INDIVIDUAL ASSET, FINANCIAL FIRM, AND THE FINANCIAL SYSTEM

In discussing liquidity management, it is important to distinguish between a liquid financial asset and a liquid financial institution. A liquid financial asset is one which can be turned into cash quickly and with little loss to the seller. Hence, a liquid asset is characterized by a relatively stable price and its speedy conversion into cash (i.e., marketability) if the seller needs cash in a hurry. In contrast, a liquid financial institution is defined in terms of the amount of liquidity needed *relative* to the ability of the firm to provide this liquidity through a reduction of financial asset holdings *or* through other means such as borrowing in the open market (liability management). A financial institution is liquid if it can meet all the demands made for cash against it at precisely those times when cash is demanded. It must maintain a sufficient reserve of cash and near-cash assets and/or be able to borrow sufficient funds to meet both anticipated and unanticipated cash drains. Moreover, whatever sources of cash the financial institution chooses to draw upon, these must be available at reasonable cost and in timely fashion. Thus, a financial institution which is forced to borrow at exorbitant rates on an "emergency" basis or is forced to sell securities at deeply discounted prices in order to raise cash is not adequately liquid.

One financial institution may have a large amount of liquid assets as compared to other firms and still be relatively illiquid at least compared to its own needs for liquidity. In contrast, another institution may have a relatively small amount of liquid assets (as compared to total assets) and still be quite liquid compared to its own needs. This distinction points up the difficulties involved for both internal management and outside analysts in determining the appropriate amount of liquidity for an individual financial institution. Given this problem, it is probably not surprising that many financial institutions maintain excessive liquidity.

The liquidity of an individual financial institution should also be distinguished from the liquidity of the financial system. Management of an individual financial institution through careful planning and anticipation of deposit and loan changes can control its liquidity to a substantial extent. Management may establish a policy of a relatively large or small amount of liquidity relative to anticipated needs for funds, depending upon risk preferences, risk factors, and other considerations. In creating such a policy, it must naturally recognize the important trade-off between liquidity and profitability. Since the yield curve usually is upward sloping—higher interest rates associated with longer-term, less liquid financial assets and lower yields associated with shorter-term, more liquid financial assets—management of a financial institution must decide if it wants to "sleep well or eat well." It can minimize its liquidity, take the funds released from the liquid assets and invest longer term in order to gain a higher return (perhaps obtaining liquidity for unexpected needs through borrowed funds), but at a greater risk, both in terms of having insufficient liquidity at a crucial time, and also with regard to the interest and perhaps credit risk associated with the longer term assets. Conversely, management can minimize its risk of illiquidity by keeping large amounts of liquid assets relative to its anticipated needs, but earn less on the short-term assets.

While individual firm liquidity is a management decision variable, the liquidity of the financial system is not under the control of the management of individual financial institutions. The liquidity of the financial system is determined basically by the Federal Reserve System. In the conduct of monetary policy the Federal Reserve may increase or decrease the system's liquidity. For example, if the Fed wished to accelerate the economy's rate of growth the various techniques of monetary control—open market operations, reserve requirement changes, and changes in the discount rate—could be used to increase the liquidity of the financial system. Conversely, if the Fed wished to curtail the expansion of the economy it would be expected to reduce the liquidity level of the economy.

BANK LIQUIDITY

Table 8–1 presents information on selected liquid assets at commercial banks expressed as a percentage of total assets: cash and due

TABLE 8–1
Selected liquidity ratios for insured commercial banks, June 30, 1978

	All banks
Cash and due from banks/Total assets	13.4
U.S. Treasury securities/Total assets	8.3
Securities of other U.S. government agencies/Total assets	3.4
Security of states and political subdivisions/Total assets	10.0

Source: *Federal Reserve Bulletin*, February 1979, p. A18.

from banks, U.S. Treasury securities, securities of U.S. government agencies, and securities of states and political subdivisions (municipals). Cash and due from banks include a variety of different items: vault cash, deposits held by member banks at Federal Reserve banks for purposes of meeting legal reserve requirements, deposits held by member and nonmember commercial banks at other commercial banks in order to "buy" services from the other banks, and cash items in the process of collection. U.S. Treasury securities include all issues which are direct obligations of the U.S. government regardless of maturity, although most holdings at commercial banks are relatively short term in nature. Federal agency securities primarily include those of the farm credit agencies (the Federal Land Banks, Federal Intermediate Credit Banks, and the Banks for Cooperatives) as well as Federal National Mortgage Association and Federal Home Loan Bank issues. Most of these federal agency issues held by commercial banks are also short term in nature. Securities of states and political subdivisions include all securities which are commonly referred to as municipals.

The data provided in Table 8–1 present only crude approximations to the liquidity position of individual banks. Not all the securities are short term in nature, nor are all cash assets (such as legal reserves) available to meet deposit needs or loan demands. Moreover, liquidity can be provided from the loan portfolio as well as from other securities. And perhaps especially important, liquidity can be provided by borrowings as well as through asset liquidation. Nevertheless, the data at least provide a basis for discussion of commercial bank liquidity.

As would be expected given the deposit structure of commercial banks, the typical commercial bank maintains a substantial share of total assets in the form of cash and short-term securities. Indeed, as of mid-year 1978, all insured commercial banks in the United States held over 25 percent of total assets in these forms. The amount of total funds devoted to these uses is, however, a function of the size of the bank. The cash and due from bank ratio rises sharply as bank size increases. The association of this ratio with bank size reflects the substantial role of larger banks in the clearing and collection of checks which, in turn, is reflected in large "cash items in the process of collection" balances.[1] In addition, the Federal Reserve requires larger commercial banks to maintain a higher proportion of demand deposits in the form of reserves. In contrast, U.S. Treasury and federal agency security holdings diminish markedly as bank size increases. Large banks may be more conscious of minimizing their short-term securities portfolio and this inverse relationship with bank size also reflects the use of purchased money (federal funds, etc.) as a mean of providing liquidity at the larger banks.

One of the most significant developments in commercial banking (and also at nonbank financial institutions) in the post-World War II

---

[1] See Chapter 6 for a more thorough discussion of this point.

period has been a sharp decline in liquid asset holdings and a change in the manner in which banks meet their liquidity needs. Commercial banks ended World War II with enormous holdings of U.S. government securities, reflecting their financing of the government's war effort. But in the postwar period, the banking system has been confronted with intense loan demand, rising costs of money and labor, and pressure on profit margins. Reflecting these factors, bank management has reduced to a substantial extent its holdings of short-term highly liquid assets. Indeed, whereas U.S. Treasury bills were once central to bank liquidity management, today many commercial banks hold few U.S. Treasury securities beyond those required for pledging purposes.

Another important development has been a shift in emphasis away from asset management to provide liquidity towards liability management. Traditionally, sources of funds at commercial banks were viewed as being determined basically by factors external to management control. However, with the development of the federal funds market, CDs, and other sources of borrowed funds, commercial banks, especially large commercial banks, have increasingly relied upon nondeposit borrowed funds to provide liquidity. It is not an exaggeration today to assert that liquidity management at commercial banks encompasses total portfolio management, using assets and liabilities together as a part of management planning. (This approach has sometimes been referred to as funds management.) More will be said about liability management later in the chapter.

PRIMARY AND SECONDARY RESERVES

Within an asset management perspective, liquidity requirements for commercial banks have been met traditionally from primary and secondary reserve holdings. Primary reserves refer to cash assets held to meet legal reserves requirements and for other operating purposes. While these assets are not all available to satisfy liquidity needs (since a large proportion must be held as legal reserves and as correspondent balances), primary reserves are still the first line of defense against daily demands for cash. Moreover, there is even some flexibility in legal reserve balances which the regulatory authorities require banks to hold. For example, reserve requirements for member commercial banks must be satisfied only on a daily average basis for a reserve week. Hence, a bank could use some of these cash assets during the week for liquidity needs as long as the average level of reserves for the entire week was satisfactory. Primary reserve holdings also include operating cash assets such as deposits at other commercial banks used to compensate these other banks for services rendered. There is some flexibility in the amount of these deposits also.

Most liquidity derived from the asset portfolio of a commercial bank is provided by *secondary reserves*. Secondary reserves refer to those assets which are primarily held for liquidity purposes; that is, those assets which can be converted into cash quickly and with little risk of loss in value. While most secondary reserves take the form of short-term, marketable securities, such as U.S. Treasury bills, portions of the loan portfolio (such as commercial paper) may legitimately be viewed as secondary reserves. In addition, not all of the short-term marketable securities portfolio of a bank should necessarily be included in secondary reserves. For example, during periods in which interest rates are expected to increase, it would be a reasonable portfolio policy to shift from long-term to short-term securities. These short-term securities would have high liquidity but their primary function is to provide income rather than liquidity.

THE MONEY POSITION IN LIQUIDITY MANAGEMENT

The money position of a commercial bank refers to those assets held to satisfy legal reserve requirements.[2] The goal of bank management should be to minimize holdings of these assets since they earn no interest. For a large bank, specialized staff would ordinarily be employed in order to anticipate changes in the availability of reserves and to dispose of excess reserves at attractive rates in the federal funds market or in other money market investments. For small banks, the amount of interest lost through idle reserves is less significant and usually does not justify the use of a specialized staff. As a result, excess reserves at large banks are normally a much lower percentage of total reserves than at the smaller banks, and frequently are zero or even negative, requiring the bank to purchase reserves from other banks overnight or for a few days in the federal funds or Eurodollar market or from the Federal Reserve's discount window.

The legal restrictions on a commercial bank in the management of its money position should be understood. Since the legal requirements for state nonmember commercial banks are specified separately for each of the states, our discussion is in terms of banks which are members of the Federal Reserve System. These banks do, of

---

[2] Of course, certain other financial institutions also must meet legal reserve requirements imposed by federal and state authorities. For example, savings and loan associations are required to hold at least 7 percent of their assets in cash and liquid securities. See Chapter 13 for a discussion of savings and loan reserve requirements.

course, hold the bulk (about three fourths) of the deposits of all commercial banks in the nation.[3]

The following rules apply to member commercial banks under the Fed's Regulation D:

First, the reserve requirement rules pertain to a given statement week. A statement week is a seven-day period which begins on Thursday and ends on Wednesday. Friday and Wednesday are especially important days—Friday since the bank's position as of the close of business on Friday counts for Saturday and Sunday, and Wednesday since it is the last day on which reserve adjustments may be made.

Second, all important variables—deposits, reserves held at the Federal Reserve, and vault cash—are measured on a daily average basis over the seven-day statement week.

Third, the reserve requirements which must be met during the current statement week are determined by the volume of deposits two weeks prior; that is, the amount of required reserves in the statement week ending on Wednesday, June 15, depends upon the volume of deposits (on a daily average basis) in the statement week ending June 1. As a result of these "lagged reserve requirements," the money manager for the bank knows at the start of the current reserve week what the bank's required reserves are for the entire week.

Fourth, the amount of vault cash which can be used to satisfy reserve requirements this week is the quantity held two weeks prior. Thus, the amount of vault cash which can be used to satisfy required reserves in the statement week ending on Wednesday, June 15, is the amount of vault cash (on a daily average basis) which the bank maintained in the statement week ending June 1. Not only does the money manager know the amount of reserves which the bank must have this week but the manager also knows the amount of vault cash which can be used to satisfy these requirements.

Fifth, any excess or deficiency in meeting required reserves during the current statement week can be carried over to the following statement week as long as that amount does not exceed 2 percent of required reserves. That is, excesses or deficiencies of up to 2 percent of required reserves in the statement week ending June 15 can be carried over and settled in the statement week ending June 22. Reserve deficiencies of more than 2 percent would require an explicit penalty charge equal to 2 percent more than the discount rate, while reserve excesses of more than 2 percent would incur an implicit penalty in potential lost income.

The money manager for an individual commercial bank then has a

---

[3] There is a trend away from membership in the Federal Reserve System, and large numbers of banks have withdrawn from the system in recent years. See Chapter 7 for a discussion of the reasons behind this development.

number of factors which must be considered in the planning process: the volume of required reserves, the amount of vault cash which can be used to satisfy these requirements, and the amount of deposits at the Federal Reserve (which can, of course, also be used to satisfy legal reserve requirements). Since the introduction of lagged reserve requirements (where required reserves and vault cash in the current statement week are based upon past levels of deposits), the money manager has known the amount of required reserves for this statement week and the vault cash usable for this statement week at the start of the week (on Thursday). Hence, management of the money position really is narrowed to controlling the volume of bank deposits at the Federal Reserve so that, on average during the statement week, these deposits are just at the right level—neither so much as to produce excess reserves (which would result in a loss of income) nor too little to produce a reserve deficiency since that would incur a penalty charge (if the amount was outside of the 2 percent limit set by the Federal Reserve for the carryover privilege). At larger banks with a multitude of transactions during a business day, this becomes a very complicated process. At smaller banks it is less burdensome.

A volume of deposits at the Federal Reserve in excess of anticipated amounts may occur during the statement week. This development may result from unanticipated deposit inflows, either directly or through a favorable clearing balance with other banks, or from prepayment of loans by businesses or consumers. As another possibility, especially for a relatively large bank, one of the bank's correspondents may have sold federal funds to the bank. If our bank is an accommodating bank, it would offer—as one of the services it provides to correspondents—to buy federal funds regardless of its own reserve position. In any case, the reserve balance at the Federal Reserve could become excessive for any of these reasons as well as for a large number of others.

Since the goal of reserve management is to keep the volume of excess reserves at a minimum, the money manager would wish to dispose of these reserves as soon as possible. There are, of course, a number of possible uses of these funds. The money manager could sell federal funds to other banks which were in need of reserves due to deposit withdrawals, adverse clearing balances, or other reasons, or the money manager could invest in other money market instruments, such as U.S. Treasury bills, bankers acceptances, or commercial paper. The particular instrument chosen would depend upon the relative yields available on these money market instruments and other factors. However, it would be affected greatly by the amount of time the money manager expects the reserve position to be in surplus. Expansion of the loan portfolio generally would not be considered unless it was expected that the reserve surplus was permanent. In the converse situation—a reserve deficiency—the money manager would again look at the alternatives available. Traditionally, with asset management, attention would be focused on the use of short-term securities, especially U.S. Treasury bills. However, with liability management, reserves could be borrowed in the federal funds market if the cost were lower. Indeed, most such short-term reserve adjustments are now made through federal funds borrowings rather than through asset liquidation.

If the reserve position of this bank was in surplus on Thursday and Friday but was expected to swing to a deficit on Tuesday and Wednesday of the same statement week, the implications for the investment strategy of the money manager would be quite different then if the reserve surplus is expected to persist for a number of weeks. In the former case, the amount of transactions costs associated with the purchase of Treasury bills today and their subsequent sale later in the same period probably would eliminate this particular money market instrument as a viable alternative and would also eliminate bankers acceptances and commercial paper. In this circumstance, federal funds transactions would be the most liquid and appropriate money market instrument. Moreover, even though the money manager might anticipate a surplus to persist for some time, there is always a degree of uncertainty associated with any such expectation. As a result, the first course of action today for most banks is to dispose of surplus funds in the federal funds market and wait to see if the surplus continues. If the reserve surplus turns out to be longer term, then the money manager can make some permanent adjustments. In both cases—short-term reserve adjustment and anticipated longer-term reserve adjustment—the money manager is likely to use the federal funds market as the primary means of initial reserve modifying actions.

As discussed briefly at an earlier point, reserve management techniques vary considerably with the size of the bank. Small banks often plan their reserve positions so that a surplus volume of deposits at the Federal Reserve builds up early in the statement week. As this excess develops, the smaller banks sell these reserves, thereby eliminating most or all of the reserve surplus by the end of the week. In contrast, many larger banks operate their reserve position in a much more aggressive manner. These banks often plan their loan and investment policies so that a reserve deficiency will develop during the statement week. If the reserve deficiency does indeed occur as planned, it is eliminated by purchasing reserves in the federal funds market or, if the deficiency is expected to persist for a longer period, by reducing liquid asset holdings or selling large CDs to business firms. Moreover, many of these larger banks seek to increase returns by anticipating intraweek changes in the federal funds rate. For example, if the money manager expected that the federal funds rate would be high early in the statement week (Thursday and Friday) but low in the latter part of the statement week (Tuesday and Wednesday), additional returns on bank assets might be obtained by selling federal funds early in the statement week (and thereby deliberately creating a reserve deficit) and buying federal funds later in the week (thereby eliminating the reserve deficit). This action is possible since legal reserve requirements do not have to be met each day, but only on average over the statement week.

MANAGING THE MONEY POSITION: AN EXAMPLE

The procedures and problems involved in managing the money position of an individual commercial bank can perhaps best be explained through the use of a simple example. As illustrated in Table 8–2, ABC National Bank has total (gross) demand deposits of about $46.2 million in the statement week two weeks prior to the current statement week. However, reserve requirements for a member bank of the Federal Reserve System are not computed on gross demand deposits, but rather on net demand deposits where net demand deposits are defined as gross demand deposits less cash items in the process of collection and also minus demand balances due from banks. In this illustration, net demand deposits are $30.9 million 46.2 − 6.7 − 8.6). The reserve requirements imposed on time deposits are related to gross time deposits. Time deposits (gross) average $25.7 million during this earlier statement week.

Reserve requirements for the current statement week can then be calculated based upon these previous deposit levels. If reserve requirements for demand deposits are 12.5 percent of the volume of net demand deposits, then total reserve requirements this statement week for demand deposits are $3.86 million. Similarly, if reserve requirements for time and savings deposits are 3 percent, then total reserve requirements for these deposits are $722,000.[4] Hence, total reserve requirements this statement week amount to $4.6 million. However, currency and coin (vault cash) holdings from the prior period ($446,000) may be used to satisfy part of these requirements. Therefore, the money manager must have on average during the

---

[4] Actually, the reserve requirement ratio is an increasing function of the size of deposits. For example, as of January 31, 1979, reserve requirements on net demand deposits ranged from 7.00 percent for the first $2 million to 16.25 percent for those net demand deposits over $400 million. A constant ratio for all deposits is used here only for purposes of illustration.

TABLE 8–2
Estimate of required reserves for ABC National Bank ($000)

Balance as of:	Demand deposits	Deductions from demand deposits		Net demand deposits	Time deposits	Currency and coin
		Cash items in process of collection	Demand balances due from banks			
Thursday	45,264	6,462	8,406	30,396	24,362	356
Friday	46,822	6,842	8,623	31,357	25,863	484
Saturday	45,222	6,432	8,422	30,368	26,402	456
Sunday	45,222	6,432	8,422	30,368	26,402	456
Monday	45,222	6,432	8,422	30,368	26,402	456
Tuesday	48,462	7,222	9,023	32,217	25,222	427
Wednesday	47,222	7,235	9,045	30,942	25,436	486
Average for statement week	46,205	6,722	8,623	30,860	25,727	446

statement week a total on deposit at the Federal Reserve Bank in its district equal to $4.14 million.

Suppose that actual deposits at the Federal Reserve on Thursday (the first day of the statement week) were $6.8 million by the end of the day due to unanticipated deposit inflows. With a reserve requirement of only $4.14 million, the bank has roughly $2.7 million in idle funds which would earn a substantial return if invested. The money manager would certainly want to put these funds to work as quickly as possible, especially if interest rates in the money market were relatively high. For example, at an interest rate of 7 percent, the lost income per day would exceed $500 if these funds were not usefully employed. And this lost income would be almost identical to lost profits since there would be few costs and little risk involved in using the funds. The only real question is where to put the funds and for how long. The initial placement would most likely be in the federal funds market. Then, as the week unfolds and as the average quantity of excess reserves becomes better known, the money manager may wish to place any excess in Treasury bills or some other asset depending upon relative yields available in the money market and the length of time for which the funds can be invested.

SECONDARY RESERVES

Management of the secondary reserve position of a commercial bank is closely related to the control of its money position. Secondary reserves refer to those assets—primarily short-term securities—which can or will be converted into cash in the near term. As such, secondary reserves automatically will become cash assets and thereby add to those assets which are usable to satisfy reserve requirements. Moreover, since most assets held as secondary reserves are highly liquid, these assets may be turned into cash prior to maturity at the discretion of management. Again, as with managing the money position, it should be kept in mind that liquidity can be provided through borrowing (liability management) as well as through liquidation of secondary reserves (asset management).

There are a number of steps involved in the management of secondary reserves. The beginning of this process is the estimation of the amount of liquidity needed. While this is a subjective judgment there are procedures which are useful in estimating the needed amount. Once the needed volume of secondary reserves *is* determined, management must then determine the manner by which this need will be met. For example, it might be that during the next six months management has estimated that total liquidity needed is $1.5 million. This liquidity could be provided by selling Treasury bills, bankers acceptances, or other money market instruments as well as by borrowing. A choice must be made among these particular instruments. Moreover, it may be that of the total $1.5 million, $250,000 is required in each month. Management could then invest in securities which mature at the time the liquidity is needed or it could invest for a longer term and sell the securities prior to maturity. Again, a choice must be made among these alternatives. As another possibility, management might not hold any particular assets to satisfy these anticipated liquidity needs but could buy the liquidity through liability management (probably in the federal funds market) at the time funds are needed.

In estimating the need for liquidity over some particular planning period, it is important to recognize that liquidity must be provided *both* for deposit withdrawals and for any increases in loans, both anticipated and unanticipated. Naturally, the bank must meet the demands of depositors for their funds. Moreover, it should plan to honor all legitimate loan requests from credit customers regardless of its funds position. There are a number of reasons why loan demands may be viewed in the same context as depositor withdrawal requests. First, financial institutions exist to serve the credit needs of the local community. As such, each institution must be prepared for unanticipated demands for funds by its business and consumer accounts. Moreover, from a narrower perspective, an intermediary must be able to provide loanable funds to customers in periods of stringency if it wishes to maintain their deposit accounts. Business firms especially tend to maintain deposit accounts where they are able to obtain satisfactory credit accommodation.

There are a number of approaches which might be employed in estimating the exact liquidity needs for an individual bank. Two are especially prominent: the structure of deposits method and the sources and uses of funds approach.[5] Both take into account the liquidity required for deposit withdrawals and in order to satisfy loan demand. These approaches are not necessarily mutually exclusive; both may be used to produce a more precise estimate of liquidity needs.

The structure-of-deposits method

This strategy for estimating liquidity needs focuses on the nature and stability of a bank's deposits and seeks to divide total deposits into groups based upon the anticipated probability of loss over some specified planning horizon. For example, deposits may be

---

[5] For a more detailed discussion of liquidity estimation, see [1].

classified according to the probability of withdrawal as short-term, medium-term, and long-term (stable) deposits. Short-term deposits would have a very high probability of being withdrawn within the planning horizon. These deposits—which would probably be dominantly demand deposits though they could also include some savings and time deposits—would require a very high liquidity reserve. Medium-term deposits would have a high probability of being withdrawn during the planning horizon though a lower probability than the short-term deposits. These deposits would require a large liquidity reserve though less than that required for the short-term deposits. Long-term or stable deposits are those which have a very low probability of withdrawal and require a low liquidity reserve. In each case, the exact liquidity reserve needed for the different types of deposits is subject to the judgment of bank management. Moreover, if necessary, the deposit categories could be divided into a much larger number of groups.

Once the liquidity needed for deposit withdrawals is estimated, it is necessary to add to this figure the liquidity needed to take care of expected and unexpected loan demand. This amount may be estimated in a number of ways. One approach is simply to examine past data and extrapolate loan demand based upon secular trend. Cyclical and seasonal factors in past loan data may also be estimated and the trend figures adjusted for their effects. Another approach is a direct forecast of loan demand based upon the best judgment of the bank's loan officers. Larger institutions will hire a professional staff of economic analysts to assist in making such forecasts. Smaller institutions frequently will rely on larger correspondent banks or economic consulting firms for estimates of economic conditions and the likely strength of future credit demand. Whatever the source of the estimates, recognition must be given to the particular phase of the business cycle in the national economy, any special local factors which might affect loan demand, and the competitive position of the bank in its relationship to other financial institutions in the local market.

Sources and uses of funds approach.   This approach begins with the proposition that, for any given planning horizon of interest to management, it *is* possible to estimate anticipated *changes* in deposits and loans. Any withdrawal of deposits or increase in loans represents a use of funds. Conversely, any increase in deposits or any decrease in loans is a source of funds. This technique requires a coordinated forecast of deposit and loan changes over the appropriate planning period. For example, in the fall of the year, management may wish to plan liquidity levels for the coming year. They might then forecast the amount of loans and deposits at the end of each month of the coming year. Month-to-month changes in these loans and deposits (added together) would then provide an estimate of liquidity needs over the planning period.

As we noted above, planning liquidity needs must also take into account external factors which are likely to affect the forecast of loans and deposits. For example, variations in business cycle conditions and monetary policy are especially significant variables in influencing the liquidity needs of an individual commercial bank. In periods of business expansion, inventory levels frequently move up substantially. Customarily these inventory accumulations are financed with short-term bank credit. As such, bank management should anticipate especially heavy loan demand during periods of business expansion. Moreover, in these periods, especially if they are associated with inflationary price movements, monetary policy is usually taking steps to curtail the availability of bank reserves and reduce the growth of bank credit. At the individual bank level, this development might be reflected in a slowdown in the growth rate of deposits or even a decline in deposit levels. Hence, bank management should be prepared for liquidity pressures to be especially severe in periods of economic expansion as loan demand rises and deposits fall off. In contrast, in periods of economic slack, liquidity pressures would be reduced as loan demand diminished and deposit growth expanded.

Management must also take into account local economic conditions. It may be that the national economic situation is buoyant and yet local loan demand may be weak due to the closing of a manufacturing plant in the local community or the existence of a drought if the local economy is agriculturally based. Conversely, the national economy may be weak and local loan demand may be buoyant. It is too often overlooked that the U.S. economy contains vast differences in types of local economic movements and that national trends may be a poor source of information about developments in the service area of the bank.

The estimation of liquidity needs through the sources and uses of funds approach can perhaps best be explained through the use of a simple example. Table 8–3 provides data on anticipated loans and deposits for a six-month period for a hypothetical bank. The estimates might be provided by the research department of a large bank or by line officers in the case of a smaller bank. In any event, the estimates assume that all legitimate loan requests will be met during the planning horizon. We note from Table 8–3 that loans are expected to increase through March and then decline from April through June (column 2). Since increases in assets represent uses of funds, the increase in loans anticipated in February and March will require that funds be provided either by inflows of deposits or liquidation of other assets. It is anticipated that deposits will expand in February (al-

TABLE 8-3
Estimation of liquidity needs ($000)

(1) Month	(2) Total loans	(3) Total deposits	(4) Change in loan deposits		(5) Funds required
January	42,000	60,000	—	—	—
February	43,500	61,000	1,500	1,000	500
March	44,000	61,000	500	0	500
April	43,500	60,000	(500)	(1,000)	500
May	43,000	60,000	(500)	0	(500)
June	42,500	59,500	(500)	(500)	0

though not by enough to provide the total funds needed for loans) and that, subsequently, deposits will fall in both April and June (see column 4). The net effect of all these movements is summarized in column 5 (funds required). This shows that with loan and deposit movements taken together, the bank can anticipate a liquidity need of $500,000 in February, and another $500,000 each in March and April. However, after April no further liquidity must be provided in May and June. Indeed, in May there will be excess liquidity amounting to $500,000.

These estimates are, of course, subject to a wide margin of error, and they leave out the reserves required for deposit increases (and thereby understate liquidity needs). Perhaps more important, these estimates are usually made as of the end of the month; that is, estimates are usually made of funds needed and provided between the end of one month and the end of another month. Intramonth fluctuations in deposits and loans may require substantial liquidity even though month-end data indicate no important liquidity needs. Finally, there are substantial problems in accurately forecasting economic and financial variables.

LIQUIDITY MANAGEMENT POLICIES

It is not sufficient for a financial institution to merely determine the amount of liquidity which it must hold over some specified planning period. The individual financial institution must also develop a strategy for meeting the anticipated liquidity demands. There are a number of different approaches to this problem that have been adopted by different financial institutions at different periods of time. As noted earlier, the traditional approach stresses *asset management* —that is, control of the mix of assets held both in terms of the nature of those assets (for example, loans versus securities) and the secondary market characteristics of the assets, (i.e., the ability to liquidate the asset prior to maturity). A more recent and more aggressive strategy is *liability management*—that is, the control of the volume of liabilities, especially nondeposit liabilities such as federal funds. In practice, most banks and an increasing number of nonbank financial institutions use both approaches (funds management). However, as a general rule, smaller financial institutions rely more heavily on asset management while the larger institutions often make heavier use of liability management. Naturally, the appropriate strategy in a given decision situation will depend to a considerable extent upon the relative cost of the alternatives as well as the risk preferences of management and shareholders. For example, if borrowing in the federal funds market was a cheaper source of funds than liquidating Treasury bills, we would expect individual financial institutions to follow the former method in satisfying their liquidity needs.

Asset management. A number of different asset management strategies have been developed over the years. One of the oldest is the "real bills doctrine" or the commercial loan theory. This approach maintains that a commercial bank should confine its loans principally to short-term, self-liquidating commercial loans. Since there will be a certain percentage of these loans maturing during any given period, the bank, it is argued, need not be concerned with the formal planning of its liquidity position. This strategy was, of course, more relevant to commercial bank liquidity management in earlier years when bank assets were concentrated in loans to businesses and primarily in short-term loans. Its relevance to today's banking system with a loan portfolio widely diversified as to type and maturity is at best questionable.

Most commercial banks today rely upon the *money market approach* to managing liquidity through the control of assets. This strategy calls for the meeting of liquidity needs by holding money market instruments, such as Treasury bills, commercial paper, or bankers acceptances. The amount and maturity of these money market instruments should correspond to the amount and timing of the expected liquidity need. For example, if a commercial bank expected that it would need $1 million in March, $2 million in April, and $4 million in May (after examining its potential loan demand and deposit flows over these periods), the bank could buy $1 million of Treasury bills which mature in March, $2 million which mature in April, and $4 million which mature in May. The bills would then be maturing as funds were needed. Moreover, if the estimates of liquidity were inaccurate and liquidity was needed prior to the anticipated dates, the Treasury bills could be sold since they do have a very good secondary market. Similar investment strategies could be followed with commercial paper or bankers acceptances, although commercial paper has a much weaker secondary market than either Treasury bills or bankers acceptances.

While the easiest strategy is to match the maturity of the liquid assets held with anticipated liquidity needs, this is not the only possible technique. For example, an aggressive commercial bank might seek to increase its yields on secondary reserves by "riding the yield curve." This strategy consists of buying securities which have a longer maturity than the expected holding period; that is, funds which are needed in March might be invested in securities which mature in October. The October maturing securities then would be sold in March prior to their maturity but at the time the funds are needed. Such a strategy might increase yields since the longer-term securities would be expected to carry a higher expected return (if the yield curve is upward sloping) than the shorter-term securities. Moreover, the yield might be increased further since the bank may realize a capital gain on the sale of the securities if the structure of the yield curve had not shifted to an appreciable extent. In contrast, however, the higher return through riding the yield curve could be eliminated through transactions costs and the possible capital loss which could be incurred if the yield curve shifted upward during the period the securities were held.

Liability management

In recent years as noted earlier, many commercial banks, especially the larger ones, have begun to manage their sources of funds (liability management) rather than only their uses of funds (asset management) in order to meet anticipated liquidity needs. This shift in strategy toward liquidity management has been a part of a larger shift toward more aggressive financial management at commercial banks and other financial institutions. Instead of investing in particular money market instruments or being concerned about the liquidity of the loan portfolio, this strategy would not explicitly provide for liquidity *until* the funds are needed. At that time, the bank would *buy* the liquidity in the money market by one of a number of different techniques. If the need was very short term (one day or only a few days), the federal funds market would most likely by used. In contrast, if the funds needed were for a longer period (say three weeks), the bank could increase the rates paid on its large certificates of deposit and obtain funds through this device. As another possibility, the larger banks could borrow funds in the Eurodollar market, probably through a London branch of a U.S. bank.

The main advantage of liability management is the potential increase in income. With liability management, the bank is able to keep a smaller quantity of funds, on average, committed to short-term investments in money market instruments and thereby can keep a larger quantity of funds invested in longer-term securities and loans. Since the yield curve is normally upward sloping, the bank should expect to increase its return on total assets. However, liability management also entails higher risk. Interest rates may be quite high at the time that the individual financial institution is seeking to acquire funds. This is especially likely if the funds requirement stems from business cycle conditions and the operation of monetary policy. Moreover, the individual commercial bank may find that funds are virtually unavailable in quantities desired by the bank. This may be especially true in periods of financial stress and concern about the stability of an individual bank. Perhaps the most appropriate policy for liquidity management is some judicious mixture of asset and liability management, depending upon relative cost, risk, and other considerations.

QUESTIONS

8–1. What is the difference between a liquid asset and a liquid financial institution?

8–2. What important trends exist in bank liquidity management? Do you expect those trends to continue? Why?

8–3. Differentiate between primary and secondary reserves. What are legal reserves? excess reserves?

8–4. What does the money position of a commercial bank refer to?

8–5. What is a statement week? Show how it is related to a bank's money position? What are lagged reserve requirements?

8–6. Into what three groups are deposits frequently classified? Of what importance are the classifications for bank management?

8–7. Differentiate between asset management, liability management, and funds management?

8–8. How would the liquidity demands placed upon a commercial bank differ over the course of the business cycle?

8–9. What are the risks and rewards involved in liquidity management?

REFERENCES

1. Baughn, William H., and Walker, Charls E., ed. *The Bankers' Handbook*, Homewood, Ill.: Dow Jones-Irwin, Inc. 1978, pp. 411–32.

2. Crosse, Howard, and Hempel, George. *The Management of Bank Funds.* Englewood Cliffs, N.J.: Prentice-Hall, 1973, chap. 8–9.

3. Reed, Edward W., Cotter, Richard V., Gill, Edward K., and Smith, Richard K. *Commercial Banking.* Englewood Cliffs, N.J.: Prentice-Hall, 1976.

4. Woodworth, G. Walter. "Bank Liquidity Management." *The Bankers Magazine,* Autumn 1967, pp. 66–78.

5. ———. "Planning Bank Liquidity Need." *The Bankers Magazine,* Summer 1968, pp. 22–32.

Problem for discussion

This chapter has discussed the procedures by which a financial institution could estimate the amount of liquidity it needs and develop a strategy for meeting that liquidity requirement. The problem situation discussed below presents the student with an opportunity to apply the principles discussed in this chapter to liquidity analysis for a large commercial bank. The student should place him/herself in the position of the bank's liquidity manager and, after reviewing the material, should address the following questions:

1. How much liquidity does the bank need? When does it need this liquidity?
2. Does the bank need additional liquid assets? If so, where should it get the added liquidity? If it has too much liquidity, what should it do with the excess funds?
3. How would interest rate forecasts affect these decisions?

The Third National Bank is a multibillion dollar, full-service commercial bank located in a major metropolitan area. While it offers a complete range of banking services, it concentrates on business lending (wholesale operations), trust services (trust assets exceed bank assets), and international banking (branches in London, Paris, and Geneva as well as in other areas around the world where it is quite active in the Eurodollar market). But perhaps its most distinctive attribute is the bank's emphasis on planning. Senior management at Third National Bank is dedicated to thorough and complete profit planning. Each fall the bank engages in an extensive review of the goals of the organization for the coming year and the specifics of how these goals are to be achieved. The process is approached with great seriousness by both junior and senior bank officers. Budgets are set with the active participation of department heads. Profit center goals are established and each loan officer is viewed as a profit center. Moreover, at quarterly intervals during the year variances (differences between the planned amount and the actual figure) for revenues and expenses are analyzed in order to isolate unfavorable factors before they have a serious impact upon the bank. These policies have met with some degree of success, although the bank has also benefited from location in an area with a robust economy. Earnings per share have increased each quarter (on a year-to-year basis) for more than five years, and the price of the bank's common stock has moved up substantially despite a lethargic stock market. The bank's price-earnings ratio is currently 14. Moreover, the loan loss experience of the bank in recent years has been quite good. Apart from a few problems with a commercial real estate development, the bank has encountered no real difficulties with the quality of its loan portfolio.

Third National Bank is located in one of the most rapidly growing areas of the "sunbelt." Based upon heavy industry (especially oil refining and petrochemicals), the local economy has experienced vigorous growth throughout the postwar period. In recent years, however, the growth has accelerated as large numbers of corporate headquarters have moved into the area. As a result, the nature of the local population has changed markedly with increased emphasis upon middle-class business and professional people and decreased importance of the blue-collar worker. The growth in the local economy has meant that local demand continually presses on the lending capacity of the bank. Unlike most banks throughout the nation in this period, Third National did not have any shortage of loan demands; indeed the bank was almost forced to ration loans even to its best customers. The major problem facing the loan function at Third National was the constant demand for loans from large manufacturing firms which exceeded the legal lending limit of the bank. (See Exhibit 1.) Since the capital base at the bank as of year-end 1978 amounted to $170 million, the bank's total loans to any one customer could not exceed $17 million. Moreover, since the community served by Third

EXHIBIT 1
THIRD NATIONAL BANK
Balance Sheet, December 31, 1978 ($000)

Assets		Liabilities and Capital	
Cash and due from banks	$ 250,000	Demand deposits (IPC)	$ 800,000
U.S. government securities	200,000	Demand deposits–banks	400,000
Federal agency securities	20,000	Other demand deposits	200,000
Obligations of states and		Savings deposits	300,000
political subdivisions	425,000	Time deposits	1,300,000
Loans	2,275,000	Capital:	
Total assets	$3,170,000	Capital stock	30,000
		Surplus	30,000
		Undivided profits	60,000
		Subordinated debentures.....	50,000
		Total liabilities and capital	$3,170,000

National Bank consists mostly of relatively small banks, the major competition for these loans is out-of-state banks and this makes loan participations with these same banks quite difficult.

Liquidity management at Third National Bank is based principally upon forecasts of interest rates, deposit flows, and loan demands made by the Economic Research Department. The information provided for the coming year is summarized in Exhibits 2 and 3. It appeared that interest rates in the short-term money market were expected to rise moderately. The three-month Treasury bill was fore-

EXHIBIT 2
Third National Bank interest rate outlook (prepared by Economic Research Department)

| | Interest rates (in percent) | | | | | |
| | 1978 | | 1979 | | | |
Short term	III	IV	I	II	III	IV
3-month Treasury bill	7.31	8.57	8.82	9.25	9.95	9.60
Federal funds	8.09	9.58	9.80	10.10	9.90	9.95
4–6-month prime commercial paper	8.03	9.83	9.85	10.25	10.50	10.32
Long term						
AAA corporate bonds	8.94	9.23	9.62	9.54	9.32	9.42
U.S. government bonds	8.53	8.78	8.92	9.04	8.94	8.92
AAA municipals	6.16	6.28	6.18	6.14	6.02	6.00

| | Deposits and loans (annual rate of change, in percent) | | | | | |
| | 1978 | | 1979 | | | |
	III	IV	I	II	III	IV
M-1	8.1	4.4	3.2	3.0	3.4	2.2
Time and savings deposits	11.3	12.4	8.4	6.2	6.4	5.3
Total loans and investments	10.8	7.7	6.5	7.2	8.3	8.2

EXHIBIT 3
Loan and deposit forecast for Third National Bank (prepared by Economic Research Department)

| | | Deposits ($000) | |
Period	Loans ($000)	Demand	Time and savings
1978 IV	$2,675,000	$1,525,000	$1,900,000
1979 I	2,575,000	1,500,000	1,950,000
1979 II	2,675,000	1,550,000	2,000,000
1979 III	2,875,000	1,575,000	2,050,000
1979 IV	3,000,000	1,600,000	2,150,000

EXHIBIT 4
Third National Bank short-term security holdings,
December 31, 1978

Security	Holdings ($000)
U.S. Treasury securities maturing within:	
3 months	$ 10,000
3–6 months	75,000
6–9 months	80,000
9–12 months	25,000
12–15 months	10,000
Obligations of states and political subdivisions maturing within:	
3 months	10,000
3–6 months	10,000
6–9 months	10,000
9–12 months	10,000
12–15 months	10,000

cast to increase from an 8.57-percent yield in the fourth quarter of 1978 to 9.60 percent in the fourth quarter of 1979, a gain of 103 basis points. Similar increases were expected for other money market rates. However, long-term rates were not expected to show much change. The liquidity manager also received a list of short-term security holdings classified by type of security and maturity as of October 31, 1978 (Exhibit 4). This list did not represent all the liquid assets held by the bank as it omitted the liquidity of the loan portfolio (including $100 million in commercial paper) as well as the cash assets that could temporarily be drawn upon.

9

Lending policies

Lending is a vital activity for most financial institutions. Not only do loans represent the largest commitment of funds for depository financial institutions (commercial banks, mutual savings banks, savings and loan associations, and credit unions), but they also produce the greatest share of the total revenue generated from all earning assets. Moreover, it is in the lending function where depository financial institutions generally accept the greatest risks. The failure of individual commercial banks and other depository financial institutions is usually associated with problems in the loan portfolio and is seldom the result of shrinkage in the value of other assets. In summary, most bank funds as well as the funds of other depository financial institutions are committed to loans, the bulk of their revenue is generated by loans, and the bulk of risk is centered in the loan portfolio.

Lending is not only significant quantitatively for the individual institution, but also plays an important part in the social function which financial institutions perform in the economy. In terms of the model presented in Chapter 1, the lending function is at the center of Stage II—the mangement of assets. Management must appraise the returns and risk characteristics of loans as compared to securities and must evaluate the relative attractiveness of different types of loans. This appraisal is complex since the loan function is central to the basic credit-granting role of the financial institution and also since loans differ widely in degrees of risk.

Lending is the basic reason-to-be for the commercial bank and other deposit-type financial institutions. Most financial intermediaries (especially the deposit type) are local in nature; their funds are drawn from a relatively local market area and their loans are usually made within an even smaller geographic area. Local consumers and businessmen depend essentially upon local financial institutions for credit. The fulfillment of this credit need by commercial banks and other depository financial institutions may be viewed as a social commitment or obligation of the institution subject, of course, to the constraints of minimum profitability and maximum risk. This social function performed by lending is perhaps even more significant for the other depository financial institutions which, for the most part, have been mutual organizations designed to pool the funds of individuals with a common bond or purpose and make loans to these same individuals.

The present chapter initially presents basic information on the composition of the loan portfolio at commercial banks—the most important U.S. financial institution in the lending field. Since this composition cannot be understood within an historical vacuum there is also some discussion of important trends in the loan portfolio. However, most of the chapter is devoted to the importance of a loan policy at a commercial bank and of the procedures involved in implementing such a loan policy. As such, the discussion is quite general in nature and is essentially applicable to any lending institution, bank or nonbank.

COMPOSITION OF THE LOAN PORTFOLIO

Table 9–1 presents a percentage classification of loans at all insured commercial banks as of December 31, 1977. The traditional emphasis on lending to businesses by commercial banks is evident from the information presented in Table 9–1. Loans classified as commercial and industrial accounted for about 20 percent of all loans while loans to farmers which are also essentially business loans, though to a particular segment of the business community, accounted for nearly 16 percent of the total loan portfolio. Moreover, real estate loans, many of which are short-term, interim construction loans to businesses, accounted for the single largest fraction of the loan portfolio.

The sharp differences in the composition of the loan portfolio at banks of different sizes is also evident from Table 9–1. For the largest

TABLE 9-1
Percentage distribution of bank loan portfolios, December 31, 1977 (percent of total loans)

Nature of loan	All banks	Banks with total assets of ($millions)					
		Under 5	5–9.9	10–24.9	25–99.9	100–299.9	300 or more
Real estate loans	33.5	24.1	29.5	34.1	37.3	37.2	29.7
Loans to farmers	15.6	30.9	25.7	17.1	7.7	2.3	1.7
Commercial and industrial loans	19.7	15.4	16.0	18.1	22.0	28.1	32.7
Loans to individuals	28.6	27.0	26.7	28.5	30.6	28.5	25.4
All other loans	2.6	2.6	2.1	2.2	2.4	3.9	10.5
Total	100.0	100.0	100.0	100.0	100.0	100.0	100.0

Source: Federal Deposit Insurance Corporation, *Bank Operating Statistics, 1977*.

size grouping (banks with total assets of over $300 million), the commercial and industrial loan was the largest single type of loan. These types of loans are not only extremely important at the larger banks but are also quite cyclical. Much of this type of lending is done for inventory expansion by the borrowing firm. Since inventory holdings of businesses are highly unstable, loan demand also fluctuates markedly. In fact, changes in business inventories are one of the most important influences on short-term fluctuations in the volume of loans outstanding at larger banks.

In contrast, commercial and industrial loans are much less important for smaller banking institutions. For example, at the smallest size group (banks with under $5 million in total assets) over 30 percent of the loan portfolio was accounted for by farm loans. Many of these smaller banks are situated in rural areas where agriculture (including both farming and ranching) is the dominant industry. This type of lending involves both short-term production loans to farmers and ranchers as well as more permanent, long-term agricultural financing. However, most bank loans to farmers are relatively short term in nature, perhaps because funds are available from the government-sponsored credit agencies to provide permanent funds at attractive rates. Moreover, loans to individuals tend to be especially important at small- and medium-size banks which frequently are located in residential areas and suburban communities. For banks between $25 and $100 million in total assets, these loans comprise about 30 percent of total loans. Loans to individuals encompass lending for the purchase of automobiles, bank credit card loans, and a variety of other types of credit directed at household needs.

The loan portfolio of commercial banks has changed drastically in recent years. In general, there has been a decreasing relative emphasis upon business lending and an increase in concentration on consumer and real estate lending. This drastic change reflects shifts in the economy and the financial system, as well as in the relative rates of return on different types of loans. Bank liabilities which were once primarily demand deposits are now mostly time and savings accounts. Reflecting the longer-term nature of bank liabilities and also the more costly aspects of these sources of funds, banks have lengthened their loan portfolios and have increased their emphasis upon real estate related loans. As an example, term loans for the purchase of equipment and buildings are now of great significance at many banks.

There has also been a revolution in the attitude of the financial system toward meeting the borrowing needs of the consumer. At one time, consumer credit was viewed as a socially unproductive use of funds by a commercial bank. With the post-World War II emphasis on the consumption of durable goods and the need to finance these p- chases, however, attitudes of bankers and others in the financial community have shifted. Commercial banks now actively solicit consumer accounts both for the purchase of durable goods and for other uses. This change in the loan portfolio has brought commercial banks into active competition with a new group of financial institutions (particularly finance companies, credit unions, and savings banks) and has tended to blur the distinction among different kinds of financial institutions.

Bank loan portfolios also reflect variations in geography. Banks located in rapidly growing portions of the nation and having substantial amounts of time and savings deposits place more emphasis on real estate lending than banks operating in more mature economic environments and depending more heavily on demand deposits as a source of funds. For example, real estate loans made up 34 percent of the loan portfolio of commercial banks in Arizona as of year-end 1977. In contrast real estate loans comprised less than 22 percent of the loan portfolio at commercial banks in North Dakota as of the same date.[1] These two states also vary widely in the degree of urbanization, the economic base, and hence the demand for different kinds of loans. To a very considerable extent the loan mix of an individual financial institution must reflect the nature of the economic base of the market area served by that institution.

LOAN POLICIES: DEVELOPMENT
AND IMPLEMENTATION

In view of the importance of lending to the financial health of the individual financial institution and to the community it serves, every financial institution must carefully plan its lending operations. Careful consideration should be given to at least two major factors. The lending institution needs some general guidelines or loan policies to assist those involved in making loan decisions. Without such guidelines, individual loan officers are likely to make judgments which are inconsistent with the goals of the organization and which are inconsistent internally from loan officer to loan officer. Moreover, the development of a loan policy forces senior management to grapple with a number of complicated issues and to face significant concerns such as how much risk the institution is prepared to accept in its loan portfolio. Also, a loan policy can be an indispensable aid in the training of new employees. Beyond establishing a loan policy, however, the institution needs to be concerned about how individual loan applica-

---

[1] Federal Deposit Insurance Corporation, *Bank Operating Statistics, 1977.*

tions are evaluated. Here, the most common approach is to establish a set of criteria for evaluating each application. These criteria are usually referred to as the *Cs of credit*.[2]

There are a number of important procedures involved in the establishment of a loan policy. The policy should be written, though the degree of formality of a written loan policy may be a function of the size of the financial institution. While it would be impossible to discuss all of the items which should be incorporated into a written loan policy, some of the most important ones should be mentioned. The policy should provide some general guidelines concerning the desired volume of lending. Since lending is the principal function of a commercial bank, for example, we would expect that the loan portfolio would dominate the asset structure. However, bank management must allocate funds to meet reserve requirements as well as to satisfy anticipated liquidity needs caused by deposit withdrawals. (The same problem is faced to varying degrees by savings banks and credit unions.) In addition, management may wish to hold a substantial amount of longer-term securities in order to achieve asset diversification as well as to minimize tax payments through municipal security investments. Moreover, the size of the loan portfolio will be affected by the credit needs of the community as well as the ability of the financial institution to meet those credit needs. For example, an intermediary may be located in an area of strong deposit potential but weak loan demand. Moreover, the management of the institution may not have the expertise to service the particular kinds of loan demand provided by the local community.

The loan policy should contain some reference to the mix of credits which the institution is to emphasize and what might be an appropriate balance of each in the loan portfolio. Such specification should be made within the framework of the demand for credit in the local economy as well as the size of the intermediary and the expertise of its management. If the local economy is based on agriculture, the loan portfolio of the institution will necessarily be heavily weighted toward credits to farmers and ranchers and business firms serving the needs of farmers and ranchers. Moreover, a small financial institution normally faces a severe limit on the size of its loans to any one customer which may, in turn, reduce the proportion of its loans to business. For example, commercial banks chartered by the federal government (national banks) and many of those chartered by the states are restrained from lending more than 10 percent of their capital, surplus, and undivided profits to any one borrower. For many banks, especially in unit banking states which prohibit branching,

---

[2] For a more complete review of these factors, see [1], pp. 541–55.

this restriction may present an important constraint in the lending program and, thereby, reduce the long-term growth of the institution.

A loan policy would also include reference to customer changes and fees for loans and related terms associated with the loan contract. There are a number of aspects of the interest rate issue which are important. The institution must appraise the degree of credit risk and other factors which should affect the interest rate charged. An important issue concerns how to adjust the rate charged as the perceived risk of the loan varies. One possibility is to group loans into risk categories and vary the interest rate from category to category. The lending institution must also decide if it is to set a fixed rate or a floating rate on its loans. If the institution desires to establish a floating rate it must decide what rate the loan contract rate should be related to. Short-term loans might be expected to have fixed rates while longer-term loans are more likely to have floating rates, though the decision to establish a fixed or floating rate depends on other factors besides the maturity of the loan, such as the strength of loan demand. Generally, floating rate loans are tied to the prime interest rate (the rate charged to the highest quality customers for short-term loans). For example, the loan contract may specify that the loan rate will be equal to the prime + 2 percentage points (200 basis points). However, this provision may run into the problem that in recent periods of high interest rates lenders, especially commercial banks, have been under political pressure to hold down increases in the prime rate.

An integral part of the loan interest decision concerns compensating balance requirements. Compensating balances refer to non-interest-bearing deposits (some commercial banks allow time deposits to be used) which the borrower is required to maintain at the lending institution as a condition of the loan. Management must decide on the amount of compensating balances required and on what types of loans compensating balances will be required. Moreover, decisions about the maturity of different kinds of loans must be made. For example, banks have increasingly been extending the maturity of their auto loans to four years or more. Such a movement reflects the increased cost of automobiles and the desire on the part of lenders to prevent a sharp increase in monthly instalment payments. Management must decide whether their institution should participate in this trend. As a part of this decision, it naturally needs to have some estimate of the implications for loan demand of the desire to restrict its lending to shorter-term car loans. Many banks incurred substantial losses on real estate related loans in the mid-1970s. Does management wish to continue its participation in this type of lending at all? These are important questions that management must confront in a fast-changing financial environment.

Additional issues in the formulation and implementation of a loan policy involve the extent to which the lender will accept different kinds of credit arrangements. Are there certain kinds of collateral the lender will not accept? Also, management must decide what types of loan commitments will be accepted. Will the lender issue letters of credit? If so, under what conditions? How is the financial institution to decide the amount and the terms of these credit lines?

These are only a few of the issues that must be dealt with in the formulation of loan policy. Perhaps their greatest importance is that they force management to consider critical questions before the lending institution drifts into an undesirable position. Potential problems are less likely to become actual problems if the intermediary anticipates these problems.

Loan policies: An illustration

A sample loan policy for commercial banks has been provided by the American Bankers Association in its pamphlet, "A Guide to Developing a Written Lending Policy," (1973). This pamphlet lists the following elements of a written loan policy: bank objectives, determination of lending policy, lending policy administration, lending authorities, loan committee organization, experience and depth of loan staff, geographic limitations, interest rates, credit criteria, coping with "grey" areas, credit file requirements, credit life policies, and substandard loans. A brief discussion of the major items follows.

Clearly, the development of a loan policy must begin with the objectives of the institution. Development and reexamination of the loan policy provides the directors with an opportunity to evaluate the role of the bank or other lending institution in community economic development, its support of small business, and other important issues. Recognition must be taken that the objectives of the institution are multifaceted, and some ranking of these objectives must be established. In fact, as discussed earlier, one of the major problems facing financial institutions' management is reconciling different and to some extent mutually conflicting objectives. Internal objectives such as earnings, liquidity, and acceptable risk levels must be specified. Once these goals have been determined, the board of directors must establish policies or rules which are consistent with these objectives. In doing this, it must be recognized that under both state and federal law, as well as common law established by judicial decisions, the board of directors remains ultimately responsible for the activities of the institution.

It is vitally important that procedures be established for the efficient administration of the lending function. The responsibility for administration of the lending function should be clear. Lending authorities for each individual and for the various committees in the institution should be specified. Most commercial banks, for example, have specific dollar limits or authority for different personnel. These limits generally increase as the responsibility and experience of the loan officer advances until—at some point—certain officials of the bank have loan authority equal to the legal lending limit of the institution. A delicate balance must be reached between establishing too low and too high loan authorities for individual officers. Loan limits which are too low will discourage the progress of individual loan officers, force senior management (including the board of directors) to review an excessive amount of small quantity loans, and perhaps drive away larger customers. Conversely, loan limits which are too high add risk to the institution's loan portfolio in that inexperienced loan officers may commit the institution to undesirable loans. Certainly, it would be expected that the distribution of loan limits among individual loan officers would vary with the size of the lending institution.

The loan policy should also describe the functions of the loan committee organization. While there are no definite patterns for the organization of a loan committee, loan committees generally meet weekly or more frequently in order to consider loans that are in excess of some particular amount or outside the normal credit standards of the organization. The loan committee should be supported by a credit analysis group which has regular contact with the loan officers and also has access to all relevant credit files. At smaller commercial banks, for example, the size of the organization precludes setting up a separate credit analysis group, and loan officers must do their own investigation and analysis. At a few large banks, where a credit analysis department is feasible, operating policies still call for individual loan officers to perform their own credit investigation as a means of maintaining closer knowledge of the prospective borrower.

Loan policy should include some reference to the trade area of the lending institution. It might specify a primary trade area within which loans should be sought and also a secondary trade area which might be investigated more fully when loan demand from the primary trade area was weak. Naturally, the relevant trade area will vary with the size of the institution. A small financial institution generally should consider the local community and its immediate environment as the primary trade area. In contrast, a medium-size lending institution may consider a particular region as its primary trade area while the largest institutions may consider the entire nation and even some foreign countries as falling within their trade area.

One important deficiency at many financial institutions in the past concerns the maintenance of records on borrowers, referred to as credit files. The exact credit file requirements for different kinds of loans should be specified in the written loan policy. Certainly the lender should have a credit file for every borrower and, in fact, may face serious difficulties with examiners if the credit files are not properly maintained. While the file may be large or small depending upon the particular characteristics of each loan, such as size and collateral, the file should provide all the important information necessary for the credit decisions, including complete financial statements for the prospective borrower. It is particularly important that the credit file contain sufficient information to justify the institution's decision on the loan application, whether that decision is positive or negative.

Commercial banks, as the most important lending institutions, have had substantial difficulty in recent years with the quality of their loans. Following the 1973–74 recession, loan losses at commercial banks mounted to particularly high levels and, at some banks, exceeded by a substantial margin the reserve for bad debts which the banks had amassed over a considerable period. Moreover, there was some evidence during this period that loan losses were not simply associated with the business cycle but also reflected improper lending standards of some institutions. Given these problems, it is vitally important that the individual financial institution include in its written loan policy some procedures for handling substandard loans. While no financial intermediary makes loans which, before the fact, it knows to be substandard, all intermediaries can expect to have some loans that turn substandard after the fact. At larger lending institutions, the number of such loans may warrant the creation of a special department staffed with seasoned loan officers and other specialists who would be available to consult with other loan officers on problem cases or who might even assume responsibility for problem loans (in which case the loans would be transferred from the loan officer to the specialized department). Such a transfer policy does have the advantage of shifting problem loans to those with specialized knowledge (and frequently the legal problems involved with these loans are great), but it has the disadvantage of not forcing the loan officer to live with prior mistakes. While such a policy would be impractical for a small intermediary, it is vital for every financial institution to have some established procedures for handling substandard loans and investments.

Loan policy development

There are a number of factors which management should consider in the development of a loan policy. These include, to name only a few, the volume of capital contributed by the owners of the firm, the character and predictability of funds sources, rates of return on alternative uses of funds, the quality and competence of management of the intermediary, and the nature of demands for funds from the intermediary's existing and potential customers. Moreover, the direct pressure of the regulatory authorities on loan demand and sources of funds should not be ignored.

Financial intermediaries vary widely in the strength of their equity base provided by investors. Some hold substantial amounts of capital while others are deficient in capital and must (over time) eliminate the capital shortage through the gradual retention of earnings or by the sale of stock. (In recent years, capital deficiencies at commercial banks have frequently been reduced through the sale of subordinated debentures.[3]) Since most of the risk in the asset portfolio of a commercial bank, for example, is centered in its loan portfolio, it would be reasonable for management to vary the size and riskiness of the desired loan portfolio with the degree of capital adequacy. Heavily capitalized banks presumably could have large loan portfolios and more risky loan portfolios without exposing depositors to excessive risk; conversely, lightly capitalized banks would need to have a smaller, less risky loan portfolio. Naturally, the size of the loan portfolio also should depend upon the degree to which loan losses on individual loans tend to occur together. Institutions whose individual loans carry large amounts of risk would be expected to have a smaller loan portfolio than those in which individual loans were relatively secure. Moreover, a lending institution whose loan portfolio is concentrated in one geographic area or in loans to one industry should have a smaller proportion of its total funds committed to the loan portfolio than another with a more diversified loan mix.

The capital structure of a lending institution and the size of its loan portfolio, therefore, are interdependent. It is an oversimplification to say that the degree of capital adequacy determines the size of the loan portfolio. Indeed, it may be argued that the size of the loan portfolio as well as the character of investments in securities determines the adequacy of a financial institution's capital. In reality, the two are jointly determined. For example, the Form for Analyzing Bank Capital developed by the Federal Reserve System for use in appraising the adequacy of capital held by member commercial banks requires $1 in extra capital for every increase in loans. Hence, the decision to expand the size of the loan account today requires more capital now and creates the potential for additional required capital in the future should the loans deteriorate in quality.

---

[3] The use of subordinated debentures by commercial banks is discussed in Chapter 11.

Another important influence on loan policy is the relative rates of return from different funds uses. While commercial banks as well as other depository financial institutions exist to provide a service to their customers and should meet the legitimate loan demands of those customers, these services naturally must be performed at a reasonable profit. Rates of return on different loan holdings may vary widely. For example, the *gross* return on consumer loans is substantially higher than the gross return on other types of loans. The Federal Reserve through its Functional Cost Analysis program estimated that the gross yield on instalment loans granted by commercial banks in 1976 was 11.6 percent while the gross yield on commercial loans was 8.9 percent. However, due to the small size of most consumer loans, the processing costs per loan are relatively high and losses on consumer loans are often higher than on business loans. In 1976, the Federal Reserve's Functional Cost Analysis program estimated that the processing costs of a bank instalment loan were 3.8 percent but were a lower percent for a commercial loan. As a result, it is not at all clear that the net rate of return on consumer loans is higher than on other types of loans, particularly after adjustment has been made for risk. It is clear, though, that bankers throughout the postwar period have acted as if the net profit from consumer loans was greater than the net rate of return on other types of bank loans and therefore have increased the proportion of their loans devoted to this use. It may be that the increased emphasis on consumer loans by bank management has lowered the rate of return on these loans so that their net rate of return is no longer higher than for other major categories of loans.

The make-up and predictability of funds sources is also an important factor affecting a financial institution's loan policies. It would be expected, for example, that an individual commercial bank could have a larger loan portfolio for a given deposit base if its deposit flows were more stable and predictable. It is generally agreed that time and savings deposits are more stable than demand deposits, so that a bank with more time and savings deposits usually could expect to commit a larger proportion of its available funds to loans. Moreover, there is greater pressure for a bank with a high proportion of time deposits to make loans since expenses for these types of deposits are high relative to demand deposits. However, in recent years the distinction between the demand deposit and the time deposit has blurred to a considerable extent as customers have increasing flexibility of shifting funds from demand to time and from time to demand deposits. It may be that differences in the stability of these types of deposits may have narrowed appreciably.

External influences also are a vital factor in determining an appropriate loan policy. A declining local economy, for example, will lead to a reduction in deposits and other funds flows and loan demand and may increase the riskiness of both new and old loans. Hence, the institution may wish to shift its relative emphasis away from loans and toward securities depending on the nature of the local economy. Conversely, if the lending institution is located in a rapidly expanding area, both the growth in funds sources and in loan demand should be heavy. Moreover, to the extent that loan markets have institutional rigidities the rates of return on loans as compared to securities may be especially attractive, and the institution making loans directly to borrowers might be expected to maintain a large loan portfolio relative to its investments in securities purchased in the open market.

The influence of stabilization policy (both monetary and fiscal policy, but especially monetary policy) is also important and related to conditions in the local economy. In periods of economic expansion, the demand for loans should be high, while there may be a reduction in the rate of growth of deposits. Conversely, in periods of easy money policies on the part of the Federal Reserve, we would expect that the demand for credit would be relatively slack and the volume of deposits and other funds sources would grow rapidly. Certainly these cyclical factors should be incorporated into the development of a financial institution's loan policies.

Implementation

It is insufficient just to state a general lending policy. Those involved in the lending function must also take these general guidelines and apply them to a specific loan situation, making the final "accept" or "reject" decision based upon both quantitative and qualitative factors. The type of analysis which lies behind the loan decision varies widely from institution to institution. At relatively small commercial banks located in rural areas, for example, great importance is often placed on personal relationships between borrower and lender and less significance is attached to financial statements and objective analysis. In contrast, in urban areas where personal relationships are frequently less stable, more reliance necessarily must be placed on "hard" evidence regarding the credit worthiness of different individuals and businesses. Moreover, in large-scale commercial lending, analysis of financial statements by the credit department of the organization becomes a vital factor.

A number of factors generally are emphasized in lending decisions. These are usually referred to as the Cs of credit. The number of Cs varies from lender to lender, but the following three are commonly used: character, capacity to generate income, and collateral.

Character refers to the personal traits of the borrower (completely apart from financial standing) which may be significant in the credit decision. Terms such as ethical, honest, and integrity are important in this regard. It is often said that character is the most important of the Cs of credit since a dishonest borrower can always find a way to avoid the restrictions imposed by the lender in a loan agreement. Certainly character should be one of the first factors examined by a loan officer. Given acceptable character, then the other Cs of credit can be explored, but if it is found that this C is inadequate, further analysis would not be warranted since, no matter how good the collateral or the financial position of the borrower, the lending institution should not provide a loan to anyone who does not meet its character standards.

Capacity to generate income refers to the ability of the borrower to generate sufficient funds either through liquidation of assets or earnings to repay the loan. Relevant to this question is the quality of management of the organization as distinct from the character of the individuals involved. In a long-term loan commitment, the lender would be inclined to look toward the earning potential of the borrower for repayment of interest and principal. Funds would be invested in permanent assets and the cash flow generated from the operation of these permanent assets would be used to retire the debt. In contrast, funds for short-term loan repayment would come from liquidation of current assets and hence the liquidity position of the firm would be crucial. For long-term loans, focus would be on interest coverage ratios (profitability related to interest payments), while on short-term loans, liquidity ratios would take preeminence. The financial analysis associated with loan applications concentrates on this C of credit.

The type of analysis which is used to evaluate capacity might best be explained through an example which is based on the procedures followed at one particular multibillion-dollar commercial bank in handling large commercial loan applications. The credit department of the bank receives a request from the loan officer to evaluate the financial characteristics of a particular loan applicant. The credit analyst then seeks information from a variety of sources. Financial statements of the applicant are essential but are not sufficient. Additional information comes from tax statements, newspaper clippings, and related sources. It is also important to have information available on the industry in which the applicant operates in order to have available a standard by which to make "good or bad" evaluations. Many such sources are readily available. Government publications and industry trade periodicals are relatively easy to obtain. Financial ratios for various industries can be found in a number of places. One excellent source is the Annual Statement Studies published by Robert Morris Associates, a group of commercial loan officers working for commercial banks. In addition, Dun and Bradstreet publishes useful lists of financial ratios. It is also important for the analyst to keep up with local business conditions, especially if the applicant is heavily dependent upon the local community for sales.

Once the data have been obtained, it is then possible to proceed with the credit analysis which will culminate in a report to the loan officer. Such a report should include at least the following: (1) the purpose of the analysis (whether the request is for a short-term working capital loan or for a long-term capital loan); (2) the previous relationships of the customer with lending institutions (of substantial importance because management is interested in the profitability of the total customer relationship and not simply the profitability of one loan); (3) the business history of the firm; (4) the characteristics of the industry within which the firm operates; and (5) the financial operating factors relevant to the firm.

Analysis of financial operating factors is especially important in determining the ability of the borrower to repay the loan. Both income statement and balance sheet data are relied upon, but the income statement is especially relevant. Trends in income statement ratios are computed. The cash flow position of the firm is estimated in which noncash expenses (such as depreciation) are added back into net profit. In addition, trends in balance sheet ratios are calculated, sources and applications of funds are used, and liquidity and leverage ratios are incorporated into the analysis. The report then concludes with a summary of the findings of the analyst.

The third C of credit is collateral. This refers to the ability of the borrower to pledge specific assets to secure the loan. These assets may be fixed in nature, such as land and buildings, or working capital, such as inventory and accounts receivable. While collateral is important in reducing risk, it should not be viewed as a substitute for adequate earnings potential. Indeed, collateralized business loans generally carry higher interest rates than noncollateralized business loans. Low-risk loans are often made regardless of collateral. Higher risk is frequently offset to some extent by requiring collateral as well as raising the rate of interest charged. However, especially high-risk loans should not be viewed as being made acceptable by collateral requirements. Such loans should not be made regardless of collateral possibilities.

It should also be recognized that lenders are increasingly constrained in their credit decisions by a variety of government regulations designed to assure equal access for all to sources of funds. While the impact of these restraints are greatest in the consumer credit area, they affect a variety of types of loans. Although usury regulations (limits on the maximum rates charged on loans) have been common for some time, the decades of the 1960s and 1970s have resulted in a large increase in the types of regulations applicable to loans made by financial intermediaries. These regulations have included disclosure requirements on interest rates under the Truth-in-Lending Act and substantial restrictions under the Equal Credit Opportunity Act. For example, the Equal Credit Opportunity Act makes illegal discrimination by creditors against potential borrowers on the basis of sex, marital status, race, color, religion, national origin, age, receipt of income from public assistance programs, and good faith exercise of rights by the borrower under the protection offered by the consumer protection acts. In addition, the Community Reinvestment Act requires that the regulatory authorities in evaluating branching and holding company requests take into account the extent to which the financial institution is meeting the credit needs of its community. The impact of such requirements on the quality of loans by banks and other financial institutions is difficult to know at this time, though these requirements obviously limit managerial discretion and increase lender costs. Moreover, the increases in costs associated with the social responsibility loans are likely to make it increasingly difficult for small financial institutions to survive and thereby lead to an even more rapid consolidation of the banking structure.

QUESTIONS

9–1. Examine the relative proportions of the different elements that make up a typical commercial bank's loan portfolio. What are the top three elements in size? What are some of the factors that might affect the relative proportions of loan funds allocated to the different elements in a loan portfolio? For example, how might the size of a financial institution or its geographic location affect the makeup of its loan portfolio?

9–2. What type of information might be found in a financial institution's loan policy?

9–3. What is a compensating balance? What role does it play in lending?

9–4. What is the difference between a fixed interest rate and a floating interest rate?

9–5. What is the purpose of a loan committee? credit files?

9–6. What are the Cs of credit? Examine the characteristics of each one.

9– 7. What factors are considered in a credit analysis of a potential loan recipient?

9– 8. How might government restrictions affect an intermediary's loan policies?

REFERENCES

1. Baughn, William H., and Walker, Charls E., eds. *The Bankers' Handbook.* Homewood, Ill.: Dow Jones-Irwin, Inc., 1978, pp. 541–610.

2. Crosse, Howard, and Hempel, George. *The Management of Bank Funds.* Englewood Cliffs, N.J.: Prentice-Hall, 1973, Chap. 10, 11.

3. Hester, Donald D. "An Empirical Examination of a Commercial Bank Loan Offer Function." *Yale Economic Essays*, Spring 1962, pp. 3– 57.

4. Hodgman, D. R. *Commercial Bank Loans and Investment Policy.* Champaign, Ill: Bureau of Economic and Business Research, University of Illinois, 1963.

5. Reed, Edward W., Cotter, Richard V., Gill, Edward K., and Smith, Richard K. *Commercial Banking.* Englewood Cliffs, N.J.: Prentice-Hall, 1976, Chap. 8– 16.

6. Wood, Oliver G. *Commercial Banking.* New York: D. Van Nostrand Company, 1978, Pt. 4.

Problem for discussion

This chapter has discussed the lending function at financial institutions such as commercial banks. Lending not only produces most of the income of commercial banks but also accounts for most of the risk embodied in the bank's asset structure. As such, the evaluation of individual loan applications—in which bank management must evaluate the loan against its lending policies and perform a credit analysis of the loan—is crucial to the success of the enterprise. The problem situation provided by City National Bank presents students with an opportunity to engage in credit analysis. Students should place themselves in the position of the credit analyst and, after reviewing the material below, should address the following questions:

1. What are the strengths and weaknesses of the loan application of Jones Manufacturing? What financial ratios are most relevant in evaluating the application? What types of industry ratios should be used for comparisons?

2. Should the loan be granted? If not, is there an alternative loan request which would be acceptable to the bank?

Jones Manufacturing is a family-owned firm engaged in the business of producing clothing of various types. Sales are primarily within the Southwest region and the output is marketed under the names of a number of large retailing organizations. The output of the firm includes slacks, shirts, and ready-to-wear suits, with casual and dress slacks accounting for about 50 percent of total sales volume. Founded by Fred Jones' father, George, immediately after World War II, the business has prospered during most of its life, although experiencing financial difficulties during some periods of adverse economic developments nationally. While the sales of Jones Manufacturing were affected to a moderate degree by national economic trends, they were subject to greater swings (as is true of the clothing industry generally) due to changes in taste, fashion, and technology. Many clothing firms which were highly profitable ten years ago are bankrupt today as they failed to adjust to the changing dimensions of the marketplace. As an example of these types of problems, Jones Manufacturing had recently experienced two successive unprofitable years in a row due to a shift in demand from cotton slacks to double knit polyester. Indeed, the most recent year (1978) had been the worst in the company's history. The senior management of the firm had failed to anticipate these developments and had been stuck with stagnating sales and substantial excess inventory which it subsequently was forced to write down in value. Moreover, the shift in sales mix from cotton to polyester also caused production inefficiencies which has further reduced the profitability of Jones (See Exhibits 1 and 2).

Jones Manufacturing was founded by George Jones in 1946. The location in a moderate-size city in south Texas was not attributable to any careful study of economic factors by the elder Jones but simply to the fact that he had served in the armed services during World War II at a local military base, had liked the city, and had chosen to stay and capitalize on his knowledge of clothing manufacturing acquired as a youth in New York City. In one sense, though, the location was fortuitous since there was an abundance of relatively cheap labor which allowed a firm using a labor-intensive production process such as the manufacturing of clothing to gain a competitive edge over rivals from higher cost locations. The firm had grown at a moderate rate in the period from 1946 to 1978 although episodes of rapid growth and high profitability had alternated with those of slow growth and diminished profitability. The instability inherent in the business had caused problems in the local community and especially with the firm's labor force. It seemed as if Jones Manufacturing was always hiring at a frantic pace or laying off at an equally frantic pace. Recently there had been some talk among the workers of attempting to unionize in order to stabilize working conditions.

George Jones had dominated the firm throughout its early life.

EXHIBIT 1
JONES MANUFACTURING
Balance Sheet

Assets	1976	1977	1978
Cash	$ 800,000	$ 600,000	$ 100,000
Accounts receivable	650,000	600,000	800,000
Inventory	1,600,000	2,300,000	2,600,000
Total current assets	$3,050,000	$3,500,000	$3,500,000
Plant and equipment (net)	1,200,000	1,000,000	800,000
Total assets	$4,250,000	$4,500,000	$4,300,000

Liabilities and Capital	1976	1977	1978
Accounts payable	$ 900,000	$1,435,000	$1,785,000
Notes payable–bank	300,000	350,000	750,000
Total current liabilities	$1,200,000	$1,785,000	$2,535,000
Long-term debt	800,000	800,000	800,000
Capital stock	500,000	800,000	800,000
Surplus	500,000	500,000	500,000
Undivided profits	1,250,000	915,000	(335,000)
Total liabilities and capital	$4,250,000	$4,500,000	$4,300,000

EXHIBIT 2
JONES MANUFACTURING
Income Statement

	1976	1977	1978
Sales (net)	$8,250,000	$8,500,000	$ 8,000,000
Cost of goods sold	6,400,000	7,200,000	7,400,000
Gross profit............................	$1,850,000	$1,300,000	$ 600,000
General and administrative expenses	1,200,000	1,400,000	1,600,000
Net profit before taxes	$ 650,000	$ (100,000)	$(1,000,000)
Income taxes	280,000	0	0
Net profit after taxes	$ 370,000	$ (100,000)	$(1,000,000)
Dividends paid	200,000	225,000	250,000

From 1946 until 1968 he had served as president and chief executive officer and currently is chairman of the board of directors. In many respects, the financial position of the firm throughout its history reflected his conservative philosophy. Recognizing the cyclical nature of the business, he had always tried to create a strong balance sheet with high liquidity and low debt which would absorb the financial pressures placed on the firm during periods of adversity. He also hoped to begin times of economic decline with a strong cash position and little short-term debt. The only long-term indebtedness of the firm reflected the expansion of the plant (and the purchase of some adjacent land for further growth in the future which was completed about five years ago). The only exception to this conservative attitude concerned dividend policy. The Jones Manufacturing Corporation had originally been financed through pooling the funds of George Jones and a number of his friends and relatives. George had remained grateful to these supporters and had increased the dividend almost every year regardless of the current profitability of the firm. Many of the original investors were now retired and depended to varying extents on the cash from these dividends for financial support. George Jones further defended this policy by saying that the dividends paid each year were dependent on the long-run profitability of the firm, not on the profits of any one year.

George Jones was playing a steadily diminishing role in the firm. Increasingly he participated only in the strategic decisions of the organization and left the tactical issues to others. In contrast his son, Fred, who had been appointed president and chief executive officer in 1976, was assuming a greater role in the major decisions of the firm. However, it remained clear to all those involved that George Jones retained a veto power over all major decisions. Fred Jones had been brought up to know the business from top to bottom. During the summers throughout high school and college he had worked on various phases of the firm's operations. Moreover, when he graduated from college he was given an intensive one-year training program in all aspects of the firm's activities. He did, however, seem to be most interested in the production side of the business (perhaps reflecting his engineering training in college) and often spent days working on schemes to reduce production costs. Moreover, there was speculation (completely unconfirmed) that George Jones was somewhat disappointed in his son's attention to the details of the business. It was known that the younger Jones spent a considerable amount of time skiing and playing golf.

The specific proposal made by Jones Manufacturing Corporation to City National Bank was the following: City National would extend a five-year, $3 million term loan to Jones for the purpose of repaying existing short-term bank debt (which totaled almost $1 million at the time of the request) and to purchase new equipment required to produce a new blend of polyester fiber slacks.* The slacks—it was said by Fred Jones—resulting from the new blend were substantially superior to any existing material and could command a premium price. Moreover, the new production process would allow output to be established at about 10 percent per unit below existing costs. It was envisioned that within two years this new type of material would allow Jones Manufacturing Company to expand output by 25 percent and that the new material would make up almost 50 percent of the total output of the firm eventually. Currently Jones Manufacturing was operating at less than 75 percent of capacity. As Fred Jones said, "once the production of our existing line gets back to normal and we add the increased output at lower cost associated with the new product, we should have no trouble servicing the debt. In fact, we might very well be able to pay the debt off before maturity."

---

* City National Bank was located 200 miles from the home of Jones Manufacturing. Jones Manufacturing did not maintain a deposit account with City nor had it ever banked from City. The request stemmed from the present friendship of Fred Jones and a senior vice president at City.

10

Investment policies

Investments at commercial banks include those securities which are held principally to provide income (as opposed to those which are held principally for liquidity), and as such are viewed as a substitute for a commitment of funds to the loan portfolio. From the perspective of the functional allocation of funds, management should commit funds initially to meeting legal reserve requirements and otherwise maintaining cash assets sufficient to provide for the necessary operations of the bank (primary reserves). It should then hold a liquidity reserve in the form of short-term securities (or more recently unused borrowing capacity) in order to accommodate unexpected movements in deposits and loans (secondary reserves). Any additional funds should then be allocated to meeting the legitimate credit needs of borrowers. Only if these commitments of funds (primary reserves, secondary reserves, and loans) are insufficient to absorb all the available resources should the bank allocate additional money to securities for the principal purpose of adding to the income of the institution.

Investments as a residual

The investment account is strictly a residual commitment of funds from this vantage point. When loan demand is strong only small amounts of funds may be available to purchase longer-term securities, and indeed existing instruments might have to be liquidated in order to provide funds to meet the higher priority loan demand. In contrast, when loan demand is weak, extra funds may be available to purchase longer-term securities. The residual nature of the investment portfolio at a commercial bank suggests that portfolio management is extremely difficult and implies that capital losses on securities in the investment portfolio should be expected during periods of rising interest rates as a recurring part of funds management. This view would suggest that the funds invested in longer-term securities for income purposes would be quite small and indeed that at some banks (those with heavy loan demand at peak periods) these investments would be zero. It also suggests that the investment account would vary in size over different time periods and for different banks.

While the amount that commercial banks commit to longer-term securities does vary substantially over the business cycle, it appears also that commercial bank management has purposely chosen to permanently commit a fraction of bank assets to the investment account. There seem to be at least two reasons for this decision. The tax factor plays an important role in investment management decisions. Since the commercial bank is exposed to the full burden of the corporate income tax rate (and since the bank's ability to reduce taxable income through loan loss provisions has been reduced in recent years), management has sought additional means to reduce the bank's effective tax rate. While the loan portfolio offers only limited tax reduction opportunities (without taking actual losses), the purchase of municipal securities whose income is exempt from federal income taxes provides an excellent vehicle to shelter income. As a result, banks have invested heavily in the obligations of states and political subdivisions (municipals) regardless of the strength of local loan demand. The success of this policy can be judged by examining the extremely low effective tax rates of some of the nation's largest banks. Moreover, even if the local loan demand is adequate to absorb all available funds, treating the investment account solely as a residual use of funds might lead to a situation in which the asset portfolio of the bank would be excessively specialized in loans based upon a few industries or a few crops in the case of agriculturally oriented banks. Through the investment portfolio, bank management is able to achieve the desired degree of diversification of assets and reduce the risk of failure associated with the faltering of the local economy.[1]

Investments versus loans

While investments and loans have similar functions in terms of providing income, there are a number of significant differences between an investment and a loan. The association between the bank and the customer is quite different for the two types of assets and more complex for loans. There is a direct, one-to-one association between the two parties for loans. Qualitative factors frequently become dominant in the loan decision. In contrast, for investments, the association between the customer and the lender is distant and indirect. Financial data necessarily must assume dominance in the investment decision. For example, it is frequently argued that one of the disadvantages to a company of using commercial paper to obtain its short-term funds as opposed to using more expensive bank credit is the impersonal nature of the commercial paper market. In time of financial distress the impersonal commercial paper market may completely eliminate the customer from short-term credit accommodation, while the bank is more likely to incorporate personal factors into the lending decision and "carry the firm" through bad times.

The originator of a loan generally is the customer. This does not mean that banks do not solicit loans in an active fashion; indeed, banks are often heavily involved in contacts with existing and potential customers for the purpose of developing new loans, and in some respects the most important talent for an aspiring loan officer is an ability to sell the bank. For a loan, however, the customer usually decides that credit is needed, then approaches the bank with a request for credit, and the bank's role is to accept, deny, or modify the credit request. In contrast, in the investment portfolio, the bank in a sense plays a much more active role with much greater flexibility. Bank management determines how many funds are available and then must choose among the many and varied investment alternatives which confront it.

Loans and investments differ also in terms of risk. While both types of assets must necessarily carry some degree of risk (both credit

---

[1] For a portfolio of securities, the appropriate measure of risk for the individual assets is the covariance of returns on the assets with the existing portfolio rather than the variance or standard deviation of the returns on the individual asset. An additional loan drawn from the local market is likely to have a high covariance (high risk) with the existing portfolio. At some point, then, the risk-return mix for securities becomes superior to the opportunities available from the loan portfolio. Moreover, with municipal securities, the bank is able to obtain both a tax shelter and a financial asset with low covariance of returns (provided it is not a local municipal obligation).

and market risk), the greatest risk is in the loan portfolio. The loan portfolio should absorb the greatest risk both because of the basic function of the bank in providing credit to the local economy and also because management, particularly for small banks, has a relative advantage in appraising the risk involved in making a loan. Management has or should have intimate knowledge of the personal and financial characteristics of the customer. Moreover, the rewards to the bank for correctly appraising risk are potentially greater in the loan portfolio than in securities.

THE NATURE OF THE INVESTMENT PORTFOLIO

Table 10–1 presents information on the securities portfolios of large commercial banks in the United States. It should be noted that

TABLE 10–1
Investment holdings of large commercial banks, December 27, 1978 ($millions)

U.S. Treasury securities		$ 41,511
Bills	$ 3,880	
Notes and bonds		
Less than one year	7,979	
One to five years	23,939	
Greater than five years	5,713	
Other securities		71,271
Obligations of states and political subdivisions	52,595	
Tax warrants	6,022	
All other	46,513	
Other bonds, corporate stocks, and securities	18,676	—
Total		112,782

Source: *Federal Reserve Bulletin*, January 1979, p. A20.

the balance sheet classification of securities is in terms of the borrower or issuer of the security (U.S. government, municipal, etc.) and maturity rather than functions (liquidity versus income), though maturity and function are closely related. Not all of the over $100 billion in total securities should be considered as a part of the investment portfolio; a substantial share would qualify as liquid securities in that they are held primarily for liquidity purposes. While the dividing line between those securities held primarily for liquidity and those held principally for income is an arbitrary one, it is conventional to treat securities with a maturity of less than one year as a part of the liquid assets of the bank and those with a maturity of more than one year as a part of the investment portfolio.[2] By this

---

[2] See Chapter 8 for a discussion of the distinction between investments and securities held for liquidity purposes.

criterion, about $20 billion of the total securities portfolio (Treasury bills, notes and bonds maturing in less than one year, and municipal tax warrants) would qualify as liquid assets, and the remaining securities would be a part of the investment portfolio.

Municipals

Those securities which qualify as a part of the investment portfolio today at most commercial banks and especially at large banks are principally obligations of states and political subdivisions (commonly referred to as municipals). Municipals include the debt securities of states, counties, cities, school districts, pollution control governmental units, and other similar governmental units. These debt securities may be either (1) general obligation bonds (GOs) in which case the "full faith and credit" (taxing power) of the governmental unit is available to secure payment of interest and principal; or (2) revenue bonds, whereby the revenue generated from the project (such as a public power authority) is used to pay principal and interest. Revenue bonds have grown faster than general obligation bonds as taxpayers have sought to limit increases in their tax burden.

The major advantage of municipal obligations to the commercial bank is their exemption from the federal income tax. Many commercial banks have found the after-tax return from municipal securities to be quite attractive as compared to taxable instruments. For example, if a commercial bank can obtain a 5 percent pretax return (and the same after-tax return since there are no federal income tax requirements on the interest) from these securities and assuming that the bank is in the 48 percent tax bracket, it would have to earn 9.62 percent on a taxable debt instrument (corporate or government) to provide an after-tax return equal to that of the municipal. It is unlikely that the capital market would provide a return equal to 9.62 percent on taxables when tax-exempt securities are providing only 5.00 percent. Indeed, the spread between municipals and taxable securities of comparable quality is usually considerably less than the 4.62 percentage points in the illustration, although this spread does vary considerably over the business cycle. For example, in December 1978 yields on AAA municipal bonds averaged 5.55 percent. In contrast, yields on AAA corporate bonds averaged 9.04 percent and long-term U.S. government bonds averaged 8.21 percent.

There is another compelling but related argument for the concentration of bank investment portfolios in municipals than higher after-tax returns on these securities. Unlike ordinary investors, the commercial bank is able to borrow funds, deduct the interest paid on these borrowed funds, and yet retain the tax exemption on the municipal securities in which the borrowed funds are invested. This possibility makes municipal investments especially attractive. For example, suppose that the commercial bank pays 5 percent for funds obtained through time and savings accounts. Assuming an effective tax rate of 48.0 percent, the after-tax cost of these funds is 2.6 percent. As long as the bank can earn more than 2.6 percent on municipal securities, it would pay bank management to continue borrowing money (through selling CDs for example) and invest the funds in municipals. At some point, of course, the reduced taxable income would make the municipals unattractive compared to taxable investments, but that point would be where the bank held a large amount of municipals and had reduced its effective tax rate to a substantial extent.[3]

Reflecting these factors, commercial bank investments in municipals have grown enormously in recent years. The major impetus for the expanded role of municipals in bank portfolios appears to be the increase in the potential effective rate of return on these securities. With inflation and the growth of the economy, the total profits of more banks have become subject to the surtax brackets of the corporate income tax. At that profit level, the investment of large sums of money in municipal securities becomes desirable.

Concentration of bank investment portfolios in municipals has created a number of problems for that market and also for individual banks. These problems have centered on the dominance of the market by a few buyers, especially commercial banks. There are only three types of buyers of municipals who are quantitatively significant: commercial banks, property and casualty insurers, and high-income individuals. Of the three, banks are most important and have come to dominate the market. For example, of the $102 billion increase in municipal securities during the 1960 to 1972 period, over $71 billion, or 70 percent, were acquired by commercial banks. Many banks, however, have already used municipals to such a degree that their effective tax rate has been reduced to near zero. Moreover, large banks in particular have found other means of reducing effective tax rates. For example, the invasion of the leasing business by commercial banking organizations has allowed some banks through the investment tax credit and accelerated depreciation associated with the ownership of real property to shield a substantial amount of income from tax. Moreover, many of the nation's largest banks receive a large share of their income from international banking activities. Taxes paid on foreign income create credits against tax liabilities domestically and thereby reduce the effective tax rate paid by these

---

[3] This illustration does of course assume that the explicit interest rate is the only cost of attracting deposits. It also assumes that the bank has taxable income to shelter. Such a policy would probably be of little interest to a new bank.

organizations and make municipal securities less attractive. In addition, as the result of the financial problems encountered in recent years by New York City, Cleveland, and other states and political subdivisions, there appears to have been some shift in attitude by investors toward the credit risk involved in purchasing municipal securities. In the immediate post-World War II era, there seemed to be little differentiation among municipal issues on the basis of credit risk and only a small credit risk premium required by the market. In contrast, recently the market appears to be more discriminating about credit risk levels involved in different kinds of municipal securities, and the risk premium on municipals generally seems to have increased. Furthermore, a number of questions have been raised about the accuracy with which ratings by Moody's and Standard and Poor's portray relative default or credit risk through bond ratings.

U.S. government issues

Banks have historically been large purchasers of U.S. government issues and today remain major holders. As of December 27, 1978, large commercial banks held $23.9 billion in Treasury notes and bonds due in one to five years and almost $6 billion due in more than five years. However, the percentage of bank assets held in the form of direct U.S. government obligations has dropped substantially in recent years. Indeed, a large part of these securities held by commercial banks today are pledged to secure government deposits; that is, are used as specific security for the deposits of the U.S. government and state and local governments. In contrast, commercial banks have become major lenders to various agencies of the federal government such as the farm credit agencies, the Federal Home Loan Banks, and other government agencies designed to foster the flow of credit into specific sectors of the economy. As a result, other bonds, corporate stocks, and securities held by large commercial banks as of December 27, 1978, amounted to almost $19 billion, most of which consisted of investments in agency securities. The principal reason for the increased commitments of bank funds to agencies as opposed to direct Treasury issues is that the agency issues generally are treated by the regulatory authorities as equivalent to direct Treasury securities, have a somewhat higher yield since they are not backed directly by the U.S. government, and also have liquidity characteristics which are almost as good as direct Treasuries. While Table 10–1 provides no information on the maturity composition of the agency issues, and while the maturity holdings will vary widely from one bank to another, holdings of agency issues at most banks are generally short term in nature. Finally, the last category of securities held by commercial banks would include corporate bonds and selected common stock issues, such as the common stock of the Federal Reserve Bank required for Federal Reserve membership.

SECURITY PRICES, RISK, AND YIELDS

The management of every financial institution should understand that the prices of bonds in its portfolio will vary with a number of factors. In particular, prices will be affected by the risk of default (credit risk) and also by changes in interest rate levels (market or interest rate risk), as well as by other considerations. Both of these factors are important in influencing bank investment strategy. However, to some extent, the flexibility of management is much greater with regard to bearing market or interest rate risk than it is with regard to bearing credit risk due to regulatory constraints on the amount of credit risk which the financial institution may accept.

Credit risk

Commercial banks are severely constrained as to the credit quality of the securities they acquire for the investment account. For national banks, there is virtually a complete prohibition of the bank owning equity securities. While member commercial banks may invest in Federal Reserve bank stock and the stock of small business investment corporations, no general investment in equities is permitted. Moreover, there are substantial limitations on the quality of fixed-income instruments in the bank's portfolio. The Comptroller of the Currency permits three groups of securities for national banks. The first kind is one that a national bank both may deal in (make a market), underwrite (create the primary market), and purchase and sell for its own account and may do so without restriction as to the quantity of the individual security in the bank's portfolio. These securities encompass direct obligations of the U.S. government, general obligations of any state or political subdivision, and obligations of federal agencies.

The second kind of securities include those which a national bank may deal in, underwrite, and buy and sell subject to the provision that the total amount of securities in the bank's portfolio from one issue not exceed 10 percent of the sum of capital, surplus, and undivided profits of the bank. This restriction, which is the same one that applies to lending to individual customers, exists to reduce the risk exposure of banks. These securities include certain international agencies such as the International Bank for Reconstruction and Development (World Bank) and revenue bonds issued by states and political subdivisions for housing, university, or dormitory purposes.

The third kind of securities include issues an individual bank may acquire and sell for its own account but may neither deal in nor underwrite. Holdings of these securities also are subject to the 10 percent rule noted above. These include primarily revenue bonds issued by states and their political subdivisions (except those discussed above) and also corporate bonds (including convertibles) and bonds of foreign corporations or governments. Moreover, a bank may not buy speculative securities. Municipal and corporate issues which are rated by the major rating agencies are presumed to be nonspeculative if they fall in the first four rating brackets (so-called investment grade issues). For unrated issues of securities held by the bank, management must be prepared to justify the nonspeculative nature of the securities.

Yield measures

The amount of risk in the investment portfolio is a function of the maturities of investments as well as their credit quality. A fixed-income security carries a coupon rate specified in the indenture. For example, a bond may be referred to as a "7." The coupon rate on this bond is 7 percent; the interest payment to the owner of this bond is 7 percent; and the interest payment to the owner of the security is $70 per year (7 percent of $1,000 which is usually the face value of bonds), normally paid in semiannual installments of $35. The yield to the investor, however, would be 7 percent only if the price paid by the investor were par or $1,000. Should the price deviate from par (as it usually does in the secondary market), the yield to the investor would be other than 7 percent. At a price above par (a premium bond), the yield to the investor would be less than the coupon rate, while at a price below par (a discount bond), the yield to the investor would be above the coupon rate.

There are two frequently used measures of market yield: the current yield and the yield to maturity. The current yield is simply the amount of total dollars received by the investor divided by the price paid for the security. If a 7 percent coupon bond is selling at $800, then the current return (yield) to the buyer of the bond excluding transactions costs is $70/800 = 8.75 percent. While this is all the investor receives currently from the bond, the investor will also obtain at maturity $1,000 (par value) for an asset which cost $800. As a result, the yield to maturity (assuming the investor holds the security until maturity) must be the current return adjusted for the capital gain to be received at maturity (or capital loss if it is a premium bond). The yield to maturity is that rate of discount which makes the present value of the semiannual interest payments during the life of the bond plus the present value of the return of principal at maturity equal to the current market value of the bond. The yield to maturity may be obtained precisely through the use of present value tables or bond books or may be estimated with the use of the following formula:

$$\text{Yield to maturity} = \frac{\text{Annual dollar payment} + \dfrac{\text{Par value} - \text{Cost}}{n}}{\dfrac{\text{Cost} + \text{Par}}{2}}$$

where n is the number of years until maturity. If the maturity of the bond issue in the above example is 10 years, the yield to maturity would be:

$$\text{Yield to maturity} = \frac{\$70 + 200/10}{\dfrac{800 + 1{,}000}{2}} = \frac{70 + 20}{900} = 10\%$$

Price, yield, and risk

A number of generalizations about price, yield, and risk are important to investors planning investment strategy. One of the more important of these concerns the relationship between market risk and maturity:

> The variability of the price of a bond for a given change in interest rates increases as the maturity of the bond increases and decreases as the maturity of the bond decreases. There is, in other words, a direct relationship between market risk and maturity for a given change in interest rates. Since the price of a bond actually represents the present value of the interest and principal payments discounted at the market rate of interest, increases in maturity should result in greater changes in the price of the bond for given changes in rate.

Another way of stating this relationship is as follows:

> The variability of the yield of a bond decreases with maturity for a given change in price. This is merely the reciprocal of the prior statement and partially explains why money market rates generally increase or decrease much more than capital market rates.

The association between market price risk and interest rate movements means that bank management must carefully evaluate its maturity options in planning investment portfolio strategy. Higher yields may be sought by investing in longer-term securities consistent with an upward-sloping yield curve. However, in order to seek this higher return, greater market risk must be accepted in terms of a larger variability of the market price of the portfolio. This price variability is especially important for the investment portfolio since investments do represent, to some extent, a residual use of funds. When loan demand increases, the investment portfolio is often reduced to provide funds to meet the loan demand. Yet increases in loan demand are likely to occur during periods of rising interest rates when liquidation of a long-term investment security would be especially costly and capital losses would be realized.

This problem is reduced to some extent by the historical pattern of rate changes over the business cycle. Longer-term bonds change in price more than short-term bonds *for any given change* in interest rates. However, interest rates in the long-term sector generally do not change as much as rates in the short-term sector. While this does reduce to some extent the extra market risk involved in buying long-term securities, it remains true that a longer-term portfolio carries greater market risk than a shorter-term security portfolio.

INVESTMENT PORTFOLIO POLICIES

All banks and other financial institutions involved in purchasing securities should have a written policy governing the investment portfolio. Such a policy will, of course, vary in terms of complexity and comprehensiveness from financial institution to financial institution. However, there are certain items which are central to every investment program.

Definition and scope

The policy should specify precisely what is meant by the investment portfolio. Since bank balance sheets prepared for accounting purposes are generally divided into cash assets, loans, investments, and other asset categories rather than according to the function performed by the asset (i.e., primary reserves, secondary reserves, loans, and investments), it is not always easy to determine just what is meant by the investment portfolio. The objectives of the investment account and the types of assets which fall within the category should be discussed. As discussed above, the investment portfolio usually consists of longer-term securities since the yield curve is generally upward sloping. However, there are periods when the investment portfolio will be comprised principally of short-term, highly liquid securities. For example, when interest rates are expected to increase, it would be desirable investment strategy for the financial institution to shift some of its investments from long- to short-term securities. This strategy is based upon the widespread argument by financial market participants that a portfolio should be lengthened in periods of rising prices (falling rates) and shortened in periods of falling prices (rising interest rates). The important consideration with regard to identifying the investment portfolio is not the maturity of the asset, but rather the purpose for which the asset is held. If the asset is held primarily to generate income and as a substitute for the loan portfolio, even if the generation of income is viewed over the business cycle, it should be considered as a part of the investment portfolio regardless of whether the security is short- or long-term in maturity.

Credit risk

Clearly one of the most important considerations in drafting a financial institution's investment policy should be the amount of credit risk which it wishes to assume. Management is constrained to a considerable degree in the selection of assets which are to be included in the investment portfolio. Yet, within these constraints, management must decide how much credit risk to assume. At one extreme, the financial institution could concentrate its holdings in U.S. government securities in which the credit risk is negligible. At the other extreme, low-quality municipal and corporate bonds could be purchased.

In making its credit quality decision, management should keep the following factors in mind. First, as discussed earlier, the commercial banks and many other financial institutions cannot purchase securities of a speculative character. This primarily limits the investment portfolio to those rated municipal and corporate securities of investment grade or better as defined by the major rating agencies. Yet there are substantial differences in quality among investment grade issues. For unrated securities, the bank should maintain records which support its contention that the securities are not speculative in nature. Second, investment portfolio policy should be formulated with the understanding that the bank most likely is at a competitive disadvantage when seeking to obtain a high rate of return through its investment portfolio rather than its loan portfolio. In its lending function, the bank usually has detailed personal knowledge of its customer and is operating in an imperfectly competitive market. In contrast, for the investment portfolio, the bank, especially the small bank, is frequently less knowledgeable than other more sophisticated investors and is operating in a highly competitive and efficient market where excess returns are difficult to realize.

Credit risk and return

There are a number of important generalizations concerning risk and return in the securities markets which might be useful to management in guiding the development of an investment policy. First is the obvious positive relationship between risk and expected return. If management wishes to obtain a higher return from its investment portfolio, it must be willing to accept a greater degree of risk. In an efficiently structured securities market there is no "free lunch," especially for the small and relatively unsophisticated investor. This statement, however, should be modified in a number of ways. There is some evidence that the realized (after the fact or *ex post*) return from lower quality securities has been higher (indeed, considerably higher) than the realized return on higher quality securities.[4] This is consistent with the notion that investors are risk averse and must be compensated for bearing risk by additional return. However, the size of the greater return for bearing risk is also consistent with another hypothesis. It is sometimes argued that many institutional investors are constrained through legal and other means to confine their investments to higher quality securities relative to lower quality securities. As a result, it is argued, yields available on higher quality securities are low relative to lower quality issues (on a risk-adjusted basis). The market does not correctly price risk, and there is an opportunity to increase return beyond what would be expected due to the greater risk by investing in lower quality issues. A second modifying comment to the expectation that risk and return are positively related in the capital market is the apparent instability over time of the risk premium. Differences between the yields available on high- and low-grade securities (the risk premium) appear to increase in periods of economic decline and shrink in periods of economic expansion. This suggests that the market overprices risk in periods of economic decline and underprices risk in periods of economic euphoria. If so, investment strategy might be directed to purchasing lower quality issues during recession and shifting to higher quality issues when economic conditions have improved.

Market risk

Another important consideration is the degree of market risk which the bank is prepared to accept. As discussed earlier, interest rate or market risk—the volatility of the market price of the securities in the investment portfolio—increases as the maturity of the portfolio expands. Also, while interest rate risk does rise with longer maturity,

---

[4] See especially Hickman [3].

the relationship between maturity and risk does not appear to be a linear one. Rather, equal additions to maturity appear to be associated with diminishing increments of interest rate risk as maturity increases. Management should specify the degree of interest rate risk it is willing to tolerate. This specification should be both in terms of the maximum maturity it will allow in the investment portfolio for different categories of securities and also the maximum average maturity of the entire portfolio. For example, the investment policy might specify that no municipal security having a maturity longer than ten years should be acquired and the average maturity (weighted by the importance of different securities in the portfolio) should not exceed five years. Naturally, this decision would be heavily influenced by the sources of funds drawn upon by the individual financial institution.

Aggressiveness of management

Commercial banks differ widely in terms of how aggressive the investment portfolio is managed. As a general rule, but with many exceptions, small banks do little explicit management of their investment portfolio while larger banks are frequently heavily involved in active portfolio management.[5] To some extent, this reflects differences in the expertise of management. It may also reflect differences in risk preferences of management and ownership of the bank. Different views on aggressiveness would affect both the maturity of the portfolio as well as the credit risk. In any case, the investment policy should contain some reference to the degree of aggressiveness considered appropriate by each institution.

At one extreme, many commercial banks have traditionally followed a spaced maturity policy. With this policy, management establishes a maximum maturity of eight years or some other number, and then divides its investment portfolio equally among each of the eight yearly intervals. Following this strategy, 12.5 percent of the total portfolio would be invested in securities with a maturity of eight years, 12.5 percent in securities with a maturity of seven years, and so on down to securities with a maturity of one year. Each year, as all the securities move one year forward in maturity, funds realized from the securities which have matured would be invested in issues with an eight-year maturity and the average maturity of the portfolio would remain of equal size.

This policy has a number of advantages. It smooths interest income though it does not necessarily maximize the return from a port-

---

[5] Many small banks have their investment portfolio strategies determined by their larger correspondents.

folio. It requires little or no expertise in security selection and, therefore, is especially suitable in small financial institutions. Similarly, management is not required to follow any particular interest rate forecast. Moreover, this policy should provide an average return over the course of the business cycle. In addition, it is sometimes argued that this policy has the advantage of providing considerable liquidity since a portion of the investment portfolio is quite short term in nature. However, this advantage is of limited validity since the purpose of the investment account is to provide income rather than liquidity. While this approach does have some advantages, it ignores the possibility that excess returns may be made by sophisticated investors through shifting maturity and credit quality in anticipation of changes in economic and financial conditions.

A much more aggressive portfolio policy would call for making major changes in the investment portfolio in response to changes in expectations regarding interest rates and security prices. When rates are expected to rise, the entire portfolio or at least a substantial portion of it would be moved toward short-term maturities. Not only would this allow the bank to avoid capital losses associated with the decline in long-term security prices as interest rate expectations are realized, but it also provides for the possibility of large capital gains when funds are later shifted long term as interest rate expectations are revised. While this type of policy provides the potential for large returns, it also opens the bank to potentially large losses. The success of the policy depends upon the accuracy of interest rate forecasts, and evidence appears to suggest that "experts" have not been able to forecast either the direction or the magnitude of interest rate changes with any degree of accuracy in recent years.

Other factors

To the extent that there are other factors which should bear upon the investment portfolio, these should be included in the policy. For example, if it is the policy of the bank to bid actively for all securities issued by local governmental units in the primary service area of the bank, this should be included in the investment policy. Similarly, the position of the bank with regard to securities pledged to secure public deposits should be specified.

CONCLUSIONS

This chapter has reviewed the nature of the investment portfolio at commercial banks, and the external risk factors that should shape the policies a bank follows toward its investments. To a considerable extent, the policies are applicable to other financial institutions also, especially depository institutions. Securities held for income as well as securities held for liquidity play an important role in total portfolio management at financial institutions. The profitability of financial institutions can be substantially affected by the success of management in controlling the maturity and credit risk levels of investment portfolios. While the principles discussed in this chapter should be helpful in portfolio management, it must be recognized that management must integrate the factors discussed here with those discussed earlier with regard to the management of liquidity (Chapter 8) and the management of the loan portfolio (Chapter 9). Indeed, the management of primary reserves, secondary reserves, loans, and investments must be accomplished within the framework of the management of the capital position of the bank as discussed in Chapter 11. While we necessarily discuss each aspect of portfolio management separately, it must be realized that portfolio management is best approached as an integrated operation.

QUESTIONS

10-1.   Before any funds become available for a commercial bank's investment account they are used to meet other funds needs and demands of the bank. What are these fund needs and demands? How do they affect the bank's investment account?

10-2.   How do securities held for investment purposes differ from those securities held for liquidity purposes?

10-3.   Why would a bank want to hold securities in an investment account? What if the returns were substantially below those on loans?

10-4.   Differentiate between a general obligation bond and a revenue bond.

10-5.   Differentiate between interest rate or market risk and credit risk. How do they affect bank portfolio management?

10-6.   What are the different characteristics associated with the three groups of securities as defined by the Comptroller of the Currency?

10-7.   What is the difference between the current yield and the yield to maturity?

10-8.   What are some of the factors that are important when considering the makeup of an investment policy?

10-9. In reference to commercial bank investment decisions, what is the spaced maturity policy?

10-10. How might a bank structure its investment policies over the business cycle?

REFERENCES

1. Baughn, William H., and Walker, Charls E., ed. *The Bankers' Handbook.* Homewood, Ill.: Dow Jones-Irwin, Inc. 1978, pp. 469-540.

2. Crosse, Howard, and Hempel, George. *The Management of Bank Funds.* Engelwood Cliffs, N.J.: Prentice-Hall, 1973, Chap. 12, 13.

3. Hickmen, W. Braddock. *Corporate Bond Quality and Investor Experience.* New York: National Bureau of Economic Research, 1958.

4. Hodgman, D. R. "The Deposit Relationship and Commercial Bank Investment Behavior." *Review of Economics and Statistics*, August 1961, pp. 257-68.

5. Lyon, Roger A. *Investment Portfolio Management in the Commercial Bank.* New Brunswick, N.J.: Rutgers University Press, 1960.

6. Reed, Edward W., Cotter, Richard V., Gill, Edward K., and Smith, Richard K. *Commercial Banking.* Englewood Cliffs, N.J.: Prentice-Hall, 1976, Chap. 17, 18.

7. Wood, Oliver G. *Commercial Banking.* New York: D. Van Nostrand Company, 1978, Chap. 15, 16.

Problem for discussion

Management of the investment account at commercial banks is a frequently neglected function, especially at small banks. Senior management at smaller banks usually has considerable expertise in lending—the "bread and butter" of banking—but often little or no knowledge of the securities markets. These banks often rely heavily upon larger banks, especially their correspondents, for investment advice. In the problem situation discussed below, the student is asked to assume the role of an outsider and evaluate the investment account of a small bank. After reviewing the material, the student should address the following questions:

1. Does the investment account at First National Bank conform to legal requirements?

2. Does the investment account at First National Bank appear reasonably balanced in terms of maturity, type of securities, and other significant characteristics?

3. What changes in the investment account would you recommend?

4. What additional services might a large bank offer to First National?

Wentworth National Bank—a multibillion dollar institution located in a regional financial center—has concentrated (with a great degree of success) its marketing effort for some years in the correspondent banking area. It has actively and aggressively promoted the services which it offers to smaller commercial banks in the area. These services include, to mention only a few, the following: the clearing of checks for correspondents, where Wentworth maintains that its service is preferable to that provided by the Federal Reserve System for member banks since Wentworth provides immediate credit for cash items and the Federal Reserve defers payment on many cash items for a period of up to two days and because Wentworth does not require expensive sorting and labeling (as the Fed does) of the cash items presented to it. Moreover, Wentworth participates in excess credit lines for its downstream correspondents while also serving these correspondents as an accommodating bank in the federal funds market. Senior management at Wentworth has told the correspondent banking officers that the message to the downstream correspondents should be: "We trust your credit evaluation and will make a decision on an overline request within 24 hours." This policy has been quite successful. Of the total loan portfolio at Wentworth of over $2 billion, close to $500 million consists of loan participations with downstream correspondents. Loan losses in these participations have been minimal, substantially below the losses on the bank's direct loans.

In addition, serving as an accommodating bank has proven to be a successful policy. Most of the downstream correspondents were consistent and predictable sellers of federal funds. While this occasionally created some difficulties for the manager of the bank's money position, it had given the bank the opportunity to expand its loan portfolio (based on regular purchases of federal funds) by a substantial amount. Federal funds purchased by Wentworth from downstream correspondents recently averaged over $600 million per day. In addition to these services, Wentworth offers various types of data processing activities, an area which has disappointed management. It was hoped originally that the use of idle time on the data processing equipment of the bank to service correspondent accounts would prove highly profitable. However, the accounting department of the bank has regularly reported that the activity is unprofitable due to the heavy overhead costs.

The portion of correspondent banking in which Wentworth takes greatest pride is that of rendering financial advice. The marketing program at Wentworth for correspondent banking services stresses the ability of the bank to offer the advice of an expert in almost any area a downstream bank would need. For example, the bank maintains a fully staffed economic research department to offer opinions on the outlook for interest rates, loan demand, and other factors. Similarly, Wentworth has a large trust department with experts on the accounting and legal aspects of trust activities as well as management of the investment portfolio. While many of the downstream correspondents of Wentworth offer trust services, few have the specialized knowledge needed in these areas. Further, Wentworth has experts in particular areas of lending such as oil and gas, real estate, and farm and ranch loans which could be made available to assist correspondents on especially difficult loan applications. Wentworth had recently placed an advertisement in *The Wall Street Journal* which gave the names and pictures of some of their personnel with specialized talent, their academic qualifications, and professional experience.

In view of the importance of correspondent activity to Wentworth (it is estimated that almost one half of total bank funds and more than 60 percent of total profits are associated with this activity), it is understandable that management reacted with some concern to a telephone call from Fred Hess, the president of First National Bank, on Wednesday May 11. First National Bank maintained more than $8 million in total deposits at Wentworth and had done so for some time. The account had relatively small activity and was therefore quite profitable for Wentworth. Moreover, this was the main correspondent account for First National, a bank with total deposits of about $70 million, located in a small, agriculturally based city of approximately 15,000 people. Despite the size of the First National Bank account Hess maintained that Wentworth had done nothing for First National except clear its checks. In particular, Hess, who had recently assumed the presidency of First National after the untimely and unexpected death of the previous president, was concerned about the investment portfolio.

Hess's concern had been prompted by a meeting the day before with a bond salesman from a brokerage house who had said that all forecasts were for sharply higher interest rates and that the bank should sell the bulk of its long-term securities and invest in short-term issues. But more generally Hess was concerned with the quality of investments in terms of maturity, mix, and risk of the securities in the portfolio. His experience included 20 years of making small retail loans and agriculturally oriented credits, and he knew little of the tax and other aspects of managing a securities portfolio. He was therefore appalled to find that no one, except the now previous president, had any real knowledge of investments. Moreover, most of the investments had been made by his secretary (presumably under instructions from the president but no one knew for sure). There was no

EXHIBIT 1
First National Bank investment portfolio, December 30, 1978

Type	Amount (cost)
U.S. Treasury securities:	
Bills—	
Within 3 months	$ 570,000
3–6 months	1,240,000
6–9 months	1,420,000
9–12 months	1,800,000
Total	$ 5,030,000
Notes and bonds—	
Within 1 year	$ 500,000
1–5 years	2,500,000
5–10 years	1,000,000
10–15 years	3,200,000
Total	$ 7,200,000
Obligations of states and political subdivisions:	
Within 1 year	
City of Dallas (AAA) GO	$ 2,500,000
City of Houston (AA) GO	2,000,000
1–5 years	
Texas Municipal Power Authority (AA)	4,000,000
Essex Pollution Control Authority (AA)	3,000,000
Total	$11,500,000
Total investment portfolio	$23,730,000

EXHIBIT 2
First National Bank selected rates of return (in percent)

	1973	1974	1975	1976	1977	1978
Return on U.S. Treasury securities	5.4	6.2	6.1	5.1	5.4	5.4
Return on municipals	3.1	3.8	4.2	4.1	4.3	4.5
Average maturity of Treasury security portfolio (in years)	1.8	2.4	2.2	1.8	2.4	2.6
Average maturity of municipal security portfolio (in years)	1.2	1.8	1.6	1.7	1.8	2.0

EXHIBIT 3
FIRST NATIONAL BANK
Balance Sheet, December 31, 1978 ($000)

Assets		Liabilities and Capital	
Cash and due from banks	$12,000	Demand deposits	$30,000
U.S. government securities	13,000	Time and savings deposits	26,000
U.S. government agencies	—	Other liabilities	1,000
Obligations of states and political subdivisions	12,000	Capital	7,000
Loans	27,000		$64,000
	$64,000		

EXHIBIT 4
FIRST NATIONAL BANK
Income Statement, 1978 ($000)

Total revenue	$3,240,000
Expenses	
Interest on deposits	1,240,000
Wages and salaries	640,000
Provision for loan losses	270,000
Other expenses	460,000
Total expenses	$2,610,000
Net profit before taxes	630,000
Applicable taxes	200,000
Net profit after taxes	$ 430,000

record of any communication about investment management between First National and Wentworth National Bank for at least the past five years. In closing, Hess said that: "If this is the best you can do for us then we just may take our deposits elsewhere. We expect more for our $8 million."

Officers of Wentworth National decided to carefully evaluate the existing portfolio of the bank (Exhibit 1) with regard to any deficiencies in terms of maturity, mix of different kinds of issues, and quality of issues. (See Exhibits 2, 3, and 4.) For purposes of developing an investment policy they took notice of the fact that First National Bank is the dominant bank in a two-bank town, that the economy of the area is stable and diversified, and that senior management expertise lies principally in the area of making loans. Moreover, the bank consistently follows a policy of keeping a small amount of excess reserves in order to reduce its risk exposure and prides itself on having sufficient liquidity to meet all loan requests of satisfactory quality.

11

Capital adequacy and capital planning

The subject of capital adequacy is one of the most important and most controversial topics in commercial banking. Bank management and the regulatory authorities are frequently in dispute about the appropriate amount of capital. Management, concerned with the rate of return on the owners' investment in the business, has often desired to reduce the ratio of capital to assets. In fact, historically there has been a sharp reduction in the volume of capital relative to loans and other risky financial assets. In contrast, the regulatory authorities, concerned with the stability of the financial system and the failure problem, have sought to maintain relatively high capital ratios. To some extent this conflict has been reduced by the authorization for national banks to sell subordinated capital notes and debentures and to count these debt instruments as a part of bank capital. Yet, the basic conflict remains due to the different orientation of the two groups. And with the relatively large number of failures in the decade of the 70s it does not appear as if the conflict will be eliminated.

The Purpose of Capital

The basic functions performed by capital must be kept in mind in order to understand the debate surrounding the capital adequacy issue. Capital exists to provide a cushion or buffer to absorb losses and to allow the institution to remain viable as a going concern during the period when problems are being corrected. From this perspective, capital is important for all financial intermediaries. This function may be viewed from a variety of perspectives. From a static point of view, capital exists to provide a cushion to absorb the risks of loss in the value of loans and investments on the books of the institution. Hence, if the ratio of capital to assets is only 5 percent, the intermediary cannot allow its assets to depreciate in value by more than 5 percent before the institution is insolvent.[1] In contrast, with a capital-to-asset ratio of 10 percent, the assets of the institution could depreciate by a much larger amount before it was technically insolvent. From a broader perspective, capital exists to provide assurance to the depositors and other creditors of the institution that it can continue to function as a viable economic unit during a period of adversity. The capital account would then be able to absorb losses until additional capital could be obtained from the generation and retention of earnings.

While there undoubtedly is validity to these arguments about the role of capital, it still remains true that from a broader perspective it is not capital which provides safety and stability to the banking and financial system, but the ability of monetary and fiscal policy to maintain a reasonably stable economic and financial environment. In a period of great economic distress, such as the 1930s, even a relatively large capital base may be unable to absorb losses. Conversely, in periods of relatively stable economic conditions, such as the period since World War II, the number of bank failures has been much reduced despite a sharply reduced capital base.

From any perspective, the amount of capital should be related to the degree of risk accepted by the banking industry in fulfilling its basic functions. For example, as observed earlier, the basic function of the commercial bank is to provide credit to local customers to meet legitimate credit needs. Necessarily, providing credit entails risk. Expected cash flow of the borrower may be insufficient to repay principal and interest at the agreed-upon times. Indeed, it is in the loan

---

[1] To some extent this problem is reduced by accounting principals in the banking industry which carry loans and securities at cost rather than market value as long as there is reasonable probability that the assets are sound. For securities especially, the ability to state value on the bank's books at cost rather than market has been important in maintaining at least an appearance of adequate capital for commercial banks.

portfolio where the commercial bank should concentrate its risk taking.

There are, however, other areas in which the commercial bank accepts risk. Any funds in excess of those necessary to meet the needs of primary and secondary reserves and to meet the legitimate loan demands of local customers should be committed to long-term securities for the purpose of generating income (the investment portfolio). Such a commitment of funds also involves risk. This risk encompasses both credit or default risk and market or interest rate risk. Again, as with the loan portfolio, there is the possibility that the borrower will be unable to repay principal and interest in a timely fashion. In addition, with relatively long maturity securities held for income, there is substantial risk of changes in the value of these securities as interest rates fluctuate. While the value of all securities fluctuates with changing interest rates, the price of a security fluctuates more the longer the maturity of that security for a given change in rates. In periods of very high interest rates those intermediaries which have heavy commitments to long-term securities face a large risk of depreciation in the value of their portfolio. While this depreciation is not recognized in the carrying value of the securities on the balance sheet, it does reduce the liquidity of the bank and increase its risk of insolvency. Finally, there is always the risk of fraud and thievery. For example, commercial banks handle large amounts of funds, including substantial amounts of currency and coin. The danger of theft of currency and coin by lower-level employees can usually be covered adequately by insurance and is unlikely to cause the bank to fail. But the threat of fraud by higher-level officials is more difficult to detect and to protect the bank against. Numerous bank failures in recent years have resulted from the manipulation of the funds of the bank by its principal officer. Perhaps the best example was the 1972 failure of the billion dollar U.S. National Bank of San Diego.

WHAT IS BANK CAPITAL?

The definition of capital in the banking industry is somewhat different than in other lines of business. Bank capital refers to the following: capital stock, surplus, undivided profits, reserves, preferred stock, and subordinated notes and debentures. Capital stock, surplus, and undivided profits need only a brief discussion. In total, they represent the amount of funds the owners have directly contributed through the purchase of common stock or indirectly contributed through retention of earnings. The amount in the capital stock account is equal to the number of shares outstanding multiplied by the par value of the stock. Hence, if there are 1 million shares outstanding and the par value is $10 per share, then the capital stock value should be $10 million. The surplus, or as it is more commonly referred to in accounting terminology, paid in capital in excess of par value, refers to the amount of funds committed by shareholders when they purchase common stock in excess of the par value of that stock.[2] Hence, in the previous example, if the common stock were purchased at $20 per share, the surplus would be $10 million. The total contribution for 1 million shares would be $20 million. Finally, the undivided profits, or retained earnings as they are more frequently called, refers to the earnings generated from the operations of the bank which have not been distributed to shareholders in the form of cash dividends. The importance of this division of total owners' equity among capital stock, surplus, and undivided profits has diminished in recent years although the amount of undivided profits is significant in affecting the legal ability of the bank to declare dividends.

The subject of "reserves" perhaps needs a more complete explanation. As discussed earlier, commercial banks face risks in their normal lending and investing activities. Such risk should properly be recognized and reserves established to provide for these losses. In actuality, the establishment of reserves is complicated by taxes and other considerations. The reserves created by commercial banks are currently divided into three groups: (1) valuation reserves; (2) contingency reserves; and (3) deferred tax reserves. Only a portion of these reserves should be viewed as part of the capital account. Valuation reserves refer to the reserves created to protect the bank from anticipated losses on loans. These reserves are increased by a charge to current income—provision for loan losses—on the income statement. They are reduced by write-offs of existing loans and also are increased by recoveries of loans which earlier had been deemed uncollectible. Each year (or more frequently if necessary) management determines in its judgment an amount which may be viewed as an expense provision for loan losses on the income statement. Such an expense adds to valuation reserves. When losses actually occur they do not directly affect current income. Rather, determination that a loan is uncollectible results in a decrease in the amount of loans and a decrease in the valuation reserves and has no income consequences. Similarly, recovery of a loan previously deemed uncollectible usually affects reserves but not income. These valuation reserves—which represent the bulk of loan loss reserves—are *not* treated as a part of the capital account. Rather, they are carried on the asset side of the balance sheet and are used to reduce gross loans to a net basis (net of valuation reserves).

---

[2] Increases in capital and surplus may also occur due to stock dividends which (in an accounting sense only) transfer funds from retained earnings to capital and surplus.

There are substantial limitations on the amounts which banks can charge off on their income statement for tax purposes. In recent years, the amounts which banks could expense for tax purposes have often exceeded the provision for loan losses which, in the judgment of management, was necessary to provide an adequate level of reserves. The added expense for tax purposes reduces taxable income and hence reduces taxes. This increases after-tax income and results in the creation of two additional reserve accounts: the contingency reserve, which *is* viewed as a part of the capital account, and the deferred tax reserve, which *is not* viewed as a part of the capital account but rather is carried on the balance sheet as "other liabilities." In short, the added expense beyond that needed to maintain an adequate valuation reserve results in funds that are not taxed in the current period. These funds have two components: the portion which would have been paid in taxes if the expense had not been taken, which is added to the deferred tax reserve, and the remainder after the deferred taxes have been subtracted, which is added to the contingency reserve.

Bank capital is not limited only to the capital provided by common shareholders. Since the early 1960s, national banks have been allowed to count preferred stock and subordinated notes and debentures in meeting their capital requirements. Since dividend payments on preferred stock are not deductible for tax purposes, however, the amount of preferred stock sold has been relatively slight. But the amount of subordinated notes and debentures sold has been substantial. Indeed, large banking organizations sold much more subordinated notes and debentures during the 1966–75 period than they did new common stock. Most of these subordinated notes and debentures were sold by bank holding companies rather than directly by individual banks, and frequently the funds raised by the holding company were used to acquire stock in the subsidiary bank.

Subordinated notes and debentures have grown immensely in importance in the capital structure of banking organizations, especially those of substantial size, for a variety of reasons. For example, during the 1966–75 period, public offerings of debt securities totaled almost $10 billion, which is more than ten times the amount of equity securities brought to market by these organizations. These debt securities provide a convenient and relatively inexpensive way to meet the needs for more capital imposed by the bank regulatory authorities and yet not create the dilution of earnings per share which would be associated with the sale of new common stock.

Since the interest expense is deductible for tax purposes, this source of funds becomes relatively inexpensive especially as compared to preferred stock. However, these subordinated notes and debentures must meet certain conditions if they are to be considered as a part of bank capital: they must be at least seven years in original maturity or they will be viewed as deposits by the regulatory authorities. If viewed as deposits, they will be subject both to Federal Deposit Insurance Corporation (FDIC) assessments, reserve requirements, and Regulation Q limitations on the maximum rates payable on all deposit liabilities. If viewed as capital, not only do they count as part of the capital structure of the bank, but also they do not require FDIC assessment, nor do they affect required reserves, nor are there any limitations on the maximum rates payable to obtain funds through this device. The regulatory authorities have imposed a maturity limitation in order to prevent commercial banks from using the notes and debentures as substitutes for deposits. In addition, the notes and debentures must be subordinated to the deposit liabilities of the bank. If the subordinated notes and debentures are to provide protection from risk to the depositors, they must necessarily be inferior in claim on the assets of the organization in case of bankruptcy.

There has been substantial controvery surrounding the use of subordinated notes and debentures as a part of the capital structure of individual commercial banking organizations. Some have argued that it is inappropriate to view a debt instrument as a part of the capital structure since the sale of the debt instrument imposes fixed obligations on the bank. Indeed, it may be argued that the sale of subordinated notes and debentures might increase the risk of failure due to the fixed nature of these obligations. This controversy has permeated the regulatory authorities. National banks may count subordinated notes and debentures as a part of the capital account in determining capital adequacy. However, the Federal Reserve does not include these debt instruments as part of the capital structure when determining capital adequacy for those banks under its supervision.

Capital trends

Capital ratios at banks, especially those related to risk assets, have experienced substantial declines over a period of some decades. For example, the ratio of total capital to total assets fell sharply during the 1930s, stabilized in the immediate postwar period, and then began to fall again after the mid-1950s. Recently, however, the ratio of capital to total assets has stabilized, though the ratio of capital to loans and other risky assets has continued to decline. Moreover, the mix of total bank capital has changed enormously.

For the entire banking system, total capital averaged almost 50 percent of bank assets throughout the first half of the 19th century. By the second half of that century the ratio of capital to assets had declined to 30 percent or less. Further decline occurred during the 20th century with the ratio of capital to assets falling to well under 10 percent by the 1970s. Numerous factors account for this substantial and persistent decline. Rapid expansion of the economy and of deposits made it simply impossible to achieve commensurate increases in capital. Declining profit margins made it desirable for bank management to allow the capital ratio to fall in order to maintain the return on equity. And, perhaps most importantly, greater stability of the economic environment has allowed the banking system to operate with reduced capital. Not only has the total quantity of capital changed relative to the size of the banking system, but the composition of bank capital has been altered, especially in the post-World War II era, with an increased role for retained earnings and subordinated debt. In contrast, capital stock and surplus have fallen in significance. Banks have found external equity to be an expensive source of funds and have concentrated on retained earnings as an internal source to bolster equity and debt as an external source. This has been especially true for larger banks.

Table 11–1 presents an analysis of the capital position of insured U.S. commercial banks as of the end of 1977. Total equity capital

TABLE 11–1
Capital measures for insured U.S. commercial banks, December 31, 1977

Measures	Size of bank (total assets in $millions)						
	Less than 5	5–9.9	10.0–24.9	25.0–99.9	100.0–299.9	300 or more	All banks
Equity capital/Total assets	10.0	9.0	8.2	7.6	6.9	6.3	8.2
Equity capital/Total deposits	10.7	9.8	9.0	8.4	7.9	7.6	9.0
Equity capital/Loans	20.9	18.0	16.1	14.7	13.7	12.7	16.1
Subordinated notes/ Equity capital	26.0	19.4	19.5	18.3	20.5	20.4	19.3

Source: Federal Deposit Insurance Corporation, *Bank Operating Statistics, 1977.*

averaged well under 10 percent of both total assets and total deposits. Yet there appears to be a marked relationship between equity capital and bank size. Larger banks appear to have less equity capital relative to total assets and total deposits than smaller banks. For banks under $5 million in total assets the ratio of equity capital to total assets averaged 10.0 percent, while this same ratio averaged only 6.3 percent for banks with total assets of $300 million or more. To some extent this inverse relationship between bank size and equity capital ratios is understandable given the greater diversification possible for larger banks. Yet larger banks also often have greater amounts of risky assets in their portfolios. It is also interesting to observe that subordinated notes appear significant for banks of all size groupings. Indeed, subordinated notes for the smallest size grouping represented a greater fraction of equity capital than for the largest banks.

MEASURES OF CAPITAL ADEQUACY

Capital exists to absorb losses stemming from making loans and investments. Since the amount of risk cannot be specified precisely, it is impossible to determine exactly how much capital is adequate. There are, however, a number of approaches to determining capital adequacy which have traditionally been used by both management and the regulatory authorities. These include the use of ratios such as the capital/asset ratio, the capital/risk asset ratio, the capital/adjusted-risk asset ratio, other formal procedures such as the Form for Analyzing Bank Capital which has been used by the Federal Reserve, and more subjective approaches such as those employed by the Comptroller of the Currency in its supervision of national banks. Historically, individual ratios, such as the capital-to-asset and capital-to-deposit ratio, appear to have been used by the various regulatory authorities until the actual banking system's ratios fell below some "normal" level, at which time the regulatory agencies usually changed to other and less restrictive ratios, such as the ratio of capital-to-risk assets, where risk assets are defined as total assets less cash and U.S. government securities.

The capital/asset ratio and the capital/deposit ratio are the simplest and oldest measures employed to ascertain capital adequacy. The total of all those items which count as capital—capital stock, surplus, undivided profits, contingency reserves, and perhaps preferred stock and subordinated notes and debentures—are added together and divided by the total amount of bank assets or deposits. Historically, the rule of thumb was that a capital/asset ratio of 7 percent would provide for adequate bank capital. This would allow the value of the bank's assets—particularly the loan portfolio—to decline by about 7 percent before the bank becomes insolvent. However, events in the past few decades have overcome this rule of thumb. Facing enormous growth of deposits due to inflation and to an expanding economy, and also under pressure in profit margins due to rising costs for labor and money, commercial banks have been reluctant to sell new equity (this has partially accounted for the sharp increase in subordinated notes and debentures). As a result, the capital/asset ratio for most commercial banks has declined appreciably and in many cases is below 5 percent. This ratio, though, remains as one of the principal ratios employed by the Federal Deposit Insurance Corporation in judging capital adequacy.

There are, however, a number of limitations to the capital/asset ratio which make it quite difficult to use as an efficient means to judge capital adequacy. The most important limitation of this ratio is that it makes no attempt to relate the amount of capital to the amount of risk carried by the banking organization. Rather, the capital/asset ratio completely ignores the risk structure of the bank's assets. For example, suppose that there were two banks with identical ratios of capital to assets, but one bank had all its funds invested in cash and short-term U.S. Treasury securities while the other had all of its funds except required reserves invested in speculative forms of loans. The capital/asset ratio would indicate that these banks are identical in terms of capital adequacy; yet, clearly, the capital adequacy of the first bank is much greater than that of the second.

In order to remedy some of these deficiencies, the ratio of capital to risk assets was developed, where risk assets are defined as total assets less cash and U.S. government securities. It is also interesting to observe that the capital-risk asset ratio became commonly used by the regulatory authorities during and immediately after World War II when the capital/asset ratio at many banks had declined below the norm and when the banks were expanding vigorously their holdings of U.S. government securities in order to finance the war. This ratio clearly represents a step forward from the capital/asset ratio in that it does recognize that capital adequacy is a function of the riskiness of assets. However, it also has a number of deficiencies; two in particular should be noted. First, it assumes that U.S. government securities, known also as governments, are riskless assets. While governments may indeed carry no credit (default) risk, these securities do carry interest rate or market risk, and for long-term governments especially, this risk is substantial. Second, this approach assumes that all assets except cash and U.S. government securities are equally risky. This last assumption also may be highly questionable. These other assets would include federal funds sold, commercial paper, bankers acceptances, short- and long-term municipals, and all varieties of loans both with respect to maturity and purpose. Clearly, these assets differ greatly in the degree of risk, with some perhaps having little more or no more risk than U.S. government securities.

Perhaps the most comprehensive quantitative technique has been developed by the Federal Reserve System with its Form for Analyzing Bank Capital (FABC). The FABC provides a comprehensive breakdown of the assets of the bank and also provides for the addition of extra capital if the liquidity position of the institution is inadequate.

Hence, the FABC recognizes that risk in banking may come from a variety of sources and provides capital for these different types of risk.

The FABC classifies the asset structure of the bank into six categories: (1) primary reserves (cash assets and federal funds sold); (2) secondary reserves (commercial paper, bankers acceptances, and securities maturing within one year); (3) minimum risk assets (securities maturing in one to five years); (4) intermediate assets (securities maturing within five to ten years); (5) portfolio assets (loans and long-term securities); and (6) fixed, classified, and other assets. Since default and/or interest rate risk increases as we move from category 1 through category six, the capital required behind each dollar of assets also increases. For example, primary reserves require no capital for either credit risk or market risk. Some intermediate risk assets require 3 percent capital for credit risk and 15 percent capital for interest rate risk. Some portfolio assets require 5 percent for credit risk and 25 percent for market risk, and bank premises require a 50 percent capital base.

The analyst may then calculate the total capital required to cover the credit and market risk embodied in the asset structure. To this the analyst should add an adjustment factor for the importance of trust activities to the bank and capital required for other special reasons. Finally, consideration should be given as to whether additional capital is needed in order to cover liquidity deficiencies. A bank with a deficient liquidity position is more likely to have to sell illiquid securities at distressed prices and therefore requires additional capital. In order to make these estimates the analyst should calculate a required liquidity number based upon the composition of deposits. For example, demand deposits would require more liquidity than savings deposits. Total required liquidity is then calculated. If the total liquidity so calculated is particularly large for this type of bank, then extra capital would be required.

Clearly the use of ratios and formulas such as the capital/asset ratio, the capital/risk asset ratio, and the FABC can only serve as guidelines. Final judgment as to capital adequacy must depend upon the subjective evaluation of a variety of factors. In fact, during the early 1960s the Office of the Comptroller of the Currency abandoned the use of ratios such as capital/asset for the determination of capital adequacy for national banks and instead relies upon the subjective judgment of the supervisory process based upon a wide variety of factors (sec. 14.1 of the Comptroller's regulations). For example, national bank examiners now base capital evaluations upon the following factors: the quality of management, the liquidity of assets, the history of earnings including the proportion retained, the quality and character of ownership, the burden of meeting occupancy expenses, the potential volatility of deposits, the quality of operating procedures, and the ability of the bank to meet the financial needs of its trade area.

Each of the tests of capital adequacy discussed above concentrates on the balance sheet of the individual commercial bank. Moreover, each is essentially static in nature. In recent years a number of additional tests have been proposed. One suggestion made by George Vojta would add to the static balance sheet test a measure of capital adequacy based upon the earnings of the bank. Moreover, the balance sheet measure would relate capital directly to the loan losses which capital exists to protect against. Under this capital adequacy approach, the earnings of the bank would be related to the expected losses on loans and securities and the capital of the bank would be related to past levels of realized losses.[3]

Another interesting approach would utilize the information provided by the financial markets in evaluating the adequacy of bank capital. Conceptually it would be expected that the cost of funds would be higher for banks which are undercapitalized. In the equity market, the cost of new funds raised through the sale of stock should be higher and in the debt market the cost of borrowed funds through deposits and subordinated debentures should be higher. While an appealing concept, application of this approach is hampered by the fact that deposit insurance at commercial banks and other depository financial institutions blunts the association between risk and the cost of funds. Moreover, the concept would be difficult to apply to smaller organizations where no market exists for their debt and equity securities.

EVALUATION OF ALTERNATIVE MEANS OF RAISING CAPITAL

Commercial banks have found it necessary in recent years to raise substantial amounts of new capital externally. This need has resulted from a combination of factors. Rapid inflation has produced a large increase in the dollar volume of bank deposits. While inflation has a number of influences on commercial banks as well as on other types of business organizations, one of the most significant is the sharp increase in the dollar size of the institution. Banks which were once $100 million institutions become $500 million in size, while $500 million dollar banks quickly become $1 billion plus in size with inflation of the currency. Yet, the increase in deposit growth does not automatically produce a comparable advance in the capital account.

---

[3] Vojta [6].

All rapidly growing business firms have difficulty in providing an adequate equity base. This growth in the commercial banking industry, though, has created special difficulties for bank management, as it has occurred at a time of intense pressure on profit margins. With growing costs of money and labor, but especially of money, commercial banks have found it increasingly difficult to maintain profit margins. The decline in margins has not only reduced the ability of commercial banks to build capital through the retention of earnings but also has reduced the willingness of banks to add to capital, since it is possible to blunt the impact of falling margins on the return on capital to some extent by allowing the capital/asset ratio to fall. In addition, there is some evidence that many bank stocks have traditionally been held by investors for dividend or income purposes, and there has been a reluctance on the part of management to reduce the dividend payout ratio to shareholders. Reflecting all of these factors, capital ratios have declined and there has been intense pressure on management to raise capital externally. The pressure has been especially intense on commercial banks subject to regulation by the Federal Reserve System. The Board of Governors of the Federal Reserve has conditioned a number of holding company acquisition approvals on the infusion by the holding company of equity capital into the acquired banks.

The capital management decision is a vitally important one as management seeks to maximize the value of the firm to its shareholders. In raising capital from external sources, bank management has essentially the following options: common stock, preferred stock, and subordinated notes and debentures. In addition, in some instances, it may be possible to satisfy the capital requirements of the regulatory authorities by selling the fixed assets of the bank and then leasing them back. In reaching its decision, management should focus on a number of different factors. In summary, these factors are income, risk, control, timing, flexibility, and other considerations.

Earnings per share.   One of the most important factors involved in the financing decision by management is the impact on the earnings per share of the organization. In general debt should have the least unfavorable (or the most favorable) effect on earnings per share as compared to the other financing alternatives. Common stock should have the greatest "dilution effect" on earnings per share, while the effect of preferred stock should be less favorable than debt but preferable to common stock.

Debt should have the least undesirable impact on earnings per share, because raising capital through selling subordinated notes and debentures does not create any additional shares of common stock. It does increase the amount of interest expense, but the effect of that change on after-tax earnings is reduced by the tax deductibility of interest. Moreover, once the earning power of the funds raised through the sale of subordinated notes and debentures is taken into account, the earnings per share after the sale of new capital should be higher than before. The earnings per share will be greater as compared to the before-sale situation as long as the funds are invested to earn a greater after-tax return than the after-tax cost of money raised. In other words, if leverage is favorable, there will be an incentive from an income perspective to proceed with financing through debt.[4] A similar argument prevails for preferred stock except that dividend payments are not tax deductible. Hence, the unfavorable impact on earnings of preferred stock dividends are more pronounced than for debt, and similarly it takes a greater return on the funds invested to create favorable financial leverage.

In contrast, the sale of common stock produces immediate dilution of earnings per share since existing earnings must be spread over a larger number of shares. Moreover, even taking into account the income generated on the funds invested, earnings per share with the sale of common stock will be less than with preferred stock or debt financing as long as favorable financial leverage results. Over the longer term, of course, as funds invested begin to generate income, the earnings per share with common stock financing should exceed the earnings per share without that financing, or from an income perspective, there would be no incentive to raise additional funds.

Risk. Different means of raising funds not only have different effects on income but also on risk. Risk in this context may be viewed from two different perspectives. The most tangible perspective is that of bankruptcy. The other is the effect on the market price of the bank's stock. The latter is less tangible but in many cases may be the most important impact from different financing alternatives. It is usually argued that risk is greatest when debt is added to the capital structure, and least when financing is done with common stock. Preferred stock falls somewhere between those two extremes.

Addition of debt to the capital structure increases the fixed charges (payment of interest and repayment of principal) faced by bank management. As such, the addition of debt can be viewed as adding to the risk that the organization will fail. However, the significance of this factor is reduced to some extent by the tax deductibility of interest (so that the after-tax cost of a $1 million interest payment is only $520,000 if the bank is in the 48 percent tax bracket, assuming of course that the bank remains profitable during the term of the bond)

---

[4] Favorable leverage would be created through the use of either subordinated notes and debentures or preferred stock.

and by the fact that bank management has numerous other fixed commitments, such as CDs, so that the addition of debt does not add greatly to the total fixed cash outflow which management is confronted with. However, an equally and perhaps more important factor is the effect on the market's perception of the risk involved in investing in shares of the organization. The additional debt may cause the price-earnings ratio of the bank's shares to decline, since the earnings available to common shareholders will be more variable with debt and since shareholders are presumed to dislike variability in the earnings and dividend stream. Hence, debt may add to the income (earnings per share) of the organization but may not increase shareholder wealth if the price-earnings ratio reduction more than offsets the impact on share value of higher earnings. However, studies have indicated that—at least up to the debt ratios prevalent through the mid-1970s—the addition of subordinated debt to the capital structure did *not* reduce the price-earnings ratio. This would suggest that management should continue to employ debt in the capital structure as long as debt increases the bank's earnings per share and as long as the price-earnings ratio does not fall.

Preferred stock also adds risk to the banking organization, but the risk is of a somewhat different nature than with debt. Dividends payable on preferred stock do not represent a legal obligation of the bank. In periods of diminished cash flow, bank management could quite legally reduce or eliminate preferred stock dividends. However, the payment of preferred stock dividends by a bank would generally be viewed as a moral commitment on the part of the organization. Moreover, failure to pay preferred stock dividends would make it impossible to pay dividends on the common shares of the bank. Hence, the sale of preferred stock also adds a noticeable degree of risk to the bank, both in terms of the risk of bankruptcy and also the risk associated with a more unstable earnings and dividend stream. In contrast, common stock creates no legal or moral commitment on the part of the bank and is, therefore, to be preferred from a risk perspective.

Control. Control refers to the possibility that an individual or groups of individuals who currently have control of the bank may lose their authority as the result of the means of financing chosen. Under this criterion, common stock is the least favorable choice since it creates additional voting shares.[5] The additional shares could fall into the hands of a new group and, along with shares already held, could be used to change control of the organization. To some extent, this

---

[5] If there is a good secondary market for the stock, however, the group seeking control also could acquire additional shares through open market purchase of existing shares.

threat is reduced by the preemptive right of existing shareholders. Under this arrangement, existing shareholders must be offered enough shares to allow them to maintain their proportionate interest in the organization. However, existing shareholders—particularly the control group—still face the difficulty of raising sufficient funds in order to buy the shares offered.

Problems with control are less pronounced with the sale of preferred stock or subordinated notes and debentures since no additional voting securities are created. However, this is not meant to imply that control is not an issue with these securities. Frequently, it is necessary for the borrower to agree to certain restrictions prior to the sale of preferred stock and/or debt instruments and especially with debt securities. These restrictions might include limitations on management salaries and on dividends payable to common shareholders to name only a few. Moreover, the borrower faces the loss of control should there be a failure to conform to the full terms of the contract under which the preferred stock or debt securities were issued. At the extreme, the board of directors could be dominated by a lender.

Timing.   Timing refers to the question of whether the present is a particularly desirable or undesirable period to sell one of the securities under debate. For example, bond prices may be unusually high, in which case bond interest rates would be unusually low. In contrast, stock prices might be unusually low. In this circumstance, the present would be a desirable time to raise funds with debt securities. However, it may be that for some reason the stock of the individual bank is selling at a historically high price-earnings ratio, in which case the timing criterion would suggest that funds should be raised with the sale of common stock. Given the enormous changes in the prices of financial assets in recent years, timing has become a consideration of great importance.

Flexibility.   In a growing economy, and particularly in an inflationary environment, it is unlikely that bank management will be able to finance only once and fulfill its capital requirements for all time. Rather, in making the capital decision today management should recognize that additional financing probably will be needed a number of times in the future. Within this context, it is important for management to consider how its financing decision today will affect the bank's ability to borrow in the future, and from this perspective common stock is clearly the preferred alternative. While the sale of debt securities today reduces future debt opportunities available to the firm and thereby reduces future financial flexibility, the sale of common stock does not use up any existing debt capacity. In contrast, the sale of common stock adds to the debt capacity of the firm by building its equity base.

Other factors. Finally, management must consider all other relevant factors not specifically covered in those above. For example, the sale of debt securities may satisfy the capital requirements of the regulatory authorities but may not add to the legal lending limit of the organization. If the legal lending limit is a matter of great importance, then this factor should be given weight in the discussion. Similarly, management may wish to expand the common stock holdings of one group, perhaps representatives of large firms in the area. In any case, there are clearly other variables to consider in making the financing decision involved in raising the required amount of capital.

QUESTIONS

11–1. What is the basic conflict over the subject of capital adequacy between management and the regulatory authorities?

11–2. What is capital? What is it composed of? What changes have recently occurred in the composition of capital?

11–3. What has been the relationship of capital to risk assets over time for the last 50 years?

11–4. What are some of the measures used in judging capital adequacy? What are their advantages and disadvantages?

11–5. How is the FABC (Form for Analyzing Bank Capital) developed by the Federal Reserve constructed?

11–6. What factors influence the structure of capital? Why have banks relied heavily on borrowed capital?

11–7. Can a bank have too much capital?

REFERENCES

1. Hahn, Phillip J. *The Capital Adequacy of Commercial Banks.* New York: American Press, 1966.
2. Landow, Wesley. "Bank Capital and Risk Assets." *National Banking Review*, September 1963, pp. 29–46.
3. Mock, Edward J. "Banks Find New Ways to Raise Capital." *Banking*, November 1964, pp. 47, 58–62.
4. Nadler, Paul S. "Can Debentures Save the Smaller Bank?" *Banking*, November 1964, pp. 43–44, 98.
5. Reed, Edward W., Cotter, Richard V., Gill, Edward K., and Smith, Richard K. *Commercial Banking.* Englewood Cliffs, N.J.: Prentice-Hall, 1976, Chap. 21.
6. Vojta, George J. *Bank Capital Adequacy.* New York: Citicorp, 1973.
7. Woods, Oliver G. *Commercial Banking.* New York: D. Van Nostrand Company, 1978), Chap. 6.

Problem for discussion

With rapid deposit growth in recent years placing pressure on capital positions, many commercial banks have been faced with the need—either because of regulations or management decisions—to raise additional capital. Moreover, the alternative sources of capital funds available to commercial banks today are much greater and more complex than in previous periods. The problem situation discussed below provides the student with the opportunity to analyze the impact of alternative capital sources on the financial position of a large bank. After reviewing the material below, the student should address the following questions:

1. What are the advantages and disadvantages of each alternative?
2. How will the earnings per share of the bank be affected by each of the alternatives?
3. What might be the impact on the market value of the bank's common stock?
4. What alternative would you recommend?

First National Bank presently serves a dynamic community of about 500,000 population. Area growth has been spurred by a heavy influx of new residents and new businesses seeking a warmer climate and by the development of new industries centered upon space technology, electronics, and commercial and residential construction. First National has captured a significant share of new business accounts and, by careful selection of branch office sites, has successfully penetrated the growing suburban consumer market.

First National's rapid growth has not been an unmixed blessing, however. For one thing, loan losses associated with the newest commercial accounts have been higher than average, principally because many of the newest firms are in relatively volatile industries subject to extreme business-cycle fluctuations. These conditions have also affected the bank's consumer loans where losses have been higher than anticipated due mainly to the bank's limited experience with many of its household customers. A second major problem is that First National frequently finds it cannot meet the total credit requirements of its commercial customers. This is due, in large part, to the legal lending limit which the federal banking agencies have placed on loans to a single borrower. When the bank receives a customer request for credit beyond its lending capacity, the overline typically is handled by sharing the loan with another bank or group of banks. Another important factor limiting the bank's lending power is the antibranching law imposed several years ago by the state legislature. A bank may establish branch offices only within the county where its headquarters is located. Thus, deposits and other local sources of loanable funds must come from a relatively restricted geographic area, and this has limited First National's growth.

Last week officials from the regional office of the Comptroller of the Currency visited with management and the board of directors. The officials had indicated only a year ago that the bank's capital position was relatively weak. This time, however, these officials insisted that steps be taken to remedy the capital deficiency—estimated to be in the neighborhood of $10.5 million. The Comptroller's office expressed concern about the volatile nature of the local economy, the limited availability of long-term nondeposit sources of funds to a bank of First National's size, the bank's modest earnings record compared to other banks of about the same size, its relatively low degree of geographic and portfolio diversification, and the intense competition in the local market area. The officials observed that First National's ratios of capital (net worth) to total assets, risk assets, loans, and deposits were substantially below comparable ratios for similar size banks. The board of directors agreed to study the situation and do whatever was necessary.

Four major alternative sources of new capital were considered by management: (1) issuance of common stock; (2) sale of capital notes and debentures; (3) sale of preferred stock; and (4) reduction of dividends and, therefore, greater retention of earnings. Management realizes the difficulty of its task, for the raising of new capital can be an inordinately difficult problem for small- and medium-size banks, principally because several avenues available to larger banks are, for all practical purposes, closed to smaller institutions. The most satisfactory approach from the point of view of the regulatory authorities is sale of stock since this directly increases the bank's equity position. However, sale of stock is one of the most expensive sources of capital and results in a dilution of earnings per share of common. Moreover, the market for the stock of smaller banks is both limited and highly imperfect. At present First National's stock is selling for $39 per share, or about 10 times earnings per share. Management has determined that First National can sell its stock at $36 per share with an underwriting cost equal to about 10 percent of the issue. Management has carried out a survey of key stockholders and found that only about 30 percent of the projected equity issue could be absorbed by current shareholders.

For most banks retained earnings are the major source of growth in capital. First National's expenses have grown rapidly in recent years, due to its aggressive program of establishing new suburban branches and the rising cost of attracting deposits in a highly competitive banking market. These factors coupled with above-normal loan losses have squeezed the bank's earnings. Management estimates that earnings in the near term will provide only a small part of the necessary increase in capital. Moreover, the bank has followed a policy since its founding in 1921 of paying an automatic dividend of 7 percent. Reduction of this dividend to build up the bank's net worth might be desirable from a capital adequacy standpoint, but would be likely to have a negative impact upon the value of the bank's stock. Reduction of dividends would lower the present value of expected dividend flows in future years and might be a signal to investors that First National's earnings were subject to more risk than in the past. Either way, a decline in the bank's stock price and price-earnings ratio would follow quickly.

Some consideration is being given by management to issuing preferred stock. A number of options are available, such as making the preferred issues callable at a fixed price at the bank's option or allowing conversion into common stock at a predetermined price at the investor's option. Convertible preferred could probably be issued at a much lower dividend yield. The bank presently has no preferred issues outstanding. Conversations with investment bankers suggest the bank could issue preferred stock, provided it is willing to pay a guaranteed annual dividend of at least 8 percent with some provision for participation in future earnings.

In recent years banks have made widespread use of senior capital (i.e., notes and debentures) subordinated to deposits. This is particularly appropriate where local economic conditions are favorable to the bank's continuing growth, but equity capital simply has not grown rapidly enough to keep pace with the growth of loans and deposits. When the debt can be issued at relatively low rates, favorable financial leverage will result, increasing earnings per share on common stock. Management has investigated the option of selling debentures and found that a seven-year capital note with a coupon of 9 percent probably could be sold in a private placement. By offering a debenture issue that is convertible into common stock, the interest rate could probably be reduced at least another percentage point and the dilution of earnings per share on common stock would be less than on nonconvertible debentures. However, underwriting fees are significantly higher on convertible issues.

In choosing which way to go management and the board of directors have in mind two main objectives: (1) the total amount of capital to be raised must be, at minimum, sufficient to satisfy the regulatory authorities; and (2) the method chosen to raise new capital should enhance the stockholders' position by maximizing their rate of return. During the past year First National Bank received total revenues of $21.1 million and had total operating expenses of $16.4 million. Its effective income tax rate is 48 percent. The bank's stock has a par value of $20 with 150,000 shares outstanding. First National Bank held $536.6 million in total assets and $489.6 million in total deposits at year-end 1978.

section
III

Nonbank financial
institutions

12

Savings and loan associations and mutual savings banks

Savings and loan associations and mutual savings banks are among the most important financial intermediaries in the American economy. These institutions intermediate primarily between individuals—receiving the bulk of their deposits from individuals and lending principally to other individuals. Savings and loans and mutual savings banks are the principal conduit for mortgage credit, especially for the financing of single-family homes. By offering individual depositors an attractive yield on their funds, these institutions attract many small savings accounts and pool these funds to make the large loans required by home buyers and apartment owners. As is true of other financial intermediaries, however, these thrift institutions increasingly are diversifying the services they offer in order to open up new markets and find new sources of profitability. The result is increasingly intense competition between savings and loans, mutual savings banks, commercial banks, and credit unions for both deposits and loans.

THE SAVINGS AND LOAN ASSOCIATION

Savings and loan associations were designed originally to serve the financial needs of the small saver. These needs include a place for the safe deposit of savings with some return on investment and credit at reasonable cost to purchase a home. The first savings and loans (frequently called building and loan societies) were set up to collect funds contributed by members and loan those funds to any member who had the capacity and desire to own a home. In turn, the mortgage loans granted to members generated income for the association and enabled it to pay interest on the deposits made by other members. The granting of credit was restricted to those who contributed their savings to the association. In this sense, the early savings and loans were similar to the modern credit union and many were run more like self-help societies than profit-making business ventures. Today, however, the savings and loan (S&L) typically is an aggressive competitor for both deposits and loans, though mortgage credit for the purchase of homes is still the dominant end product of S&L operations.

THE STRUCTURE OF THE SAVINGS AND LOAN INDUSTRY

Savings and loan associations may be chartered by either the federal government or by the individual states. Federally chartered associations are supervised by the Federal Home Loan Bank System and comprise about 40 percent of all savings and loans operating in the United States. An S&L may be chartered today either as a mutual institution or as a permanent stock association. Nearly all federal savings and loans are mutuals, though in recent years a few federally chartered, stockholder-owned S&Ls have been created by action of the Federal Home Loan Bank Board. Roughly one quarter of state-chartered associations are stockholder owned and the rest are mutuals. A mutual association is formed without capital or paid-in surplus and depends upon reserves accumulated from earnings to serve as a cushion against loss. The depositors literally "own" a piece of the organization when they open an account. In contrast, permanent stock associations are owned by their shareholders who hold common stock, as is true of any other business corporation. Depositors in a stockholder-owner S&L are creditors of the organization, not owners.

On December 31, 1977, there were 4,770 savings associations operating in the 50 states, the District of Columbia, Puerto Rico, and Guam. Of this total 4,023 were mutuals and 747 were stockholder-owned S&Ls. Since 1973, the number of stock associations has grown in response to rapid population increases in areas of the nation where stockholder-owned S&Ls are important (principally the Midwest and western United States) and a sharp increase in the demand for mortgage credit.[1] Assets held by mutual associations amounted to nearly $353 billion in 1977, while stock associations held total resources of $107 billion. Stockholder-owned associations controlled 23 percent of the industry's assets at year-end 1977, yet represented only about 16 percent of the total number of S&Ls. By this reckoning it is obvious that stock savings and loans are larger on the average, than the mutuals.

The distribution of assets among large and small savings and loans reflects considerable concentration in the industry's resources. A large number of relatively small S&Ls hold a minor proportion of all industry assets. (See Table 12–1.) At year-end 1977, for example,

TABLE 12–1
Distribution of savings associations by asset size, December 31, 1977

Asset size ($millions)	Number of associations	Percent of total	Total assets ($millions)	Percent of total
Under $10	1,036	21.7%	$ 4,227	0.9%
$10 and under $50	1,952	40.9	55,891	12.2
$50 and under $100	800	16.8	60,208	13.1
$100 and under $500	838	17.6	172,523	37.6
$500 and over	144	3.0	166,423	36.2
Total	4,770	100.0%	$459,282	100.0%

Note: Columns may not add to totals due to rounding error.
Source: Adapted from Federal Home Loan Bank Board; and United States League of Savings Associations, *Savings & Loan Fact Book, 1978*, p. 53.

slightly over 1,000 associations (or about one fifth of the total) held total assets of less than $10 million apiece, but controlled less than 1 percent of the industry's resources. The few largest associations with $500 million and more in total assets held more than a third of all industry assets. However, there has been dramatic growth in the number of associations moving into larger asset size categories. The average size S&L increased more than sixfold between 1970 and 1977.

Both the number of mergers among savings and loans and the formation of new branch offices have accelerated in recent years. For

---

[1] Stockholder-owned S&Ls have more options in raising funds since they may issue stock as well as offer deposits. In addition, two of the most rapidly growing states of the Union—Texas and California—permit the chartering of stock associations. Of the 747 permanent stock associations operating at year-end 1977, 86 were headquartered in California and 226 in Texas. California's stock associations dominated in asset size, holding about 51 percent of the assets of all stockholder-owned S&Ls in the United States. See, in particular, United States League of Savings Associations [10], pp. 48 and 51–52.

example, between 1970 and 1977, there were 735 mergers among savings associations belonging to the Federal Home Loan Bank System, more than in the entire decade of the 1960s. This acceleration in merger activity reflects, in part, rising costs (particularly the cost of raising funds) and an attempt by individual associations to reach for greater economies of organization and operation. In addition, the increasing complexity of the savings and loan business has made it more difficult for individual associations to find capable management. Finally, the Federal Savings and Loan Insurance Corporation (FSLIC) has relied heavily upon mergers to combine those associations in danger of failing with fiscally sound institutions in order to preserve public confidence in the industry.

Savings and loan associations generally have more liberal branching rules than commercial banks. For example, even in states which completely prohibit full-service branching by commercial banks, associations may establish branch offices within a 100-mile radius of the home office. In 1967, federally chartered associations were permitted to operate mobile branches serving communities not large enough for full-time branch offices. During the early 1970s the Federal Home Loan Bank Board (FHLBB) authorized the establishment of satellite offices, more commonly known as "minibranches," which are located principally in retail stores and shopping malls. Minibranches may be completely automated or manned by tellers. The same forces which have accelerated mergers within the industry also have caused a dramatic increase in branching activity. There were more than 13,000 S&L branch offices at year-end 1977, roughly triple the number in 1970.

Reflecting the large number of mergers and more liberal branching rules, the total number of savings and loans has been declining since 1960. As shown in Table 12–2, there were 1,550 fewer associations in 1977 than in 1960 and nearly 900 less than in 1970. The decline in numbers is the work of a number of powerful forces, includ-

TABLE 12–2
Number of savings and loan associations by type of charter (year-end figures)

Year	Federally chartered associations	State-chartered associations			Industry totals
		Total	FSLIC-insured	Noninsured	
1950	1,526	4,466	1,334	3,132	5,992
1960	1,873	4,447	2,225	2,225	6,320
1970	2,067	3,602	2,298	1,304	5,669
1977	2,012	2,758	2,023	735	4,770

Source: Adapted from Federal Home Loan Bank Board; and United States League of Savings Associations, *Savings and Loan Fact Book, 1978*, p. 48.

ing increased competition between banks, savings and loans, and credit unions and a more restrictive chartering policy. The individual states have been far less liberal in granting new charters than federal authorities, and the number of state-chartered associations has been declining for more than two decades.

As we noted earlier, a significant number of associations have converted from mutual to stock-type savings and loans in recent years. Among the most frequently cited advantages of the stock form of ownership are the following:

1. A stock association can raise funds through equity capital as well as by offering deposits to the public.
2. Capital stock may make the structure of the industry more flexible by making mergers easier to carry out, increasing the opportunity for greater economies of scale.
3. Access to equity as a source of funds may make S&Ls more competitive and better able to attract skilled management by offering stock option plans.
4. Equity capital may strengthen the financial position of individual savings and loans because it will augment their net worth position and enable associations to withstand greater loan losses.
5. Management decision making may improve since officers of a stock association are responsible to stockholders who presumably wish to maximize the return on their investment.
6. The consumer will have more options with both stockholder-owned and mutual associations to draw upon.[2]

The foregoing are *potential* advantages of stockholder-owned savings and loans over mutuals, which may or may not be achieved in practice. Recent research does tend to favor the stockholder-owned savings and loan, although there is considerable debate over the validity of the findings. In one recent study mutual associations were compared to federally chartered stock S&Ls in California where there is considerable direct competition between the two.[3] The mutuals seemed to place greater emphasis upon expenses rather than profits and their market share declined substantially during the study period. Stock associations used more advertising than did mutuals; and, when they advertised, stockholder S&Ls generally stressed interest rates offered on deposits, while the mutuals referred to the strength of their reserves and the safety of depositor funds. Stock associations appeared to be more aggressive merchandisers and—where per-

---

[2] See, in particular, the statement of FHLBB Chairman, Thomas A. Bomar, to the Subcommittee on Financial Institutions of the Senate Banking Committee [2], pp. 2–3.

[3] See Nicols [8].

mitted by law—used both premiums and bonuses to attract new depositors. The mutuals grew more slowly, reported lower gross operating income (relative to assets), and paid lower dividend rates to savers than did the stock associations.

SOURCES AND USES OF FUNDS FOR SAVINGS AND LOANS

Uses of funds

Since savings and loan associations are specialists in financing the construction of homes and apartments, it is no surprise that mortgage loans are their principal asset. At year-end 1977, for example, mortgage loans represented more than 80 percent of the indus-

TABLE 12–3
Balance sheet (statement of condition) for all U.S. savings and loan associations, year-end 1977

Sources and uses of funds	Amount in $billions	Percent of total
Assets		
Mortgage loans	$381.2	83.0%
Insured mortgages and mortgage-backed securities	12.7	2.8
Mobile home loans	2.6	0.6
Home improvement loans	3.8	0.8
Loans on savings accounts	2.8	0.6
Education loans	0.6	0.1
Miscellaneous consumer loans	0.5	0.1
Cash and investments eligible for liquidity	34.3	7.5
Other investments held	4.9	1.1
Federal Home Loan bank stock	3.2	0.7
Investments in service corporations	1.5	0.3
Building and equipment	6.1	1.3
Real estate owned	1.9	0.4
Miscellaneous assets	3.2	0.7
Total assets	$459.3	100.0%
Liabilities and Net Worth		
Savings deposits	$386.9	84.3%
Advances from the Federal Home Loan banks	20.0	4.3
Other borrowed funds	7.9	1.7
Loans in process	9.9	2.2
Other liabilities	9.5	2.1
Net worth	25.2	5.5
Total liabilities and net worth	$459.3	100.0%

Note: Columns may not add to totals due to rounding error.
Source: Adapted from Federal Home Loan Bank Board; and United States League of Savings Associations, *Savings and Loan Fact Book, 1978*, p. 80.

try's total resources and amounted to $381 billion. (See Table 12–3.) Indeed, the industry's ratio of mortgages to total assets has changed little since the 1930s.

Recently, however, new types of credit have come to play a larger role in the industry. Notable here are mortgage participation certificates (PCs) and mortgage-backed securities. PCs are financial instruments representing an undivided interest in a relatively large and geographically diversified portfolio of high-quality mortgages. The most well-known issuer of PCs is the Federal Home Loan Mortgage Corporation (FHLMC, or "Freddie Mac"), set up by Congress in 1970 to increase the flow of funds into the residential mortgage market and to encourage the development of a viable secondary market for home mortgages. In addition to issuing PCs, FHLMC raises funds by borrowing from the Federal Home Loan Bank System and by selling bonds and certificates. It uses the funds to carry on an active program of purchasing both conventional and government-guaranteed (Federal Housing Administration and Veterans Administration) mortgages from thrift institutions and other lenders. PCs, first introduced in 1971, are sold today in denominations of $100,000, $200,000, $500,000, and $1 million and are freely transferable. They are quite attractive to savings and loan associations because they are exempt from federal lending limitations and qualify as mortgages on real property for tax purposes. PCs also may be used as collateral when a member savings and loan wishes to borrow reserves from the Federal Home Loan banks to shore up its cash position.

A related type of investment of growing importance to savings and loans and other thrift institutions consists of so-called mortgage-backed securities. The most familiar type are supervised by the Government National Mortgage Association (GNMA, or "Ginnie Mae") which guarantees these securities. GNMA was set up in 1968 to improve the secondary market for housing-related mortgages and to help stabilize the mortgage market. Mortgage-backed securities are issued against a pool of mortgages held by federally approved lenders and are retired as repayments on mortgages in the pool are made. The most common type of GNMA mortgage-backed security is the "pass-through" certificate which pays interest and principal monthly to the holder. Bonds backed by mortgages also may be issued by the federal mortgage agencies which pay interest on a semiannual basis. GNMA mortgage-backed securities have grown dramatically in response to heavy demands for mortgage credit in recent years.

Savings and loans also provide credit for the purchase of mobile homes. Such loans were first authorized for federally chartered associations by the Housing and Urban Development Act in 1968.

Mobile home loans totaled almost $2.6 billion at year-end 1977, but still represented less than 1 percent of total industry assets. There is a definite trend toward more diversified lending by S&Ls where state and federal regulations allow. Some states now permit associations to make consumer instalment loans for the purchase of automobiles, home appliances, and other durable goods.

Cash, U.S. government securities, and other marketable securities are the most liquid assets held by savings associations. The Federal Home Loan Bank Board stipulates that a certain percentage of an association's withdrawable savings deposits and short-term borrowings must be held in certain "qualified" assets—cash, short-term commercial bank deposits, short- and medium-term U.S. government and federal agency securities, bankers acceptances, and municipal securities with maturities of two years or less. The FHLBB can vary the required percentage of liquid asset holdings between 4 and 10 percent of total savings deposits and short-term borrowings. As of mid-1979 the required liquidity ratio was set at 7 percent, 3 percent of which had to be held in short-term (generally under one year) instruments. The regulatory authorities typically lower the required liquidity ratio when saving by the public drops in order to expand the volume of credit available to the housing market and raise the liquidity ratio when savings deposits are growing rapidly.

Sources of funds

Savings and loans are thrift institutions and, therefore, their principal funds source is savings deposits. At year-end 1977 associations held a total of nearly $387 billion in savings deposits, representing more than 80 percent of all funds raised by the industry. The proportion of S&L funds represented by savings deposits, while dominant in size, has by no means been stable. Fluctuations in interest rates, changes in economic activity, and changes in government credit policies have produced significant changes in the ability of savings and loans to attract deposits and to retain the deposits they already hold. During the 1966–67, 1969–70 and 1978–1979 periods, for example, there were large federal budget deficits, rapid inflation, and restrictive money and credit policies which pushed interest rates in the money and capital markets to record levels. Savers reacted to this unsettling environment by transferring funds out of their savings accounts into other investments, including marketable securities. During 1972 and 1976–77, in contrast, there were unprecedented increases in savings funds, particularly in the larger certificate-type, interest-sensitive deposits, as the economy slowly recovered from a recession and interest rate increases were relatively moderate.

In response to competitive pressures, regulatory actions, and market conditions, savings and loans frequently have changed the mix of savings plans offered the public, especially during the past decade. For most of the postwar period passbook savings accounts, which generally permit the saver to withdraw funds at will, were the dominant type of savings deposit. These accounts carry a maximum interest rate of 5.25 percent today. Within the past few years, however, new regulations have permitted S&Ls to offer a much broader array of savings instruments, varying in the rates of interest paid, maturity, and minimum amounts. One of the most important is the certificate of deposit (or CD), issued in fixed amounts with a set maturity not to exceed 10 years.

Another more recently developed savings instrument arousing considerable investor interest is the so-called money market certificate, carrying a minimum denomination of $10,000 with an interest rate which fluctuates with the yield on six-month U.S. Treasury bills. Money market certificates have been of great assistance to S&Ls in reducing the potentially damaging effects of disintermediation in periods of rapidly rising interest rates such as prevailed during 1978 and 1979. Much longer in average maturity are the new individual retirement accounts (IRAs) and Keogh plan accounts authorized for savings institutions, including savings and loans. These accounts are designed primarily to provide pension programs for individuals who do not have access to employer retirement plans. Funds placed in these accounts are sheltered from federal income taxes until withdrawal, which can occur after age 59½. All certificate accounts earn higher interest rates than passbook accounts.

The second largest source of funds for savings and loans is net worth, representing about 6 percent of all funds raised. Net worth includes retained earnings (or undivided profits), paid-in surplus, and reserves. The net worth account is designed to protect depositor funds. While net worth has been growing in dollar terms, it has been declining relative to borrowings and deposits as a source of industry funds in recent years.

Just as commercial banks which are members of the Federal Reserve System may borrow reserves from the central bank, member savings and loan associations may secure credit from the Federal Home Loan bank (FHLB) headquartered in their district. FHLB advances represented about 4 percent of total funds sources in 1977. This funds source has been rather erratic due to fluctuations in economic activity and general credit conditions. Savings and loans use

FHLB advances as a residual source of funds, borrowing more heavily in periods when deposit growth slackens and repaying their borrowings when deposit growth accelerates.[4]

Data from the Federal Reserve's Flow of Funds Accounts, industry trade groups, and federal and state regulatory agencies highlight a number of important trends in S&L sources and uses of funds in recent years. Savings inflows have become much more volatile in response to fluctuations in interest rates and economic conditions. For a period stretching from the end of World War II through 1965 the industry grew rapidly, but the rate of deposit growth was relatively stable. Beginning, however, in the late 1960s and continuing to the present day, marked fluctuations in interest rates, government credit policy, and economic conditions frequently have led to abrupt changes in the inflow or outflow of savings deposits. In years of high and rising interest rates, such as 1966, 1969, 1973, 1978, and 1979, savings deposits at S&Ls became less attractive compared to other market investments, forcing a sharp cutback in mortgage lending and industry growth. In contrast, during periods of lower rates and stimulative monetary policy, such as 1967, 1971–72, and 1975–77, rates offered on S&L deposits look attractive and frequently funds flow in large volume back into savings deposits. These marked fluctuations in savings deposits have forced the industry to draw more heavily upon nondeposit sources of funds, particularly borrowing from the Federal Home Loan Banks. This phenomenon of shifting funds sources between savings deposits and borrowings suggests the importance today for financial managers of S&Ls of forecasting interest rates, especially short-term rates associated with deposit flows.

The Flow of Funds Accounts reveal that net acquisitions of mortgages continue to dominate the growth of savings and loan assets. During 1977 mortgage holding of associations rose a record $58 billion, led by a $47 billion rise in holdings of mortgages against single-family homes. The previous high was in 1976 when net mortgages acquired during the year totaled more than $44 billion. As is the case with savings deposits, however, the growth of mortgage loans has fluctuated widely in recent years. For example, the net gain in mortgage acquisitions during 1974 was only $13 billion while in 1976 and 1977, as indicated above, mortgage acquisitions were three to four times that figure. The critical factor here is the demand for

---

[4] Savings and loan also use the mortgage-backed bonds discussed earlier as a source of funds, issuing these securities against pools of previously acquired mortgages. Regulations limit the use of this source of funds to a maximum of 5 percent of an S&L's savings deposits. Mortgage-backed bonds are sold in the open market by larger S&Ls while smaller associations tend to use private placements. Both government-guaranteed and conventional mortgages serve as collateral for these bonds.

single-family mortgage loans. When credit is relatively scarce and expensive, demand for home mortgage credit falls and the growth of S&L loans slows. These recent fluctuations in mortgage credit extended by S&Ls again underscore the necessity for using effective forecasting techniques in the industry.

Earnings, dividends, and expenses of savings and loans

A glance at the sources of income for savings and loan associations shows clearly the key role of this institution as a mortgage lender and thrift deposit institution. Income from mortgages represented about fourfifths of S&L revenues in 1977. This percentage has been quite stable over time; in fact, in 1960, it was 83 percent. Other revenue sources include income from service corporations and investment portfolios.

Following a rapid increase during the 1950s and early 1960s, the industry's operating income and net after-tax earnings leveled off in the middle and late 1960s as S&Ls attempted to adjust to higher interest rates and more volatile fluctuations in savings deposits and mortgage demands. More recently, however, operating income has risen rapidly, reflecting the beneficial effects of higher average mortgage rates, more efficient use of available funds, and an increase in lending in areas having high mortgage rates. In 1977 association income totaled almost $35 billion, a substantial increase over the 1976 level of about $29 billion.

Interest paid to savers amounted to $23 billion during 1977, or almost exactly two thirds of industry operating revenues. (See Table 12–4.) From 1950 onward, interest on deposits grew by a few per-

TABLE 12–4
Earnings, dividends, and expenses of U.S. savings and loan associations, 1977

Source of revenue or expense	Amounts in $billions	Percent of operating income
Total operating income	$34.7	100.0%
Operating expenses	5.4	15.6
Net operating income	$29.3	84.4%
Interest paid on savings deposits	23.1	66.6
Interest expense on borrowed money	1.5	4.4
Net income before taxes	$ 4.8	13.7%
Taxes	1.5	4.2
Net income after taxes	$ 3.3	9.5%

Source: Adapted from Federal Home Loan Bank Board; and United States League of Savings Associations, *Savings & Loan Fact Book, 1978*, p. 88.

centage points each year, reaching a high of 69 percent of operating income in 1967. Since then, the industry's cost of attracting savings deposits has fluctuated within a relatively narrow range. Other operating expenses, including salaries and wages, represent about one sixth of S&L operating income and generally have been falling relative to other expenses throughout the postwar period. Despite gains in operating efficiency, however, the industry has experienced a general decline in net earnings (relative to assets or revenues) during the postwar period, especially since the early 1960s. Certainly higher interest costs on savings deposits and on other forms of borrowed money have accounted for a substantial proportion of the squeeze on the industry's net income. Of nearly equal importance, however, has been the secular uptrend in the industry's tax burden—a trend common to most depository financial institutions in recent years.

Beginning in 1951, savings associations were brought under the same federal tax rules as commercial banks and other business corporations. However, the industry was granted an exemption in the form of tax-free additions to reserves for losses on assets. Taking advantage of this privilege, few associations paid any taxes until the early 1960s when permissible additions to reserves were significantly reduced. The Tax Reform Act of 1969 further restricted tax-deductible additions to reserves, gradually lowering the allowable percentage of net income transferable to loss reserves to more closely approximate actual loss experience. In addition, taxes were imposed upon so-called preference items such as accelerated depreciation on real property and capital gains on assets.

In order to take advantage of the special federal tax concessions that remain, a savings and loan must qualify as a "domestic building and loan association." As such, it must be supervised by a federal or state regulatory agency or be insured by the Federal Savings and Loan Insurance Corporation. In addition, at least three quarters of its operating revenue must come principally from mortgages. Despite the availability of tax shelters, the industry's tax burden has risen dramatically in recent years and its *effective* tax rate is on a par or, in certain years, even greater than that faced by commercial banks and many nonfinancial corporations.

REGULATION OF SAVINGS AND LOANS

Savings and loans are subject to reserve requirements on their deposits and minimum capital (net worth) requirements just like commercial banks. The Federal Savings and Loan Insurance Corporation (FSLIC) requires each association whose deposits it insures to hold liquid reserves amounting to 5 percent of its savings deposits. The deposit base used in figuring the reserve requirement is an average of year-end savings deposit balances over a 5-year period. At the same time, each S&L must hold a minimum level of net worth. Savings and loans choosing to hold more risky loans must also hold greater levels of net worth for the protection of their depositors and other creditors.

Interest paid on deposits by savings and loans was brought under regulation by passage of the Interest Rate Adjustment Act of 1966. Under this law the Federal Home Loan Bank Board sets maximum rates that may be offered on savings accounts. These rate ceilings have been modified a number of times in recent years to preserve competitive equality with rates offered by commercial banks and other depository institutions and to keep abreast of open market interest rates. Currently, for most time and savings accounts, savings and loans pay an interest rate only a quarter point higher than do commercial banks. At the time this book went to press, interest rate ceilings on savings deposits offered by FHLB member associations ranged from 5.25 percent on regular passbook accounts to 8 percent on certificates of deposit with a minimum maturity of eight years or more. As in the case of commercial banks, certificate accounts of $100,000 or more carry no rate ceilings, regardless of their maturity.

The future of the savings and loan industry

A number of recent developments are likely to have a profound influence upon the future of the savings and loan business. Included in this list would be new electronic devices (particularly for the transfer of funds), new financial instruments (especially variable rate mortgages and NOW accounts), and recent proposals to reform the financial system. These new developments are discussed at length in Chapters 20 and 21. Therefore, only a few brief comments on these topics are presented here.

A variable rate mortgage (VRM) is a lien against real property in which the interest rate adjusts up or down, depending upon changes in some market "reference rate." The reference rate—such as the prime commercial loan rate charged by banks or the rate on long-term U.S. government bonds—is chosen to reflect changes in prevailing credit conditions. What benefits might accrue to S&Ls if they offer VRMs? VRMs presumably would allow savings associations to attract and hold deposits regardless of economic and financial conditions because their revenues would more readily adjust to fluctuations in market rates of interest. Deposit-rate ceilings could then be eliminated because much of the need for them would have disappeared. There still would be some disintermediation effects because mortgage rates might not move up or down as rapidly or as much as rates on other financial instruments. However, the savings and loan association that offers both the variable and the more conventional fixed-rate mortgage would experience a more even flow of revenues and deposits and perhaps would be able to adjust more easily to periods of monetary restraint or ease.

A number of legislative proposals have been put forward in recent years to aid savings and loans. For example, the president's Commission on Financial Structure and Regulation—more popularly known as the Hunt commission—made a number of reform proposals in 1971 that were accepted by the Nixon and Ford administrations, modified somewhat, and passed on to Congress. Among the more specific Hunt commission recommendations affecting savings and loans were the following:

1. Over a five and one-half year period, interest rate ceilings on time and savings deposits would be removed.
2. Savings and loan associations would have the authority to offer checking accounts.
3. Tax laws would be amended so that commercial banks and S&Ls could operate with greater equality.
4. Interest rate ceilings on home mortgages backed by the Federal Housing Administration (FHA) and the Veterans Administration (VA) would be eliminated.
5. Savings and loans would be able to devote a larger proportion of their total assets to consumer loans and corporate securities.

It is clear from these proposals that the Hunt commission felt it advisable for savings and loans to seek greater diversification in their assets and sources of funds. In theory, this would increase the stability of the industry, particularly in periods of intense credit restraint, and perhaps indirectly improve the flow of funds to the housing sector. The commission also favored equal treatment under both law and regulation for all thrift institutions so that all deposit-type intermediaries could compete on equal terms. It believed, as many experts do today, in encouraging greater competition in the financial sector, especially between commercial banks and nonbank thrift institutions.

MUTUAL SAVINGS BANKS

We now turn to a financial intermediary which is similar to savings and loan associations in many respects, yet markedly different in others. The deposit-type thrift institution known today as the "mutual savings bank" began in Scotland in the early 19th century. The original idea, still followed today, was to create an outlet for the savings of low- and middle-income families and thereby encourage family thrift. In turn, the savings bank would invest the public's funds in long-term capital market instruments (principally bonds and mortgages) in order to pay interest on the deposits. As we saw earlier, savings and loans also were started in order to encourage thrift among savers of modest means, but their deposits were specifically earmarked for the financing of new homes.

STRUCTURE OF THE INDUSTRY

The first mutual savings banks headquartered in the United States opened in Boston and Philadelphia in 1816. By year-end 1977, there were a total of 467 mutuals active in 17 states. (See Table 12–5.)

TABLE 12–5
Number, total assets, and average assets of mutual savings banks in selected years, 1900–1977 ($millions)

Year	Number of mutuals	Total assets	Average assets
1900	626	$ 2,328	$ 3.7
1910	637	3,598	5.6
1920	618	5,586	9.0
1930	592	10,496	17.7
1940	540	11,919	22.1
1950	529	22,446	42.4
1960	515	40,571	78.8
1970	494	78,995	159.9
1977	467	147,287	315.4

Source: Adapted from National Association of Mutual Savings Banks, *National Fact Book of Mutual Savings Banking, 1978,* p. 15.

These institutions operated 2,781 offices and held 33 million savings accounts amounting to $134 billion. Growth has been rapid; the average savings bank nearly doubled in size between 1970 and 1977.

The industry is concentrated both geographically and by size of institution. The majority of mutual savings banks are situated along the East Coast of the United States, principally in the New England and Mid-Atlantic regions. As of year-end 1977 Massachusetts had the largest number of savings banks with New York second, followed by Connecticut, Maine, and New Hampshire. The mutuals located in Connecticut, Massachusetts, and New York represent almost three quarters of all U.S. savings banks and hold more than 80 percent of industry resources. About 90 percent of all deposits held by mutuals are accounted for by savings banks headquartered in only five states—Connecticut, Massachusetts, New Jersey, New York, and Pennsylvania.[5]

Most mutuals are relatively small. (See Table 12–6.) More than half hold deposits of less than $100 million; while only 15 percent

TABLE 12–6
Distribution of mutual savings banks according to size and state of location,
December 31, 1977

State	Number of mutual savings banks	Number reporting total deposits of: ($millions)					
		Less than 25.0	25.0 to 49.9	50.0 to 99.9	100.0 to 249.9	250.0 to 499.9	500.0 and over
Massachusetts	166	21	34	47	47	12	5
New York	115	—	7	20	27	16	45
Connecticut	65	2	9	27	18	5	4
Maine	30	5	10	10	4	1	—
New Hampshire	26	3	7	12	3	1	—
New Jersey	20	1	2	2	5	6	4
Washington	9	—	—	3	2	2	2
Pennsylvania	8	—	1	—	2	—	5
Rhode Island	6	—	—	1	3	1	1
Vermont	6	1	—	3	1	1	—
Indiana	4	—	2	2	—	—	—
Maryland	4	—	—	1	—	—	2
Wisconsin	3	2	1	—	—	—	—
Alaska	2	—	—	1	1	—	—
Delaware	2	—	—	—	1	—	1
Minnesota	1	—	—	—	—	—	1
Oregon	1	—	—	—	—	1	—
Totals	467	35	73	129	114	46	70

Source: Adapted from National Association of Mutual Savings Banks, *National Fact Book of Mutual Savings Banking, 1978,* p. 15.

hold deposits of $500 million or more. While smaller savings banks numerically dominate, the average-size mutual has risen sharply in recent years to hold about $215 million in total assets—more than three times the average asset size for both commercial banks and savings and loan associations.

Mutual savings banks, legally, are owned by their depositors and are operated for their benefit. Savers who deposit their funds in a mutual receive all earnings (less any additions to reserve accounts as required either by law or by the policies of the individual institution) in the form of quarterly or semiannual crediting of interest to their accounts. Though the depositors legally are the owners of a savings

[5] See Harless [5], p. 24.

bank, policy making and control of management is reserved for a board of trustees who often serve without pay. New trustees may be chosen by the existing board or elected according to the dictates of state law. Whatever method of selection is used, state laws and the bylaws of each savings bank set out detailed rules to govern the board of trustees and the mutual's officers.

Savings banks are regulated almost exclusively by the states with only limited involvement by the federal government. In fact, they are the only financial intermediary accepting deposits that is chartered exclusively by the states. The federal role is limited to the insurance of deposits for mutuals that qualify and the setting of deposit-rate ceilings. In contrast, state laws encompass nearly every aspect of savings bank operation, including the selection of management and board of trustees, the kind and quality of assets that may be acquired, the types of customer services that may be offered, and the distribution of earnings. Regular examination of individual institutions also is carried out by state agencies, though savings banks insured by the Federal Deposit Insurance Corporation and mutuals belonging to the Federal Home Loan Bank System are subject to examination by these two federal agencies.

Responding to increasing competition for funds, the industry has sought and won important regulatory concessions within the past decade. Mutual savings banks appear to be striving toward the goal of becoming "department stores of finance," offering a wide range of financial services similar to those offered by commercial banks. (See Table 12–7.) These services include thrift deposits, mortgage credit, family financial counseling, life insurance, safe-deposit boxes, money orders, traveler's checks, credit cards, and passbook loans. The service package offered by the industry has expanded in the 1970s to encompass third-party payments services (particularly NOW accounts) and retirement plans. A number of states now permit the offering of credit cards and the transfer of funds to and from savings accounts for stipulated purposes. Moreover, there is a trend in the industry toward more effective utilization of marketing techniques, evidenced by increased use of cash-dispensing machines providing readily available money on a 24-hour basis and the provision of financial counseling services to individuals and families. Further expansion in service offerings is expected in future years as the industry strives to retain its share of deposit and loan markets and compete successfully with credit unions, commercial banks, and savings and loan associations.

Probably the most important new service offered by mutual savings banks is the account with third-party payment powers. Actually, there are three basic types of these accounts in use today: (1) regular

TABLE 12–7
Number of mutual savings banks offering selected services in 1977

Types of services offered	Number of mutual savings banks offering the service
Automated tellers	64
Bank money orders	462
Checking accounts	219
Overdraft privileges on checking accounts	107
Check verification	59
Club accounts	420
Collateral loans	406
Credit cards	101
Direct deposit	411
Education loans	372
Home improvement loans	452
24-hour cash dispensing facilities	52
Individual retirement accounts	394
NOW accounts	256
Passbook loans	466
Payroll deductions	304
Personal loans	311
Point-of-sale services	15
Safe-deposit boxes	380
Savings bank life insurance	333
Savings payout plan	96
School savings	113
Self-employed retirement savings (Keogh)	276
Telephone bill-paying	39
Traveler's checks	458
Total savings banks included	469

Source: Adapted from National Association of Mutual Savings Banks, *National Fact Book of Mutual Savings Banking, 1978,* p. 59.

checking accounts; (2) interest-bearing negotiable orders of withdrawal (NOW) accounts; and (3) noninterest-bearing negotiable orders of withdrawal (NINOW) accounts. In June 1972 mutuals introduced NOWs in Massachusetts through a loophole in that state's banking regulations. Almost immediately, New Hampshire savings banks began offering NOWs on similar legal grounds. Congress legitimized the NOW account for all deposit-type intermediaries in Massachusetts and New Hampshire effective January 1974.[6] In September 1975 checking account powers were granted to Oregon savings institutions through a new law in that state—a move soon followed by the states of Connecticut, Delaware, Maine, and New York. Federal prohibitions against the offering of NOW accounts were removed in Connecticut, Maine, Rhode Island, and Vermont during

---

[6] For a more complete discussion of the NOW phenomenon see Chapter 21.

1976. NINOWs were legalized for savings banks in Pennsylvania and Minnesota during 1977. So rapid and so sweeping has been the movement to give savings banks third-party payments services that by 1978 97 percent of the mutuals then in operation could legally offer payment services.

Sources of funds

Historically, the major source of funds for mutual savings banks has been the deposits of individuals and families. The majority of these savings accounts offer a fairly modest yield, but also possess the important features of liquidity and safety which are so important to savers of relatively limited means. Significant changes are now occurring in the sources of savings bank funds, as we noted above, due to the rise of NOW accounts and other third-party payments services. While, historically, passbook savings deposits have represented the principal source of funds for mutuals, the growth of NOWs and higher-yielding time deposits has been much faster in recent years. The appeal of mutuals to the small saver has not diminished noticeably but even the small saver has become more cognizant of the alternative and frequently more profitable uses of funds available. At year-end 1977, higher-yielding time deposits and other special thrift accounts represented about two fifths of total savings bank deposits, compared to only about one fifth in 1971. The growth in higher-yielding, longer-term savings deposits has had profound effects on the savings banking industry.

The principal insurance fund for deposits in mutual savings banks is the Federal Deposit Insurance Corporation (FDIC), which insures individual accounts up to a maximum of $40,000. Few savings bank deposits are not fully protected by some form of deposit insurance. While the FDIC will insure qualified savings banks in every state, the state of Massachusetts also has set up an agency which insures 100 percent of the deposits held by savings banks in that state. The availability of deposit insurance has definitely spurred the growth of the industry because this feature is particularly attractive to the small saver—the major source of funds for mutual savings banks.

Savings banks are limited by law in the interest rates they are permitted to pay on deposits. Insured mutuals are subject to ceiling rates set by the Federal Deposit Insurance Corporation in cooperation with the Federal Reserve Board (which sets deposit-rate ceilings for member commercial banks) and the Federal Home Loan Bank Board (which determines maximum deposit rates for savings and loans). Only certificates of deposit in amounts of $100,000 or more, offered by mutuals as well as commercial banks and savings and loans, may be offered free of any legal ceiling on rates paid. However, mutual savings banks deal mainly in small savings accounts and, therefore, are more restricted by rate ceilings than are commercial banks. As shown in Table 12–8, federal deposit-rate ceilings applicable to mutual sav-

TABLE 12–8
Comparative federal deposit interest rate ceilings on consumer thrift deposits at commercial banks, mutual savings banks, and savings and loan associations (as of June 1, 1978)

Type of account	Mutual savings banks	Commercial banks	Savings and loan associations
Ordinary savings deposits	5.25%	5.00%	5.25%
Time deposits, by maturity:			
90 days–1 year...................	5.75	5.50	5.75
1–2½ years	6.50	6.00	6.50
2½ years or more	6.75	6.50	6.75
4–6 years*	7.50	7.25	7.50
6–8 years*	7.75	7.50	7.75
8 years or more*	8.00	7.75	8.00

Note: No time deposits of more than $100,000 are included. Table does not include money market CDs authorized in 1978 whose ceilings rates are equal to the auction discount yield on six-month U.S. Treasury bills plus 25 basis points for those certificates issued by mutual savings banks and savings and loan associations. Commercial banks may issue money market CDs at the six-month Treasury bill yield.
  * Minimum denominations of $1,000.
  Source: Adapted from data from the Federal Deposit Insurance Corporation, the Federal Home Loan Bank Board, and the Federal Reserve Board; and National Association of Mutual Savings Banks, *National Fact Book of Mutual Savings Banking, 1978*, p. 43.

ings banks range from 5.25 percent on passbook accounts to 8.00 percent on $1,000 minimum, eight-year deposits. In addition, mutual savings banks along with other deposit-type intermediaries were authorized, effective June 1, 1978, to offer money market CDs carrying a flexible ceiling rate equivalent to the auction discount rate prevailing each week on six-month U.S. Treasury bills plus 25 basis points (i.e., one fourth of 1 percent). These CDs carry six-month maturities and must be sold in $10,000 minimum denominations.

Uses of funds

Mutuals are closely regulated in the loans and investments they are permitted to make. For example, securities purchased must come from a list sanctioned by the appropriate state supervisory agency. U.S. government securities are always acceptable as investments as are high-quality municipal and Canadian securities, World Bank securities, secured utility and railroad obligations of investment quality, highly rated industrial bonds or their equivalent, and high-quality common and preferred equity shares. Investments in open market securities in recent years have averaged just under 25 percent of industry assets, led by corporate bonds and stocks, while the bulk of remaining funds have flowed into first mortgage loans. Only a minor percentage of total industry resources normally are devoted to the most liquid assets, which include U.S. government securities, federal agency obligations, mortgage-backed bonds, municipals, and cash. (See Table 12–9.)

The liquidity needs of mutual savings banks are very low since their deposits are predominantly savings balances whose fluctuations are much more predictable than are commercial bank demand deposits. The primary liquidity reserve consists of cash (including bank deposits), short-term U.S. government securities, and prime-quality marketable securities. In a pinch savings banks can borrow short-term funds from commercial banks or other lenders, warehouse some of their loans, or sell their more marketable securities; however, the industry has no government-created "lender of last resort" such as the Federal Reserve System for commercial banks or the Federal Home Loan Bank System for savings and loans. The proportion of funds devoted to more liquid financial assets (especially demand deposits and currency, time deposits, and U.S. government securities) increased beginning in the late 1970s as mutuals attempted to rebuild their liquidity reserves after a period of severe disintermediation in 1973 and 1974. Another factor leading to the recent growth in liquid assets may be the growth of special accounts, particularly NOWs and other payments accounts. It seems reasonable to assume that as mutuals become more like commercial banks in the deposit services they offer, their liquidity requirements will increase and the composition of their assets will change accordingly.

Mutuals are limited by state law and regulation in the kinds of loans they may grant. Most commonly, first mortgage loans on improved real property are allowed as are loans to customers against their savings deposits. A few states allow savings banks to make instalment and home improvement loans but limit these to a relatively small percentage of total assets. However, the industry's major lending activity centers around mortgage credit, either originated by mutuals or purchased from other lenders. As a whole, mortgages represent about three fifths of industry assets. About 70 percent of these are conventional mortgage loans for the purchase of commercial and residential properties, and the remainder are about equally divided between government-guaranteed FHA and VA residential mortgages. Because mutuals face no significant geographic restrictions on their real estate lending (as do savings and loans, for example), they often

TABLE 12–9
Assets and liabilities of mutual savings banks, December 31, 1977

Item	$millions		Percent of total assets
Assets			
Cash and due from banks		$ 2,401	1.6%
U.S. government obligations		5,895	4.0
Federal agency obligations		3,338	2.3
State and local obligations		2,828	1.9
Mortgage investments		96,526	65,5
Mortgage loans	$88,195		59.9%
GNMA mortgage backed	8,331		5.7
Corporate and other bonds		21,498	14.6
Corporate stock		4,751	3.2%
Other loans		6,210	4.2
Guaranteed education loans	783		0.5
Consumer instalment	989		0.7
Home improvement loans	588		0.4
Federal funds	2,081		1.4
Passbook loans	789		0.5
All other loans	980		0.7
Bank premises owned		1,281	0.9
Other real estate		462	0.3
Other assets		2,096	1.4
Total assets		$147,287	100.0%
Liabilities and Reserves			
Regular deposits		$132,744	90.2%
Savings	$78,005		53.0%
Time	54,739		37.2
School and club		202	0.1
Other deposits		1,070	0.7
Total deposits		$134,017	91.0%
Borrowings and mortgage warehousing		622	0.4
Other liabilities		2,670	1.8
Total liabilities		$137,309	93.2%
Capital notes and debentures		350	0.2
Other general reserves		9,628	6.5
Total general reserve accounts		$ 9,978	6.8%
Total liabilities and general reserve accounts		$147,287	100.0%

Source: Adapted from National Association of Mutual Savings Banks, *National Fact Book of Mutual Savings Banking, 1978*, pp. 11–12.

make loans far removed from their local market area. The added risk protection and standardization afforded by FHA- and VA-guaranteed mortgages are attractive features to mutuals, though the low interest rate ceilings on these government-guaranteed mortgage instruments have resulted in a shift of industry residential lending more toward conventional mortgage loans in recent years.[7] Purchases of GNMA mortgage-backed securities, totaling a record $2.5 billion in 1977, also have become an important element in the industry's support of the U.S. mortgage market.

Of course, net acquisitions of mortgage loans and other assets depend upon market conditions and the alternative investments available to savings banks. Mutuals have much greater flexibility in asset selection than savings and loans and are not restricted by law to investing mainly in mortgages. Net holdings of mortgages rose $6.5 billion in 1977, considerably more than the $4.4 billion purchased in 1976. Both years' net mortgage acquisitions were well above purchases of mortgages during 1974 and 1975 when interest rates and deposit flows were less favorable. In contrast, industry holdings of corporate bonds mushroomed during 1975 and were also heavy in 1976 after only a slight increase during 1974 and a substantial decline the previous year. The explanation lies principally in the rising mortgage rates available and the heavy demand for real estate loans during 1973 and again in 1976 and 1977, while 1975 ushered in a period of attractive prices on corporate and other bonds. Thus, the management of mutual savings banks, like that of other intermediaries, is highly sensitive to relative yields on financial instruments, shifting their investments as the spread between rates of return on various securities changes.

Holdings of state and local government obligations have grown quite rapidly in recent years, especially since 1974. Changes in tax laws account for some of the growth in savings bank municipal holdings, but market prices of municipal bonds also have been extremely attractive, reflecting favorable conditions in the bond market as a whole. This favorable trend in bond yields and prices is also reflected in recent gains in holdings of U.S. government bonds and federal agency obligations. Uncertain conditions in the stock market have resulted in corporate shares losing ground to other securities in the portfolio holdings of savings banks. Another factor adversely affecting stock acquisitions by mutuals was the 1976 ruling by the Financial

---

[7] Mutuals have become more innovative in their mortgage lending. Some institutions, located principally along the East Coast, have offered mortgages with flexible interest rates, shorter maturities, and graduated monthly payments. The most widely used of these mortgage instruments is the variable rate mortgage (VRM) discussed earlier in this chapter. (See Chapter 21 for a more complete discussion of the VRM.) Canadian roll-over mortgages also have been offered by some savings banks. These instruments require the borrower to renegotiate the mortgage loan more frequently (frequently every five years) and therefore offer greater flexibility in their interest rate on the loan. Graduated-payment mortgages, which permit smaller monthly installment payments in the early years of a loan, also have been offered by some mutuals in recent years.

Accounting Standards Board that equity investments should be valued at the lower of their cost or market value.

GROWTH OF THE INDUSTRY

The growth of mutuals has been somewhat erratic, especially during the past decade as credit conditions and interest rates have fluctuated widely. There is increasing evidence that the assets and liabilities of the industry are becoming more volatile, reflecting changes in conditions in the nation's financial markets and a shift in the mix of services offered to the public. For example, during the credit crunches of 1966, 1969, and 1973–74, savings bank deposit growth dropped precipitously, only to resume again in the period following when interest rates were lower and credit was easier to obtain. The result has been to put greater pressure on management to adopt more flexible policies and to offer new services to attract savers.

Despite these sharp fluctuations in inflows of funds, accompanied by corresponding changes in the industry's assets, the long-term growth of mutuals has been respectable. By war's end in 1945 total financial assets held by the industry were just under $17 billion, but this figure had more than doubled by the late 1950s. At year-end 1977 assets totaled $147 billion, an increase of more than 600 percent since 1945. The average savings bank has grown over the same period from an institution with about $30 million in total resources to well over $300 million. While merger activity and consolidations have reduced the population of savings banks, the number of branch offices has advanced significantly, aiding individual banks in increasing the size of their operations.

Like all financial intermediaries, savings banks operate simultaneously in two markets—borrowing funds and making loans and investments. In those areas of the nation where they have concentrated their operations, savings banks are an extremely important conduit for loanable funds. For example, in total, the industry accounts for about a third of the volume of savings accounts in the 17 states where it is represented. As Harless notes, in four states—Connecticut, Massachusetts, New Hampshire, and New York—deposits held by mutuals total more that the savings deposits of commercial banks, credit unions, and savings and loans put together.[8] For the nation as a whole mutuals hold about 15 percent of all savings deposits held by individuals and families in deposit-type financial intermediaries. In this respect, they are a much more significant factor in the savings market

---

[8] See Harless [5], p. 30.

than are credit unions, though the latter are growing considerably faster. Mutual savings banks rank third in the nation behind commercial banks and savings and loan associations in the total amount of savings deposits held.[9]

On the lending and investing side of the balance sheet, mutuals exert their most significant impact upon the nation's mortgage market. Mutuals hold more FHA-insured mortgages than any other lender and rank second in their acquisitions of VA-insured loans. Mutuals make both residential and commercial mortgages. At year-end 1977 residential mortgages held by the industry totaled $73 billion while other (principally commercial) mortgages were about $15 billion. Within the residential category, mortgages on one- to four-family dwellings totaled nearly $58 billion, while mortgage loans on multifamily dwellings amounted to approximately $15 billion. The relative growth of these different types of mortgage loans varies with market conditions. For example, between 1973 and 1974 net additions to savings bank portfolios of mortgages on one- to four-family dwellings rose only $400 million as the housing market slid into its greatest recent recession due to high interest rates, unemployment, and rapidly rising building costs. Additions to holdings of other mortgages—multifamily, commercial, and farm—where market conditions were more favorable—totaled $800 million. In contrast, during 1977—a year in which the demand for new homes was very strong—holdings of home mortgages by mutuals rose almost $5 billion, which was nearly three times the gain in the industry's holdings of commercial, farm, and multifamily mortgages.

Revenues, expenses, and taxes

Revenue flows at mutual savings banks have remained strong throughout the postwar period, especially during the past decade. As interest rates in the open market have risen, rates of return on savings bank loans and investments also have increased. Mutuals during the postwar period generally have received lower rates of return on their assets than savings and loans but higher returns than commercial banks. In the most recent years, however, earnings of mutuals generally have lagged behind both banks and savings and loans. This is due to sharp increases in savings bank expenses, especially in years of rapidly rising interest rates. The earnings squeeze has been exacer-

---

[9] At year-end 1977 mutuals held nearly $133 billion in time and savings deposits compared to $379 billion in thrift deposits held by savings and loans and $386 billion held by commercial banks. See, especially, National Association of Mutual Savings Banks [7], p. 22.

bated by a general shift of depositor funds from relatively low-yielding savings deposits to higher-yielding time deposits.

A partial offset to the effect of rising costs on net earnings may be found in the relatively lenient tax situation faced by mutuals. However, there is a trend toward higher effective tax rates resulting principally from provisions of the 1969 Tax Reform Act. The law requires savings banks to pay ordinary corporate income tax rates on net income left over after interest is paid to depositors. However, as in the case of savings and loans, a portion of net earnings may be sheltered through additions to bad debt reserves based upon the savings bank's actual or estimated loss experience. For "nonqualifying loans" (principally loans not connected with the financing of real property) tax-free additions to reserves for losses must be related to actual loan loss experience. In the case of "qualifying loans," the savings bank may employ the greater of either actual loss experience or a fixed proportion of taxable income. The 1969 Tax Reform Act stipulated that by 1979 no more than 40 percent of otherwise taxable income could be used for tax-free additions to bad debt reserves.

CONCLUSIONS

In this chapter we have taken a close look at the savings bank industry, represented by mutual savings banks and savings and loan associations. Overall, it must be said that the outlook for this industry is somewhat clouded. A period of more moderate growth seems likely in future years, provided the industry can adapt its structure and service package to the changing market for financial services. Among other things, successful adaptation will require greater diversification of assets—a step recommended by numerous authorities in the field—and more aggressive use of branching, mergers, electronic equipment, and marketing of financial services. The aggressiveness with which the industry has penetrated the payments system with such devices as NOW accounts and computer terminals for withdrawing and depositing funds is a hopeful sign for the future. As in the case of other financial intermediaries, however, much of the industry's future success depends upon the willingness of the regulatory authorities to loosen the bonds of regulation and permit greater innovation.

QUESTIONS

12-1. How may a savings and loan association be chartered? What is the difference between a mutual and a permanent stock association?

12–2. What is the most important regulatory agency in the savings and loan industry? What are its principal powers?

12–3. What are some of the potential advantages accruing to a savings and loan association when it is chartered as a permanent stock association? Can you suggest any advantages which may accrue to customers? Any disadvantages?

12–4. What are the major assets and liabilities of savings and loan associations? mutuals savings banks? Compare and contrast the sources and uses of funds of these two savings institutions.

12–5. What is a variable rate mortgage? What potential advantages could it offer the management of savings associations and savings banks?

12–6. Why do you think savings banks and savings and loans are interested in becoming active participants in the payments mechanism along with commercial banks? What are the potential benefits and costs of NOW accounts to deposit-type financial intermediaries?

12–7. Both the number of savings and loan associations and the number of mutual savings banks have been declining in recent years. Explain why this is happening. Do you think this trend will continue?

12–8. The growth of mutual savings banks and savings and loans has become much more volatile in recent years, leading to greater uncertainty in the financial management of these institutions. List the principal factors which have led to more volatile changes in the assets and deposits of these institutions. In what ways can management deal with this problem effectively?

REFERENCES

1. Benston, George J. "Savings Banks and the Public Interest." *Journal of Money, Credit, and Banking,* February 1972, pt. II, pp. 133–226.

2. Bomar, Thomas A. "Conversion." *Federal Home Loan Bank Board Journal,* May 1974.

3. Daly, George G. "Financial Intermediation and the Theory of Firm: An Analysis of Savings and Loan Association Behavior." *Southern Economic Journal,* vol. 37 (January 1971), pp. 283–94.

4. Friend, Irwin. *Study of the Savings and Loan Industry.* vol. 1–4 (Washington, D.C.: Federal Home Loan Bank Board, 1969–70).

5. Harless, Doris E. *Nonbank Financial Institutions.* Federal Reserve Bank of Richmond, October 1975.

6. Lapp, John S. "Market Structure and Advertising in the Savings and Loan Industry." *Review of Economics and Statistics,* vol. 58, no. 2 (May 1976), pp. 202–8.

7. National Association of Mutual Savings Banks. *National Fact Book of Mutual Savings Banking, 1978.*

8. Nicols, Alfred. "Stock versus Mutual Savings and Loan Associations: Some Evidence of Differences in Behavior." *American Economic Review,* May 1967, pp. 341–45.

9. Shows, E. Warren. "Conversion of Savings and Loans: Some Aspects of Equity in the Transition." *Altanta Economic Review,* January–February 1974, pp. 31–34.

10. United States League of Savings Associations. *Savings and Loan Fact Book, 1978.*

Problem for discussion

As we have seen in this chapter, savings and loan associations and mutual savings banks make thousands of residential real estate loans each year. This is one of the most complicated areas for the lending of funds because home mortgage loans typically carry 20- to 30-year maturities and both the borrower and the lending institution face substantial risks over this long period. Property values may decline or borrowers may suffer serious financial reverses and be forced to give up their homes. The risks of home mortgage lending have led many financial institutions active in this field to prefer FHA- or VA-insured mortgages, though most home mortgage loans granted today are conventional nonguaranteed loans.

In this problem suppose you are a loan officer employed by Hardy Building and Loan Association to interview prospective mortgage borrowers. You have recently interviewed Mr. and Mrs. Robert Warren concerning the application they submitted last week for a conventional residential mortgage loan on a newly constructed three-bedroom home. You must decide whether to recommend to the association's loan committee if a mortgage commitment should be made to the Warrens.

The construction company has priced the one-story, three-bedroom structure, which has 1,500 square feet, at $49,500. The Warrens have been residents of the local community for about three years, but have been renting a home during that period. Their monthly rental is $240, significantly less than what the monthly mortgage payments would be on their new home. Information on monthly mortgage payments under a variety of assumed interest rates from 8 percent to 10 percent is shown in Exhibit 1. In the market area served by Hardy Building and Loan Association,

EXHIBIT 1
Monthly mortgage payments per $1,000 of mortgage loan

Maturity of loan in years	Annual interest rate on the loan								
	8%	8¼%	8½%	8¾%	9%	9¼%	9½%	9¾%	10%
15	$9.56	$9.71	$9.85	$10.00	$10.15	$10.30	$10.45	$10.60	$10.75
20	8.37	8.53	8.68	8.84	9.00	9.16	9.33	9.49	9.66
25	7.72	7.89	8.06	8.23	8.40	8.57	8.74	8.92	9.09
30	7.34	7.52	7.69	7.87	8.05	8.23	8.41	8.60	8.78
35	7.11	7.29	7.47	7.66	7.84	8.03	8.22	8.41	8.60

mortgage loan rates on 90 percent loans have ranged in recent weeks between 9½ and 9¾ percent.

Mr. Warren works as a salesman for an auto insurance company. His salary is about $16,000 annually, netting about $1,200 per month in take-home pay. He has held his present job—his first full-time job after college—for about three years. Sally Warren works part time as a secretary, a position she has held for eight months, and brings home net about $250 per month. The Warrens have two children attending public school.

An appraisal report on the property and a credit check also have been made. A member of Hardy's credit appraisal staff estimates that the new home has a current market value of about $50,000. Two weeks ago the Warrens applied for a conventional mortgage loan at the First National Bank, but were told that the bank could lend no more than 80 percent of the property's appraised value with a maximum maturity of ten years. Because Mr. Warren graduated from college only three years ago and the family has had little opportunity to build its savings, they can come up with no more than a 10 percent down payment. A check of the Warren's financial statements shows little additional financial strength beyond the family's two monthly paychecks. Mr. Warren carries a $20,000 term insurance policy and holds a few corporate and government bonds valued at $2,500. The family's two-year-old Chevrolet station wagon is valued at $3,300. Their passbook savings account, held at First National Bank, has a balance of $750. The family is covered by a health insurance group plan through Mr. Warren's employer, but Mr. Warren has no disability insurance.

Hardy Building and Loan Association normally would prefer to make a conventional mortgage loan in this instance because of its greater flexibility. Currently, government-guaranteed FHA loans carry a ceiling rate of 8½ percent. In contrast, there is no legal interest rate ceiling applying specifically to conventional mortgages, though an existing state usury law limits the rate on loans to individuals to a maximum of 10 percent. For the 90 percent conventional loan sought by the Warrens, the Mortgage Guaranty Insurance Corporation (MGIC), which will insure acceptable conventional mortgage loans against default, levies an initial fee of one half of 1 percent of the amount of the loan plus an annual renewal fee of one fourth of 1 percent of the amount of the unpaid balance for the first ten years. However, conventional mortgage credit carries no government guarantee behind the borrower's obligation as does an FHA or VA loan. FHA insures 97 percent of the first $25,000 of appraised value; then 90 percent of the residual value up to $35,000; and 80 percent of any amount over $35,000.

There are a number of additional costs (usually referred to as "closing costs") associated with the making of residential real estate loans. Hardy charges a loan commitment fee of 1¼ percent of the face amount of the loan. Mortgage title insurance will cost an additional $250. In addition, a reserve of $550 must be set aside in escrow for property taxes and insurance. The lender must be presented at the time of closing with a mortgagee's home insurance policy whose principal value is at least equal to the amount of the mortgage loan. If the Warrens seek FHA insurance, there is an FHA appraisal charge of $50 and a mortgage discount fee of 2 points. If a 90 percent conventional loan is made, Hardy Building and Loan Association will automatically seek insurance coverage from MGIC.

If the Warrens are able to put 10 percent down, they will need to borrow $44,500 in order to purchase their new home. There are, however, some risks which need to be carefully assessed by the loan officer. First, there is some feeling among businessmen in the area that the local economy is due for a major downturn. To be sure, the city and surrounding county are currently in the midst of a population boom, due to the rapid influx of new residents seeking a milder climate and better job opportunities. But, there are rumors of a drastic slowdown or even cutback in government employment in the near future. Indeed, the local community's unemployment rate is slightly higher today than a year ago. If the situation worsens, conditions in the local real estate market will quickly turn sour with adverse effects on property values. Adding to the problem, a boom in apartment construction is well underway—a delayed response to the earlier growth of government jobs.

The Warren's personal financial situation raises some questions. Mr. Warren, the family's principal breadwinner, works on commission in a highly volatile industry. If the local economy turns down, auto insurance sales are likely to do the same. Moreover, his employer, the Gilbert Insurance Agency, has the reputation of frequently transferring its salespeople to new locations. Salesmen who do not produce an adequate volume of new premiums and policy renewals are eased out; those who do perform well usually are transferred to more challenging jobs in four to five years. Mr. Warren is probably approaching a critical period in his present job, having been with the company nearly three full years. On the plus side, however, the Gilbert Insurance Agency indicated on the verification of employment form sent to it by Hardy that Mr. Warren's future employment prospects with the agency were excellent and his probability of continued employment was about 95 percent. The Warrens owe $2,550 to the local bank for an auto loan (monthly payments of $133), $450 to a credit card plan for vacation expenses, $455 to an appliance store for a refrigerator and stove (monthly payments of $65), $950 to a furniture company for living and dining room furnishings (monthly payments of $50), and $150 to a department store for fall clothing. However, the report from the local credit bureau gave the Warrens a rating of "good" on their payment record, indicating that on only one or two occasions have late payments been made.

The substantial fixed charges incurred coupled with the family's fluctuating income may make it difficult for the Warrens to meet monthly mortgage payments and also to keep up the value of their property. Rising costs for fuel, taxes, and home repairs make home ownership far more expensive today than even a few years ago. Hardy Building and Loan Association, like many savings and loans, tries to limit its residential mortgage loans to a maximum of two to two and one half times the gross annual income of the borrower. It prefers a situation where the home mortgage payment plus all other instalment obligations are no more than about a third of the borrower's monthly gross income. However, Hardy will grant exceptions to this rule where the borrower's future earnings prospects appear exceptionally bright. The Warrens are anxious to purchase their new home and probably can secure the financing they need at a neighboring savings and loan or mutual savings bank which extends more liberal credit terms. You must, therefore, consider the Warren's request with great care.

13

Credit unions

One of the most specialized and also one of the fastest growing of all financial intermediaries is the credit union. The financial institutions we have discussed to this point are generally business-oriented firms, attempting to earn the highest possible returns for their owners consistent with regulations and the principles of sound financial management. Credit unions, on the other hand, are cooperative associations rather than businesses operated for profit. Credit union members pool their funds to earn interest and then make loans to each other. Harless [6] describes the credit union by means of a simple equation:

A group of people + A common interest + Pooled savings + Loans to each other = A credit union.

The early history of credit unions was marked by relatively slow growth. The small saver and borrower whom credit unions serve did not really come into prominence until the 20th century, especially after World War II. Reflecting the rise of the small saver and borrower during the postwar period, the number of credit unions increased rapidly, doubling during the 1950s alone. In the decade of the 1960s membership in U.S. credit unions doubled, while credit union assets more than tripled.

By year-end 1978, nearly 22,000 credit unions—with more than 40 million members and resources of almost $65 billion—were functioning within the United States. (See Table 13–1.) In recent years their membership has grown by 2 to 3 million a year and their asset and deposit growth has exceeded that of other depository intermediaries by a wide margin.

TABLE 13–1
Growth in credit union membership, assets, and savings, 1945–1978*

Year	Number of credit unions	Number of members	Savings shares and deposits ($millions)	Loans outstanding† ($millions)	Total assets ($millions)
1978	21,935	40,289,198	$52,592	$50,636	$62,631
1977	22,407	36,860,406	46,740	41,907	54,182
1976	22,615	33,760,396	39,150	34,280	45,013
1975	22,703	31,151,763	33,116	28,218	37,937
1974	22,964	29,502,615	27,566	24,434	31,953
1973	22,999	27,488,416	24,669	21,771	28,418
1972	23,115	25,753,543	21,628	18,675	24,533
1971	23,284	24,094,257	18,367	16,164	21,134
1970	23,699	22,797,193	15,492	14,108	17,960
1965	22,119	16,753,106	9,249	8,095	10,552
1960	20,456	12,037,533	4,975	4,377	5,653
1955	16,201	8,153,641	2,447	1,934	2,743
1950	10,591	4,610,278	850	680	1,005
1945	8,683	2,842,989	369	128	435

* 1978 figures are preliminary.
† Loans to other credit unions are included in the figures shown prior to 1960.
Source: Adapted from National Credit Union Administration; and Credit Union National Association, Inc., 1979 Yearbook.

Despite their impressive growth, deposits in credit unions still are quite small in comparison to other financial institutions. Credit union deposits represented only about 4 percent of total savings held in U.S. deposit-type financial intermediaries at year-end 1978. Nevertheless, the trend of growth in savings accounts relative to competing institutions is impressive, as shown in Table 13–2. The savings deposits of U.S. credit unions increased 287 percent between 1969 and 1978, significantly faster than savings deposits held by commercial banks and savings and loan associations and more than double the rate of growth of savings accounts at mutual savings banks. Of course, the relatively small base from which the industry started explains part of its rapid growth rate. The other principal cause, as we shall see in this chapter, is the aggressive and innovative spirit which characterizes credit union management today.

TABLE 13–2
Growth of savings accounts at U.S. deposit-type financial institutions, 1969 and 1978

Type of institution	Total savings accounts held ($billions)		Percentage increase, 1969–1978
	1969	1978	
Commercial banks	$193.7	$600.3	209.8%
Savings and loan associations	135.7	431.1	217.8
Mutual savings banks	67.0	142.7	112.9
Credit unions	13.7	53.0	287.2

Source: Adapted from Credit Union National Association, Inc., *1979 Yearbook.*

THE STRUCTURE OF THE CREDIT UNION INDUSTRY

Credit unions began operations early in the 19th century. At one time their sole purpose was to meet the needs of lower-income individuals for inexpensive credit. Today, however, credit union membership includes individuals from a wide variety of social classes and income strata as reflected in a recent survey conducted by the Credit Union National Association (CUNA), the major industry trade association, and Opinion Research Corporation.[1] Credit union members tend to make greater use of credit cards, checking accounts, and home mortgage credit than the general population. In fact, the extremely rapid growth of credit unions during the postwar era is a direct reflection of the industry's ability to offer financial services appealing to middle-income individuals and families.

Credit unions are chartered by both state and federal governments. At year-end 1977 the 12,750 federally chartered institutions represented 57 percent of the total number of U.S. credit unions. There has been a substantial decline in the number of state-chartered credit unions in recent years, while the number of federally chartered associations has remained comparatively stable. The number of charters is closely linked to population size and population growth. The states of California, New York, Pennsylvania, and Texas with large populations have accounted for a disproportionate number of credit union charters in recent years.

Type of membership

Most credit unions (about 80 percent) are organized by occupational groups. Traditionally, credit union charters require a mini-

---

[1] For a summary of the survey findings see Credit Union National Association [2], pp. 4–9.

mum of approximately 100 potential members. However, business firms which are too small to charter a separate unit frequently are able to affiliate with an existing union. As shown in Table 13–3, close to three fifths of all U.S. credit unions are organized around a job or

TABLE 13–3
Distribution of U.S. credit unions by common bond (percent)

Type of bond	1969	1978*
Associational	17.79%	13.61%
Occupational†	56.88	57.35
Governmental	7.19	9.63
Residential	14.76	15.77
Total	100.00%	100.00%

* Includes only those credit unions reporting.

† Includes credit unions whose members are employed in manufacturing, wholesale and retail trade, and other private business sectors.

Source: Adapted from Credit Union National Association, Inc. 1979 Yearbook.

occupation in private industry. About one sixth are related to government employment, and close to 10 percent to employment with an educational institution. There are also credit unions connected to associations which include churches, labor unions, lodges, and, more recently, students. Members of residential credit unions share a common place of residence, such as a state or local community. Relatively speaking, there have been only minor shifts among membership types in recent years. Associational membership has declined slightly percentagewise, while residential-based credit unions have gained somewhat. There has been a tendency in recent years for governmental agencies issuing new charters to become more liberal in defining groups with sufficient common interest to form a credit union. For example, residents of a neighborhood, city, or state have been held to constitute a group of people with sufficient common interest to organize their own credit union.

Concentration of assets

Although there has been little change in membership structure in the industry, a significant shift in the concentration of assets among large and small credit unions and in the average size of these institutions has occurred. As revealed in Table 13–4, the credit union under $100,000 in asset size has declined sharply in relative importance. The greatest growth has taken place in the size category of $1 million

TABLE 13–4
Distribution of U.S. credit unions by asset size,
1969 and 1978

Size Category	1969	1978
Under $100,000	37.86%	11.93%
100,001–500,000	36.42	35.08
500,001–1,000,000	11.10	17.21
1,000,001–2,000,000	7.15	14.37
2,000,001–5,000,000	4.94	10.97
5,000,001 and over	2.53	10.44
Total	100.00%	100.00%

Source: Adapted from Credit Union National Association, Inc.,
1979 Yearbook.

or more in total assets which now includes 36 percent of all credit unions compared to less than 15 percent a decade ago. Credit unions are still very small compared to other deposit-type financial intermediaries, reflecting the fact that the bulk of their individual deposit accounts are quite modest in size. The average-size savings deposit at federal credit unions, according to the National Credit Union Administration, is about $1,135, substantially smaller than at either commercial banks or savings and loan associations.

In large part, this size disparity reflects the nature of deposit accounts offered by the industry and permitted by regulation. Until year-end 1977 all deposits offered by U.S. credit unions were similar to passbook savings accounts at commercial and savings banks. These deposits carry the lowest rates of return permitted by law and turn over quite rapidly since they may be withdrawn virtually at will by the customer. The nature and mean size of credit union thrift deposits is likely to change rapidly in the years ahead as a result of legislation passed by Congress during 1977. On December 30, 1977, federally chartered credit unions were authorized to offer variable-rate share certificates. Many state regulatory agencies have followed suit in order to grant their member associations more options in raising funds. The new authority to offer higher-yielding, longer-term thrift deposits undoubtedly will increase credit union operating costs, but may also bring greater stability to the industry's deposit flows and permit the granting of longer-term loans to customers.

As indicated by the data in Table 13–1, there is a trend toward fewer (but larger) credit unions. The number of associations peaked in 1969 at 23,876 and then declined by more than 1900 through 1978. In the meantime the number of members, the value of savings accounts, loans, and total assets grew rapidly. The result, of course, was a dramatic rise in the size of the average association. The decline in numbers and the increasing size of most credit unions reflect the increasingly aggressive competition among financial intermediaries and the high cost of the many new financial services being offered by individual credit unions today. Competition and costs have encouraged the consolidation of existing credit unions into larger and more efficient units. Moreover, if the industry continues to expand its services at the present rate in order to compete more fully with commercial and savings banks for the consumer's funds, the pressures for consolidation into fewer, but larger credit unions are likely to intensify.

Operating structure of credit unions

Credit unions elect boards of directors from among their membership to serve without compensation. The board of directors is the chief administrative unit of the institution—setting policies, procedures, and the scope of services which will be provided. The membership also selects a credit committee which must approve or disapprove of all loan applications. Supplementing these decision-making groups are two appointed committees in charge of financial auditing and education of members. The education committee informs actual and potential members concerning available services. Committee members usually serve without pay and are highly instrumental in bringing in new members.

The principal officers of a credit union include the president, vice president, treasurer, and secretary. Usually these officers, with the exception of the treasurer, are nonpaid volunteers. The president normally presides over meetings of the board of directors and makes periodic reports to the association's membership. The vice president acts in the president's absence and may chair one or more of the standing committees. The treasurer is responsible for the records and daily operation of the organization, including supervision of any office managers, loan officers, and clerical staff. Finally, the individual association's secretary keeps minutes of all meetings and aids in the preparation of reports to the membership.

As is true of most industries, the credit union business contains a hierarchy of organizations designed to serve individual institutions. The credit unions within a given community or geographical area frequently join together to form a chapter, which undertakes public relations projects and sponsors educational programs. A somewhat higher level grouping is the statewide credit union league, now present in all 50 states, Washington, D.C., and Puerto Rico. These organizations provide information to individual credit unions on pending legislation, organize conferences and seminars, and assist in the growing problem of training management and staff in credit union policies and procedures.

The Credit Union National Association (CUNA) is a nationwide confederation set up in 1934 to provide legislative, public relations, research, and development support for member associations. Credit unions which are not members of a state league may affiliate directly with CUNA. Today, more than 90 percent of all U.S. credit unions are affiliated with CUNA, which has 51 member leagues. At an even higher level, the World Council of Credit Unions is a global association, serving over 50 million credit union members in 67 countries. The purpose of the World Council is to strengthen international ties between the credit union industry in member countries and to coordinate the efforts of national and regional confederations.

SERVICES PROVIDED BY CREDIT UNIONS

As indicated earlier, the two principal functions of credit unions are to accept savings deposits and to make low-interest loans to members. In their lending activities credit unions appear to have significant advantages over other consumer lending institutions such as commercial banks and finance companies. Since their average-size loans are smaller, generally secured, and made exclusively to members, they have less need for extensive credit information from the customer and also experience lower default rates on loans. Due to the volunteer policy-making and managerial services provided by members, the average cost of making and servicing instalment loans is less than at most other lending institutions, and this holds loan rates down.[2] However, credit unions, like other financial intermediaries today, increasingly are diversifying the services they offer the public, and this movement has profound implications for their cost structure. If the experience of the commercial banking industry is an appropriate indicator, diversification into new service lines typically brings rising unit costs, greater volume, but also a declining profit margin.

An almost bewildering array of new services has been developed by the industry in recent years. For example, most credit unions offer and some require borrowers to take out life insurance for the term of a loan. Frequently, the credit union pays the premium for this insurance. Some associations have ventured further into the insurance field by acting as brokers and working with insurance firms to establish group plans for members. Increasingly, the services offered by

---

[2] Flannery [5] estimates that the average annual cost of making and servicing an instalment loan is $20 for a credit union, $48 for a commercial bank, and $51 for a consumer finance company.

credit unions are bringing them into direct competition with commercial banks for deposits, loans, and related financial services. For example, the State Department Federal Credit Union, like many commercial banks, operates 24-hour automated teller windows at various locations where members work. With a special identification card members can make withdrawals from their accounts when cash is needed. A few credit unions offer traveler's checks for their members, while many provide vacation planning services, retail store discounts, and money orders where permitted by state law.

For many years commercial banks faced little or no competition in the payments field because only they possessed the power to accept demand deposits (checking accounts). By year-end 1978, more than 1,600 U.S. credit unions were offering so-called *share draft* services. These permit depositors to write drafts against their account balances and pay bills just as they would with a bank check. Federal regulations issued by the National Credit Union Administration authorize all federally chartered credit unions to offer the service, and many states have granted similar authority to the credit unions they charter. By the end of 1978 U.S. credit union members held $968 million in share-draft balances. The new service is expected to spread rapidly as more credit unions see tangible benefits from entering the nation's payments system.

The share draft is similar in many ways to a bank checking account. However, it has several additional features which a bank check does not possess. When a share draft is written by a credit union member in payment for goods and services, a carbonless duplicate is automatically created, lessening the importance of the customer remembering to write down every item in a register. Share drafts are usually truncated so that when the draft reaches the final bank, the essential information is microfilmed. All further processing is handled by computer and the paper draft is not returned to customers or to their credit unions. Instead, the credit union and the customer receive a printout of all drafts written against their accounts, thus providing a convenient summary of all financial transactions, but minimizing the transfer of paper items.

Perhaps the most important advantage of the share draft account is that it generally pays dividends on the average or minimum balance remaining on deposit during the dividend period. The National Credit Union Administration in Washington, D.C., has set a ceiling interest rate of 7 percent on share draft accounts. To most customers the ability to earn interest on funds that are easily and instantly accessible is the single most important feature of this new credit union service. However, U.S. credit unions do not expect to hold this edge for long as NOW accounts, offered principally by commercial and savings banks, are becoming ever more popular and the areas of the nation in which NOWs are permitted are widening.[3] Moreover, credit unions have had to carry significantly greater operating costs for the privilege of offering share drafts. The cost of processing share drafts, including return-item charges, account maintenance fees, and data transmission charges, has been estimated at 6 to 10 cents per draft. Frequently, the customer is charged only a penny for each share draft written.

In their penetration of the nation's payments system through share drafts, credit unions appear to be looking ahead to an era when most payments are made electronically and not by paper. As we will discuss in Chapter 21, the United States is rapidly moving forward with plans to link computers and provide electronic clearance of drafts against financial institutions involved in the payments process. Moving more slowly, but also becoming a reality are electronic transfers of funds (EFTS) between customers and their banking institutions, such as through point-of-sale terminals in shopping centers and retail stores. Someday it will be possible for all transactions to be carried out by telephone with the aid of precoded plastic identification cards. The new payments technology will all but erase the traditional distinction between checking and savings deposits since funds can be moved from one account to another instantaneously. However, credit unions and other nonbank deposit-type intermediaries must gain entry to the payments process soon if they are to share in the market for electronic funds transfer of the future.

Of particular concern to credit union managers is: what will happen to the consumer's dollar when automatic electronic deposit of payrolls spreads nationwide? Deposit of payroll checks in a financial institution via computer tape instead of pieces of paper will give a strong competitive edge to those institutions that are already part of the payments mechanism, especially commercial banks. The customer's entire paycheck will be deposited with one financial institution, resulting in a potential loss of funds to other institutions. Credit unions today are participating in the direct deposit of federal social security payments and military payrolls. An effort is being made in the industry to obtain direct deposits of payrolls from private employers—a service provided by commercial banks for a number of years. One major step in this direction occurred in 1977 when credit unions were admitted to 28 of the 33 automated clearinghouses (ACHs) which now span the United States and provide for electronic

---

[3] See Chapter 21 for a discussion of the nature and growth of NOW accounts.

transfer of funds among financial institutions. At the retail service level some credit unions have introduced automated tellers (ATMs) and point-of-sale (POS) terminals in stores and shopping centers.

Among other important new services offered by credit unions are credit cards. During 1977 several large U.S. credit unions began offering VISA credit cards to their membership. At least initially, the majority of the associations offering cards assess lower instalment rates on credit balances than do commercial banks. Credit unions are also moving rapidly into the mortgage loan field. Prior to 1977 only state-chartered credit unions could engage in long-term mortgage financing in those states specifically authorizing the service. However, following congressional action in that year the National Credit Union Administration has issued new regulations permitting federally chartered credit unions to grant up to 30-year home mortgage loans to members. While only a minority of credit unions actually hold first mortgage loans, the volume of such loans is expected to increase dramatically over the next decade, bringing credit unions into direct competition with commercial banks and savings and loans in the financing of single-family residences. Regardless of future developments, the present array of services offered by the industry represents a radical change in the role of credit unions within the U.S. financial system. Just as other financial intermediaries have broadened their services, so must the credit union if it is to survive and grow in the increasingly intense competition for the consumer's deposit and credit needs.

REGULATORY STRUCTURE

Prior to 1970, federally chartered credit unions were supervised by the Bureau of Federal Credit Unions in the Department of Health, Education and Welfare. This agency was abolished in 1970, and replaced by the National Credit Union Administration (NCUA), an independent agency within the executive branch of the federal government. NCUA is financed solely by funds received from federal credit unions in return for services performed and for providing deposit insurance to all qualified associations. NCUA exercises its supervisory responsibilities through the National Credit Union Board, consisting of three persons appointed by the president of the United States. The board meets quarterly to provide advice and counsel to the NCUA administrator with respect to the regulation of member institutions. State-chartered credit unions are supervised by regulatory agencies within each state. All states except Alaska, Delaware, Hawaii, Nevada, South Dakota, and Wyoming charter credit unions. The rules and regulations for issuance of a charter vary from one state to the next, but some consistency among state requirements exists due largely to the efforts of CUNA and NCUA.

Until recently there was no institution to serve as a "lender of last resort" to the industry in order to deal with short-run cash shortages. Credit union leagues had lobbied for the creation of a federal credit agency that would supply such funds in time of need, similar to the Federal Reserve System's discount window which makes short-term loans to member commercial banks. Following several unsuccessful attempts to persuade Congress, the industry chartered the U.S. Central Credit Union (CCU) in Kansas in 1974. CCU channels short-term funds and provides cash management services to individual associations through 41 designated corporate central credit unions. The proliferation of new services has created a need for the credit union financial system now growing up around CCU and the corporate central unions. The development of credit card and share draft services, for example, places individual associations under added liquidity pressures, resulting in surplus cash at certain times and cash shortages at others. The new financial system centered in the CCU permits members to pool their liquid funds to help individual associations with temporary cash deficits and earn a rate of return adequate to help offset the industry's rising costs. In 1978 Congress passed new legislation authorizing the creation of a Central Liquidity Facility (CLF) which would act as a lender of last resort for emergency credit needs and interface with the CCU system.

LOAN, INVESTMENT, AND DEPOSIT POWERS

Since the creation of NCUA in March 1970, the Federal Credit Union Act has been amended several times, reflecting the increasing political sophistication of the industry's spokesmen. Under the terms of the act, a federally chartered credit union is empowered to make contracts, purchase and dispose of property, and perform other functions related to the business of accepting and loaning funds. However, credit unions are severely limited in the types of assets (loans and investments) they are permitted to acquire in order to protect the deposits of members. Both secured and unsecured loans may be made to consumers—an association's principal category of assets. Credit unions also may invest in fully guaranteed U.S. government obligations, savings accounts at savings and loan associations and mutual savings banks, share certificates and deposits of federally insured credit unions, and obligations of approved federal agencies (such as the Federal Land Banks). A few states allow their associations to acquire high-grade corporate bonds and state and local government obligations.

The lending powers of federally chartered credit unions were increased significantly when Congress passed Public Law 95-22 on April 19, 1977. Permissible maturities for most loans were increased to 12 years. Residential real estate loans to finance one- to four-family dwellings and secured by a first lien on the property may have maturities of up to 30 years, instead of the previous limit of only 10 years.[4] This new provision is expected to result in a significant expansion of real estate lending by the industry. Loans of up to 15 years may be granted on purchases of mobile homes or for home improvements provided they represent a lien against a member's residence. Self-replenishing lines of credit may be granted borrowers provided the maximum amount is stated. Loans to other credit unions may not exceed 1 percent of an association's paid-in capital, unimpaired capital, and surplus. Finally, credit unions may participate out loans with other credit unions or other financial intermediaries, but the credit union originating the loan must retain an interest of at least 10 percent of the amount of the loan.

Credit unions are restricted in their dividend payments on member deposits to a maximum of 7 percent per annum on regular share accounts. New forms of variable rate savings accounts and share certificates are now authorized by federal regulations which became effective in December 1977. These new rules permit credit unions to pay up to 7¾ percent per annum on share certificates and up to 7 percent on variable-rate accounts. Dividends may be paid at any interval of time authorized by the board of directors. Immediately before the payment of each dividend, the gross earnings of the credit union must be determined. Based upon this amount, certain sums must be set aside as reserves against loan losses.

Deposit insurance

Until recently, very few credit union depositors had their savings protected by insurance. Beginning in 1970, all federal credit unions were required to be insured by the NCU Share Insurance Fund, administered by NCUA. The plan is similar to the FDIC insurance plan for commercial banks and protects deposits up to $40,000 per member account. State-chartered credit unions also may be covered

---

[4] Following the passage of public law 95-22 NCUA issued new regulations governing real estate lending by federal credit unions. Such loans must be a first lien against residential property no larger than a one- to four-family dwelling, and the dwelling must be the principal residence of the member-borrower. The original loan must be limited to either 80 percent of the purchase price of the property or 80 percent of its appraised value, whichever is less. The remaining amount may also be secondarily financed by a credit union so long as the institution's total indebtedness does not exceed 95 percent of the property's value.

by federal deposit insurance provided they meet its qualifications. By the end of 1977, more than 3,800 state-chartered credit unions had become a part of the federal insurance program. Combined with federal credit unions which must be insured, a total of more than 16,600 associations were federally insured in 1977, representing 74 percent of all U.S. credit unions.

TAXATION OF CREDIT UNIONS

A credit union is considered a nonprofit organization and, as such, is exempt from income taxation by the federal government and by most states. A credit union does business only with its owners who hold one share per so many dollars (typically $5) held on deposit. The earnings from its operations belong to members in proportion to the amount of business they have conducted with the institution. As a result, the credit union is obligated to divide its earnings among its members, and following the division of earnings, there is no significant income left to tax. This privilege of tax exemption has been under attack recently from commercial banking groups who argue that if credit unions are going to offer bank-type services (such as checking accounts), they should be taxed on any profits earned at a rate comparable to banks.

CREDIT UNION PORTFOLIOS

Only limited information is currently available on the sources and uses of funds of many U.S. credit unions. NCUA provides reasonably complete data on both federally chartered and federally insured credit unions. Statistics on uninsured state-chartered credit unions are more difficult to obtain. Accordingly, most of the discussion on sources and uses of funds which follows pertains to federally chartered credit unions.

As shown in Table 13–5, loans to members are the largest single item in the credit union portfolio, representing about three quarters of all industry assets. Since loans are the highest-yielding asset for a credit union, their growth has been rapid in recent years, paralleling the substantial increases in member deposits. Federal credit unions loaned more than $23 billion to members in 1977, about 21 percent more than in 1976. The ratio of total loans to deposits (shares) increased to nearly 89 percent by year-end 1977, and the average-size loan climbed to $1,898 in 1977.

A survey of federal credit unions conducted by NCUA in 1977 indicates that 35 percent of the volume of loans and 24 percent of the number of loans are for the purchase of automobiles. Loans for per-

TABLE 13–5
Distribution of sources and uses of funds in federal credit unions,
1967 and 1977 (percent)

Item	1967	1977	Change 1967–1977
Sources of funds:			
Members' shares	87.3%	86.1%	−1.2
Reserves and undivided			
earnings	7.6	5.7	−1.9
Notes payable	1.7	5.5	3.8
Other sources	3.4	2.6	−0.8
Total	100.0%	100.0%	—
Uses of funds:			
Cash	5.8%	2.9%	−2.9
Loans to—			
Members	75.4	76.5	1.1
Other credit unions	1.9	0.6	−1.3
U.S. government			
obligations*	3.3	12.6	9.3
Savings and loan shares	12.4	3.5	−8.9
Shares and deposits in other			
credit unions	—†	1.8	1.8
Other uses	1.2	2.1	0.9
Total	100.0%	100.0%	—

* Item includes federal agency securities and common trust investments in 1977.
† Item not applicable prior to 1968.
Source: Adapted from National Credit Union Administration, *Annual Report*, 1977.

sonal needs or to cover household and family expenses ran a close second, representing nearly 33 percent of the amount of loans granted and nearly half of the total number of loans made. (See Table 13–6.) Third in importance were loans for home furnishings and appliances, accounting for about 7 percent of the number and 4 percent of the dollar volume of all approved loans. Loans to acquire boats and mobile homes ranked fourth. Within the category of loans for personal needs and household expenses, debt consolidation loans were the most important—accounting for 8 percent of the total number of approved loans in 1977. Next in importance in the personal expenses category were loans to finance vacations and to pay dental, medical, and funeral bills.

The majority of credit union loans—about three quarters in 1977—are secured. The principal security used is automobiles followed by comakers and pledged shares (deposits). Most loans are comparatively short in maturity with about half carrying maturities of two years or less. Only 16 percent of the number of loans granted by the sampled federal credit unions had maturities of more than three years. Most short-term credit union loans cover personal, fam-

TABLE 13–6
Purpose of loans granted by a sample of federally chartered credit unions, 1977

Purpose of loans	Number of loans	Percentage distribution	Amount of loans ($000)	Percentage distribution
Total durable goods	16,136	37.8%	$43,043	45.9%
New autos	4,869	11.4	20,574	22.0
Used autos	5,318	12.4	12,491	13.3
Furniture and household appliances	2,927	6.9	3,868	4.1
Boats, mobile homes	944	2.2	3,224	3.4
Other	2,078	4.9	2,886	3.1
Total personal, household, and family expenses	19,682	46.1	30.522	32.6
Nondurable goods	1,512	3.5	1,985	2.1
Vacations....................	2,073	4.9	2,693	2.9
Education	634	1.5	1,219	1.3
Medical, dental, and funeral expenses.............	1,424	3.3	2,234	2.4
Taxes	965	2.3	1,641	1.8
Insurance	798	1.9	1,228	1.3
Debt consolidation	3,446	8.1	6,567	7.0
Other	8,830	20.7	12,955	13.8
Residential repair and modernization	5,149	12.1	11,166	11.9
Total real estate	958	2.2	6,432	6.9
Farm	201	0.5	1,245	1.3
Nonfarm	757	1.8	5,187	5.5
Business	798	1.9	2,556	2.7
Total	42,723	100.0%	$93,719	100.0%

Source: Adapted from the National Credit Union Administration, *Annual Report*, 1977.

ily, and household expenses. Loans on durables, real estate, and businesses generally are the longest term loans in a credit union's portfolio.

Under federal and most state laws credit unions may charge no more than 1 percent a month on the outstanding balance of a loan, including all charges incident to granting the loan. This represents an annual percentage rate (APR) of 12 percent. The majority of associations give their members credit life or other protection insurance free. Default and delinquency rates on credit union loans generally are quite low. A study by NCUA in 1977 showed that only 3.6 percent of the number and 2.2 percent of the volume of loans extended by federal credit unions were two months or more delinquent. Smaller credit unions generally have a greater problem with delinquencies and defaults since many are manned by volunteers or part-time employees who frequently have less expertise in credit analysis. As a result of the few bad loans made, the number of failures in the industry is also relatively low. For example, 143 federal associations were involuntarily liquidated during 1977, or about 1 percent of all federally chartered credit unions, due to insolvency problems.

Investments in securities and cash

Investments in securities and deposits of other intermediaries represented about 18 percent of the total assets of federal credit unions in 1977. (See Table 13–5.) During the past decade investments have increased as a percentage of total assets due principally to an upsurge in holdings of U.S. government and federal agency securities. The attractive yields and excellent marketability of these securities have caused many credit unions to substitute government securities for deposits in savings and loans as the principal liquid asset held by the industry. More recently, investments have been declining relative to loans due to heavy credit demands from credit union members. For example, during 1977 total investments at federal credit unions rose about 14 percent, while loans to members increased 24 percent. Holdings of cash also have been on the decline as the industry has responded to the credit needs of its members and the rising opportunity cost of idle funds. For example, cash holdings represented nearly 6 percent of total assets at federal credit unions in 1967, but had fallen to less than 3 percent in 1977.

Share capital and other funds sources

The principal source of funds for credit unions is member share accounts (deposits). Shares represented 86 percent of total sources of funds for federally chartered credit unions in 1977. The growth of credit union shares has been especially rapid since federal insurance through the National Credit Union Share Insurance Fund (NCUSIF) was set up in 1970. In addition, larger-size deposits have flowed in since the creation of NCUSIF. For example, data released by NCUA indicates that federal credit union deposits larger than $5,000 increased about fivefold between 1970 and 1976. Still, about three quarters of the total number of credit union share accounts contain less than $1,000 each, and these shares average about $180 each. Share deposits of $20,000 or more represent less than 1 percent of total deposits. Only about 1 percent of all shares held in federal credit unions are not covered by insurance.

Generally, shares held by members have declined as a source of credit union funds since 1975. The same has been true of reserves and retained earnings, as shown in Table 13–5. Like commercial banks, credit unions are relying more heavily upon borrowed sources of funds (notes payable), principally in the form of certificates of indebtedness, to finance their operations. The relative decline in reserves and undivided earnings is partly the result of lower reserve requirements imposed on federal credit unions since 1970. Under the law federal associations must set aside at least 6 percent of the amount of their "risk" assets (defined as loans to members minus government guaranteed loans and those secured by share deposits) as a reserve for losses. This reserve is built up over time by diverting a portion of each year's gross income into the regular reserve account.

Revenues and expenses

Just as loans are the principal asset on the balance sheets of credit unions, so interest on loans is their principal revenue source. As

TABLE 13–7
Income and expenses of federal credit unions, 1977

Income and expense items distribution	Amount ($millions)	Percentage distribution
Interest on loans	$2,143	83.1%
Income from investments	404	15.7
Other income	33	1.3
Total income	$2,580	100.0%
Employee compensation	309	31.9%
Borrower's protection insurance	79	8.2
Life savings insurance	46	4.8
Association dues	14	1.4
Examination and supervision fees	13	1.3
Interest on borrowed money	91	9.4
Office occupancy expense	30	3.2
Educational and promotional expense	20	2.1
Office operations expense	95	9.8
Professional and outside services	57	5.9
Conventions and conferences	17	1.8
Annual meeting expense	8	0.8
Share insurance premiums	18	1.9
Other expenses	172	17.8
Total expenses	$ 968	100.0%
Net income	1,612	—

Source: Adapted from the National Credit Union Administration, *Annual Report*, 1977.

shown in Table 13–7, revenue from loans accounted for 83 percent of the income of federal credit unions in 1977. A distant second in importance is income from investments in securities and deposits. Due to rapid growth in loan demand, the proportion of revenues accounted for by loans has increased during the 1970s while investment income generally has declined in relative terms.

Credit union expenses increased somewhat faster than revenues in 1977, squeezing net income. As reflected in Table 13–7, wages, salaries, and fringe benefits paid to employees were by far the most important expense category for federal credit unions. Other major expense items include insurance services provided members who borrow, office operations, and interest on borrowed money. The most rapidly growing expense item is interest on borrowed money due to the increasingly heavy use of borrowed funds by associations. Note that interest paid on deposits is not technically an expense item for a credit union since the depositor is really an owner and receives a portion of the association's net income after expenses as dividends.

Dividends and interest refunds

The majority of credit union income (about 53 percent in 1977) is returned to members in the form of dividends. Indeed, the percentage of income accounted for by dividends has risen in recent years reflecting both higher dividend rates and more frequent crediting of member dividends. In 1974 federal credit unions were permitted to credit members with dividends as frequently as daily, instead of quarterly as called for by earlier provisions of the Federal Credit Union Act. Average dividend rates paid by U.S. credit unions have risen sharply in recent years. For example, in 1977 federally chartered associations paid an average dividend of 6.33 percent compared to only 6.15 percent just one year before. The higher rates paid are traceable to greater competition from other financial institutions and an attempt by credit union managers to protect their deposits against disintermediation due to higher prevailing interest rates. Many credit unions pay interest refunds to their borrowing members. Such refunds, of course, reduce the effective interest rate on loans. Refunds in the 10 to 11 percent range are the most prevalent with a trend toward larger refunds in recent years as credit unions have aggressively responded to competition.

CREDIT UNIONS IN THE FUTURE

Although in terms of asset size still a relatively minor financial institution, credit unions are rapidly increasing in importance. In the field of consumer instalment credit they are highly competitive today with both commercial banks and finance companies. Their share certificates and share deposits represent a larger and larger share each year of the market for thrift deposits served also by commercial banks, savings and loan associations, and mutual savings banks. Credit unions offer a number of relatively unique services which give them an advantage when competing against other financial institutions for the consumer's savings and credit needs. They occupy convenient locations, usually near the customer's home or place of work. Credit unions generally pay close to the highest interest rates allowed by law on short-term, consumer-type savings deposits; the maximum permissible rates on these deposits are higher than rates permitted on similar deposits offered by commercial banks, savings and loan associations, and mutual savings banks. Credit union members frequently volunteer their time and talents to an association, helping it to keep operating costs relatively low. Finally, we have observed that the average-size credit union deposit is significantly smaller than the average-size thrift deposit held by a commercial or savings bank. These smaller deposits tend to be less volatile and less interest sensitive than deposits held by banks, providing a more stable base from which to make credit union loans.

Few of these advantages appear immune from significant changes in the future, however. Certainly the widespread use of electronic transfer of funds (EFTS) will reduce the convenience advantages of credit unions. Commercial banks are likely to be the principal beneficiaries of the automatic deposit of payroll checks unless nonbank thrift institutions, such as credit unions, are able to make significant inroads into the nation's payments mechanism in the years ahead. Moreover, as we pointed out earlier, the average size of credit union share accounts is growing, which could increase the interest sensitivity of their deposits. However, as long as the demand for consumer instalment credit continues to grow rapidly and convenience continues to have a high priority among consumers, credit unions probably will increase their share of both the savings deposit market and the market for consumer loans.

QUESTIONS

13–1.   In what ways is the credit union different from other financial institutions previously discussed, especially commercial banks and savings banks?

13–2.   Discuss the reasons behind the recent rapid growth of U.S. credit unions.

13–3.   What do the abbreviations CUNA, CCU, NCUA, and NCUSIF stand for? Describe the functions of these institutions.

13–4.   What advantages do credit unions have over other consumer lending institutions (especially commercial banks and finance companies) in their lending activities? in attracting savings deposits? Which of these advantages appear to be long lasting and which only temporary?

13–5. What are share drafts? What advantages do they offer the customer? the individual credit union? Can you foresee any significant financial management problems for a credit union stemming from the offering of share drafts?

13–6. List the principal sources and uses of funds for a credit union. What are the major sources of revenue and expenses? Cite any recent trends which appear to have influenced the pattern of funds flows through credit unions.

13–7. Why is the population of U.S. credit unions declining? What are the probable consequences of this for credit union management?

REFERENCES

1. Cargill, Thomas F. "Recent Research on Credit Unions: A Survey." *Journal of Economics and Business*, vol. 29, no. 2 (Winter 1977).
2. Credit Union National Association, Inc., *1978 Yearbook*, Madison Wis.
3. Credit Union National Association, Inc., *1979 Yearbook*, Madison, Wis.
4. Dougall, Herbert E., and Gaumnitz, Jack E. *Capital Markets and Institutions*. 3d ed. Englewood Cliffs, N.J.: Prentice-Hall, 1975.
5. Flannery, Mark J. "Credit Unions as Consumer Lenders in the United States." *New England Economic Review*, Federal Reserve Bank of Boston, July–August 1974.
6. Harless, Doris E. *Nonbank Financial Institutions*. Federal Reserve Bank of Richmond, 1975, chap. 10.
7. Hempel, George H., and Yawitz, Jess B. *Financial Management of Financial Institutions*. Englewood Cliffs, N.J.: Prentice-Hall, 1977, pp. 129–31, 148–52.
8. Jacobs, Donald et al. *Financial Institutions*. Homewood, Ill.: Richard D. Irwin, Inc., 1972.
9. National Credit Union Administration, *Annual Report, 1977*, Washington, D.C., June 1978.
10. Smith, Paul F. *Economics of Financial Institutions*. Homewood, Ill.: Richard D. Irwin, Inc., 1971.

14

Life insurance companies

Life insurance companies are among the most important financial intermediaries in the American economy. Life insurance in force totaled more than $2.5 trillion in 1977 with 86 percent of all families in the United States holding policies from one or more legal reserve companies. Life companies operate as financial institutions by collecting revenues from policyholders and investing those dollars in securities available in the money and capital markets. Although the primary product sold is protection against loss of income due to premature death, both contractual savings and the accumulation of an estate also are major services provided by these companies today. Life companies are able to grow at a relatively rapid pace because the payment of premiums by policyholders generally occurs prior to the payment of insurance claims and the latter are highly predictable.

In this chapter we review the growth and development of life insurance companies in the United States since World War II. The first section discusses the major services offered by the industry. The second explores briefly the process of investment decision making and planning as used by most life insurers, while the third discusses recent growth trends. Later sections of the chapter examine recent changes in the sources and uses of funds by U.S. life companies and review major regulations and the structure of the industry. In the concluding section we look at recent problems and the long-term outlook for the life insurance business.

LIFE INSURANCE SERVICES

A life insurance contract is designed to shelter an individual or family against financial loss in the event of the premature death of the policyholder. Actually, life insurance companies over the years have evolved into highly complex financial institutions which provide protection against financial losses associated with death, disability, and old age. As a matter of fact, cash paid out to customers still alive (in the form of annuities, dividends, accumulated cash saving, endowments, and medical care benefits) in recent years have been roughly triple the death benefits paid to policyholders or their beneficiaries by U.S. life companies. For example, during 1977 payments to beneficiaries associated with death claims reached $10.2 billion. In contrast, cash awards made during the lifetime of the policyholder amounted to $16.3 billion. (See Table 14–1.) These figures do not include health and medical benefits which totaled nearly $17.5 billion in 1977.

TABLE 14–1
Benefit payments by U.S. life insurance companies, selected years, 1940–1977
($millions)

Year	Death payments	Matured endowments	Disability payments	Annuity payments	Cash surrender values	Policy dividends	Total
1940	$ 995.0	$269.2	$103.5	$ 176.5	$ 652.0	$ 468.1	$ 2,664.3
1950	1,589.7	495.1	99.6	319.4	592.3	634.6	3,730.7
1960	3,346.1	673.1	123.8	722.0	1,633.4	1,620.1	8,118.5
1970	7,017.3	978.3	232.9	1,757.1	2,886.4	3.577.4	16,449.4
1977	10,195.7	931.7	495.0	4,167.5	4,308.9	5,913.2	26,462.0

Source: Adapted from the American Council of Life Insurance, *Life Insurance Fact Book*, 1978.

Life insurance provides a system of protection against the risk of income loss by distributing the burden of adequate financial protection over a large number of individuals. The insurance contract consolidates a large number of individual, unpredictable risks into a stable system of predictable risks. The well-known insurance principle suggests that a risk, such as the timing of death, while not generally predictable for an individual can become quite predictable for a sufficiently large group of individuals. For the individual policyholder, the payment of a stream of mandatory insurance premiums compensates for the uncertainty of death by establishing an estate as soon as a new policy is written and thereby providing some degree of financial security.

Actuaries can estimate mortality rates for categories of people with significant precision, and the forecast mortality rates may be used to determine the annual premiums which should be assessed policyholders. The gross annual premium per policyholder is approximately equal to the ratio of the total amount of expected benefit claims divided by the number of policyholders. Of course, the actual process of determining the appropriate premium rate on life policies is somewhat more complex than this since the insurance company must consider not only the probable number of deaths among its policyholders, but also its annual expenses, expected investment funds earned, desired profit margin, and the prices and package of benefits offered by competitors. The expenses of running the company (including commissions earned by salesmen, rental charges, office equipment and supplies, assessments, taxes, and a minimum targeted rate of return) will be passed on to policyholders in the form of larger payments for insurance protection. To take account of its investment return from purchases of securities in the money and capital markets, the company must calculate the current value of expected benefit claims discounted at the projected rate of return on its security holdings.

Insurance companies offer a wide variety of death benefit and living benefit plans. The most important form of death benefit policy is *permanent insurance*, often known as normal or whole life insurance. This form of protection usually requires premium payments each year for the life of the policyholder. It builds cash value whereby the policyholder can borrow at a favorable rate of interest. Life companies rapidly build up their reserves from such policies and invest these reserves principally in long-term financial assets, such as corporate bonds and mortgages. Another major form of death benefit protection is *term insurance*, which protects the policyholders' beneficiaries from financial loss merely for a period agreed upon (such as 20 or 30 years) as set out in the insurance contract. The net cash flow generated by a term policy is significantly smaller than for permanent insurance. However, term insurance has been growing as a proportion of the annual sales of life companies and as a percentage of total life insurance in force. In 1977, for example, term policies accounted for about 50 percent of the volume of industry sales of life insurance and about a third of all life insurance in force.[1] (See Table 14–2 for a summary of different kinds of life insurance purchased in the United States.)

Saving is also an important component of the package of services offered by life companies. Permanent insurance policies build up cash

TABLE 14–2
Types of policies purchased from U.S. life insurance companies, 1967 and 1977

Type of policy	Percent of policies purchased		Percent of amount of policies in force	
	1967	1977	1967	1977
Permanent insurance	27%	35%	25%	26%
Limited pay life	21	15	9	7
Endowment policies	7	4	4	2
Retirement income	3	2	2	1
Modified life insurance	4	6	4	4
Level or decreasing term				
insurance	9	17	21	34
Family plan	5	2	4	2
with additional term	3	1	5	2
Regular policy	4	5	5	5
with F/P rider and additional				
term	2	1	5	3
Combination policies	14	12	16	14
Progressive and other	1	—*	—*	—*
Total	100%	100%	100%	100%

* Less than one half of 1 percent.
Source: Adapted from the American Council of Life Insurance, *Life Insurance Fact Book*, 1978.

values throughout the period of the policy, providing a reserve for the policyholder to meet financial emergencies or to be used in retirement years. Term insurance policies typically do not accumulate cash values and, therefore, have little or no savings value. A popular form of insurance with a substantial savings component is the *annuity*—a contractual obligation by a life company to pay a given amount of money over a designated period irrespective of whether the policyholder lives or dies. Annuities guard against the possibility of outliving an individual's accumulated wealth by providing guaranteed current or future income. Sales of annuity contracts have been

---

[1] Various package policies have been developed in recent years combining the benefits of permanent and term insurance. For example, under so-called *family plans* several members of the same family can be included under the same life insurance contract. The most common form of such a contract provides for permanent insurance for the principal wage earner and smaller term policies on other members of the family. So-called *combination* insurance plans also provide both permanent and term insurance coverage.

increasing rapidly in recent years, due principally to the sale of annuities for individual pension programs. More than 4 million individual and supplemental annuity contracts were active at year-end 1977, while annuity payments by life companies exceeded $4 billion during that year.

Related to term insurance is the *endowment* policy which pays the policyholder or designated beneficiaries a fixed sum when the policy matures. Endowment policies in the United States totaled about $52 billion in 1977, yet represented only about 4 percent of total ordinary and group insurance in force. *Limited pay* life insurance requires premium payments only for a set period or until the policyholder dies. Policies of this type amounted to more than $123 billion in 1977, representing about 10 percent of ordinary life policies in force. *Group* life insurance provides coverage under a master policy for employees of business firms or governmental units and for those who are members of labor unions, professional associations, or other groups. This form of coverage has grown dramatically from about 20 percent of all life policies in force in 1950 to more than 40 percent in 1977. *Industrial* life policies are small insurance contracts with premiums collected weekly or monthly. The roughly $39 billion in industrial life policies carried by U.S. companies at year-end 1977 represented no more than 2 percent of all outstanding life policies. Another form of term insurance is *credit life* issued through a lender of funds, such as a commercial bank, credit union, or savings bank, to guarantee repayment of a loan in the event the borrower dies prematurely. While dwarfed in importance by individual and group policies, credit life insurance has been increasing rapidly and totaled nearly $140 billion by year-end 1977. As the composition of the types of policies written by life companies changes, this changing mix affects their growth and the composition of their investments in the capital market. We will explore in more detail the effects of policy mix upon life insurance company investment policies in later sections of this chapter.

THE INVESTMENT PROCESS FOR LIFE COMPANIES

Since the liabilities of life companies are long term and highly predictable, funds obtained from policyholder premiums may be invested principally in long-term, interest-bearing securities. Liquidity needs are relatively low because of the stability and predictability of benefit claims and also because of the stability of income flows from investments. Since life company cash flows can be predicted with great accuracy, these firms are able to commit themselves to long-term financial instruments with more confidence, investing principally in capital market securities (especially corporate bonds and mortgages) with maturities stretching over several years. The investment policies of life companies are of critical importance to policyholders. If there is effective competition in the industry, higher earnings on aggregate investments tend to lower the net cost of insurance protection, influencing both premiums charged and dividends paid to policyholders.

The investment process for life companies centers upon determining *expected* cash flows from policy premiums and other revenue sources, since commitments frequently must be made to borrowers (mainly in the form of agreements to acquire corporate bonds and residential and commercial mortgages) well in advance of funds actually received. In practice, life insurance firms forecast their cash flows as much as 30 months in advance of cash receipts. However, these forecasts are revised frequently (usually monthly or weekly) as new data becomes available. The most important cash inflows include policy premiums, interest, dividends, and capital gains from investments, sales or redemptions of securities, and miscellaneous income. Principal cash outflows include life and annuity benefits, operating expenses, dividends, loans to policyholders, and federal and state taxes. Investment decisions depend heavily upon reliable estimates of these inflows and outflows. If actual cash inflows are greater than or equal to scheduled commitments (or uses of funds), the company's investment portfolio is expanded through the taking on of new securities. Indeed, additional investment outlets must be found as soon as possible to prevent loanable funds from remaining idle and foregoing interest or dividend income. With high and rising interest rates in recent years the pressure on life companies to make efficient use of any cash surpluses, however temporary they may be, has increased dramatically. The more serious situation is when inflows of funds are *less* than the volume of scheduled commitments. This problem usually is handled in one of two ways: (1) commitments of funds to borrowers may be postponed until adequate financial resources are available or (2) additional cash may be raised through the sale of securities or through borrowing. Many companies use "warehousing" of securities to raise short-term cash, getting another lender of funds (such as a commercial bank or mortgage company) to provide interim financing of commitments to borrowers until the life company obtains sufficient funds to repurchase those commitments.

GROWTH OF LIFE INSURANCE COMPANIES

Total assets of U.S. life companies have grown from $64 billion in 1950 and $120 billion in 1960 to nearly $352 billion by year-end 1977. Paralleling the growth in assets, life insurance in force has increased from $242 billion in 1950 to more than $2.5 trillion in 1977. (See Table 14–3.) The long-term growth of industry assets has occurred at a relatively steady pace. Until recently, the cycle of business expansions and recessions appeared to have only limited influence upon the

TABLE 14–3
Growth of U.S. life insurance companies and policies, selected years, 1950–1977

Year	Total assets of U.S. life companies (in $billions)	Number of policies (in $millions)	Amount of life insurance in force (in $billions)
1950	$ 64.0	210	$ 242.0
1960	119.6	308	618.2
1970	207.3	402	1,506.5
1977	351.7	448	2,788.7

Source: Adapted from the American Council of Life Insurance, *Life Insurance Fact Book*, 1978.

growth of premiums written and life insurance in force, differing from the experience of other major segments and industries in the U.S. economy. While this is still true to some extent, the attitude of the public appears to be changing. More and more individual savers are stressing the substitutability of financial claims and the idea of "self-insurance" through personal investments. Personal savings in the form of acquisitions of bank deposits, stocks, bonds, and money market instruments frequently take the place of life insurance purchases today.

In this kind of environment, both premium payments and borrowings by policyholders against the cash value of their policies have become more cyclically sensitive and have reduced the stability and predictability of life company cash flows. This has been especially evident during the decade of the 1970s. For example, industry growth averaged only about 6 percent a year between 1970 to 1975—a period which included a deep recession—and more than 10 percent a year for the 1976–77 period when economic conditions were more buoyant.

PRINCIPAL SOURCES OF FUNDS

The two major sources of funds drawn upon by life companies are premiums received from policyholders and earnings on investments in a variety of financial assets. (See Table 14–4.) In 1977 total revenue of U.S. life companies was nearly $98 billion. About three fourths of the industry's income comes from policy premiums, about one fifth from earnings on investments, and the residual from miscellaneous

TABLE 14–4
Sources of funds for U.S. life insurance companies, selected years, 1950–1977 ($millions)

Year	Premium receipts				Net investment income	Other income	Total sources of funds
	Life insurance premiums	Annuity consider- ations	Health insurance premiums	Total premium receipts			
1950	$ 6,249	$ 939	$ 1,001	$ 8,189	$ 2,075	$1,073	$11,337
1960	11,998	1,341	4,026	17,365	4,304	1,338	23,007
1970	21,679	3,721	11,367	36,767	10,144	2,143	49,054
1977	33,765	14,974	23,580	72,319	21,713	3,953	97,985

Source: Adapted from the American Council of Life Insurance, *Life Insurance Fact Book*, 1978.

sources. Premiums amounted to $72 billion—a figure which was almost exactly double the 1970 level. Net investment income totaled nearly $22 billion during 1977, reflecting the fact that life companies earned almost 7 percent before taxes on their invested assets that year. There has been a sharp uptrend in the industry's average rate of return on its investments in recent years due to higher interest rates on securities purchased in the open market and shifts in industry investment policies toward securities with greater returns. As recently as 1973, U.S. life companies earned a before-tax net rate on investments of only about 6 percent.

The major sources of funds drawn upon by life companies have changed over time as the industry has altered its package of financial services in response to demand and cost pressures. For example, premiums from the sale of ordinary life insurance policies represented only 46 percent of total premium receipts in 1977 compared to nearly 60 percent in 1970. Premium receipts from annuity contracts represented only 10 percent of premium income in 1970, but grew to more than 20 percent in 1977. Health insurance premiums climbed to a third of all premium receipts in 1977, compared to about 30 percent in 1970. Further relative gains in annuity premiums, due to burgeoning retirement income needs, and in health insurance premiums, due to soaring medical costs, are anticipated in future years.

PRINCIPAL USES OF FUNDS

Life insurance companies must be prudent in their investment policies since benefits owed to policyholders are an obligation that must be paid when due. Because of the need to safeguard their funds, enforced by government regulations, these companies generally refrain from investing in high-risk securities. Rather, they seek "adequate" returns within the bounds of safety of principal and prudent investment policies. Most securities acquired have an investment rating of Baa or higher and the industry continues to hold substantial quantities of riskless U.S. government and federal agency securities as well as state and local government (municipal) and foreign government debt obligations.

Investment strategy calls for holding long-term bonds and other financial assets to maturity. Securities will be sold only if unusually attractive reinvestment opportunities appear or if certain securities decline in quality. For this reason, life companies frequently avoid call privileges on corporate bonds. Because most corporate bonds sold in the open market do allow the issuing firm to call its securities in at a future date, life companies (especially the larger ones) have turned to the market for *private placements* for a substantial share of their investment needs. In this market the borrower places securities directly with the insurance company; therefore, the company can tailor more effectively the terms of securities it takes on in order to match its specific investment needs. While average effective yields do appear to be higher in the private placements market, borrowers in this market generally are smaller and somewhat more risky so that risk-adjusted interest rates may be comparable to those available in the open market.

Government securities

Marked changes have occurred in recent years in the types of securities acquired by life insurance companies. As a general rule, the industry has lowered its holdings of more liquid securities and expanded its investments in longer-term, higher-yielding assets. For example, as shown in Table 14–5, holdings of liquid government securities amounted to 25 percent of industry assets in 1950. By 1960, the proportion had dropped below 10 percent and by 1970 to about 5 percent. Since then industry holdings of government issues have risen and now account for close to 7 percent of total assets.

The industry's total investment in government securities may be divided into holdings of federal, state, local, and foreign government issues. The largest proportion of life company holdings of government securities are in U.S. government (Treasury and federal agency) issues which amounted to $9.3 billion at year-end 1977, or about 40 percent of total industry holdings of government securities. Holdings of state and local obligations totaled about $6 billion, or about one quarter of total government issues held by life companies. Securities issued by foreign governments (mainly Canadian governmental units) and inter-

TABLE 14–5

Distribution of assets held by U.S. life insurance companies, selected years, 1950–1977

Year	Government securities	Corporate securities		Mortgages	Real estate	Policy loans	Miscellaneous assets	Total assets
		Bonds	Stocks					
				(amounts in $millions)				
1950	$16,118	$ 23,248	$ 2,103	$16,102	$ 1,445	$ 2,413	$ 2,591	$ 64,020
1960	11,815	46,740	4,981	41,771	3,765	5,231	5,273	119,576
1970	11,068	73,098	15,420	74,375	6,320	16,064	10,909	207,254
1977	23,555	137,889	33,763	96,848	11,060	27,556	21,051	351,722
				(percentage distribution)				
1950	25.2%	36.3%	3.3%	25.1%	2.2%	3.8%	4.1%	100.0%
1960	9.9	39.1	4.2	32.9	3.1	4.4	4.4	100.0
1970	5.3	35.3	7.4	35.9	3.0	7.8	5.3	100.0
1977	6.7	39.2	9.6	27.5	3.2	7.8	6.0	100.0

Source: Adapted from the American Council of Life Insurance, *Life Insurance Fact Book*, 1978.

national agencies totaled a little more than $8 billion, or about 35 percent of the government security portfolios held by U.S. life insurance companies.

U.S. government securities represent a store of reserves for life insurance firms—i.e., a residual source of funds to be drawn upon quickly as the need for cash arises. These liquid securities are particularly useful to the company's investment officer when promises for credit have been made to borrowers but expected cash inflows do not materialize. Federal securities can easily be marketed, usually with minimal capital losses, to cover immediate cash needs. In the majority of years during the postwar period life companies were either net sellers or purchased only negligible amounts of U.S. government obligations. The major shift was out of U.S. government securities into corporate bonds and real estate mortgages which carry substantially higher yields. More recently, with increased demands of policyholders for loans against their insurance policies and the rapid growth in total assets, the need for liquidity has increased and there has been some renewed interest in U.S. government issues. Life companies buy both short-term (under one year) and long-term (over one year) U.S. government securities. These securities are used principally to put temporarily idle funds to work until those funds are needed to meet long-term investments, especially purchases of mortgages and corporate securities.

State and local government obligations enjoyed a brief period of popularity among life company investment managers between 1950 and 1960 due to their attractive after-tax yields. The interest income on these obligations, as we have seen, is exempt from federal income taxes, though capital gains are fully taxable. However, both the dollar and percentage amounts of life company investments in these securities declined during the 1960s, then rebounded during the 1970s as yields on state and local securities climbed relative to yields on corporate securities and mortgages. Life insurance companies purchase a wide range of state and local government issues, including both general obligation and revenue bonds. Nevertheless, as a percentage of total assets, state and local securities are very small because the effective income tax rates paid by life companies are much lower than those paid by most other businesses.

Corporate stock

The need for stable cash flows and safety of invested funds as well as restrictive state regulations have constrained greater holdings of equities by U.S. life insurance companies. Common and preferred stock investments totaled almost $34 billion at year-end 1977, or slightly less than 10 percent of total assets. Close to 30 percent of equity investments are in preferred stock and the remainder in common stock. Stock holdings increased in volume and as a percentage of total investments in the majority of postwar years until 1973 when total holdings declined. However, in both 1975 and 1976 the industry's holdings of both common and preferred stock rose by more than $6 billion, then fell back slightly during 1977. Life companies are not a major factor in the stock market today since they hold only about 3 percent of all corporate shares. However, the role of life companies in the stock market is growing due to the expansion of insured pension and variable annuity plans. While direct acquisitions of corporate stock by life companies are severely restricted by regulations, state laws allow substantial purchases of equity securities for pension and annuity plans provided these securities are placed in a *separate account*, not a part of the company's resources associated with its insurance underwriting operations.

Corporate debt securities

In 1945, corporate debt securities held by U.S. life companies totaled $10 billion, or nearly 23 percent of total industry investments. At the close of 1977 the figure had increased to nearly $138 billion, or almost 40 percent of total industry resources. The high yields available from these securities explain much of their attractiveness to life companies. Life insurers are the largest institutional investor in corporate bonds and notes. The most remarkable growth in the corporate bond area has been in industrial issues, which have risen from about 2 percent of total assets in 1950 to nearly 27 percent in 1977, reflecting the dynamic growth of the U.S. manufacturing and industrial sector and its burgeoning demands for long-term credit. Life companies also make substantial investments today in public utility bonds, in railroad bonds, and in the securities of foreign corporations.

Mortgages

Mortgages are secured by a lien on real property, including family residences, apartment houses, condominiums, shopping centers, office buildings, and manufacturing and service establishments. Life companies have always been significant investors in financing these foms of real property, though their mortgage holdings have declined relative to other assets in the most recent period. At year-end 1977 nearly $97 billion was invested by U.S. life insurance firms in mortgages, representing more than a quarter of industry assets. The original maturity of life company loans on real property generally ranges between 20 and 30 years and interest rates typically are fixed for the life of the loan. The industry's heavy investments in real estate mortgages over the years may be explained by their relatively high yields, high investment quality, and maturity distribution which matches the companies' cash flow patterns and investment yields.

Total mortgage holdings have been declining as a percent of industry assets since 1974, when close to a third of total assets were invested in this financial instrument. Investments in home mortgages have been on the decline since 1966. For example, mortgage loans on one- to four-family dwellings represented just 15 percent of total real property loans made by the industry in 1977 compared to nearly 45 percent only ten years earlier. However, other (principally multifamily apartments, commercial, and farm) mortgages have increased each year with net purchases averaging $3 to $4 billion annually during the 1970s. The difference is due mainly to interest rate ceilings on FHA-VA home mortgages which have held their yields below market levels. Yields on commercial mortgages, on the other hand, are not constrained by legally imposed rate ceilings and fluctuate with market conditions.

Other investments

The asset side of life company balance sheets includes a category for "other assets" which normally are small in volume compared with those items already discussed. For instance, investments in residential and commercial properties and company office properties accounted for only about 3 percent of the industry's total assets at year-end 1977. For many years now life companies have been active in the construction and ownership of multifamily apartments, shopping centers, and office buildings.

Another asset—loans to policyholders—nearly doubled in dollar amount during the 1970s. These loans have represented about 8 percent of industry assets for several years running and totaled close to $28 billion at year-end 1977. The substantial growth in the dollar value of policy loans during the past few years is a response of policyholders to the high and rising rates of interest on other sources of loanable funds. Life insurance policies specify a fixed rate of interest on loans to policyholders and this rate generally has been lower than rates charged by other lenders. Until recently, the maximum loan rate on most policies issued was in the range of 5 to 6 percent. Either way, loans against insurance policies are a relatively cheap source of funds for individual policyholders.

A policy loan represents borrowing against the cash value built up over time in a life insurance policy. If the insured dies, designated beneficiaries receive the face value of the policy minus the amount of funds borrowed and any interest due. However, most individuals drawing loans against their policies anticipate earning greater returns on the funds borrowed than the interest cost incurred. This expectation of a surplus return over cost usually increases when interest rates in the economy rise. Hence, policy loans tend to increase rapidly during periods of credit restraint and high interest rates, as occurred during the 1973–74 and 1978–79 periods for example. The result of this increased borrowing by policyholders is, of course, a smaller volume of funds available for investment by the industry at a time when much higher returns are generally available in the financial markets.

Earnings and taxes

Because of the nature of life insurance operations, net income consists almost entirely of income from investments. The actual volume of net income generated by policy premiums after all benefit payments are made is difficult to estimate because benefits usually are distributed to policyholders well after the time insurance policies are purchased. Although payments of $26 billion to beneficiaries, annuitants, and policyholders were recorded during 1977 and total premium payments amounted to $72 billion, the difference of $46 billion does not represent actual net income from policy premiums. Rather, the outlay of cash benefits in the future should absorb any premiums paid by policyholders in current and prior years.

Life insurance firms are taxed at all three levels of government in the United States. In the case of federal taxation, effective income tax rates are significantly lower than rates paid by other U.S. business corporations, though the effective rate has approximately tripled since 1960. State and local governments frequently impose taxes on the gross premium income of companies operating within their jurisdictions. However, two thirds of the aggregate taxes paid by life companies take the form of federal income taxes. The tax burden of the industry has increased significantly during the past two decades, especially after passage of the Life Insurance Company Tax Act of 1959. U.S. life companies paid federal, state, and local fees, licenses, and taxes of more than $4 billion in 1977.

REGULATION

The activities of life insurance companies are deemed to be inseparable from the public interest and these companies, therefore, have been closely regulated for many years. An insurance department or commission supervises the activities of life insurers active in each state. Periodic financial statements are required so that the regulatory authorities can check on the soundness and financial stability of each company. From time to time the regulatory agencies verify these financial statements by making on-the-spot examinations of the companies' operations and records.

Prior to World War II the life insurance business was regulated exclusively by state and local units of governments. While the federal government's role has increased in recent years as a result of new tax rules and regulations over securities transactions, the bulk of government regulation of life insurance operations in the United States still is exercised by the states. State governments through commissions and agencies control the chartering of new companies, liquidation of failing companies, licensing of insurance agents, the content of policy forms, premium rates, and the character of permissible investments. Numerous hearings are held at the state level each year to consider insurance rate and service adjustments.

The form in which assets may be held also is laid down explicitly in state laws and regulations. These regulations, along with the decision making and skill of management, are the principal determinants of the quantity and quality of assets a life insurance company holds, its level of earnings, and growth. For example, life company holdings of common stock are probably substantially below what market conditions and rational portfolio management practices would dictate. In general, only assets contained on lists sanctioned by state authorities or assets which a "prudent man" would acquire may be added to life company investment portfolios.[2]

While regulation of the insurance industry may prevent certain abuses and offers some protection to the public, it is not necessarily true that such government intervention leads to the social optimum. At times regulatory bodies seem to be more responsive to the needs of the industry rather than to the needs of consumers of insurance services. At other times the regulatory rules imposed seem needlessly restrictive against company activities and make it exceedingly difficult for the industry to earn a competitive return on its invested funds. The situation is further complicated by the character of the industry itself which offers a great variety of policies and other financial services that sometimes are difficult for consumers to evaluate. Regardless of how the analysis is conducted, the central conclusion seems to be that the existing system of insurance regulation is in need of major revisions for the good of the public and the industry.

---

[2] See Robinson and Wrightsman [7], p. 51.

STRUCTURE OF THE INDUSTRY

Commercial life insurance firms in the United States fall into two broad categories: stock companies and mutual companies. A *stock* company is owned by its shareholders, similar to any other private corporation. A *mutual* company, on the other hand, legally is owned by its policyholders. In a sense, a mutual firm is a cooperative effort on the part of policyholders to pool their premiums for the protection of the whole group. At the close of 1977, there were about 1,750 life insurance companies chartered to operate in the 50 states. (See Table 14–6.) About 140 of these were mutuals and the rest were stockholder

TABLE 14–6
Number of U.S. life insurance
companies, selected years,
1900–1977

Year	Number of companies
1900	84
1910	284
1920	335
1930	438
1940	444
1950	649
1960	1,441
1970	1,780
1977	1,750

Source: Adapted from the American Council of Life Insurance, *Life Insurance Fact Book*, 1978.

owned. However, the mutual companies—which typically are both older and larger than the stockholder-owned firms—owned approximately 60 percent of the industry's resources. There are, of course, several large stock companies; however, the large majority of these are small compared to the mutuals.

The number of life insurance companies advanced at a healthy pace in the early postwar years to keep up with demands for financial services from a growing U.S. population. The growth rate slowed markedly during the decade of the 1960s, however, and the total number of companies peaked in 1970. Over the past decade a gradual decline in numbers of firms has occurred. The majority of life companies which disappeared were merged into larger firms and a few converted to property-casualty insurance companies. Rising costs, the scarcity of highly specialized management personnel, and the need to diversify operations and offer new financial services have favored larger companies and encouraged both mergers and the exit of smaller firms.

CONCLUSIONS

A little more than 200 years have passed since the first life insurance company was established in the United States. In that relatively short span of time, as we have seen, the assets of life companies reached more than $350 billion with approximately 1,750 companies offering insurance protection to the public. Today life insurance policies represent one of the most important outlets for household savings in the U.S. capital market. Life insurers are a dominant force in U.S. markets for corporate bonds and mortgages. U.S. citizens—two thirds of whom are insured—hold more than $2.5 trillion in life insurance policies with both legal reserve companies and fraternal organizations.

The foregoing statistics seem to imply that the future of the industry is assured. However, a number of recent trends cast some doubt that the future growth of the industry will be as rapid as in the past. For example, the growth of policy loans, which in tight money periods have approached 8 to 9 percent of industry assets and, because of regulations, carry submarket yields, is a continuing source of concern. The industry has not been particularly successful at getting permissible interest rates on these loans adjusted to market levels in order to reduce the outflow of funds. As noted previously, increased borrowing by policyholders absorbs funds normally available for investment and slows the accumulation of assets.

A second source of concern is the decline in the relative importance of whole or ordinary life policies and the rise in term insurance. As we have noted, term policies do not generate as many dollars for investment as do ordinary life policies since their premiums are significantly lower. As the mix of policy sales has shifted toward term insurance, the flexibility of the industry in investing long-term funds has been correspondingly reduced. Since it is basically upon sales of ordinary life policies that the industry has built its impressive long-term growth record, future industry growth is more uncertain. Many observers feel that continued inflation will support the shift in public demand from ordinary life policies to term insurance as the public seeks new outlets for its savings and relies upon insurance exclusively for protection against risk rather than as a savings instrument.

Probably the most encouraging development is the *innovation* increasingly practiced by life companies. Innovation opens up new sources of revenue and promotes the long-term growth of the industry. One example is the development of variable annuities for individual retirement programs. Offering a hedge against inflation, variable annuities generate income that fluctuates with either the market value of a portfolio of securities or are tied to some general economic index. This service, developed in the early 1960s, has gained wide customer acceptance and the number of group retirement plans carrying a variable annuity provision has grown quite rapidly. As with all changes in this heavily regulated industry, the future success of variable annuities is likely to depend more upon regulatory acceptance than effective public demand. Not all states expressly permit variable annuities.

Another recent innovation within the industry is the sale of shares in mutual funds devoted principally to common stocks. This new service permits life companies to offer a financial package embracing protection against both income risk and inflation through capital appreciation in stock prices. Once again, it is likely to be the force of government regulation, more than public acceptance, which shapes the future of this particular financial innovation and of other innovations that life companies may develop in future years. Indeed, life insurance companies today face an unusual mix of significant opportunities and significant challenges. The future success or failure of this industry in gaining increased consumer acceptance of its services—both new and old—will have profound implications for the evolving structure of the nation's financial system.

QUESTIONS

14–1. Against what kinds of financial losses do life insurance companies provide compensation?

14–2. Explain the differences between permanent or ordinary life insurance and term insurance. What is a life insurance annuity? an endowment policy? limited-pay insurance? group insurance? industrial life? credit life? In what ways do these different policies influence portfolio management practices at life companies?

14–3. What are the principal assets held by a life insurance company? How has the composition of life company asset portfolios changed in recent years?

14–4. What are the principal sources of funds drawn upon by U.S. life insurance companies?

14–5. Why do many insurance companies prefer private placements in acquiring corporate bonds rather than purchasing bonds in the open market?

14–6. List the types of regulations involved in the operation of a life insurance company. Why is this industry so heavily regulated? What are the principal goals of regulation?

14–7. What are policy loans? Explain how fluctuations in these loans affect the growth and investment policies of life companies.

14–8. Discuss recent trends in the profitability and growth of life insurance companies. Try to explain the factors behind these trends.

14–9. Why is innovation important today in the life insurance business? Explain why innovation may be even more important to the long-run viability of life companies in future years.

REFERENCES

1. American Council of Life Insurance. *Life Insurance Fact Book*. Washington, D.C.: 1978, 1977.

2. Dougall, Herbert E., and Gaumnitz, Jack E. *Capital Markets and Institutions*. Englewood Cliffs, N.J.: Prentice-Hall, 1975.

3. Harless, Doris. *Nonbank Financial Institutions*. Federal Reserve Bank of Richmond, October 1975.

4. Hempel, George H., and Yawitz, Jess B. *Financial Management of Financial Institutions*. Englewood Cliffs, N.J.: Prentice-Hall, 1977.

5. Life Insurance Association of America. *Life Insurance Companies as Financial institutions*. Englewood Cliffs, N.J.: Prentice-Hall, 1962.

6. Noback, Joseph C. *Life Insurance Accounting*. Homewood, Ill.: Richard D. Irwin, Inc., 1969.

7. Robinson, Roland I., and Wrightsman, Dwayne. *Financial Markets: The Accumulation and Allocation of Wealth*. New York: McGraw-Hill Book Co., 1974.

Problem for discussion

In this chapter we have discussed the nature of financial services offered and investments made by life insurance companies. We have noted how the highly stable and predictable nature of benefit claims against life companies allows these firms to divert nearly all of their net cash flow into long-term commitments of funds to borrowers. Life insurance companies today are active lenders in the fields of commercial, multifamily, and single-family mortgage lending and in providing long-term capital funds to corporations for the purchase of equipment. Life insurers usually must make commitments of large amounts of funds to commercial or housing projects on the basis of *expected* net cash flows and then make fine adjustments in their cash position as projections are translated into realized revenues and expenses.

In this problem imagine that you are a credit analyst and investment specialist for Mutual Insurance Company—a life insurer active for more than 50 years in the market for both commercial and residential mortgage loans. A group of organizers led by Mr. J. D. Reynolds has been planning for the past eight months to build a new office building and commercial complex in North Bend to house small retail businesses, doctors, lawyers, and dentists. Your company has been asked to take on the permanent financing of the project in the form of a 15-year loan in the amount of $3,275,000.

North Bend is a rapidly growing suburban area adjacent to Center City—a standard metropolitan statistical area (SMSA) with a population in excess of 300,000. Population growth in the area has been above the national average for the past two decades, due principally to the influx of electronics and aircraft firms into the greater metropolitan area. In addition, a large military base operated by the Strategic Air Command lies on the southern fringe of the community. The need for office space has been acute in some sections of the metropolitan area, particularly in those locations near the air base, the larger manufacturing and assembly plants, and the downtown area. In other parts of the city the demand has been much less strong and the commercial real estate market, more uncertain. It is in one of these latter areas that the proposed office complex would be constructed.

Construction of the complex would begin in 90 days provided both construction financing and a permanent takeout commitment for a mortgage loan is granted. The Reynolds group has applied to First State Bank for construction financing at an interest rate of 10 percent. The project's organizers are hoping the insurance company will agree to taking on the permanent mortgage financing at an interest rate of about 9 percent.

A number of recent developments have raised some serious questions concerning the appropriateness to the insurance company of granting the commercial mortgage loan as requested. There appear to be substantial risks associated with the project and with local business conditions. For one thing, the federal government plays a substantial role in North Bend's economy and the future magnitude and direction of government spending in the area are highly uncertain. For example, three years ago the air base employed 2,500 people, including service personnel and local firms under contract for construction and maintenance of base property. Currently less than 2,000 are employed there due to government cutbacks and curtail-ments. Last month, the Department of Defense announced that some military bases were being considered for possible closing or for further cutbacks in personnel. Speculation has been rampant in the local business community that the SAC base might be on the Defense Department's cutback list.

Private business activity in the area tends to be highly volatile. Electronics and construction firms account for at least 30 percent of the local labor force and both industries typically experience marked fluctuations in sales coincident with movements in interest rates, government spending, and foreign imports. During the most recent recession unemployment in the local construction industry approached 25 percent due to record high interest rates and a severe drop in the demand for new mortgage loans. The failure rate for local retail establishments has doubled since 1970 due to fluctuations in spending and employment.

In the wake of these recent developments a careful review of this credit application seems in order. The proposed commercial complex would be located three miles from a freeway and within a mile and a half of two shopping centers. Due to the rapid growth of North Bend the adjacent freeway is highly congested, especially in the morning and after five o'clock with commuter traffic from outlying areas. Reynolds and his group have argued that a substantial number of businesses would be interested in the new office facilities because of their proximity to the city, the air base, local industrial firms, the shopping centers, and the freeway. There are several other commercial buildings located in this particular area and a number under construction nearby. Right now, there appears to be a seasonal low in rentals of office space with a number of commercial complexes in the area reporting vacancy rates of about 12 percent.

A construction loan of $3,275,000 is requested for a year from First State Bank in order to build the three-story structure and adjacent parking facilities. When completed, the building would include about 100,000 square feet of floor space. Building costs in the area are rising rapidly—the Chamber of Commerce says 1 percent a month—so that reliable figures on the cost of the proposed project are somewhat difficult to obtain. Based upon estimates and architect's plans submitted by the organizers, it appears that construction costs will be about $3,150,000. Interest costs and other financial charges associated with the construction phase will be approximately $81,000. Other miscellaneous costs (including architect's fees, building permits, utility assessments, and city service fees) will probably total about $41,000. First State Bank has agreed to make the construction loan of $3,275,000 provided a commitment for permanent financing is secured from another qualified lender of funds. Reynolds and the other project organizers already own the land needed for the structure, having purchased it last year for $560,000 with a 60 percent loan from another bank. This loan is to be paid out in five years and bears an interest rate of 8¾ percent.

The project organizers have estimated that annual gross revenues from the project will be about $780,000 provided all office suites and shop space are completely filled. Annualized operating expenses are estimated at $240,000. Mortgage costs will vary, of course, with the interest rate awarded on the loan, but the organizers have assumed a 9 percent annual interest rate in their cash flow calculations.

As the credit analyst for Mutual Insurance Company you must resolve a number of important issues associated with this loan application. Among the most important are the following:

1. Have the developers adequately researched the market for commercial office space?
2. Should the interest rate on the loan be higher or lower or the maturity shorter or longer?
3. Is the amount of credit requested too much considering the earnings potential of the project?
4. How much weight should be given to the volatile nature of conditions in the local economy?

Try to formulate answers to these questions and then reach a decision on whether to recommend this project for permanent mortgage financing.

15

Property and casualty insurance companies

Property-casualty insurers protect their policyholders against the risks of property or income loss due to accidents, personal negligence, crime, or acts of nature. These companies are sometimes called "department stores of insurance," because they offer such a wide variety of policies to protect their customers against loss. Indeed, the range of insurance services offered by this industry has been expanding rapidly in recent years in response to competitive pressures, inflation, and rising costs. Similar to life insurance companies, property and casualty companies invest their funds in long-term marketable securities and build up reserves to meet the future claims of policyholders. In this chapter we examine the types of services offered and the sources and uses of funds for this important group of financial intermediaries.

STRUCTURE OF THE INDUSTRY

Several different kinds of firms are active in the property-casualty business: (1) mutuals, (2) stockholder-owned companies, (3) life and casualty insurers, (4) domestic Lloyd's (5) workers' compensation insurers, and (6) reciprocals. In total, the industry contained nearly 2,950 firms with total resources of approximately $135 billion at year-end 1977. However, less than 1,000 property-casualty insurers offer policies in a majority of the 50 states and these sell the bulk of all new policies issued each year. The remaining, predominantly small insurance firms provide protection for persons in local areas or serve customers with unusual or unique insurance needs, such as entertainers and physicians.

Mutual insurance companies are owned by their policyholders, who provide the bulk of funds for their operation and growth. Thus, the capital accounts of mutuals are usually referred to as policyholders' surplus, reflecting the fact that policyholders are technically owners and the capital safeguards their investments. Policyholders' surplus increases as a result of underwriting operations and earnings on investments after all operating costs and taxes are met. The mutuals represent about one quarter of the total assets of all property-casualty insurers but outnumber the stockholder-owned companies. *Stockholder-owned companies*, on the other hand, are like any other business corporation in that the stockholders are the sole owners, accepting the risks of ownership and receiving any dividends voted by each company's board of directors. The stockholder-owned companies include some of the largest firms in the industry and, in fact, hold close to three quarters of the assets held by all U.S. property-casualty insurers.

The remaining types of property-casualty insurers are relatively small in number and in total resources. For example, there are an estimated 50 reciprocal companies in the United States. *Reciprocals* represent groups of policyholders who cooperate to pool their resources in order to acquire relatively low-cost insurance protection. *Lloyd's* organizations, while important in Great Britain, are comparatively unimportant in the United States. Scarcely more than a dozen such companies were active in the United States during the early 1970s, though there is some evidence the number has grown since then in response to rapidly growing commercial insurance needs. These groups of unincorporated individuals provide financial protection for abnormal business risks normally avoided by most property-casualty firms. The individual underwriters which make up a Lloyd's organization each assume an agreed-upon percentage of the potential liability under policies written and may reinsure their risk with other companies. *Workers' compensation insurers* protect employees against job-related hazards. These companies frequently are created by state law in order to provide medical care and rehabilitation and make up for lost income for injured workers. In the event of accidental death related to a worker's job, benefit payments may be made to dependents as well. Finally, *life and casualty insurers* offer both property and life insurance plans along with casualty coverage. These companies include both stockholder-owned firms and mutual associations.

Many companies in the industry today are *multiple-line* companies, offering many different kinds of policies to cover a wide range of business and consumer risks. Whatever kind of property-liability coverage the customer has, this includes coverage for damages or other losses only up to the maximum amounts specified by contract. The insurance company seeks to indemnify a policyholder only for actual loss as measured by expenses stemming from repairs or restoring what has been lost. In the case of bodily injury, this calculation of loss can be exceedingly complicated since medical problems can be long term in nature and the victim's future income-earning potential may be impaired. Moreover, as we will soon discover, most losses covered by property-casualty insurance are affected directly by inflation. For example, automobiles and home repairs, medical care, and hospitalization have risen dramatically over the past decade in response to inflationary pressures. These developments have sharply increased the underwriting costs of property-casualty insurers, increased the risks of underwriting operations, and narrowed the industry's margin of profitability.

INSURANCE SERVICES OFFERED BY PROPERTY-CASUALTY COMPANIES

Property-casualty insurers can protect their customers against any risk which has reasonable predictability. However, most companies devote their resources to writing policies to cover only a few major kinds of risk. Table 15–1 indicates the relative importance of the principal types of premiums written by U.S. property-casualty companies in 1977. The industry has experienced rapid growth in recent years, especially during the 1970s due to sharply increased demands for both business and consumer insurance protection. Aggregate net premiums written by the industry for all lines of insurance coverage rose from nearly $33 billion in 1970 to more than $72 billion in 1977, an increase of more than 120 percent. During 1977 alone business and consumer purchases of property-casualty insurance coverage rose nearly 20 percent.

Automobile liability and damage protection.   Protection against property damage and death or physical injury resulting from owning and operating a motor vehicle is by far the dominant form of insurance written by this industry. Auto insurance coverage accounted for more than two fifths of the total volume of property-liability premiums in 1977. Claims may result from individuals injured or otherwise damaged by an owner's vehicle or the owner may file a

TABLE 15–1
Net premiums written by U.S. property-casualty insurers, 1977 ($millions)

Private passenger auto liability	$15,000	Fire insurance and related lines	$4,500
Commercial auto liability	3,950	Homeowners' multiple peril	6,800
Total auto liability	$18,950	Farmowners' multiple peril	400
Private auto physical damage insurance	9,625	Commercial multiple peril	4,975
Commercial auto physical damage insurance	1,925	Workers' compensation insurance	9,350
Total auto physical damage	$11,550	Inland marine coverage	1,600
Total of all automobile insurance coverage	$30,500	Ocean marine coverage	975
		Surety and fidelity insurance	950
Medical malpractice insurance	$ 1,225	Burglary and theft insurance	130
Other liability coverage	5,875	Crop and hail damage	340
Total nonauto liability coverage	7,100	Boiler and machinery coverage	215
		Glass insurance	35
		Credit insurance	45
		Aircraft coverage	150

Source: From *Insurance Facts*, 1978 Edition, by permission. Copyright 1978, Insurance Information Institute; and Alfred M. Best Co., Inc., *Best's Aggregates and Averages, Property-Liability*, annual ed.

claim resulting from the theft of or accidental damage to a motor vehicle. Both the largest number of auto policies and the greatest volume of auto insurance premiums are accounted for by consumers—families and individuals—rather than commercial accounts. For example, during 1977, of the nearly $31 billion in net auto insurance premiums written, individuals accounted for about $25 billion, or 80 percent, while commercial customers accounted for only $6 billion, or slightly less than 20 percent of the total.

Intense competition for auto insurance business prevails among the companies writing this form of insurance coverage. The costs of auto repair have skyrocketed in recent years as have medical costs of those injured each year in thousands of auto accidents. According to the Insurance Information Institute, the total dollar cost of traffic accidents in the United States rose about 17 percent in 1977 alone. The average claims for personal injury and property damage related to auto accidents both have more than doubled over the past decade. As a result, many auto insurance programs have reported substantial underwriting losses during the 1970s. Claims against policies from auto accidents relative to auto premiums earned and operating expenses associated with auto policies compared to auto premiums written have displayed definite upward trends. Still auto insurance lines generate a significant amount of cash flow which enables property-casualty insurers to compensate to some extent for underwriting losses through their earnings on investments.

Fire insurance and related policies. The two fields of fire insurance and extended coverage for damage caused by wind, water, earthquakes, and civil disturbances at one time were the principal business of property-casualty companies before the rapid rise of auto insurance. Today, these traditional insurance lines, though smaller in relative terms, remain among the more profitable of the industry's insurance services. While fire losses in the United States amount to billions each year, improved fire fighting techniques and effective prevention programs have gradually lowered the industry's loss ratio in this field. Nevertheless, one problem of concern to property-casualty insurers is the rapid increase in arson-caused fires in major U.S. cities—one of the fastest growing serious crimes during the 1970s. As shown in Table 15–2, at year-end 1977 fire insurance cov-

TABLE 15–2
Premiums written on fire insurance and allied
property-casualty insurance lines, 1957–1977
($millions)

Year	Fire insurance premiums	Allied insurance premiums*
1957	$1,594.0	$ 712.5
1960	1,667.4	738.9
1965	1,548.1	667.3
1970	2,199.4	948.0
1971	2,293.7	878.5
1972	2,463.2	942.5
1973	2,392.1	1,025.0
1974	2,368.3	1,087.5
1975	2,510.2	1,180.9
1976	2,810.5	1,291.3
1977	3,050.0	1,450.0

* Allied insurance lines include protection from earthquakes, explosions, riots, windstorms, and water damage.
Source: From *Insurance Facts*, 1978 Edition, by permission. Copyright 1978, Insurance Information Institute.

erage totaled just over $3 billion, up more than 50 percent from a decade earlier. Related policies for property losses associated with earthquakes, floods, high winds, and civil disturbances have grown very rapidly, particularly since the mid 1960s, due to sharp increases in building and repair costs.

Liability insurance policies. Insurance claims stemming from property ownership or performing a task under contract, from selling or distributing goods, from operating equipment, or from performing professional services are covered by liability insurance. Compared to auto liability insurance, the general liability insurance business is relatively small; net premiums written totaled about $7 billion in 1977. However, this kind of risk protection is one of the most rapidly growing forms of property-casualty insurance. Two major causes were the substantial increases in medical malpractice suits against physicians and surgeons and other organizations in the health care field and product liability suits against manufacturers for damages due to defective merchandise. An Interagency Task Force set up by the federal government estimated that at least 60,000 and perhaps as many as 70,000 product liability claims were made during 1976, while the number of product-claim lawsuits entered on federal court dockets increased more than 10 percent during fiscal 1977.[1] As a result, the industry's loss ratio on this form of insurance has increased noticeably.

Workers' compensation insurance. Those injured in work-related accidents may receive benefits to recover medical costs and income lost. Workers' compensation protection also pays benefits to families whose principal wage earner has been killed on the job. The particular employees covered by workers' compensation vary from state to state, but there has been a trend toward covering more and more workers. This is evidenced by the fact that sales volume has more than tripled over the past decade. Generally the employer pays the cost of workers' compensation insurance according to rates set by state law. Loss rates associated with this form of risk protection generally have been rising in line with the general increase in employee benefits.

Multiple peril policies. This kind of "package" insurance, bundling together several different kinds of risk, was developed early in the postwar period. These new policies were developed with business and consumer convenience in mind. Instead of different policies to cover acts of nature, loss from crime, and negligence, insurance agents can now offer combined coverage at a lower price. Multiple peril insurance has become extremely popular in a relatively short space of time. Premiums written for homeowners' multiple policies rose from less than $3 billion in 1970 to almost $7 billion in 1977. The commercial version of these policies increased nearly four fold over the same period. It should be noted that nearly all the traditional property-casualty insurance lines (except credit and aircraft coverage) have continued to grow at an impressive pace in recent years.

---

[1] See, in particular, Insurance Information Institute, *Insurance Facts*, 1978 ed., p. 7.

Miscellaneous property-casualty policies. In the miscellaneous category are property-casualty policies designed to cover a wide range of risks. Inland marine insurance, for example, provides protection for goods involved in water transport. Personal property also is covered today by this form of insurance. While multiple peril insurance has assumed some of the business in this field, premiums written for inland marine insurance continue to grow rapidly. The volume of sales nearly tripled over the decade ending in 1977. Losses related to water transport also are covered today through ocean marine insurance. Ship hulls and cargos on both commercial and pleasure craft are protected by this form of coverage. Not surprisingly, with the rapid development of international commerce and pleasure boating in recent years, the volume of premiums written for ocean marine coverage has grown quite rapidly, increasing more than fourfold in two decades.

Surety and fidelity policies guard against failures to deliver goods or complete a project or against dishonest acts committed by a firm's employees. Familiar examples in this area include contractors working on a building project who may fail to meet completion deadlines and defendants who promise to show up in court on an appointed date and fail to do so. Premiums written under surety bonds have grown steadily over the years. Fidelity bond premiums each year are less than half as much as for surety coverage; however, substantial future growth is expected in this area as a growing number of retail and manufacturing firms now recognize the benefits of securing protection against the dishonest actions of a few employees. Fidelity bonding is most common today in the financial institutions' sector due to the large sums of money involved.

Other specialized forms of property-casualty insurance include crop and hail insurance, boiler and machinery coverage, glass insurance, and protection against burglary and theft. The volume of premiums written to cover property losses from burglaries and related crimes involving property declined in the early 1970s, then climbed quite steeply later in the decade. Inflation has played a role here in sharply escalating the value of property losses from crime. Particularly noteworthy has been the upsurge in burglaries and auto thefts which have reached alarming proportions in major metropolitan areas. Moreover, there is evidence of a substantial increase in recent years of "white collar" (nonviolent) crimes against businesses, resulting in economic losses variously estimated at $25 to $50 billion annually.

This brief survey of services offered by property-casualty insurers suggests perhaps the appropriateness of the term often applied to firms in this industry—"department stores of insurance." This is one of the most innovative of all financial industries, generally sensitive to customer needs and quite willing to provide new forms of insurance protection where the new services appear to be economically viable in the long run. It is also a highly competitive industry at the local market level. Frequently regulations limit price competition, so that individual insurers stress customer convenience, effective advertising, and aggressive retailing of services.

FUNDS FLOWS FOR
PROPERTY-CASUALTY COMPANIES

Analysis of insurance company balance sheets is a difficult task for most outside observers of the industry, not only because of differences in accounting systems from company to company, but also because of differences in basic accounting terminology between the property-casualty insurance business and other industries. The major categories of assets include bonds, common and preferred stocks, mortgages, real estate owned, collateral loans, cash (including demand deposits and currency), premium balances, and miscellaneous assets. On the sources of funds side the major categories include long- and short-term debt, paid-in capital, surplus, and equity-related reserves. Paid-in capital represents common stock held by the individual company's owners if the firm is stockholder owned rather than being a mutual organization. Net surplus reflects retained or accumulated earnings after taxes less dividend distributions to shareholders in a stock company or to policyholders in a mutual company. Additions to retained earnings arise principally from underwriting profits and interest, dividends, and capital gains received on investments. The earnings account is reduced through payment of dividends, investment losses, underwriting losses, and payment of taxes to federal, state, and local governments. Equity reserves are a contingent liability related to disputed claims by policyholders that may result in actual losses to the company. Claims in process which the company expects to pay, advance payments by policyholders not yet earned, and, of course, borrowings from banks, nonbank financial institutions, and in the open market typically are listed in the liability accounts.

Allocation of funds by property-casualty insurers

The assets held by property-casualty companies fall into two major categories—financial assets and other assets. Included in "other" assets are receivables from policyholders (frequently called premium balances), real estate owned, office supplies and equipment, and similar items accounting for about one fifth of the industry's total resources. The remainder of the industry's assets consist principally of cash, bank deposits, and marketable securities. Traditionally, casualty companies have relied upon revenues from investments to provide the bulk of their net income, while hoping to roughly "breakeven" on their underwriting operations. The composition of their investments, then, is considerable importance to the short-run profitability and long-run viability of property-casualty insurers.

Financial assets held by U.S. property-casualty companies for selected years during the 1967–77 period are shown in Table 15–3, which is derived from the Flow of Funds Accounts provided by the Federal Reserve System. A number of interesting trends in industry investments are evident in this data. As with other major financial intermediaries during the postwar period, there has been a sharp decline in asset liquidity as reflected in holdings of cash (i.e., demand deposits and currency) which fell from 3.2 percent of total financial assets in 1967 to only 2 percent in 1977. The industry's reserve cash needs are modest due to the reasonable predictability of cash inflows and outflows associated with premium payments, interest income from investments, and claims of policyholders. Moreover, as individual insurance companies have grown in size they have managed to economize on cash balances. Finally, the rise in interest rates since the late 1960s has increased the opportunity cost of cash balances, encouraging property-casualty insurers to reach for higher-yielding assets.

Investments in corporate stock (both common and preferred) also have declined in recent years due to accounting regulations requiring the valuation of equity investments at market rather than cost and adverse developments in the stock market. Corporate equities represented about 32 percent of total industry financial assets in 1967 and less than 16 percent in 1977. Filling the gap left by declining holdings of corporate stock are industry holdings of corporate and municipal bonds, especially the latter. Reflecting the fact that property-casualty insurers are subject to the full corporate income tax rate, the industry has shown increasing interest in the relatively high tax-exempt yields available on state and local obligations during the 1970s. In fact, property-casualty insurers rank second to commercial banks as major buyers of municipal obligations. Municipal holdings rose a full 10 percentage points to 44 percent of total industry financial assets at year-end 1977. The industry's interest in municipal bonds tends to fluctuate with its earnings however. Acquisitions of municipals tend to decline in years of poor profit performance and increase during more profitable years when additional tax sheltering of income is required.

Industry holdings of federal government securities have been quite volatile. Until the mid-1970s investments in U.S. Treasury securities

TABLE 15–3

Financial assets held by property-casualty insurers, selected years, 1967–1977 ($billions)*

Items	1967 Assets	Percent	1970 Assets	Percent	1973 Assets	Percent	1975 Assets	Percent	1977 Assets	Percent
Demand deposits and currency	$ 1.3	3.2%	$ 1.4	2.8%	$ 1.5	2.2%	$ 1.7	2.2%	$ 2.2	2.0%
Corporate equities	13.0	31.8	13.2	26.5	19.7	28.3	14.2	18.4	17.1	15.7
U.S. Treasury securities	4.3	10.5	3.4	6.8	2.8	4.0	4.7	6.1	9.8	9.0
Federal agency securities	1.2	2.9	1.6	3.2	2.3	3.3	3.3	4.3	4.4	4.0
State and local government obligations	13.5	33.0	17.0	34.1	28.5	41.0	33.3	43.1	48.2	44.3
Corporate bonds	4.3	10.5	8.6	17.2	8.0	11.5	12.2	15.8	16.9	15.5
Commercial mortgages	0.2	0.5	0.2	0.4	0.2	0.3	0.2	0.3	0.4	0.4
Trade credit	3.2	7.8	4.4	8.8	6.5	9.4	7.7	10.0	10.0	9.2
Total financial assets	$40.9	100.0%	$49.9	100.0%	$69.5	100.0%	$77.3	100.0%	108.8	100.0%
Profit taxes payable	$ 0.1	0.4%	$ 0.2	0.6%	$ 0.3	0.6%	$ 0.3	0.5%	$ 0.5	0.6%
Policy payables	25.0	99.6	34.2	99.4	47.4	99.4	58.5	99.5	79.8	99.4
Total liabilities	$25.1	100.0%	$34.4	100.0%	$47.7	100.0%	$58.8	100.0%	$80.3	100.0%

* Column figures may not add exactly to column totals due to rounding errors.

Source: Adapted from Board of Governors of the Federal Reserve System, *Flow of Funds Accounts: Assets and Liabilities Outstanding, 1967–77*, Washington, D.C.

declined steeply as other securities with higher yields were sought. More recently, industry holdings of U.S. Treasury issues have risen in response to higher rates available on these securities and greater liquidity needs. Investments in federal agency securities have risen steadily to about 4 percent of total financial assets, reflecting the improved marketability of agency issues and their slightly higher yields compared to U.S. Treasury issues. Mortgage holdings have been remarkably steady at less than 1 percent of total financial assets.

TABLE 15–4
Changes in holdings of financial assets by property-casualty insurers between 1967 and 1977

Items	Change between 1967 and 1977 in $billions	Percentage terms
Total financial assets	$67.9	166.0%
Demand deposits and currency	0.9	69.2
Corporate equities	4.1	31.5
U.S. Treasury issues	5.5	127.9
Federal agency securities	3.2	266.7
State and local government obligations	34.7	257.0
Corporate bonds	12.6	293.0
Commercial mortgages	0.2	100.0
Trade credit	6.8	212.5

Source: Adapted from Board of Governors of the Federal Reserve System, *Flow of Funds Accounts: Assets and Liabilities Outstanding, 1967–77*, Washington, D.C.

Table 15–4, also based upon the Federal Reserve's Flow of Funds Accounts, shows even more graphically recent changes in the property-casualty industry's holdings of financial assets. Between 1967 and 1977 industry holdings of total financial assets increased 166 percent. Obviously, those categories of financial assets growing faster than this increased their share of the industry's portfolio. Holdings of corporate bonds grew the most rapidly in response to the unusually attractive yields on these securities over most of the past decade. The growth of federal agency and municipal obligations was also extremely rapid for the reasons discussed previously. In contrast, cash assets, corporate stocks, commercial mortgages, and U.S Treasury securities grew far more slowly than the increase in total financial assets and, therefore, declined relative to other portfolio assets.

Funds received by property-casualty insurers

The two major sources of funds for property-casualty insurers are premiums paid by policyholders and net income from investments.

The net amount of funds available for investment from the flow of policyholder premiums is highly uncertain, since claims against policies can be quite unpredictable. The net gain or loss from underwriting may be measured by the difference between premiums written and the sum of operating expenses and claims paid. On balance, the industry's net underwriting gain has averaged close to zero in recent years and frequently has been negative, as shown in Table 15–5. For

TABLE 15–5
Underwriting and investment income of U.S. property-casualty insurers, selected years, 1957–1977 ($millions)

Year	Underwriting gains (or losses) after policyholders' dividends	Investment income*	Combined net income before taxes
1957	$ –409.1	$ 579.7	$ 170.6
1960	149.8	767.9	917.7
1965	–709.5	1,131.6	422.1
1970	–425.8	2,005.1	1,579.3
1971	826.2	2,421.5	3,247.7
1972	1,061.7	2,799.7	3,861.4
1973	6.1	3,325.3	3,331.4
1974	–2,644.9	3,832.7	1,187.8
1975	–4,226.8	4,150.2	–76.6
1976	–2,188.7	4,805.9	2,617.3
1977	1,112.0	6,120.0	7,232.0

*Investment income for all U.S. property-casualty insurers minus expenses of making investments before taxes.
Source: From *Insurance Facts*, 1978 edition, by permission. Copyright 1978, Insurance Information Institute.

example, while property-casualty companies recorded net underwriting gains of $1.1 billion (after policyholder dividends) in 1977, underwriting losses of more than $2 billion were recorded during 1976 and more than $4 billion in 1975.

Investment income of property-casualty companies has advanced steadily. Net investment income in 1977 was an estimated $6.1 billion, 27 percent higher than the 1976 figure of $4.8 billion. The sum of income from investments and net underwriting gains (or losses) yields the before-tax net income of property-casualty insurers which amounted to $7.2 billion in 1977. This last figure was almost three times the previous year's before-tax income and reflected both higher average yields on holdings of financial assets and positive underwriting gains following three consecutive years of losses. Measured against net worth, the industry's return on capital was nearly 20 percent in 1977. This represented a sharp recovery from a declining trend experienced throughout most of the 1970s. For example, the return on equity accounts was less than 2 percent in 1975.

Once federal and state tax obligations and policyholder or stockholder dividends are met, any net income remaining to property-casualty insurers goes to build up the industry's financial strength (or net worth). Additions are made to capital and equity-related reserves, providing greater security for policyholders against unanticipated underwriting losses. The principal index of the industry's financial condition is the policyholders' surplus account, analogous to the net worth account in most corporations. As shown in Table 15–6,

TABLE 15–6
Total assets and policyholders' surplus of property-casualty insurers, selected years, 1957–1977 ($billion)

Year	Total assets	Policyholders' surplus
1957	$23.4	$ 8.9
1960	30.1	11.9
1965	41.8	17.1
1970	58.6	18.5
1971	67.3	22.7
1972	78.9	28.2
1973	83.9	27.1
1974	82.1	20.9
1975	94.1	25.3
1976	112.8	31.4
1977	135.1	37.3

Source: From *Insurance Facts*, 1978 edition, by permission. Copyright 1978, Insurance Information Institute; and Alfred M. Best Co., Inc., *Best's Aggregates and Averages, Property-Liability*, annual ed.

policyholders' surplus rose about $6 billion in both 1976 and 1977—a notable change after significant declines earlier in the decade due principally to large underwriting losses. The rise in net earnings as reflected in the surplus account was paralled by a substantial gain (nearly 20 percent) in industry assets to $135 billion in 1977. These gains in total footings and in the surplus account are indications that the industry has learned to make more efficient use of its available funds in the face of inflation-accelerated damage claims, increased litigation especially in the product liability and professional services fields, and more volatile fluctuations in interest rates and security prices. Superior tax management practices also have played a major role in improving the industry's after-tax returns, as evidenced by its growing holdings of tax-exempt municipal bonds.

The growth of the net worth or policyholders' surplus account is of great importance to the industry's present and future financial position and should be carefully studied. By definition, net worth or policyholders' surplus is the difference between total assets and industry liabilities. For stockholder-owned companies net worth consists of capital stock, surplus, and equity-related reserves. Mutual companies include net surplus, guarantee funds, and equity reserves in this account. The size of a company's policyholders' surplus account, both in dollar terms and relative to total claims against the company, is a key determinant of both the risks the firm will insure (i.e., the service mix it tries to achieve) and the investments it will make. Net worth is the principal cushion for unexpected claims against the insurer and the protective shield against significant deterioration in the value of a company's assets. Other factors held constant, a company with a larger and stronger net worth position will tend to take on somewhat more risky, longer-term investments and assume somewhat greater risks in its underwriting operations.

REGULATION AND TAXATION OF PROPERTY-CASUALTY INSURERS

Property-casualty insurance companies are regulated principally by the states rather than the federal government. The setting of insurance rates charged the public, financial reporting standards, agent licensing procedures, standards for investments, and procedures for examining individual companies are all controlled by insurance commissions at the state government level. While regulations vary widely, their general purpose is to assure an adequate return to the companies and, at the same time, to protect the public against excessive insurance rates, poor service, and the financial insolvency of individual insurers. These goals conflict to some extent, making the regulatory process a difficult one. Rates charged for major lines of casualty insurance differ from region to region and are a function of both regulation and the industry's loss experience—that is, the frequency and cost of claims—in a given area. The regulatory authorities must be especially careful that rates permitted on all insurance lines are high enough to protect the financial integrity of each company in order to meet the claims of policyholders and also high enough to ensure that the public is adequately served. When insurance rates are set too low, for example, property-casualty insurers, operating in their own economic interest and in the interest of existing policyholders, tend to be less aggressive in marketing their risk-protection services. If rates are set too high, an excessive volume of resources may be devoted to providing insurance services and the industry may receive windfall profits. Typically the setting of insurance rates lags behind changes in underwriting costs. In recent years these costs have generally spiraled upward, putting downward pressure on industry earnings and increasing insurance risks.

With a few exceptions the earnings of property-casualty companies are subject to the same federal tax rules as any other business corporation. Stockholder-owned companies are assessed the full corporate income tax rate on net earnings from investments and net profits (if any) from underwriting operations. Mutual companies may deduct policyholder dividends before taxes and may postpone tax payments on certain categories of underwriting income into future years through a special loss reserve account. The states levy a premium tax on the gross income of both life and property-casualty insurers. This tax levy totaled more than $2.3 billion in 1977 and was almost evenly split between property-casualty and life companies. Insurance companies also pay property taxes, sales taxes, and, in some areas, various local income taxes and use fees.

RECENT DEVELOPMENTS IN THE INDUSTRY

The property-casualty insurance business is changing rapidly in response to competitive pressures, regulation, and action in the courts. We have commented on some of these trends in earlier sections of this chapter; others deserve a brief mention as well. One problem is a fundamental change in the risk parameters surrounding major insurance lines, making the industry's previous experience less helpful in setting rates to adequately cover future claims. Inflation has been a major problem (especially for auto repairs and health care) requiring companies to more accurately forecast price trends in order to protect their reserves and return on equity. Innovation in insurance services, while necessary to attract new customers and retain existing clientele, also increases the industry's risk since it is much more difficult to set rates at levels necessary to defray the costs of services provided when loss experience is limited. Finally, entirely new forms of property and personal injury risk have appeared in recent years, such as those related to nuclear power plants and pollution of the environment.

A prominent example of recent innovation and changing risk parameters in the property-casualty field is the rapid rise of *no-fault* automobile insurance. No-fault insurance allows persons injured in an auto accident, regardless of who is at fault, to be compensated for certain expenses (such as medical costs and lost income) by their own insurer. Only about half the states have adopted such a plan for handling auto accident claims in hopes of reducing litigation in the courts and bringing about speedier settlement of policyholder claims. Proposals have been introduced in Congress for several years running to make no-fault insurance compulsory nationwide. The problem with this form of insurance is that it changes the basic risk characteristics of the largest insurance line carried by property-casualty companies. Whatever the benefits to consumers of this form of insurance coverage, it appears to complicate the task of insurance management in ensuring adequate service to the public and an adequate return on the industry's invested capital.

Additional problems facing the industry in recent years include an apparent rise in man-made and natural disasters, changes in insurance regulations, increases in crime rates (especially arson, burglary, and white-collar crimes), and more liberal settlements of policyholders' claims in the courts. At the same time the concept of expanded product liability on the part of manufacturing firms and those offering professional services has led to a rapid rise in lawsuits, increasing both the amount of successful claims and the costs of litigation borne by property-casualty companies. Finally, there is considerable evidence that the insurance business is sensitive to stages of the business cycle. Industry revenues decline during periods of recession, while loss and expense ratios rise during periods of expansion, especially when inflationary conditions prevail. When the two—inflation and recession—occur together, the industry experiences a particularly difficult time in earning a satisfactory rate of return on its invested capital and in providing a satisfactory volume of services to its customers.

QUESTIONS

15-1. List the major types of insurance coverage provided by property-casualty companies.

15-2. Explain how the following property-casualty companies differ from each other:
   a. Stockholder-owned companies.
   b. Mutuals.
   c. Domestic Lloyds.
   d. Reciprocals.
   e. Workers' compensation insurers.
   f. Life and casualty companies.

15-3. How do the liquidity needs of life insurance companies and property-casualty companies differ? Explain how these differences are reflected in the composition of each industry's assets.

15–4. Explain why the proportion of property-casualty assets held in senior securities has been on the rise over the past several years. What has happened to holdings of common and preferred stock and why?

15–5. What are the principal sources of funds drawn upon by property-casualty insurers?

15–6. What has happened to the earnings from underwriting operations recorded by property-casualty companies in recent years? What are the principal reasons behind the industry's reduced underwriting income?

15–7. What is the major source of net earnings for property-casualty companies? Explain how this earnings source might be affected by government monetary and fiscal policy.

15–8. List some recent innovations in insurance services provided by property-casualty companies. What are the potential benefits of diversification to the companies? potential risks?

REFERENCES

1. Athearn, James L. *Risk and Insurance.* 2d ed. New York: Appleton-Century-Crofts, 1969.

2. Bickelhaupt, David L. *General Insurance.* 9th ed. Homewood, Ill.: Richard D. Irwin, Inc., 1974.

3. Harless, Doris. *Nonbank Financial Institutions.* Federal Reserve Bank of Richmond, October 1975.

4. Insurance Information Institute. *Insurance Facts.* 1977, 1978 eds.

5. Jacobs, Donald P., Farwell, Loring C., and Neave, Edwin H. *Financial Institutions.* 5th ed. Homewood, Ill.: Richard D. Irwin, Inc., 1972.

6. Mehr, Robert I., and Cammack, Emerson. *Principles of Insurance.* 5th ed. Homewood, Ill. Richard D. Irwin, Inc., 1972.

7. Mehr, Robert I., and Hedges, Bob A. *Risk Management: Concepts and Applications.* Homewood, Ill.: Richard D. Irwin, Inc., 1974.

Problem for discussion

As we have seen in this chapter, the decade of the 1970s presented enormous difficulties for the financial management of property and casualty insurance companies. One of the major outlets for funds—the equity market—stagnated in a period in which escalating inflation substantially increased the cost of claims. Moreover, the sharp fluctuations in the stock market caused earnings to be erratic, making planning for purchases and sales of municipal securities especially difficult. In the problem situation discussed below the student is asked to determine the investment strategy of a property and casualty insurance company in a period of great uncertainty. After reviewing the material below, the student should address the following questions:

1. Under what conditions would a property and casualty insurance company devote a substantial fraction of its assets to municipal securities? Does the coming year appear to present such conditions?
2. What are the alternative investment opportunities? What are the risk and return characteristics of each of these?

Old Reliable Casualty Company is a full-line insurance company specializing in property and casualty insurance. Established originally to write fire insurance for the New England textile industry in the late 19th century, the company had grown substantially, if irregularly, throughout the years and had gradually expanded into other lines of casualty insurance. Moreover, in the early post-World War II period, Old Reliable (a motto used extensively in its advertising) had established a life insurance subsidiary. However, writing life insurance policies remained a minor part of the total premium income of the firm and was generally unprofitable. Indeed, there had been rumors that senior management of the company had planned to sell the life insurance business to another firm.

Perhaps the most significant development in the recent history of Old Reliable occurred in 1966 when the company was purchased by a large conglomerate heavily involved in international and domestic manufacturing, real estate development, and oil and gas exploration. At the time, the founding family of Old Reliable, which did not play an active role in management, had viewed the exchange of its stock in Old Reliable for the stock of the conglomerate as an ideal way to diversify its investments, obtain greater liquidity, and perhaps achieve substantial capital gains. The stock of the conglomerate was selling at 43 times its expected earnings and had appreciated substantially in the recent past. Moreover, the majority owners of Old Reliable believed that affiliation with the conglomerate might increase the insurance company's access to the capital market, especially in times of adversity. There was no public market for the shares of Old Reliable and the firm's bankers had been placing increasing pressure on the firm to expand its equity base.

Unfortunately, affiliation with the conglomerate did not achieve the desired benefits either for the founding family or for Old Reliable. The fascination of the stock market with the conglomerate movement collapsed shortly after the acquisition, so that within a year the market value of the conglomerate's stock had been reduced by more than 50 percent. Moreover, the conglomerate was unable to provide any capital to Old Reliable and indeed had a severe capital deficiency of its own. Perhaps most significantly, the conglomerate substantially altered the senior management of Old Reliable and also expanded markedly the regional coverage of the firm and the number of different types of insurance lines offered. As a result, costs increased dramatically—both operating costs associated with a more extensive network of branch offices and also the costs of claims—but the revenues derived from these expanded operations did not rise proportionately.

The ten-year period following the acquisition of Old Reliable turned out to be a very difficult period for the company and the economy. Severe economic and financial instability occurred, including the most severe recession since the Great Depression of the 1930s. The equity market—in which Old Reliable had more than one half of its total investments—fluctuated substantially with no apparent trend. (See Exhibit 1.) And, perhaps most important, inflation had become

EXHIBIT 1
Interest rates in the money and capital market, 1976–1978

Money market	December 1976	December 1977	December 1978
Prime rate	6.0%	7.75%	11.69%
Three-month Treasury bill rate	4.5	6.10	9.11
Federal funds	4.7	6.50	10.06
Capital market			
Municipal bonds	5.8	5.60	6.50
Corporate Aaa bonds	8.0	8.30	9.20
Long-term Treasury securities	7.4	7.80	8.90
Preferred stock dividend/price ratio	8.0	7.60	8.80
Common stock dividend/price ratio	3.8	4.60	5.40

Source: *Federal Reserve Bulletin*, various issues.

institutionalized in the economic system and had reached double-digit levels in the middle and late 1970s. These developments had a substantial and adverse effect on Old Reliable. The stagnating stock market made it difficult for the company to earn a reasonable rate of return. Moreover, declining stock values reduced the capital position of the company. (See Exhibit 2.) Indeed, the severe stock market decline in 1974 had lowered the capital position of Old Reliable to the point where it was in violation of the minimum statutory capital position required by state law. Further, the inflation produced escalating claims at a time when consumer pressure and intensified competition made it more difficult to obtain higher rates for policies, especially for automobile insurance.

EXHIBIT 2
Common stock prices

	1976	1977	December 1978
New York Stock Exchange			
(December 31, 1965 = 50)	54.4	53.7	53.7
Industrial	60.4	57.8	58.4
Transportation	40.0	41.1	42.5
Utility	37.0	41.0	38.1
Finance	52.9	55.2	55.8
American Stock Exchange			
(August 31, 1972 = 100)	101.6	116.2	149.9

Source: *Federal Reserve Bulletin*, various issues.

It was within this general background that the management of Old Reliable pondered its municipal investment strategy. Yet the year (1978) which was about to close was one of substantial profitability for the company. While stock prices declined slightly, the company had been highly profitable in the past year and substantial additions were made to the municipal investment portfolio of Old Reliable. But the coming year (1979) was expected to be one of reduced profitability so that the attraction of additional municipals would be limited. (See Exhibit 3.) Moreover, should the coming year be one with an

EXHIBIT 3
Forecasts made by experts

The coming year (1979) should be one of intense pressure in the money and capital markets. Interest rates in the money market should advance by 100–150 basis points and by 50–100 basis points in the capital market.

The inflation outlook is unfavorable. The rate of inflation should accelerate from an annual rate of 6 percent late in the current year to an annual rate of over 10 percent toward the end of the coming year.

It appears likely that commercial banks will be under intense pressure by their business customers for loan accommodation. Deposit inflows should be limited but loan demand from all types of customers should be substantial.

Stocks are cheap. Now is the time to buy. The price-earnings ratio on the Dow Jones Industrials is at historically low levels. The risk-reward ratio is presently exceedingly attractive.

operating loss then tax-exempt municipal income would be especially unattractive. Furthermore, depreciation of the value of investments made by Old Reliable—either in the equity market or in debt securities—could severely harm the capital position of the firm.

16

Pension funds

One of the most important functions performed by financial intermediaries and financial markets is to give economic units an opportunity to more closely match the time distribution (temporal allocation) of actual expenditures with desired expenditures. The receipt of cash by individual economic units frequently occurs in a discontinuous fashion while desired expenditures are often more continuous. Moreover, viewing actual and desired expenditures over a longer time perspective, there is frequently a substantial mismatch between the receipt of income and desired expenditures.

Analyzing the lifetime earnings curve of an individual, the typical pattern is for earnings to mount rapidly during the early working years, then to reach a peak in late middle age, decline slightly from late middle age until retirement, and then to fall precipitously at retirement. Yet, desired expenditure patterns need not conform to this time series at all. Desired expenditures may rise throughout the working life of the individual (although not necessarily at a constant rate) and increase sharply in later years and following retirement. Without financial markets and institutions individuals could earn no return on their invested savings from surplus years (periods when income exceeded desired consumption) and would not have the opportunity to borrow against future income in years when desired consumption exceeded income. Without financial institutions and financial markets, the individual economic unit would be forced to constrict expenditures to match income. In contrast, with financial institutions, the individual should be able to invest surplus funds today for consumption tomorrow and borrow today against future income for consumption today. With this intertemporal shifting of such flows the individual more closely matches desired and actual consumption patterns over his or her entire lifetime. Hence, with financial institutions, the individual should be able to achieve a higher level of economic well-being (utility) then if no financial institutions and markets existed.

While all financial institutions and markets play a role in the reallocation of individual expenditures over time, the pension fund is an especially important financial institution from this perspective. The pension fund as a financial intermediary exists to bridge the gap between rising desired expenditures for most individuals following retirement and the abrupt decline in income at the cessation of the individual's working lifetime. This gap is closed (partially or fully) by the accumulation of funds (savings) over the working lifetime of the individual (through both employer and employee contributions), and the investment of these funds in a portfolio of financial assets (stocks and bonds) and sometimes in real assets (real estate). With knowledge of the amount of funds contributed in each period as well as the earnings rate on the accumulated funds, it is possible to determine fairly precisely the amount of retirement income. With this knowledge, the individual can plan more effectively his or her current expenditures.

It must be admitted, however, that rapid inflation makes this planning process much more difficult. It is possible to actuarially determine the amount of retirement benefits in money income from information on the volume of contributions and the earnings on those contributions, but it is not possible from this information to ascertain the amount of retirement benefits in real income or constant dollar terms. Unfortunately, many individuals who planned carefully for retirement have found that rising prices have made their retirement incomes far too small.

Pension funds as important financial intermediaries are principally a post–World War II phenomenon. With rising incomes, the breakdown of the extended family, and increasing concern over financial security throughout an individual's lifetime, there developed both in private business and the government the feeling that contributions should be made toward providing an actuarially sound benefit program for employees at the termination of their working life. This attitude produced the social security program in the 1930s which was designed to establish a floor on retirement income for many individuals (and since has been broadened substantially) and a proliferation of employer-sponsored plans both in the public and private sector after World War II in order to provide more substantial retirement. Indeed, pension programs now cover most of the labor force even without considering the extensive coverage provided by social security. For example, private pension plans covered almost 50 million people in 1975, while government-administered plans provided potential retirement benefit for almost 20 million more. And the social security system encompassed over 110 million people.

With large contributions from participants in the plans and with relatively few retirees in the early years of the retirement plans to draw funds out, the size of pension assets has grown at an enormous rate. For example, total noninsured assets held by both private and state and local government pension funds amounted to less than $7 billion in 1946. In contrast, by year-end 1977, total assets of these funds were over $300 billion (and these figures do not include the pension fund assets which are administered by life insurance companies which are themselves substantial, at almost $100 billion).

The rate of growth has been so rapid and the assets of pension funds have become so large that it has been suggested by some that pension funds are becoming dominant owners of Amercian business, a development which may have substantial implications for control, dividend policy, and other aspects of the management of corporate business in the United States. Moreover, the growth of pension fund assets may have substantial implications for the saving behavior of individuals. Higher saving through pension funds may reduce saving through other means. In any case, pension funds have become a major force in financial markets, especially in the equity market where in many years they been the largest single purchasers of equity securities.

CHARACTERISTICS OF PENSION FUNDS

Pension funds may be classified in a number of ways. One especially important distinction when pension funds are viewed from the perspective of the financial intermediation process is between funded and unfunded plans (or some mixture of these two which would be a partially funded pension program). A funded pension program is one in which the sponsor places some amount of assets under the control of a trustee after it has been determined that—at some appropriate rate of return on the assets—this contribution would produce a sufficient amount of assets at retirement in order to meet the benefits promised to the employees. In contrast, an unfunded pension program is one in which the employer accepts the responsibility to provide retirement benefits to employees but does not set aside today any funds to meet that obligation. Of course, many plans lie somewhere between these two extremes and are termed partially funded programs. In past years, many pension programs have been unfunded or only partially funded. For example, the social security program is only partially funded (actually a very small fraction of total benefits are funded), while many state and local retirement plans have been completely unfunded. However, recent pension reform legislation has placed increasing emphasis on the funding of such programs. Only funded (or partially funded) pension programs qualify as financial intermediaries and play a role in the saving and investment process.

Funded pension programs may be further classified as insured or noninsured. An insured pension program is one in which administration of the program is under the control of an insurance company. The employer agrees to provide a certain amount of funds each year and the insurance company agrees to provide a retirement annuity to the employees in the program beginning at the time of retirement, with the amount of the annuity based upon some assumed rate of earnings on the funds during the time of accumulation prior to the beginning of retirement pay. These insured pension programs may take a variety of forms. Some are conventional group annuities in which the annual contributions purchase paid-up annuity units for those participating in the plan. Others are programs in which the annual contributions accumulate funds and the cost of retirement benefits of the individual are charged to that fund at the time of retirement. Still another variety is a program in which a separate annuity contract is usually offered to each employee. But all of these programs have a common feature in that they are usually fully funded or almost fully funded. Insured pension fund programs comprise a substantial and growing share of the assets of life insurance companies.

Noninsured (not administered by a life insurance company) pension funds, in contrast, are administered by trustees chosen by the employer. And, as revealed in Table 16–1, noninsured pension funds are much larger than insured pension funds. The trustees may be employees of the firm or some other individual or institution. The investment policies of the fund are then determined by the trustees subject to the influence of the employer. In many cases, the trust departments of commercial banks serve as trustee for the fund during the accumulation period and also administer payment of benefits during the retirement period. Indeed, commercial bank trust departments compete vigorously to obtain management of large noninsured pension funds. Trusteed pension funds also come in a variety of forms. They may represent corporate pension funds estab-

TABLE 16-1
Assets of all private and public pension funds—Book values, end of year ($billions)

	1970	1977
Total private	$138.2	$279.6
Insured pension funds	$ 41.2	$ 98.1
Noninsured pension funds	97.0	181.5
Total public	$123.7	$221.9
State and local government	58.1	130.8
U.S. government		
Federal Old Age and Survivors Insurance	32.5	32.5
Federal disability insurance	5.6	3.4
Civil service retirement and disability program	23.1	52.6
Railroad retirement fund	4.4	2.6
Total private and public	$261.9	$501.5

Source: Securities and Exchange Commission, *Statistical Bulletin*, May 1978, p. 8.

lished voluntarily for executive and nonexecutive employees. As another possibility, the fund may be established because of union pressure and the trustees may, in fact, be officers of the union. This would be most common in an industry in which there are a large number of small employers but one large labor union as the bargaining agent for the employees. Still other trusteed plans have been established for employees of state and local governments.

Pension programs also may be separated into those sponsored by the federal government either for its own workers or for the general population and those sponsored by the private sector (including state and local governments). The U.S. government has sponsored a number of pension programs. The best known is more accurately termed the Old Age, Survivors, and Disability Insurance Fund. This program is funded only to a small extent. Indeed one of the most important developments in the pension system in recent years has been the growing financial difficulties of the social security system. The social security trust fund shrank dramatically during the decade of the 1970s despite large increases in social security taxes. Moreover, with a growing number of retired persons compared to the total work force expected in coming decades, the financial problems of the social security system may not have ended. Recent large increases in the tax rates for both employer and employee may postpone the financial problems of the system. While social security is the largest and best known of the retirement programs of the U.S government, there are a number of other sponsored retirement programs which should be noted. The Civil Service Retirement Program covers federal government employees. It is also only partially funded and depends upon Congress for a substantial share of the benefits. Also the Railroad Retirement Fund is a special fund established by the federal government in order to provide retirement benefits to employees of the railroad systems of the United States.

FACTORS WHICH INFLUENCE PENSION FUND INVESTMENT POLICIES

The investment policies of pension funds are influenced and affected by a number of factors. These include:

Stability of sources of funds. The pension fund has one of the most stable sources of funds of all financial intermediaries. Inflows into the fund from the contributions of the employer and employee are contractual in nature and therefore highly predictable. Moreover, outflows from the fund in the form of retirement benefits are also highly predictable and can be anticipated well in advance of the date of the need for funds. Premature death and other causes for withdrawal from the fund prior to retirement are less predictable uses of funds, but these demands represent a small fraction of the cash flow for most pension funds. Moreover, during the early years of a growing pension fund, the stability is even more pronounced since benefits can frequently be paid from the cash contribution from future beneficiaries without liquidating existing assets nor even using the earnings of the existing assets for the necessary cash.

Examination of data on the receipts and disbursements of private noninsured pension funds provides some interesting information on these points. In 1975, total receipts of private noninsured pension funds were $26.6 billion. Of this total, employer contributions were $19.8 billion, employee contributions totaled $1.6 billion, and investment income was $6.7 billion. Yet total benefits paid out were only $12.3 billion and expenses and other disbursements were just $263 million.[1] Not only did the pension funds not need liquid assets in order to pay benefits, since employer and employee contributions together amounted to almost double total benefits paid out, but investment income alone on accumulated assets would have provided more than one half the funds needed to pay the benefits required.

The extreme stability of sources of funds coupled with the fact that the pension funds' time horizon is quite long means that these intermediaries are not active in short term or even very much in intermediate-term investments. The pension fund has little need for liquidity. It is essentially an investor in capital market instruments and, within the capital market, in the largest segment of the maturity structure of fixed income instruments—in equity securities—both

---

[1] Securities and Exchange Commission, *Statistical Bulletin*, November 1976, p. 555.

preferred and common stock. Indeed, as will be discussed more fully below, the pension fund has become the dominant purchaser of equity securities in the U.S. capital market.

Taxes. Taxes are a factor in influencing the policies of pension funds. Taxes affect both the mix of contributions by employer and employee and the nature of fund investments. Since contributions to pension funds by the employer are not taxable to the employee as earned income until actually received there is an incentive for pension fund contributions to come primarily from the employer. In fact, employers have contributed about 80 percent of combined employer-employee contributions in recent years. Moreover, the fund itself pays no taxes. Generally the money paid into the fund is before tax (at least in the case of the employer's contribution) and the funds accumulate within a tax shelter. When benefits are paid to the employee at retirement, these benefits are taxable at whatever individual income tax rate is applicable to the beneficiary at the time he or she receives payment. The lack of taxation on the earnings of the fund during the accumulation period has a number of important influences on the investment policies of these firms. While pension funds are principally capital market investors, their interest in municipal securities is virtually nil since municipals are valuable only to investors in high marginal income tax brackets. In addition, the pension fund need not differentiate between returns on investment in the form of ordinary income or capital gains, since it pays no taxes on either. The return to the pension fund which is significant is the total return, the sum of dividend or interest income plus capital gain. In contrast many investors in high marginal income tax brackets prefer a portion of their return in the form of capital gains—either on equity securities or deep discount bonds since this increases their after-tax income.

Management pressure. One important factor influencing the investment policy of many pension funds is pressure by management for a high return on the funds placed with the pension program in order to insure the payment of promised retirement benefits at minimum cost to the employer. While this would be most relevant to private pension funds administered by employers, it would also have significance for state and local government retirement funds. After all, contributions by the employer, and in most private pension funds most of the contributions are made by the employer, are expenses of the firm. The employer would like to reduce these expenses as much as possible. Yet, from a labor relations perspective, the employer seeks to promise as high benefits as possible. These conflicting goals can be made compatible (to a degree) if the rate of return on the fund can be increased. The amount of the retirement benefit which can be actuarially promised to employees is a function of the amount of funds contributed each year and the assumed rate of earnings on those funds during the accumulation period. To the extent that the employer is able to obtain higher returns on the fund's assets, the employer is able to reduce contributions and thereby expenses. In recent years, this factor has resulted in substantial investments in common stock.

Nature of obligations. The types of investments which pension funds make will of course be determined to some extent by the nature of the obligations which have been promised to beneficiaries at retirement. There are two basic types of obligations: the fixed annuity and the variable annuity. The fixed annuity is one in which the amount of a beneficiary's retirement income is fixed at the time of retirement and remains unchanged during the payment period. Traditionally, the fixed annuity has been the dominant form of pension fund obligation. With the rapid increase in prices in recent years, many individuals have become concerned about the prospect that inflation during retirement years would reduce the value of retirement income from adequate to subsistence level or even below. As a result, the variable annuity was developed in which payment to the beneficiary at retirement is variable and depends upon the performance of the contributions made prior to retirement and in subsequent years.

A fixed annuity obligation on the part of the pension fund would suggest an investment policy which concentrates on fixed-income instruments such as bonds and mortgages. In contrast, the variable annuity obligation would suggest investment in equity securities such as common stock. There are, of course, combinations of programs. The variable annuity need not have all of its investments in equities; it could be a "balanced fund" with part debt and part equity. Moreover, the fund could be devoted to equity securities during the accumulation period and then transferred to a fixed annuity at retirement. Such a policy would dictate investments in common stock during the accumulation period and in bonds and mortgages after retirement.

Limitations on Trustee investment policies. The investment policies of pension funds are frequently constrained by limitations in the contract establishing the fund. This is most common in public investment programs where there are substantial restraints designed to reduce the risk exposure of the fund. For example, it is often required that public pension funds invest no funds in land. In addition, at one time many public pension funds were required to invest some fraction of their assets in the bond issues of the state or local government for whose employees the fund was established. While economically this requirement has little merit (and it did reduce the return available to the beneficiaries at the time of retirement), the restriction was justified with the argument that public employees should support the employer with their funds. Certainly such a requirement should have made it easier for some governmental units to sell their debt issues.

PENSION FUND INVESTMENTS

Private pension funds

Private pension fund investments are heavily concentrated in two types of capital market securities: corporate equities and corporate bonds. (See Table 16–2). Indeed, as of the end of 1977, corporate

TABLE 16–2
Financial assets of noninsured pension funds, 1977 ($billions)

	Private	State and local government
Demand deposits and currency	1.7	1.8
Time deposits	4.8	—
Corporate equities	101.9	30.0
U.S. Government securities	15.9	6.4
Agency issues	4.2	6.2
Corporate bonds	45.6	74.3
Mortgages..............................	2.7	8.2
Municipals		3.6
Other	8.7	—
Total financial assets	185.5	130.5

Source: Federal Reserve Flow of Funds Accounts.

equities accounted for almost 60 percent of total financial assets, and corporate bonds totaled another 25 percent for noninsured pension funds. This concentration on equities is a relatively new development. In 1956, for example, the investment in equity securities by private pension funds amounted to only about one third of the total financial assets of this financial intermediary. This increase in investments in the equity market reflects a number of factors. Certainly, the growth of variable annuity retirement funds has played an important role. Moreover, the pressure by management to expand the assumed earnings used in calculating the contribution necessary to make the pension program actuarially sound is also important. But perhaps most significant was the change in attitude on the part of many investors toward the risk/return opportunities available in equities. The post–World War II "bull market" in equities (which appears to have ended in the mid-1960s) convinced many investors that the risks in equity securities were relatively limited (at least for the long-term investor) while the returns were substantial.

The amount of funds contributed to the equity market in recent years has been enormous. Indeed it has been argued that one of the main reasons for the post–World War II bull market in equities was the substantial amount of funds contributed by pension funds. For example, in 1956, private pension funds committed $941 million to the equity market—representing less than one half the net acquisition of financial assets by private pension funds and about one fourth the net new funds committed to equity securities. In contrast, in 1966, private pension funds committed $3.5 billion to the purchase of equities, representing about 50 percent of their net acquisition of financial assets and more than 75 percent of the net increase in funds committed to equities. Hence, private pension funds were increasing their influence on the equity market not only because their total assets were expanding (and at a very rapid pace), but also because the proportion of that expansion in available funds that was devoted to equities was rising.

The enormous concentration of pension fund investments in this period reflects a number of factors. First, the excellent performance of the stock market in the immediate post–World War II period encouraged many fund managers to believe that returns on equities would be substantially higher than returns on fixed-income securities. Given the greater risks assumed by the investor in equity securities, it would be expected that the return would be higher. In addition, many studies in the academic community of realized rates of return over a large number of past periods suggested long-run returns from equities that were considerably in excess of returns in long-term bonds. For example, Fisher and Lorie investigated the average annual return which could have been obtained through a random selection of stocks listed on the New York Stock Exchange in the period from 1926 to 1965. On a before-tax basis the average annual return over the entire period from 1926 through 1965 was 9.3 percent.[2] Moreover, variable annuity policy sales were increasing as investors looked to equities as a means of hedging against inflation. Finally, while the pension funds were pulled by the apparent attractiveness of the yields available in equities, they were pushed by the pressure of management seeking to lower pension costs through increasing the assumed rate of earnings on investments in the pension fund.

Concentration of new money in equities has diminished in recent years as the relatively poor performance of the stock market resurrected the fact that equity prices could fall as well as rise. For example, in 1974, private pension funds committed less than 25 percent of

[2] Fisher and Lorie [4].

their net acquisition of financial assets to equities. The year 1974, of course, was a period of extremely high interest rates with attractive returns in the corporate bond market, so that almost half of the total flow of funds at private pension funds was devoted to corporate bonds. However, even in 1977 equities absorbed less than 25 percent of the net new funds invested by private pension funds. Barring some renaissance of the equity market, it seems unlikely if private pension funds will again devote most of their funds to equities. Rather, it seems likely that many private pension funds will seek roughly a 50-50 split in investment of new funds between equities and fixed-income instruments.

State and local government pension funds

Investment policies of state and local government pension funds, as revealed by Table 16–2, have been quite different than private pension funds. Primarily because of more detailed regulation and control over investment policies, and perhaps because of less pressure for higher returns, state and local government pension funds have not invested as greatly in equity securities as private pension funds. In recent years, the restrictions on the investment policies of these institutions have been relaxed to a considerable extent. Increasingly both private and public noninsured pension funds are following similar types of investment policies. Private pension funds appear to be reducing their contributions to equities, while public pension funds seem to be increasing their contribution to the corporate stock market.

At the end of 1977, state and local government pension funds held almost $131 billion in financial assets. Most of these assets were held in the form of fixed-income instruments, principally corporate bonds ($74.3 billion). A small amount of these funds were devoted to municipal securities despite the unattractiveness of this kind of security for a tax-free investor, probably reflecting the hangover of previous restrictions which forced these funds to support the bond issues of local governmental units. Yet if we look at the Flow of Funds Accounts, we see some striking changes in the investment policies of these institutions. For example, in 1971 state and local government retirement funds committed almost 50 percent of the net flow of funds to equities and in 1977 the percent committed to equities was about 30 percent, a much larger share than had been common in earlier years.

Federal government pension funds

The retirement program established by the federal government has been less significant from the perspective of financial intermediation for two important reasons. First, since the program has been only partially funded the amount accumulated in the funds has been relatively small. As Table 16–1 shows, total assets of all federally sponsored retirement programs (including disability plans) amounted to less than $100 billion in 1977. Moreover, in recent years benefits paid have exceeded contributions so that the sizes of many of the funds have diminished. Second, the funds have been invested entirely in government securities (special issues of the U.S. Treasury). Because of concern for safety as well as the possibility that should these funds ever become large they might dominate American business through stock ownership, their policies have been to invest most funds in special U.S. Treasury issues. Hence, the direct result of federal government retirement programs has been to reduce the amount of funds required in the credit markets by the U.S. Treasury.

ERISA

One of the most significant events in the recent history of pension funds occurred in 1974 when the Employee Retirement Income Security Act of 1974 (ERISA) became law. This law, which resulted from intensive investigation of abuse in the administration of pension plans, made a number of changes in the existing law regulating pension programs. These changes covered those employees who are eligible for enrollment in the pension program, what length of service is necessary before the individual has "vested" benefits, and what kind of funding requirements are imposed on the employer.[3] The general purpose of these changes was to make sure that individuals who work for a company for some considerable number of years do, in fact, receive pension benefits. If the employer chooses to sponsor a pension program, ERISA makes certain demands on the employer in order to ensure fair treatment of the employee.

ERISA covers a wide variety of items relevant to pension programs and is highly technical in nature. While it would be impossible to present the complete details of the act, it may be desirable to focus on some of the more significant changes which ERISA bought about. The ERISA requirements include the following: any employee who is at least 25 years of age and has at least one year of service with an employer must be permitted to enroll in the company's pension plan. Employees have a number of options in vesting, ranging from full vesting after a specified number of years (with no vesting prior to that point) up to partial vesting when the sum of an employee's age and

---

[3] *Vesting* refers to the right of the employee to obtain the pension. A pension is fully vested if the employee has complete rights to obtain the pension regardless of future employment.

years of service add to 45 and additional vesting beyond that point. Minimum funding schedules are established with requirements for gradual funding of unfunded past liabilities (pension promised for which no funds have been set aside). In addition, a pension program insurance plan, the Pension Benefit Guaranty Corporation, was established to guarantee a portion of vested benefits and is financed by employer contributions. Finally, ERISA placed additional fiduciary responsibility on the managers of the assets of the fund.

ERISA has been an extremely controversial piece of legislation. It has been charged that ERISA has caused many smaller pension programs to be discontinued because of the large amount of paperwork necessary to meet the requirement of the act. Opponents of the act argue that many employees are now worse off than before. While before they had an imperfect pension plan, now they have no plan at all. Moreover, the Labor Department and the Internal Revenue Service have been extremely slow in developing detailed guidelines to implement the act. One noticeable development has been the shift of many plans from self-management by the employer to management by a financial institution due to the increased liability imposed on the fund manager by ERISA.

FUTURE TRENDS

As discussed earlier, pension funds have grown enormously in recent years and have moved from a relatively small force in the financial spectrum prior to World War II to become one of the major financial intermediaries. Moreover, their influence in the equity market has been especially notable. Yet it is unlikely that this rapid growth in assets under management will continue in the future. The extremely fast expansion of pension fund assets has been fueled by two factors, both of which appear to be weakening. First, there have been a substantial number of employees contributing to the programs and yet few beneficiaries. Moreover, many funds attained relatively high rates of return, at least until the difficulties in the stock market in the late 1960s and 1970s. It is not surprising that the pension funds grew rapidly when there existed both a large net inflow of funds and high earnings on the funds' assets. But in recent years there has occurred a shift in the ratio of beneficiaries to contributors and this shift should become more pronounced in the future. Indeed, the age structure of the population is projected to change dramatically in the coming decades with fewer workers relative to retired persons. Undoubtedly this will have a major influence on the growth of pension fund assets.

A second and perhaps more significant factor from a long-run perspective is the growing realization of the immense cost of pension benefits. In the early post– World War II period, with rapid growth in the economy, tight labor markets, and limited inflationary effects on employee compensation, employers liberalized pension benefits to a very considerable extent. Moreover, with the expectation of a high return on funds contributed to the pension program, pension benefits could be improved to a substantial extent without boosting pension costs by an appreciable amount. But, in recent years, with pressure on profits from rising labor costs and with poor performance in the equity markets between 1966 and 1979, employers have begun to resist increases in pension benefits. It appears likely that employer contributions to pension funds will grow less rapidly in future years than in the recent past.

QUESTIONS

16– 1. Discuss methods by which variances in income levels and consumption levels over time are accommodated. What exactly is a pension fund? How does it operate?

16– 2. Differentiate between funded and unfunded pension programs both insured and uninsured. Which type is most significant as a financial institution?

16– 3. What are the major assets and liabilities of a typical pension fund? Differentiate according to kind of pension funds. What factors explain these differences?

16– 4. What tax advantages do pension funds enjoy?

16– 5. What factors are expected to influence the future growth of pension funds?

16– 6. What is ERISA? What are its principal purposes and likely effect?

REFERENCES

1. Andrews, Victor, ed. "Noninsured Corporate and State and Local Governments Retirement Funds in the Financial Structure," in *Private Capital Market*. Englewood Cliffs, N.J.: Prentice-Hall, 1964, pp. 381– 531.

2. Bernstein, Merton C. *The Future of Private Pensions*. New York: Free Press, 1964.

3. Ehrlich, Edna E. "The Functions and Investment Policies of Personal Trust Departments." Federal Reserve Bank of New York *Monthly Review*, October 1972, pp. 255– 70.

4. Fisher, Lawrence, and Lorie, James H. "Rates of Return on Investments in Common Stock: The Year-by-Year Record, 1926– 1965." *Journal of Business*, July 1968, pp. 291– 315.

5. McCandlish, Raymond W. "Some Methods for Measuring Performance of a Pension Fund." *Financial Analysts Journal,* November–December 1965.
6. McGill, D. M. *Fundamentals of Private Pensions.* 2d ed. Homewood, Ill.: Richard D. Irwin, Inc., 1961.
7. Melone, Joseph J., and Allen, Everett T. *Pension Planning.* Homewood, Ill.: Dow-Jones, 1966.
8. Murray, Roger F. *Economic Aspects of Pensions: A Summary Report.* National Bureau of Economic Research, Inc. New York: Columbia University Press, 1960.
9. *The Private Pension Controversy.* New York: Bankers Trust Company, 1973.

Problem for discussion

The importance of behaving as a "prudent man" is fundamental to the investment policy of pension funds. In practice, prudent investment policy has traditionally meant the acquisition of high-quality stocks and bonds and substantial diversification of the portfolio within each of these broad categories of financial assets. Yet in an inflationary era, is it really prudent to confine the pension fund portfolio to financial assets or should various real assets (such as ceramics, gold, paintings, and real estate) also be acquired? The problem for discussion described below deals with this question.

> After reviewing the material, the student should make a list of the advantages and disadvantages of such a change in investment policy and should evaluate such a policy from the perspective of the employer and employee.
>
> Should the pension fund buy real assets and, if so, which assets and how much?

The ABC Pension Fund is a company-sponsored plan for the employees of ABC Manufacturing Corporation. Contributions to the fund are made only by the employer (a noncontributory plan) while the trustees are selected by the company. Major investment decisions for the pension fund are made by the treasurer of ABC Manufacturing Corporation with the advice of staff personnel in the treasurer's department and with additional information provided by the management of a local security broker. The level of contributions by ABC Manufacturing Corporation to the plan are determined each year during an annual review of the plan by a consulting actuary.

The ABC Pension Fund is reasonably typical of most pension funds. The program was begun by the employer in the early 1950s as an aid in obtaining skilled employees in a labor-short environment. With few employees retiring in the 1950s, 1960s, and throughout the 1970s the total assets of the fund expanded sharply. By early 1979 the assets of ABC Pension Fund exceeded $50 million. Moreover, the investment strategy of the fund was also fairly representative of the pension fund industry. In the early 1950s, the trustees were reluctant to commit a substantial share of the fund's assets to common stock. The memory of the 1930s was too strong along with the forecasts of another depression following the end of World War II. Yet as equity prices moved sharply upward during the 1950s and early 1960s, the trustees became increasingly interested in common stock. In fact, by 1965 over 50 percent of the portfolio of the fund was invested in common stock, most of which were regarded as "emerging growth stocks." And in the early 1960s this portfolio mix proved quite successful as the fund averaged a total return (dividends plus capital appreciation) of 12.2 percent per year.

Unfortunately the ABC Pension Fund increased its equity commitments toward the end of the postwar bull market in common stocks. In the 12 years ending in 1978, the total return on the pension fund was only 3.4 percent, not particularly poor as compared to the performance of other pension funds but certainly unsatisfactory in a period of high inflation rates. The performance of the fund was especially troubling to the trustees as it was less than the assumed return used by the actuaries in calculating the annual contributions made by the company in order to maintain the fund as a sound financial base. Moreover, employees of the ABC Manufacturing Corporation were pressing for liberalization of benefits since those previously promised were now inadequate due to rising prices. In fact, the company was voluntarily supplementing the pension payments to its retired employees since the benefits under the existing program had been so seriously eroded by inflation.

Given this environment, the trustees were intrigued by the idea that pension funds perhaps should diversify outside of the traditional stocks and bonds (financial assets) into a variety of real assets which might appreciate more rapidly during inflationary periods. In this regard, the trustees noted that investors in paintings, gold, diamonds, land, and other real assets had done much better in the past few years than investors in stocks and bonds. For example, as Exhibit 1 shows, common stocks achieved a compound annual growth in value of only 2.8 percent in the 1968–78 period, yet Chinese ceramics grew in value 19.2 percent per year in the same period and gold returned an annual gain of 16.3 percent to the investor. In that period, the annual growth in value for high-grade corporate bonds was substantially in excess of the return on common stocks, and the inflation rate was more than double the return on common stock. It seemed as if the pension fund

EXHIBIT 1
Returns on alternative investments, 1968–1978

Investment	Compound annual growth in value, 1968–1978
Chinese ceramics	19.2%
Gold	16.3
Stamps	15.4
Old master paintings	13.0
Coins (U.S. nongold)	13.0
Diamonds	12.6
Crude oil	11.5
Farmland	10.6
Single-family home	9.2
Silver	9.1
High-grade corporate bonds	6.1
Common stocks	2.8

Source: Salomon Brothers, July 3, 1973, p. 1.

could preserve the purchasing value of its funds only by investing a portion of its portfolio in real assets. Yet questions of liquidity and prudence were certainly of importance in the decision to diversify into real assets. Moreover, the trustees and their investment adviser lacked expertise in evaluating the merits of these real assets.

17

Finance companies

In this chapter we examine a set of financial intermediaries, commonly called finance companies,
that specialize in loans to businesses and consumers. As we shall soon see, there have been substantial changes in both the sources and uses of funds in
the finance industry in recent years. Moreover, finance companies today face increasing competition
from commercial banks, credit unions, savings and
loan associations, and other lending institutions.
As a result of both competitive and cost pressures,
finance companies of all kinds have diversified their
functions, reaching simultaneously into both business and consumer loan markets. There also has
been a trend toward consolidations and mergers
within the industry, substantially reducing the
number of independent firms. The foregoing structural changes all have occurred against the back-
drop of increasing penetration of the industry by
affiliates of bank holding companies. Competition
from bank holding companies is likely to increase
in the period ahead as banks seek more profitable
investment opportunities in the business and consumer loan fields.

TYPES OF FINANCE COMPANIES

Probably the most widely known finance company is the *consumer finance company*, which engages principally in making instalment loans to individuals and families. Finance company loans to individuals are made on both a secured and unsecured basis at rates generally higher than on similar loans made by commercial banks, credit unions, and other consumer leaders. As Jacobs, Farwell, and Neave observe, "The unsecured loans are based on the borrower's character and ability to repay. The secured loans are usually made on a chattel mortgage basis against furniture or automobiles or electrical appliances."[1] Historically, the loan pricing policies of consumer-oriented finance companies have been based upon the premise that most of their customers are unacceptable risks for commercial banks and other more conservative lenders. It has been argued that the typical small-loan customer earns a lower income and is more occupationally unstable than the clientele with whom banks typically deal.

In addition to companies specializing in small loans to consumers, other firms in this industry specialize in *sales finance* and *commercial finance*. Companies specializing in sales finance carry on both retail and wholesale credit operations. Their most important activity is the purchase of instalment paper from dealers selling goods to the public—particularly autos, home appliances, and furniture. Firms specializing in sales finance activities maintain close ties with dealers writing instalment paper. It is common for a single company to purchase virtually all of a given dealer's instalment contracts. Indeed, some finance companies are "captive companies" that fall under the control of a single dealer or merchandise manufacturer. Prominent examples are Sears Roebuck Acceptance Corporation—a subsidiary of Sears, Roebuck and Company, and General Motors Acceptance Corporation—a subsidiary of General Motors Corporation. The captive finance company buys most of a particular dealer's paper or handles contracts covering most of a specific manufacturer's merchandise.

Another important facet of sales finance activity is "wholesale finance" aimed principally at providing working capital for the carrying of business inventories or for other commercial operating needs. Retailers obtaining wholesale financing can purchase goods for resale with the finance company paying the manufacturer and holding title to the goods as evidenced by a trust receipt. As the goods are sold, the retailer repays the note to the finance company, remitting either cash

---

[1] See Jacobs, Farwell, and Neave [8], p. 479.

or instalment contracts which customers have signed. One prominent example of this financing technique is the so-called floor plan loan used extensively by automobile dealers to acquire inventories of new cars. A line of credit is extended to an auto dealer by the sales finance company, and the manufacturer is authorized to deliver new cars to the dealer's lot. Payment is made to the manufacturer by means of a draft against the finance company which technically holds title to the automobiles until they are sold and the dealer can pay back the finance company for the amount of credit extended.

Commercial finance operations encompass a wide variety of credit plans, though most involve the provision of working capital to business firms secured by accounts receivable or other acceptable collateral. Under true accounts receivable financing the finance company may merely ask for an assignment of customer credit accounts to serve as collateral for the loan. Under a factoring plan, on the other hand, the company purchases the receivables outright. Under these two broad options, however, are still other options common in the industry. For example, some agreements between the business borrower and the finance company call for notice to the customer that the instalment contract is involved in the loan against the merchant's receivables. On the other hand, if the finance company's loan is collateralized and the business borrower is responsible for all collections and repossessions, then the customer whose trade account is involved probably will not be notified of the financing arrangement.

Today, commercial finance companies do much more than merely provide accounts receivable financing. For example, finance company loans secured by a mortgage on fixed assets, pledge of inventories, or other acceptable collateral are common as are leasing arrangements whereby the finance company purchases machinery, equipment, or rolling stock for customer use. In most instances the customer maintains and repairs the leased equipment until the agreement terminates, though there are numerous exceptions and a wide variety of leasing arrangements in use.

RECENT CHANGES IN THE FINANCE INDUSTRY

The distinctions drawn in the preceding section between consumer, sales, and commercial finance companies are fading into history. These distinctions, to be sure, are still useful because many finance companies today still specialize in one or another of these activities. Some still prefer making small personal loans while others still prefer providing working capital to businesses. However, companies of any size now deal in *both* commercial and consumer credit markets. The trend of recent changes may be seen by examining the nationwide surveys of finance companies carried out by the Federal Reserve System in 1955, 1960, 1965, 1970, and 1975. During the 1950s and 1960s the Federal Reserve Board surveyed separately three categories of finance companies—sales, personal, and business—and reported separate financial statements for each type of institution. By 1970, the board reported that "this distinction was no longer meaningful because the trend toward diversification—already important in 1965—had broadened activities of many companies substantially further."[2]

Types of credit extended by finance companies

Business credit represents the largest share of gross receivables in the finance company industry today. At mid-year 1977, for example, according to data released by the Federal Reserve Board, business receivables of U.S. finance companies totaled $50.4 billion compared to $40.7 billion in receivables associated with consumer credit. Moreover, business and miscellaneous receivables have grown much faster than consumer credit in recent years—a reflection of both increased competition for consumer loans from other lenders (especially commercial banks and credit unions) and greater diversification of services offered. As Table 17–1 indicates, between the 1965 and 1975 Federal Reserve surveys of the industry, consumer receivables fell from 63 percent of total credits to 50 percent in the latter year and have declined further in relative terms during the late 1970s. Business credit climbed from 36 to 46 percent of the total and "other" receivables advanced from 1 to 4 percent over the decade ending in 1975, when the last Federal Reserve survey of the industry was completed. The growth in dollar volume in all categories of receivables is impressive. Total credit extended by the industry advanced from $57 billion in 1970 to $91 billion in 1977, a gain of about 60 percent.

Considerable diversification has occurred within the various loan categories, reflecting a strong emphasis upon innovation in the industry. As the Federal Reserve Board noted in its 1970 survey, "even within the traditional types of specialization, lending had grown most rapidly in those areas where finance company participation had

---

[2] See especially Board of Governors of the Federal Reserve System [3], p. 958. The Federal Reserve System surveys finance companies at five-year intervals. The five surveys beginning with 1955 were each based upon the financial reports of finance companies as of a single day, June 30. As a result, the findings are subject to considerable variation, characteristic of single-date reports, and also reflect, to some extent, differences in economic conditions around the time of each survey. Nevertheless, each survey provides a reasonable benchmark for broad trends in portfolio composition and sources of financing in the industry as a whole.

TABLE 17-1
Types of credit extended by U.S. finance companies, 1965–1975*

Types of credit	Amount of credit ($billions)			Percentage change between Federal Reserve Board surveys		Share of total receivables		
	1965	1970	1975	1965–1970	1970–1975	1965	1970	1975
Consumer	$22.4	$31.8	$42.8	42%	35%	63%	56%	50%
Business	12.9	23.0	39.3	78	71	36	40	46
Other	0.2	2.3	3.9	1,107	69	1	4	4
Total receivables	$35.5	$57.1	$86.0	61%	51%	100%	100%	100%

* Figures are as of June 30 for each indicated year. Columns may not add to totals due to rounding.
Source: Adapted from Board of Governors of the Federal Reserve System, references [2], [3], and [4] at end of chapter.

been on a small scale in 1965—such as mobile home financing and leasing—and the tendency to move into nonbanking operations—already evident in 1965—had also continued."[3] The 1975 board survey indicated "a slower but continuing trend of finance companies to move into areas such as financing of revolving credit, second mortgages, mobile homes, and leasing, and out of the financing of passenger cars."[4] Many of these changes are illustrated in Tables 17–2 and 17–3 which reflect the composition of business and consumer credit extended by domestic finance companies in 1965, 1970, and 1975.

In the consumer loan field, personal cash loans made by finance companies held steady as a percentage of consumer receivables through 1975. However, these loans rose sharply in the late 1970s in response to soaring inflation and energy costs. By mid-1977 personal cash loans extended by U.S. finance companies totaled $19.5 billion and represented nearly 48 percent of all consumer receivables in the industry. At the same time, loans on passenger cars dropped precipitously as a percentage of all consumer receivables through 1975, reflecting the increased popularity of smaller cars, but then recovered in percentage terms as other forms of credit extended directly to consumers declined. By mid-1977 retail automotive credit granted by domestic finance companies totaled $13.2 billion, representing 32 percent of outstanding consumer credit. Mobile home loans climbed rapidly through 1975, representing 8 percent of industry consumer receivables, as did loans to purchase other retail consumer goods—principally apparel, merchandise, furniture, appliances, and recreational equipment. However, these trends appeared to moderate during the late 1970s due to competition from other lenders and a shift of emphasis by finance companies toward greater lending to business. Both mobile home loans and credit extended for other retail consumer goods leveled off. Nevertheless, mobile home loans still represented close to 8 percent of finance company consumer receivables in 1977.

In the business loan sector the most notable development was the expansion of leasing activities. While figures on the volume of leases granted by finance companies were not reported in the 1955 and 1960 Federal Reserve surveys, data covering the 1965–70 period showed dramatic increases in this form of financing and the growth continued during the 1970s, though at a somewhat slower pace. (See Table 17–3.) The long-term growth in lease financing reflects efforts by various businesses to curtail capital expansion, reduce the proportion

---

[3] Ibid., p. 958.

[4] Board of Governors of the Federal Reserve System [4], pp. 197–98.

TABLE 17-2
Consumer receivables held by U.S. finance companies, 1965–1975*

Types of consumer credit	Amount of credit ($billions)			Percentage change between Federal Reserve Board surveys		Share of consumer receivables		
	1965	1970	1975	1965–1970	1970–1975	1965	1970	1975
Passenger cars	$ 8.8	$ 9.3	$ 9.9	5%	8%	40%	29%	23%
Mobile homes	1.1	2.3	3.5	108	49	5	7	8
Other consumer goods†	3.5	7.6	12.6	101	62	16	25	30
Revolving credit	n.a.	n.a.	5.8	n.a.	n.a.	n.a.	n.a.	n.a.
Other	n.a.	n.a.	6.9	n.a.	n.a.	n.a.	n.a.	n.a.
Personal cash loans	8.7	12.4	16.7	42	35	39	39	39
Secured by second mortgage	n.a.	n.a.	1.9	n.a.	n.a.	n.a.	n.a.	n.a.
Other	n.a.	n.a.	14.8	n.a.	n.a.	n.a.	n.a.	n.a.
Total consumer receivables	$22.4	$31.8	$42.8	42%	35%	100%	100%	100%

* Figures as of June 30 for each indicated year. Columns may not add to totals due to rounding; n.a. indicates not available.
† Includes home improvement loans not shown separately.
Source: Adapted from Board of Governors of the Federal Reserve System, references [2], [3], and [4] at end of chapter.

TABLE 17-3
Business receivables held by U.S. finance companies, 1965–1975*

Types of business credit	Amount of credit ($billions)			Percentage change between Federal Reserve Board surveys		Share of business receivables		
	1965	1970	1975	1965–1970	1970–1975	1965	1970	1975
Wholesale	$ 4.2	$ 7.5	$10.9	76%	47%	33%	33%	28%
Retail	4.0	6.6	11.1	63	69	31	29	28
Leasing	0.8	3.8	8.1	352	112	7	17	21
Other	3.8	5.1	9.2	34	78	29	22	23
Commercial accounts receivable	1.0	1.4	3.4	41	134	8	6	8
Factored accounts	0.8	1.5	1.4	82	−5	8	6	4
Advances to factored clients	n.a.	n.a.	0.2	n.a.	n.a.	n.a.	n.a.	1
Miscellaneous	2.0	2.2	4.2	14	88	15	10	10
Total business receivables	$12.9	$23.0	$39.3	78%	71%	100%	100%	100%

* Figures as of June 30 for each indicated year. Columns may not add to totals due to rounding; n.a. indicates not available.
Source: Adapted from Board of Governors of the Federal Reserve System, references [2], [3], and [4] at end of chapter.

of business debt, and secure tax advantages. The early 1970s, in particular, saw a serious recession develop which reduced demands for consumer and other goods and created a shortage of liquidity in the corporate sector. To firms caught in this situation, leasing appeared to represent a more attractive and less costly alternative than either borrowing or equity financing. Lease receivables increased more than 350 percent between 1965 and 1970 to almost $4 billion (or from only 7 percent of all business receivables to 17 percent) and rose further to over $8 billion by 1975 (or to 21 percent of total business credit).

The dominant type of business credit extended by finance companies throughout the postwar period is represented by wholesale and retail paper, which arises principally from the manufacture and sale of business, industrial, and farm equipment and motor vehicles.[5] Both wholesale and retail paper declined in relative importance to make room for newer and more innovative forms of business financing, such as leasing, during the 1960s and early 1970s but then recovered, reflecting strong business demand for investment goods. Wholesale and retail paper combined represented 62 percent of total business credit extended by domestic finance companies in 1970, dropped to 56 percent in 1975, but recovered to about two thirds of all business receivables in 1977. However, the composition of wholesale and retail paper acquired by U.S. finance companies has changed markedly. Loans on commercial vehicles and loans for business, industrial, and farm equipment climbed sharply to more than $23 billion in 1977, or more than 45 percent of outstanding business credit at domestic finance companies. At the same time purchases of wholesale paper declined as a proportion of total business credit, while loans on accounts receivable and factored accounts remained about unchanged as a percentage of total business credit.

Sources of funds

Not only have the loans made by finance companies changed, but their sources of loanable funds also have shifted in recent years. Finance companies are sometimes called "secondary intermediaries" because they depend mainly on other financial institutions for their sources of funds. In contrast, a "primary intermediary," such as a commercial bank, derives its funds principally from the ultimate

---

[5] The Federal Reserve Board defines wholesale and retail paper as contracts arising from transactions between manufacturers and dealers that are secured by passenger cars, commercial vehicles, mobile homes, trailers, motor homes, boats, airplanes, helicopters, and business equipment; retail credit stemming from sales of business equipment and commercial vehicles; and other wholesale operations not elsewhere classified. See, in particular, Board of Governors of the Federal Reserve System [3] and [4].

saver (i.e., businesses and households). Historically, finance companies have relied upon a comparatively small equity capital base, depending mainly upon debt as a source of funds. The most important sources of their borrowed funds are commercial paper, long-term senior debt obligations, bank loans, and other short-term notes. However, as Table 17–4 reflects, the relative importance of these different funds sources has varied considerably over time as long- and short-term interest rates have changed relative to each other.

During the early 1960s long-term and short-term borrowings of finance companies grew at approximately the same pace. By mid-1965 the aggregate liabilities of domestic finance companies were almost evenly divided between short- and long-term debt. However, in the period from 1965 through 1970, long-term borrowings increased only 27 percent, while short-term debt more than doubled. By mid-1970 commercial paper (short-term unsecured IOUs) was by far the largest source of funds for the industry, followed at some distance by long-term debt and bank loans. In fact, short-term obligations accounted for nearly two thirds of all debt owed by finance companies in 1970; and commercial paper represented close to three quarters of all short-term borrowings. This heavy emphasis upon short-term debt was a negative response to the record high long-term interest rates prevailing in the economy during this period. In their rush to enter the commercial paper market on a large scale, finance companies also reduced their reliance on commercial banks as a source of loanable funds. Indeed, banks became a much less reliable source of industry financing during the late 1960s and early 1970s due to tight credit conditions and a resulting shortage of reserves. As a result, finance companies turned increasingly to short-term borrowing in the open market.[6] Moreover, investors willingly absorbed the large increase in finance company short-term IOUs due to the comparatively high yields available in the commercial paper market.

By the mid 1970s the primary sources of funds used by finance companies had changed again. With more favorable long-term rates prevailing, the industry returned to the financing mix employed a decade earlier with a more nearly equal balance between long-term and short-term borrowings. Stockholders' equity, as in previous years, provided only about one sixth of total funds. Debt—both short term and long term—accounted for about three quarters with miscellaneous liabilities making up the remainder of total funds needed. As

---

[6] Fluctuations between long-term and short-term debt in response to relative interest rates, changes in monetary policy, and so on are centered primarily in the larger finance companies. Smaller companies generally have much higher ratios of equity to total sources of funds and have displayed a greater dependence on long-term debt and bank credit, even in recent years.

TABLE 17–4

Sources of funds used by domestic finance companies, 1965–1975*

Sources of funds	Amount outstanding ($billions)			Percentage change between Federal Reserve Board surveys		Percentage of total funds sources		
	1965	1970	1975	1965–1970	1970–1975	1965	1970	1975
Bank loans	$ 5.6	$ 7.6	$ 8.6	36%	14%	15%	13%	10%
Short term	5.3	6.6	7.9	24	20	15	11	9
Long term	0.3	1.0	0.7	260	−26	1	2	1
Commercial paper	8.9	22.1	25.9	147	17	25	36	29
Directly placed	7.7	19.2	23.7	151	23	21	32	27
Dealer placed	1.3	2.8	2.2	125	−22	3	5	3
Other short-term notes ..	0.5	1.0	2.8	78	189	2	2	3
Deposit liabilities	0.7	0.6	1.5	−10	132	2	1	2
Other current liabilities ...	2.2	3.5	3.1	57	−10	6	6	4
Other long-term senior debt	9.2	11.2	23.4	22	110	25	18	26
Subordinated debentures	3.5	4.3	5.6	24	29	10	7	6
All other liabilities	0.2	0.4	3.8	93	802	1	1	4
Capital and surplus	5.4	9.9	14.0	83	40	15	16	16
Total liabilities and capital	$36.3	$60.6	$88.7	67%	47%	100%	100%	100%
Memo								
Short-term debt	$14.7	$29.6	$36.6	101%	24%	41%	49%	41%
Long-term debt	13.0	16.5	29.7	27	81	36	27	34
Total debt	$27.7	$46.1	$66.4	67%	44%	76%	76%	75%

* Figures are as of June 30 for each indicated year. Columns may not add to totals due to rounding.
Source: Adapted from Board of Governors of the Federal Reserve System, references [2], [3], and [4] at end of chapter.

in prior years, most finance company debt was short term, accounting for about 40 percent of total funds raised in 1975, down from about 50 percent in 1970. But long-term debt had climbed to 34 percent of total sources of funds from only 27 percent in 1970. By mid-1977, according to Federal Reserve Board data, finance companies had shifted even more heavily into long-term borrowings. Their senior debt obligations and other long-term IOUs totaled almost $35 billion in June 1977, while short-term commercial paper outstandings amounted to $27.5 billion. Bank loans were only $5.7 billion of total funding sources, followed by other forms of short-term debt at $5.5 billion. Equity funds (including capital, surplus, and undivided profits) amounted to $14.4 billion, or less than half the industry's long-term debt.

One of the most important and, at times, one of the more volatile of the industry's financing sources is commercial paper. The so-called credit crunches of the late 1960s and early 1970s heightened finance company interest in this short-term IOU. Long-term rates had risen to historic highs and commercial banks were having trouble making and keeping commitments on their credit lines, due principally to massive disintermediation of deposits and heavy loan demand. By mid-1970 commercial paper represented 36 percent of all funds raised by domestic finance companies, and total commercial paper borrowings stood at $22 billion compared to less than $9 billion in 1965. Five years later, in June 1975, commercial paper accounted for about 30 percent of all funds raised by the industry. And, by June 1977 finance company paper represented 33 percent of industry liabilities, but only 28 percent of total sources of funds. The general decline in industry reliance on commercial paper as a source of funds reflected the adverse reaction of some investors to real or imagined changes in the quality of borrowers in the paper market.

Only a minor proportion of all finance companies issue commercial paper. Due to the fact that commercial paper is unsecured, only the largest and best-known companies can attract investors. Also, most paper issued by finance companies (about 90 percent) is "directly placed" rather than marketed through securities dealers. That is, the company posts the rates it is willing to pay on various maturities and sells the paper directly to interested investors. No securities dealer or other intermediary is used to identify buyers or arrange the sale. On June 30, 1977, directly placed finance paper outstanding totaled $24.8 billion, while dealer-placed issues by finance companies amounted to only $2.7 billion.

Companies adopting the "direct placement" method must be large firms with an efficient marketing program and established contacts in the financial community. Not surprisingly, directly placed paper usually can be sold at a lower rate (higher price) than paper sold through dealers. As the Federal Reserve Board notes: "Selling indirectly through dealers usually is the method used by issuers with only seasonal needs for funds or with a name not well enough known to sell without dealer contacts. In general, such paper carries a somewhat higher interest yield than paper placed directly, and in addition, the issuer always pays ⅛ of a percentage point to the dealer for his services."[7] According to the Federal Reserve survey of the industry, only 128 companies reported outstanding commercial paper liabilities at mid-year 1975, down from 138 to 1970. These companies represented less than 4 percent of the total number of firms in the industry and were heavily concentrated among the largest size groups.

The industry's heavy reliance upon short-term financing is not without its dangers. It tends to make finance companies highly susceptible to fluctuations in credit conditions and particularly to changes in short-term interest rates. Heavy reliance on short-term debt introduces greater volatility into the earnings of finance companies, increasing the degree of investor risk and further increasing their borrowing costs. Moreover, the higher cost of borrowed funds typically is translated into higher loan charges to consumers and other users of finance company services. Of course, the interest rates and fees paid by customers also are influenced by the labor and administrative costs of making loans. The costs of credit examination, collection, and related administrative expenses are included in the rates charged by these companies as is an acceptable rate of return on invested capital relative to the risks assumed by the company. However, these administrative and operating expenses are not nearly as volatile as are the costs of borrowing in the open market.

STRUCTURE OF THE INDUSTRY

Number and distribution of firms

The total number of all types of finance companies in the United States—consumer, commercial, and sales—is unknown, principally because many firms are extremely small and cater exclusively to local markets. The Federal Reserve Board's survey of the industry in 1975 received responses from 3,376 companies, up from slightly less than 3,000 in 1970. While most of these companies are small, there is considerable concentration at the national level with a few firms operating hundreds of offices across the nation through local or

---

[7] See Board of Governors of the Federal Reserve System [4], p. 200.

statewide subsidiaries and accounting for the bulk of total loans outstanding. The Federal Reserve estimated in 1975 that only about 6 percent of all domestic finance companies held about 94 percent of the industry's gross receivables. (See Table 17–5.) These same com-

TABLE 17–5
Size structure of the U.S. finance company industry, 1970 and 1975

| Size of company* ($000) | Number of companies | | Percent of | | | |
| | | | Number of companies | | Total receivables* | |
	1970	1975	1970	1975	1970	1975
Under $100	826	863	27.9%	25.6%	0.2%	0.1%
100–249	554	641	18.7	19.0	0.1	0.1
250–499	511	563	17.3	16.7	0.2	0.2
500–599	424	415	14.3	12.3	1.6	0.3
1,000–2,499	271	338	9.2	10.0	0.5	0.7
2,500–4,999	128	162	4.3	4.8	1.7	0.8
5,000–24,999	112	204	3.8	6.0	1.6	3.7
25,000–99,999	77	102	2.6	3.0	8.4	6.1
100,000 and over	58	88	2.0	2.6	85.7	88.0
Total	2,961	3,376	100.0%	100.0%	100.0%	100.0%

* Total short-term and intermediate-term loans outstanding.
Source: Adapted from Board of Governors of the Federal Reserve System, references [3] and [4] at the end of chapter.

panies (with at least $25 million in total receivables each) held about 94 percent of all consumer receivables and 97 percent of all business receivables carried by domestic finance companies. In contrast, the smallest finance companies (having less than $5 million in gross receivables) held only about 3 percent of the total volume of consumer credit and 1 percent of all business receivables, but represented 88 percent of the total number of U.S. finance companies.[8]

The size of a finance company has an important influence upon its operations and, in particular, upon its sources and uses of funds. For example, the Federal Reserve Board found in its most recent survey of the industry that the largest companies held more diversified portfolios of loans than the smallest and were more actively involved in diversifying their activities. In contrast, the smallest firms tended to concentrate their activities on consumer loans, especially personal cash loans. Moreover, business credit extended by the smaller firms tended to be in the more traditional fields of accounts receivable financing and factoring, while the larger companies placed consid-

[8] Board of Governors of the Federal Reserve System [4], p. 200.

erably more emphasis on new types of commercial lending, such as leasing. Of course, larger finance companies have better access to the capital markets than smaller firms and, therefore, are more able to vary the volume and mix of their borrowings to suit financial conditions. For example, during the 1970–75 period, the larger companies replaced a substantial volume of short-term borrowings with long-term debt, while smaller finance companies reported little or no change in the maturity composition of their borrowings. Also, the smaller companies are forced to use more equity capital and less debt in financing their operations (i.e., are less heavily leveraged) due to their heavier use of more risky short-term financing and less diversified loans.

For the industry as a whole it is widely believed that competition for funds and for loan customers is intense, at least in local markets where national, regional, and local companies may all be represented and engage in direct competition with each other. Besides the half-dozen major national companies, there are numerous smaller chain organizations specializing principally in small loans to individuals and families which operate perhaps 30 to 200 offices.[9] Locally oriented companies probably number at least 1,000, each operating a small number of offices clustered in a fairly well-defined region. Smaller, independent firms apparently are able to compete effectively with the larger national and regional companies, at least for consumer credit. This may reflect the fact that effective scale economies are relatively modest in this industry and its product is regarded as relatively homogenous by the individuals and families who regularly use the industry's financial services.

Recent structural changes

There is evidence of considerable structural change going on in the finance company field. One important facet of this change is *diversification* into more profitable credit lines, as mentioned earlier. In 1970 the Federal Reserve Board reported that:

> Two of the largest . . . consumer finance companies have entered the field of commercial financing on an important scale. Another company has purchased a funiture business, some have entered the field of commercial financing, wholesale financing is being carried on by some companies, and the insurance business is becoming more common as well.[10]

---

[9] See especially Michelman [9] and Chapman and Shay [5].
[10] See Board of Governors of the Federal Reserve System [3], p. 958.

Several factors account for this trend toward diversification. One is the purchase of small loan companies by larger conglomerates or congeneric organizations which have the resources necessary to carry out large-scale diversification. For example, bank holding companies have purchased or started *de novo* both small loan companies and credit insurance affiliates to open up new markets for loans. Moreover, recent increases in borrowing costs (especially in 1966, 1969, 1974, and 1978–79) have squeezed earnings, encouraging the search for new and more profitable product lines, as well as the absorption of smaller companies.

Competition has also played a key role in the finance industry's trend toward diversification. Commercial banks and credit unions pose a serious threat to finance company participation in the consumer lending field today. In fact, the share of the nationwide consumer instalment loan market accounted for by finance companies has declined sharply during the postwar period. (See Table 17–6.) While consumer instalment credit extended by finance companies

TABLE 17–6
Consumer instalment credit extended by major lenders

End of period	Total	Commercial banks	Finance companies	Credit unions	Miscellaneous lenders	Retail outlets
		Financial institutions ($billions)				
1940	$ 3.9	$ 1.5	$ 2.3	$ 0.2	*	$ 1.6
1950	11.8	5.8	5.3	0.6	0.1	2.9
1955	24.4	10.6	11.8	1.7	0.3	4.5
1960	36.7	16.7	15.4	3.9	0.6	6.3
1965	61.1	29.0	23.9	7.3	1.0	9.8
1970	88.2	45.4	27.7	13.0	2.1	13.9
1975	154.2	82.9	36.0	25.7	9.6	18.2
1977	206.5	112.4	44.9	37.6	11.6	23.5
		Percentages of total consumer credit extended by financial institutions				
1940	100.0%	38.5%	59.0%	5.1%	*	
1950	100.0	49.2	44.9	5.1	0.8	
1955	100.0	43.4	48.4	7.0	1.2	
1960	100.0	45.5	42.0	1.1	1.6	
1965	100.0	47.5	39.1	11.9	1.6	
1970	100.0	51.5	31.4	14.7	2.4	
1975	100.0	53.8	23.3	16.7	6.2	
1977	100.0	54.4	21.7	18.2	5.6	

* Less than $50 million or 0.05 percent.
Source: Adapted from Board of Governors of the Federal Reserve System, *Federal Reserve Bulletin*, selected issues.

rose from $2.3 billion in 1940 to nearly $45 billion in 1977, the market share represented by these companies declined from almost 60 percent to less than 22 percent during the same period. The rate of decline in the finance company share of instalment credit accelerated in the late 1950s and 1960s. Especially notable has been the drop since 1960 with the industry's share of total instalment credit almost exactly cut in half.

The share of the consumer debt market lost by finance companies has been taken over largely by commercial banks and credit unions. These intermediaries, like finance companies, have faced a profit squeeze, brought on by the rising cost of funds. As a result, they have aggressively and successfully sought out instalment credit customers. The increased competition for instalment credit has caused net rates of return in the market to fall and the quality of receivables available for purchase to decline. Confronted with lower profit margins and increased risk in the instalment loan field, finance companies (particularly the sales finance variety) have turned to other types of loans to protect their earnings, including mobile homes, leasing, and factoring. Several companies have acquired or launched new nonfinancial subsidiaries, in both domestic and foreign markets, in such widely diverse areas as insurance, manufacturing, and retailing.[11]

During the 1960s the number of U.S. finance companies declined dramatically, while the average size of individual companies remaining in the industry rose substantially. For example, in 1960 the Federal Reserve Board counted slightly more than 6,400 companies. By 1965 the industry population was under 4,300 and by 1970 less than 3,000. Thus, the industry has been subject to much the same pressures for consolidation and merger as have many other financial industries during the postwar period, including commercial banks, credit unions, and savings banks. It is significant to note, however, that the number of companies increased by more than 400 between the 1970 and 1975 Federal Reserve surveys. A substantial part, if not most, of this growth may be attributed to entry into the field by bank holding companies which have opened large numbers of *de novo* firms.[12]

Competition with other financial intermediaries

There is an overlap of markets served by commercial banks, credit unions, savings banks, and finance companies. Each institution has

---

[11] See especially Board of Governors of the Federal Reserve System [3], p. 959.

[12] See Chapter 21 for a discussion on bank holding company activities in various nonbank fields including finance companies.

tended to concentrate on that sector of the market for loanable funds where it has the greatest comparative advantage in offering its services. Commercial banks generally prefer to make larger, less risky loans which carry lower average yields. Credit unions extend loans to members only and are able to charge lower rates, in part because they draw their funds from relatively small personal savings accounts. In contrast, finance companies stress convenience and the ability to extend more risky loans than any of the other competing institutions usually are willing to make. Still, many of the consumer loans extended by finance companies are acceptable to commercial banks, credit unions, and savings and loan associations empowered to make consumer loans. While consumers (unlike most business borrowers) are often ignorant of the credit alternatives open to them, many *are* aware and will shop around for credit. In this instance banks and finance companies are in direct competition with each other, especially where each institution aggressively solicits consumer accounts.

Future competition between finance companies and other financial intermediaries should intensify as a result of changes now occurring in the U.S. financial sector. Finance companies increasingly are looking for new product lines and investments to diversify their operations and stabilize their cash flow. At the same time deposit-type financial intermediaries continue to penetrate the markets for consumer loans and consumer savings and transactions balances with new services. These intermediaries should continue to wrest a larger share of the consumer loan market from finance companies in the years ahead. At the same time commercial banks through their holding company organizations undoubtedly will enlarge their foothold in the finance industry through both acquisitions of existing companies and *de novo* entry. The result will be increased pressure on independents in the finance company field to further diversify their operations and find new sources of profitability. It is quite likely, however, that the public will be a net beneficiary of increasing competition from within and without the finance industry. In a free market economy competition ensures that the consumer of financial services will be served effectively and efficiently.

QUESTIONS

17–1. Name the three different types of finance companies. What are the essential characteristics that differentiate one type of finance company from another?

17–2. What changes have occurred recently in the sources and uses of funds of finance companies? Try to explain why these changes have occurred.

17–3. Explain how it is possible for a finance company to charge a higher interest rate on a loan than a commercial bank located just across the street.

17–4. What is a "captive" finance company? What advantages and disadvantages would such a firm have relative to independent finance companies?

17–5. Examine some of the recent structural changes occurring in the finance industry. Why has the number of finance companies declined over the past two decades? Can you explain why diversification has become so dominant a trend among finance companies?

17–6. Differentiate between dealer-placed and directly-placed commercial paper. Which type is used mainly by the larger finance companies? Why?

17–7. In what areas do finance companies compete directly with commercial banks, credit unions, and savings banks? Do you think this competition will increase or decrease in future years? Please explain why.

REFERENCES

1. "Big Change in Small Loans." *Business Week*, June 13, 1970.
2. Board of Governors of the Federal Reserve System. "Survey of Finance Companies, Mid-1965." *Federal Reserve Bulletin*, April 1967.
3. ———. "Survey of Finance Companies, 1970." *Federal Reserve Bulletin*, November 1972.
4. ———. "Survey of Finance Companies, Mid-1975." *Federal Reserve Bulletin*, March 1976.
5. Chapman, John M., and Shay, Robert P., eds. *The Consumer Finance Industry: Its Costs and Regulation.* New York: Columbia University Press, 1967.
6. "Finance Companies: An Era of Change." *Banker's Monthly*, July 1975.
7. Harless, Doris E. *Nonbank Financial Institutions.* Federal Reserve Bank of Richmond, October 1975.
8. Jacobs, Donald P., Farwell, Loring C., and Neave, Edwin H. *Financial Institutions.* 5th ed. Homewood, Ill.: Richard D. Irwin, Inc., 1972.
9. Michelman, Irving S. *Consumer Finance: A Case History in American Business.* New York: Augustus M. Kelley, 1970.
10. "The Finance Industry--A Review of the Decade." *Banker's Monthly*, April 1970.

Problem for discussion

In this chapter we have seen that finance companies make a wide variety of credit plans available to individuals, households, and businesses. These firms are most familiar to consumers for the relatively small loans they make to individuals and families for living expenses, moving costs, medical care, and purchases of consumer durables such as automobiles, furniture, and appliances. Operating out of convenient, locally based offices consumer-oriented finance companies frequently take on credit customers that other lenders, such as commercial banks, refuse to accommodate.

In this problem for discussion imagine that you are the manager and principal credit officer in the local office of Gulf Finance Company. Mr. Ralph Williams earlier this week submitted an application for a personal loan to consolidate some outstanding debts and make some repairs on the family car and home. In total, Williams has asked to borrow $2,700 for one year. Mr. Williams estimates that his gross earnings and those of his wife will total about $17,000 this year. Out of this, Williams projects the family will spend about $5,200 for housing (including utilities, taxes on the home, and insurance costs), about $4,000 for food, and another $4,000 for transportation, clothing, medical care, and other personal expenses. Federal and state income and employment-related taxes will be about $3,000. Williams hopes to save net about $400 in the coming year and make a few small charitable contributions.

Mr. Williams is a high school graduate and attended college for two years before dropping out. He is presently employed as a clerk in Ward's Hardware Store where he works about 45 hours a week, including Saturdays. Frequently he does odd jobs to supplement the family's income, such as selling shoes and men's clothing during the Christmas season and working at the neighborhood gasoline station. The hardware store hired Williams nearly two years ago and the manager rates his probability of continued employment as "good," but there is apparently little or no opportunity for advancement in that position. The store is owned and managed by a small family corporation. Mr. Williams' previous employer was ABC Salvage Company where he worked for a year and a half until the firm closed its local office.

The Williams family has four children, including three school-age girls (ranging in age from 8 to 11) and a four-year-old boy. His wife, Jacquelyn, also a high school graduate, works as a secretary and file clerk 30 hours per week at a local aluminum siding company. During casual conversation in the finance company's office, Mr. Williams mentioned that he and his wife were thinking about having another baby.

The Williams' family has few liquid assets or other forms of saving. They hold no bonds or stocks, but have a $325 deposit in a local credit union. Mr. Williams has a $20,000 life insurance policy, but each year he has borrowed against its cash value and now has a policy loan in the amount of $975. There is no remaining cash value in the policy at present. Neither Mrs. Williams nor the children have any life insurance in force. The family has no medical insurance coverage and Ward's Hardware Store does not have a group health insurance plan nor does Williams have any disability insurance protection.

A check with the credit bureau showed that the Williams carried a "fair" credit rating. Approximately eight months ago the family was slow in making payments on some charge accounts. This occurred after Mrs. Williams lost her job with a local department store due to a dispute with her supervisor over some missing merchandise. The department store indicates they would not hire her back, but her present employer, Hardy Aluminum Products, considers her prospects for continued employment as "good."

The Williams own their own home which is mortgaged to the Mutual Building and Loan Association. Monthly mortgage payments are $275, including property insurance coverage. Utility costs average $100 per month on this 1,400 square-foot home, while property taxes are $700 per year. The house was appraised two years ago at $30,000 when the Williams purchased it for $29,500 with a 95 percent mortgage loan. The Williams have taken on a number of instalment obligations in recent years to upgrade their standard of living. On the credit application filed by Mr. Williams the debts shown in Exhibit 1 were listed.

EXHIBIT 1
Debt obligations and monthly payments

Lender	Monthly payments	Balance due on loan
Mutual Building and Loan Association (home mortgage)	$275.00	$27,000
Co-operative Employees Credit Union	110.00	1,100
First State Bank and Trust	75.00	450
Quinlan Furniture Company	43.00	459
Mitchell's TV and Stereo Shop	27.50	360
Dr. S. R. Kemp, Pediatrician	Open	125
Bank credit card	Open	650

The family auto is a Dodge Crestwood station wagon now five years old with about 75,000 miles on the speedometer. The car is in need of several repairs and is having transmission problems, one of the reasons for Mr. Williams' loan request. The Williams still owe $450 on the vehicle to First State Bank. The family's home also needs some new flooring in the kitchen and den, repairs to the backyard fence, and a new heating unit.

Given the foregoing facts would you make this loan to the Williams' family as requested?

If not, are you prepared to offer them a loan on terms perhaps more suited to their credit needs?

18

Investment companies

Investment companies—or investment trusts as they are often known—are financial institutions which obtain funds from a large number of investors through the selling of shares. These funds are then placed in a pool under professional management, and securities (financial assets) are purchased for the benefit of all the shareholders. While investments in the fund may be made by either large or small savers, the investment company exists primarily to offer the small saver a means to diversify asset portfolios in a manner unattainable except with a very large portfolio.

Investment companies have a long and checkered history, although their existence as a significant financial institution in the United States is relatively recent. The Societe Generale de Belgigue, formed in 1822, is generally credited as the first investment company. The movement spread throughout continental Europe during the 19th century and reached special importance in England toward the close of the century. In the United States, the period from the end of World War I until the stock market crash of 1929 represented the initial period of investment company growth. However, investor experience with the returns provided by this financial institution during the 1920s was quite poor, not only because of the problems in the equity market during the period, but also because many of the investment companies were poorly managed and were organized more for control of the firms in which they invested than simply as passive investors. Not until after World War II did the investment company occupy a significant place quantitatively in the galaxy of American financial institutions. Conditions were favorable for the development of the investment company movement after World War II with the expansion of money incomes as well as the spread of this income among many people who were relatively unsophisticated financially. Moreover, the upsurge in the equity markets in the immediate postwar period also contributed to the growth of funds under management by investment companies. As a result, the number of shareholders expanded from about 3 million in 1945 to over 50 million in 1967, and the total assets of investment companies grew from $2 billion to almost $50 billion during the same period.

While all investment companies have a number of common characteristics, there are substantial differences in goals and form of organization. Most (measured in terms of total assets) have the growth of capital as their primary objective. Others exist for the purpose of maximizing current income subject to reasonable stability of principal. Still others are established to invest exclusively in money market instruments. And, recently, a large number of investment companies have been formed to invest in tax-exempt municipal bonds. Moreover, some investment companies stand ready to buy and sell their shares to potential investors in any amount at the request of their customers. Others have a fixed number of shares and buy or sell these shares to their investors only infrequently. Still other investment companies have two sets of shares (income and capital); one set obtains all the capital gains and the other receives all the income. Finally, some investment company shares are sold at a price equal to the underlying asset value of their portfolio, while others are sold at a price above the underlying asset value of their portfolio, and still others may be bought in the market at a price below the value of underlying assets.

Regardless of these differences, all investment companies do have a number of features in common with other financial intermediaries. They provide a variety of important services to the public and it is these services which have accounted for their rapid growth since World War II. These services include risk, denomination, and maturity intermediation as well as convenience. Risk intermediation is performed both through the administration of the portfolio of the institution by skilled analysts and portfolio managers and also through the ability of the investor to achieve a more broadly diversified portfolio by investing indirectly through an investment company rather than by investing directly in primary securities. Even if it can be shown (and there is substantial evidence to support this view) that professional management is of little value in making equity investments (i.e., that professional investors cannot obtain a higher return than the market portfolio without taking on greater risk), still through the greater diversification made possible by indirect investing in the investment company the individual investor should be able to obtain a higher rate of return for a given risk level or a lower risk level for a given rate of return. This should be especially important for the small investor who finds adequate diversification without excessive transaction costs virtually impossible to achieve.

Individual investors should benefit from denomination intermediation whereby they are able to obtain equity investments in denominations which are more suitable to their individual needs than is possible through direct investments in equity securities. Many investment companies permit initial investment of as little as $50 or $100. In addition, maturity intermediation is of some consequence. Through an investment company, the investor is able to obtain an indirect financial asset which has greater liquidity than individual primary securities. The importance of this maturity intermediation is intensified when that liquidity is viewed not only as the ability to turn an asset into cash quickly but also to do so at little loss in value. The diversified portfolio offered by the investment company should have greater price stability than the portfolio which the investor could construct for himself or herself from primary securities or any individual security which might represent the investor's undiversified portfolio.

Investment companies are managed by professional management companies which arrange for the clerical and recordkeeping services necessary for the fund and also supervise the portfolio management decisions. These mutual fund management companies are often affiliated with large life insurance companies (for example, American General Insurance Company has over ten mutual funds under its management) or are independent of other financial institutions (Dreyfus Corporation, for example). These management firms receive a fee for their portfolio management services—usually something less than 1 percent per year of the assets of the fund. It is interesting to note that the fee is usually a function of the size of the fund rather than the performance of the fund. Since there are large economies of scale in managing financial assets, this type of fee structure particularly encourages a proliferation of different types of mutual funds under one corporate management umbrella.

As with other financial institutions, mutual fund management companies exist to achieve profit and/or wealth maximizing goals.

However, there are a number of differences between this type of organization and other financial institutions which sets the mutual fund apart. Most financial institutions can be viewed simply in terms of the model presented in Chapter 1. The institutions have a capital base on which they seek to borrow funds by offering financial assets to the investor which have desirable risk, denomination, and return characteristics. These funds (from stage I production) then become loanable funds (the output from stage I), and these loanable funds are invested following asset portfolio management decisions (stage II production). But with the mutual fund and its management company, stage II (the management of assets) is the primary stage. The mutual fund exists to manage assets. The sources of funds represent the ownership interests of the investors on which no specific promises have been made. In fact, most mutual funds cannot—with but minor exception—use borrowed money. Yet, it is the success of the management company in devising a portfolio strategy which determines the ability of the mutual fund to compete for savings in the marketplace and thereby to generate revenues for the mutual fund management company.

TYPES OF INVESTMENT COMPANIES

Open end versus closed end. Investment companies may be classified either as open end or closed end. Open-end investment companies stand ready to repurchase shares from the holders in any quantity and whenever the holder should desire. In addition, the open-end investment company will sell shares in any amount to prospective investors at whatever time the investor should determine. These open-end investment companies are generally referred to as *mutual funds*. The price of shares in the open-end investment company is determined by the net asset value of the funds' shares where net asset value refers to the total market value of the assets in the funds' portfolio less any fund liabilities divided by the number of fund shares outstanding. The fund may be offered at the net asset value per share or at the net asset value per share plus a sales charge which may be as high as 10 percent of the net asset value (the sales charge generally goes to brokers involved in the distribution of the fund's shares). Such funds are referred to as "load" funds and most mutual funds are load funds. In contrast, the funds may be offered at the net asset value. Such funds are referred to as "no load" funds. While only a minority of funds are no load, the preponderence of growth in the mutual fund industry in recent years has been among no load funds, despite the requirement that no load funds be bought directly from the fund rather than from a broker.

The enormous growth in the post–World War II period in the

volume of assets under management by the investment company industry has centered among the open-end funds, and today total assets of open-end funds are many times the total assets of closed-end funds. As pointed out in Table 18–1, total net assets of open-end investment

TABLE 18–1
Distribution of mutual fund assets, 1965–1977 ($billions)

Year	Total net assets	Cash and equivalents	Corporate bonds	Preferred stocks	Common stocks
1965	$ 35.2	$1.8	$ 2.6	$0.6	$30.3
1970	47.6	3.6	4.3	1.1	38.5
1975	42.2	3.2	4.8	0.5	33.2
1977	45.0	3.3	6.5	0.4	30.7
		(percent)			
1965	100.0%	5.1%	7.3%	1.7%	85.9%
1970	100.0	7.7	9.0	2.4	80.9
1975	100.0	8.9	11.3	1.2	78.6
1977	100.0	7.3	14.4	0.9	68.2

Note: Columns may not add to totals due to rounding.
Source: *Mutual Fund Fact Book*, 1978.

companies (mutual funds) exceeded $40 billion at the end of 1977. At the same time, closed-end, equity-oriented funds had total assets of less than $3 billion.

Closed-end funds are quite different in many respects from open-end mutual funds. The most important distinction is in terms of the number of shares outstanding. These funds issue a fixed number of shares. The shares are traded in the open market and supply and demand for the funds' shares determines their price. Purchases of shares by the fund or the sale of additional shares by the fund are quite infrequent. There is only a loose association between the net asset value of the closed-end fund and the market price of the shares of the fund. Most closed-end funds which invest in equity securities have sold at discounts from net asset value in recent years. Indeed, in some cases, there is a very substantial discount, sometimes as large as 30 percent or more. These discounts have given rise to the notion that the investor could obtain a greater return by investing in the closed-end funds since the investor is purchasing $1 worth of earning assets but paying substantially less than that in many cases.[1] One explanation for the persistence of the discounts is that there is no one (i.e., no broker) to sell shares in closed-end funds as compared to open-end

---

[1] See especially Malkiel [7].

funds. In contrast to equity closed-end funds, some closed-end funds which invest in bonds often sell at premiums over net asset value. Another difference between closed-end and open-end investment companies concerns capitalization. Open-end investment companies generally choose a simple capital structure with little or no use of financial leverage. In contrast, closed-end investment companies often have a complex capital structure with securities convertible into capital stock and with substantial amounts of financial leverage.

Objective of fund. Investment companies also differ widely in their objectives. Most mutual funds have the increase in the capital value of the shares of the fund as their principal objective. This objective may be approached through a variety of different kinds of equity securities. Hence, these are known as common stock funds. Some of these funds specialize in "blue chip" common stocks, buying the shares of firms which are established leaders in their fields and have a long history of paying cash dividends. Others may specialize in so-called growth stocks which pay relatively modest cash dividends, have low payout ratios (i.e., high earnings retention ratios), and are located in areas where the demand for their product or service is expanding very rapidly. Some investment companies specialize in the issues of a particular industry such as the utility, airline, or chemical industries, while others concentrate in specialized kinds of stocks (natural resource related, for example) regardless of industry. As examples of the different types of common stock funds, the Dreyfus fund, with total assets of over $2 billion, had the following companies as its five largest holdings as of the end of 1977: Philip Morris (4.5 percent of assets), American Telephone (3.0 percent), R. J. Reynolds Industries (2.0 percent), Polaroid (1.8 percent), and Amerada Hess (1.8 percent). In contrast, the Rowe Price New Horizons Fund, a smaller, higher risk type fund, had the following companies as its five largest holdings at the end of 1977: W. W. Granger (2.8 percent of assets), Wall-Mart Stores (2.8 percent), American Television and Communications (2.8 percent), Leaseway Transportation (2.6 percent), and Mervyns (2.5 percent).[2]

The common stock fund accounts for the great bulk of the total assets under the control of investment companies (especially mutual funds) and has been the basic source of growth of the industry in the post–World War II era. This is made clear by reference to Table 18–1 which provides the distribution of assets in open-end investment companies for a number of years. However, the funds with other objectives—generally more conservative objectives—have become of growing importance in recent years. One of these types of funds is the

---

[2] *Investment Companies, 1978,* Weisenberger Financial Services, New York.

balanced fund. The balanced fund emphasizes both appreciation of capital and income and seeks these objectives through a balanced portfolio of equities and fixed-income instruments. The portfolio of such a fund might contain a mixture of the following: common stock, preferred stock, bonds, and convertible bonds. Given such a portfolio, it might be expected that in an efficient financial market both the return and the risk to the investor would be less than with a common stock fund. For example, the American Balanced Fund had 65 percent of its portfolio in common stock, 31 percent in bonds and preferred stocks, and 4 percent in cash and cash equivalents as of the end of 1977.

There are also a wide variety of specialty funds. Two in particular have shown substantial growth in recent years. They are the *bond fund* and the *money market fund.* The bond fund is primarily concerned with the generation of current income through investing in fixed income securities, although frequently this type of fund seeks capital appreciation by active management of the portfolio. In recent years there have been a large number of new bond funds brought to market. These include both open-end and closed-end funds, although a particularly large amount of these types of funds have been closed-end in nature. While the open-end bond funds usually stress the advantage of active portfolio management, the closed-end bond funds often have a fixed portfolio. Also, these bond funds exist both for investments in corporate debt and municipal securities. Prior to 1977 the law did not allow open-end funds to pass through tax-free income to shareholders. However, following legislative changes, open-end mutual funds were formed in large numbers for the purpose of investing in municipal securities. The poor performance of the stock market since the mid-1960s and the high interest rates of the period have been of considerable significance in fostering the growth of bond funds. The rapid rate of inflation which has pushed people of relatively modest means into high tax brackets also has played an important role in the development of tax-exempt bond funds.

One interesting investment company developed in recent years is the money market fund.[3] Money market funds are investment trusts which exist for the purpose of holding money market instruments—U.S. Treasury bills, commercial paper, and other varieties of short-term, low-credit-risk financial instruments. These funds also may be either closed or open end, although most are open end. Money market funds also may be either load or no load, although most are no load.

Money market funds are a relatively new phenomenon in the investment community, dating back to early 1974. Their development

---

[3] For more details, see Fraser [2].

came principally in response to two factors. First, interest rates on short-term financial instruments (money market instruments) reached unprecedented levels in 1974. For example, the prime bank rate rose to 12 percent, and the rate on three-month Treasury bills was almost 10 percent. Second, the returns available to the small investor (consumer or businessman) at commercial banks were restrained to low levels by Regulation Q interest rate ceilings on deposits. In a sense, the development of the money market fund represents an attempt by market participants to avoid artificial restraints on investors which limit the efficiency of financial markets and provide an excellent example of the ability of financial markets to avoid artificial restraints on the flow of funds in accordance with risk/return considerations.

Fund managers quickly moved into this gap with the money market fund. Shares in money market funds were offered as being attractive not only to consumers, but also to business firms which were not large enough to effectively manage their own liquidity position, and also to fiduciary institutions such as trust departments in relatively small commercial banks. Growth of assets under management and expansion in the number of funds was explosive. From virtually nothing in 1973, total money market fund assets rose to over $2 billion by later 1974 and to almost $4 billion by the end of 1975. Similarly, the number of money market funds grew from a handful in 1973 to over 30 by late 1974 and to 50 by late 1977. Open market interest rates peaked in late 1974 and declined in the following months. As a result of the narrowing gap between open market rates and the rates payable by banks and savings and loan associations, the rate of growth of the assets of money market funds slowed throughout 1975 and 1976. However, the large increase in money market rates in 1978 and 1979 again encouraged the growth of money market funds. Indeed, by late 1979, total assets of all money market funds exceeded $30 billion.

One of the important reasons for the rapid growth of money market funds is the special services they offer. For example, a number of these funds offer expedited redemption procedures. Shareholders may contact the fund by toll-free telephone or by letter and have all or a portion of the value of their holdings transferred to their individual bank on the next business day. Moreover, many money market funds have checkwriting redemption privileges available. By this technique, the fund maintains a program with a commercial bank whereby the investor may write a check (for an amount above some minimum) against the assets in the fund. When the check is presented to the bank for payment through the normal clearing mechanism, the bank sells a sufficient number of shares to provide the necessary funds to pay the check. One advantage of this procedure is that the holder of shares in the money market fund continues to receive interest until the check clears the bank. Hence, the shareholder can "play the float game." In addition, many mutual fund management companies have established money market funds in order to offer a full range of investment vehicles to their customers. In a number of cases the investor may shift from one fund to another (bond to stock to money market fund, for example) of the same management company at no extra charge, thereby offering substantial convenience to the customer.

Another interesting although quite small investment company group is the *dual purpose fund.* Started in 1967, all dual purpose funds (which are entirely closed-end funds) have two shares of stock: income and capital. Moreover, there is a termination date for the existence of the fund at which time the assets will be liquidated and the funds distributed to shareholders. The income shareholders receive all the dividends earned on the contributions by both income and capital shareholders plus a promised amount of liquidating dividend. The capital shareholders obtain no income distributions but are entitled to all capital gains distributions during the life of the fund plus, at the termination of the existence of the fund, distribution equal to the difference between the liquidating value of the fund and the promised payment to income shareholders. The basic idea behind the dual purpose funds, which number less than a dozen, is that each shareholder—whether income or capital—obtains leverage through having $2 at work for each $1 invested. However, the performance of the dual purpose funds after their beginning in 1967 has not been very favorable. Most of the funds have sold at substantial discounts in the secondary market. Part of the explanation is the poor performance of the stock market in the years immediately following the founding of these funds. There also appears to be an inherent contradiction within the fund between the goals of the income and capital shareholders which may cause portfolio management problems.

MANAGEMENT, SIZE, REGULATION, AND TAXATION

Investment companies, whether closed end or open end, have their portfolio and other policies determined by an investment advisor. This investment advisor may be an insurance company or its subsidiary—in recent years there has been a substantial penetration of the mutual fund management business by life insurance companies—or a firm which specializes in money management through mutual funds and other devices. Due to the economies of scale involved in managing funds, there is some advantage to the mutual fund management company in offering a variety of funds, thereby seeking to obtain a large amount of assets under control. Hence, there are a number of mutual fund management companies such as Dreyfus, T. R. Price, and Scudder which offer a substantial variety of funds with different objectives to the public and which have billions of dollars under management. For these services, the mutual fund management company receives a management fee which constitutes its income and is one of the principal operating costs of the fund itself. The management fee is completely separate and distinct from the load. The management fee is paid to the company regardless of whether the fund is load or no load, and is usually stated as some percent of the assets of the fund regardless of the performance of the fund. Hence, benefits to the mutual fund management company accrue from increasing the size of the fund rather than maximizing the rate of return to fund shareholders, although conceptually these variables should be related.

Size. Table 18–2 presents information on the number of open-end mutual funds and the total assets in these funds in the period

TABLE 18–2
Number of mutual funds and total assets under management, 1945–1975

Year	Number of funds	Total assets ($billions)
1945	73	$ 1.3
1950	98	2.5
1955	125	7.8
1960	161	17.0
1965	170	35.2
1970	361	47.6
1975	426	45.8
Money market funds	(36)	(3.7)
1977	477	48.9
Money market funds	(50)	(3.9)

Source: *Mutual Fund Fact Book*, 1978.

from 1945 through 1977. The total asset numbers reflect net sales of the funds (sales minus redemptions) as well as changes in the market value of the securities in the portfolios of the funds. In short periods, change in market conditions may dominate net sales, since most of these assets consist of common stock, subject to wide fluctuations in value.

A number of important facts are highlighted by Table 18–2. First, as discussed earlier, the mutual fund industry is essentially a post–World War II phenomenon. In 1945, total assets under management for all open-end funds amounted to only slightly more than $1 billion. Second, the bulk of the growth in the mutual fund industry occurred in the 1950s and the 1960s which were periods of generally rising stock prices. Third, since 1970, there has been no net growth in assets under management except for money market funds. Part of the recent development reflects the poor market conditions for common stock in the 1970–75 period which depressed total asset values. Sales of bond funds and money market funds have been substantial, while common stock funds have suffered from net redemptions of a substantial magnitude. Fourth, despite the impression of many that mutual funds dominate the equity market, in fact, mutual funds are a relatively small proportion of total equity holdings. As discussed in Chapter 16, pension funds are a much more significant influence in quantitative terms than mutual funds. However, as a general rule, turnover of shares by mutual funds is more rapid than for pension funds, so that the significance of mutual funds in the trading of securities is greater than their share of total common stock holdings would indicate.

Regulation. There is substantial regulation of investment companies both at federal and state levels. The major acts which relate to mutual funds are the following: the Securities Act of 1933, the Securities Exchange Act of 1934, the Investment Company Act of 1940, and the Investment Advisers Act of 1940. The Securities Act of 1933 requires registration with the Securities and Exchange Commission (SEC) for an offering of new securities and requires that the offering firm provide extensive information to the SEC and to shareholders. Since open-end investment companies offer shares continuously, they are always legally in registration under the rules of the Securities and Exchange Commission. The Securities Exchange Act of 1934 requires periodic reports of the investment companies and also requires that the funds provide shareholders with the prospectus before soliciting the purchase of shares. But perhaps the Investment Company Act of 1940 is most significant in its impact on mutual fund management. This act regulates the composition of the board of directors of the investment companies and the nature of the contract between the investment company and the management company. The mutual fund must file with the Securities and Exchange Commission a statement indicating its investment policies, and these policies may be changed only through vote of the shareholders. Shareholders must be allowed to elect at least two thirds of the directors of the fund. The management contract between the fund and the management company cannot exceed two years in duration and must be approved by shareholders. Moreover, there are substantial limitations on the capital structure of the funds, especially with regard to the amount of financial leverage (i.e., borrowed funds) that may be used.

Taxation. Investment companies conforming to the appropriate statute do not pay any tax on their dividends or capital gains. The investment company must meet a number of conditions including paying out each year at least 90 percent of net ordinary income. Moreover, at least one half the assets of the fund must be in cash or diversified securities and no more than 25 percent of the assets may be invested in the securities of any one issuer. Investment companies are viewed as "conduits" which simply flow the dividends and realized capital gains through to shareholders. The shareholders rather than the fund itself then become responsible for the taxes on the dividends and capital gains at their individually appropriate income tax rates.

RATES OF RETURN ON MUTUAL FUND SHARES

The rate of return earned by shareholders in a mutual fund has been examined in great detail by a number of researchers. Results of this research have been relatively consistent and have not been favorable to the mutual fund industry.[4] In particular, it has been demonstrated that investors could have usually achieved as good a rate of return by purchasing and holding a market portfolio (perhaps selecting the individual securities in the portfolio by a random process) as by investing in mutual funds. For example, as Table 18–3 shows, of

TABLE 18–3
Comparison of mutual fund performance with the Standard & Poor's stock average (percent change)

Type of fund	10 years ending 1978
Maximum capital gains	−5.1
Long-term growth	+13.1
Growth and income	+23.6
Balanced	+26.6
Standard & Poor's 500 stock average	+28.1

Source: *Management Results*, Wiesenberger Investment Companies Services, December 1978. Copyright 1978, Warren, Gorman & Lamont, Inc.

four broad groupings of mutual funds by objectives, none performed better than the unmanaged Standard & Poor's stock average in the ten years ending in 1978. While the S&P index rose 28.1 percent, the maximum capital gains mutual fund group fell 5.1 percent in a period of high inflation, long-term growth funds increased 13.1 percent, growth and income funds rose 23.6 percent, and balanced funds in-

---

[4] See Friend, Blum, and Crockett [3].

creased almost as much as the S&P Index with a gain of 26.6 percent. This suggests that over periods as long as a decade, mutual funds are not able to outperform the market. Indeed, in recent years, a large percentage of mutual funds have done considerably worse than the market. Moreover, the findings are not limited to mutual funds but may be generalized to other institutional investors in common stock such as pension funds, life insurance companies, and property and casualty insurance companies.

There appear to be reasonable explanations for these findings. First, it is argued by some that investment analysts employed by mutual funds for individual security selection are not able to pick securities with exceptionally high returns for a given amount of risk. For example, security analysts generally employ two different approaches to select securities with the potential for above-average returns: fundamental analysis and technical analysis. *Fundamental analysis* attempts to examine the fundamental earnings potential of a firm by looking at the products of the company, their markets, and potential. The traditional approach used in fundamental analysis would be to project the economy, the industry, and the firm's market share and from these to project the earnings of the firm. Based upon the earnings potential, the fundamental analyst would determine the intrinsic worth or value of the company's stock by capitalizing the expected earnings at some appropriate multiple. If the intrinsic value exceeded the current market price, then the security is undervalued and is a candidate for inclusion in the fund's portfolio. Conversely, if the intrinsic value was less than the current market price, then the security is overvalued and should not be included in the fund's portfolio. If that security is currently held in the institution's portfolio, then it should be sold as soon as possible. In contrast to this extensive analysis of the characteristics of the company used by fundamental analysts, the technical analyst relies only upon past price behavior of the company's stock. The technician argues that all relevant information is embodied in the movement of the price of the shares of stock. By examining these past movements, the financial analyst is able (in this view) to predict future movements and know whether to buy or sell the security.

The notion that fundamental and/or technical analysis can predict individual securities with excess returns has been challenged by the efficient markets literature. The *efficient markets* hypothesis argues that all relevant information which should influence the price of the stock of a firm is quickly embodied in that price so that there is — without inside information — no opportunity for the analyst to pick securities with above normal returns.[5] The efficient markets hypothe-

---

[5] See Malkiel [6] for a useful discussion of the implications of efficient markets.

sis would argue that the intrinsic value and the current market price of a security are identical; that there are neither undervalued nor overvalued securities. A large number of studies have indicated that the equity market is relatively efficient; much less is known about the efficiency of the bond market. In addition, extensive evaluation of various decision rules based upon technical analysis has been unable to find consistent evidence of excess returns produced by technical analysis over more random selection implied by the efficient markets hypothesis.

The evidence seems to indicate that portfolios of securities selected by mutual funds are not able to consistently outperform the market. Yet, there are costs involved in administering these portfolios. Brokerage and other costs are substantial since the portfolio turnover of mutual fund assets is often quite high. Moreover, there is some evidence that mutual funds hold more securities than necessary in order to approach the performance of the markets. This extreme diversification which seems to produce no tangible benefit is, of course, achieved at some cost to the investor. Hence, it is not surprising that the return on many mutual funds is less than the market return.

These findings of academic research along with the disillusionment of the investor with the actively managed fund have resulted in the creation of another type of mutual fund: the index fund. The index fund is a passively managed mutual fund in which the objective is not to "beat the market" but to "equal the market." The objective is sought by structuring a portfolio of securities which is representative of the entire market. If this portfolio allocation is successful, then the fund will do as well as, though no better than, the overall market except for the cost of management. With passive rather than active management, the management fee should be less than for most mutual funds.

This discussion is not meant to imply that mutual fund shares may not be beneficial to the investor. Clearly, for the small investor, investment companies do offer degrees of diversification that are impossible to realize through direct investment. But these results do indicate that, under most circumstances, the investor should not expect to achieve abnormally high returns through mutual fund shares. There is one important exception to this generalization. Returns above the market return should be possible if the investor is willing to accept a risk level above that of the market. If investors wish to achieve excess returns, they should then choose a fund with excess risk.

Mutual funds had a difficult time selling their shares throughout the early and mid-1970s. As shown in Table 18–4, net sales were generally over $1 billion each year from the late 1950s until the early

TABLE 18–4
Sales and redemption of mutual fund shares ($billions), 1950–1977

Year	Sale of own shares	Repurchase of own shares	Net issuance
1950	518.8	280.7	238.1
1955	1,207.5	442.6	764.9
1960	2,097.2	841.8	1,255.4
1965	4,358.1	1,962.4	2,395.7
1970	4,625.8	2,987.6	1,638.2
1971	5,147.2	4,750.2	397.0
1972	4,892.5	6,562.9	(1,670.7)
1973	4,359.3	5,651.1	(1,291.8)
1974	3,091.5	3,380.9	(289.5)
1975	3,307.2	3,686.3	(379.1)
1976	4,360.3	6,801.2	(2,440.9)
1977	6,399.7	6,026.0	373.7

Note: Excludes money market funds.
Source: *Mutual Fund Fact Book*, 1978.

1970s. But in 1972, 1973, and 1974 there were net redemptions exclusive of the sale of money market funds. Given the poor performance of the equity market, it is not surprising that the performance of mutual funds also was disappointing and that investors sold more fund shares than they bought. Yet, there is more to the problem than the poor performance of the market. Many investors were sold mutual fund shares with the unrealistic expectation of returns substantially higher than the market. Research associated with the efficient markets literature suggests that these expectations were unreasonable and should not have been created in the first place. The mutual fund investor must recognize that return is a function of risk and that in our efficient securities market there is no "free lunch."

QUESTIONS

18–1. What is an investment company? What are the different kinds of investment companies? What are some of the areas of specialization that investment companies have developed?

18–2. In terms of risk and rate of return, what might be the advantages for a small investor to purchase shares in an investment company?

18–3. With regards to investment companies, what is the advantage of maturity intermediation?

18–4. What is a mutual fund? Differentiate between load and no load funds. Differentiate between open-end and closed-end funds.

18–5. What is a balanced fund? What is a specialty fund?

18–6. What is the difference between an active portfolio and a fixed portfolio?

18–7. Examine the development of the money market fund. What factors were important in the growth of this market? What is an expedited redemption procedure? What is a checkwriting redemption privilege?

18–8. Examine different aspects of investment companies in terms of management, size, regulation, and taxation.

18–9. Differentiate between fundamental analysis and technical analysis as attempts to select securities with the potential for above-average returns.

REFERENCES

1. Baumol, William J. *The Stock Market and Economic Efficiency.* New York: Fordham University Press, 1965.

2. Fraser, Donald R. "The Money Market Fund as a Financial Intermediary." *MSU Business Topics,* Spring 1977, pp. 5–11.

3. Friend, Irwin, Blum, Marshall, and Crockett, Jean. *Mutual Funds and Other Institutional Investors.* New York: McGraw-Hill Book Co., 1970.

4. Jensen, Michael D. "The Performance of Mutual Funds in the Period 1954–1964." *Journal of Finance,* May 1968.

5. Litzenberger, Robert, and Sossin, Howard. "The Structure and Management of Dual Purpose Funds." *Journal of Financial Economics,* March 1977, pp. 203–30.

6. Malkiel, Burton. *A Random Walk Down Wall Street.* New York: W. W. Norton and Co., 1975.

7. ———. "The Valuation of Closed-End Investment Company Shares." *Journal of Finance,* June 1977, pp. 847–59.

8. Securities and Exchange Commission. *A Study of Mutual Funds.* Washington, D.C.: U.S. Government Printing Office, 1967.

9. ———. *Public Policy Implications of Investment Company Growth.* Washington, D.C.: U.S. Government Printing Office, 1961.

19

Other financial institutions

Previous chapters have discussed a number of major financial institutions in considerable detail in terms of sources and uses of funds, industry characteristics, management decision problems, and other important features. This chapter attempts to touch briefly upon three financial institutions which—while not especially large in the total flow of funds in the U.S. economy—do play an important role in specialized parts of the economy: mortgage banks, leasing companies, and real estate investment trusts (REITs).

These three financial institutions possess a number of similar features. All are involved in the long-term commitment of funds for the purpose of making purchases of capital goods such as new homes, machinery, and transportation equipment. Mortgage banks and real estate investment trusts are generally associated with the financing of housing, with the mortgage bank usually connected with the financing process for single-family residences, and with the real estate investment trust involved in the financing of apartments and other income-producing property. Leasing companies also frequently engage in the financing of income-producing property, such as office buildings, although their financing activities tend to be more diversified than either mortgage banks or REITs. A further similarity between these types of financial institutions exists in terms of their historical development. All three became significant in the post–World War II period. While mortgage banks and leasing firms did exist prior to World War II, it was a special set of economic and financial circumstances after World War II which contributed to the rapid growth of these institutions. In contrast, REITs were given birth by special legislation of the United States Congress enacted in 1960.

While there are a variety of similarities among these three types of financial institutions, there are also some great differences. Leasing companies and real estate investment trusts essentially lend their own funds and act as a principal in financial transactions. Each of these two financial institutions has an equity base upon which it pyramids large amounts of financial leverage (debt). The funds provided by owners are combined with the funds provided by creditors and the financial institution acquires for itself either financial assets such as mortgages or real assets (such as an office which is then leased). In contrast, the role of the mortgage bank is generally as an agent rather than principal, and as such the mortgage banking firm is more akin to the stock brokerage firm. The mortgage banker finds those who wish to acquire real property (such as a single-family home) and matches this need with those who wish to make a loan on a single-family home (such as a life insurance company, mutual savings bank, or savings and loan association). In this case, the mortgage banker may act both as agent and as principal.

As another important difference among these financial institutions, the recent growth and future prospects of each institution must be mentioned. The mortgage banking industry and the leasing industry have enjoyed enormous growth in the postwar period and this growth shows no signs of ending. In contrast, the real estate investment trust exhibited remarkable expansion during the late 1960s and early 1970s during periods of monetary stringency, but in recent years the industry has experienced enormous problems with defaulted loans and a number of the leading firms in the industry have gone bankrupt. The future of the real estate investment trust, at least as presently constituted, is very much in doubt.

MORTGAGE BANKING

Mortgage banks (or mortgage companies as they are frequently called) are not easy firms to define since the industry encompasses firms which differ greatly in both size and function. Moreover, in contrast to the financial institutions discussed earlier, the degree of regulation of the industry is very slight. It has been suggested that one of the reasons for the rapid growth of mortgage banking in recent years is the comparative absence of regulation. In the broadest sense, a mortgage bank is any firm which both lends money on improved real estate *and* offers the securities to other investors as a dealer, or is an investor in real estate securities, or is an agent of an insurance company or other purchaser of first mortgage securities. Such a definition would cover a multitude of individuals and corporations. But, in its essence, the basic function of the mortgage bank is to originate and service mortgage loans for institutional investors. The mortgage banking firm must then be greatly concerned with finding sources of demand for mortgage loans and simultaneously with finding a source of funds to meet that demand from life insurance companies, mutual savings banks, and savings and loan associations. Moreover, once the loans have been originated and financed, the mortgage banker provides (for a fee) the servicing functions of collections, paying insurance, and taxes for the institutional investor.

The mortgage banker is first concerned with the origination of the loan. As such, prospective borrowers must be found. The successful mortgage banker usually will develop close relations with real estate brokers and builders, both of whom are likely to have intimate knowledge of the needs of individuals for financing real property. In this regard, many mortgage bankers employ solicitors whose function (either on a commission or salary basis) is to obtain loan applications for the firm. Once loan applications are obtained, the financing of the loan must be secured. Most mortgage bankers have relationships, carefully cultivated and developed over the years, with institutional investors. Since the supply and demand for money capital in the United States is not balanced geographically, these institutional investors are often located some distance from the office of the mortgage banker. For example, rapidly growing areas in the West, Southwest, and Southeast would be expected to have a capital deficit while slowly expanding areas such as the Northeast would be expected to have a capital surplus. The flow of money then is often from the Northeast to these more rapidly growing parts of the nation.

Mortgage bankers may place a loan with an institutional investor in one of several different ways. First, the loan may be made only after the investor has approved the transaction. While the safest approach from the perspective of the investor, it is also the most cumbersome. Since the process necessarily is quite slow, it risks loss of the borrower to another lender. As another possibility, the mortgage banker may make the loan out of its own funds (usually borrowed from commercial banks) and then offer the loans for sale to one or more institutional customers. Obviously, the latter approach provides the customer with a more rapid decision on the credit application, although with limited funds the mortgage banker generally cannot handle all its operations in this manner. In either case, the mortgage banker must be quite careful of the credit quality of the prospective customer.

Once the loan is closed the mortgage banker handles all the details of the loan until the maturity of the financial instrument. Such details involve processing current payments, inspecting the property at reasonable intervals, changing records when the property is sold, and protecting the owner of the mortgage in case of a delinquency. For this service the mortgage banker receives what is referred to as a servicing fee—which is the principal source of income for many companies.

The mortgage banking firm generally obtains its income from three sources. First, as already mentioned, it earns a servicing fee on loans placed with institutional investors. Institutional investors, who are often located at a considerable distance from the property financed, have neither the expertise nor the inclination to service the loans and would prefer to see the mortgage banker engage in this necessary function. Mortgage banking firms argue that they can perform this function more efficiently than institutional investors because of economies of scale and because they have additional sources of income besides the servicing fee. Mortgage bankers also may earn income from selling mortgages to an institutional investor (on those mortgages where the mortgage company acts as a principal) at a price higher than the mortgage company paid. In a period of falling interest rates this can be a source of sizable profit. Finally, the mortgage banker may obtain income from the sizable fees associated with the transfer of real property. In addition to the fees associated with change of title, the mortgage banker may obtain commissions from writing insurance on the property and may obtain property management fees in some cases.

The dimensions of the mortgage banking industry are difficult to determine. The firms range in size from one-man operations to national firms with branches in most major cities of the nation. Some mortgage banking firms are indeed very large. Table 19–1 provides information on the ten largest mortgage banking firms based upon the volume of mortgages serviced as of mid-year 1976. Lomas and Nettleton Financial Corporation serviced over $5 billion in mortgages representing over 300,000 individual mortgages. Moreover, those mortgages were held by about 700 investors. Perhaps the most striking aspect of the industry is its recent growth. There has been more than a doubling of the number of mortgage companies since World War II. Moreover, the assets of mortgage banking firms expanded even more rapidly and, perhaps most significantly, the share of

TABLE 19–1
Ten U.S. largest mortgage banking firms, June 30, 1976

Name of firm	Dollar volume of mortgages serviced ($billions)	Number of mortgages serviced	Number of investors
Lomas and Nettleton Financial Corp.	$5.2	331,717	730
Advance Mortgage Corp.	2.8	136,700	334
Colonial Mortgage Service	2.6	106,017	472
Cameron-Brown	1.9	95,036	405
Western Mortgage Corp.	1.9	79,984	187
Pennamco	1.9	102,197	334
Kissell Co.	1.8	109,357	870
National Homes Acceptance Corp.	1.8	133,850	1,094
Stockton, Whatley, Davis and Co.	1.7	74,314	221
James T. Barnes and Co.	1.5	64,255	237

Source: Reprinted with permission from the October 25, 1976 issue of *American Banker.*

single-family mortgages serviced by mortgage banking firms rose dramatically. While there are a number of reasons for this growth, one in particular stands out—the postwar expansion in insured mortgage operations of the U.S. government, especially the program sponsored by the Federal Housing Administration. The existence of insured mortgages created a financial instrument which was suitable for investment by capital market institutions which sought the yields available on mortgages but were unwilling to accept the risks of conventional mortgages on single-family homes. At the same time, these institutional investors were often located at some distance from where property expansion was occurring and did not wish to set up their own facilities for investigation of a large number of small loans. The mortgage banker fulfilled the needs of the large institutional investors by offering insured mortgages and taking care of the servicing of these mortgages.

One of the most significant recent developments in the mortgage banking industry has been its penetration by commercial banks. Many commercial banks have owned mortgage banking subsidiaries for some years. But with the development of the bank holding company movement and the approval by the Federal Reserve Board of mortgage banking activities for bank holding companies, many commercial banks shifted their mortgage banking firms from bank subsidiaries to holding company subsidiaries. Moreover, many bank holding companies have acquired independent mortgage banking firms and have started *de novo* mortgage banks. Bank holding companies today are estimated to control over 50 percent of the total dollar volume of mortgages serviced by the 100 largest mortgage banking firms.

LEASING

Leasing as a means of obtaining the use of capital equipment has grown enormously in recent years. There are a number of reasons for this interest. From the perspective of the lessee, leasing may sometimes be transacted at a lower rate than borrowing. Since the lessor is often able to obtain substantial tax benefits from accelerated depreciation and the investment tax credit, the lessor often passes a part of these benefits on to the lessee in the form of a lower implicit rate of interest on the lease contract. Lease payments can often be structured so that they approximate the useful life of the asset more closely than loan payments. Leasing can be construed as a hedge against inflation for the lessee since lease payments will be paid with dollars having reduced purchasing power.[1] Capital limitations may prevent a purchaser from making the down payment associated with a purchase. Leasing may allow for "off balance sheet" financing—the lessee can charge the use of the equipment as a current operating expense rather than capitalizing the asset, thereby avoiding the appropriate liability on the balance sheet, and depreciating the equipment on the income statement. Recent pronouncements from the Financial Accounting Standards Board make it increasingly difficult to follow this procedure. In the early years of the lease, the lease process may provide a more desirable cash flow than purchasing, and especially desirable as compared with other forms of borrowing (such as term loans) which do not provide 100 percent financing. Leasing may also minimize reductions in book earnings, especially during the early years of the lease.

From the perspective of the lessor financial institutions, especially commercial banks, have found leasing to be an attractive endeavor for several reasons. For a bank especially, leasing can benefit the institution indirectly through the attraction of new customers and thereby increase deposits. By filing consolidated tax returns and taking advantage of the investment tax credit, financial institutions are often able to shelter substantial amounts of nonleasing income through benefits from leasing. Yield potential on leases are often considerably higher than the maximum interest allowed under usury laws. As an example, return on investment for a leasing company frequently exceeds 20 percent. Moreover, it is sometimes argued that

---

[1] Any type of borrowed funds would, of course, provide a similar type of protection.

a commercial bank can accept loans of greater risk through a leasing subsidiary rather than directly through the loans of the bank.

Lease contracts can be immensely complicated and vary in a number of ways. However, certain generalizations can be made. One approach is to classify leases according to the method of origination. By this approach leases may be dealer-generated or direct. The dealer-generated lease involves a procedure whereby a lender purchases leases generated or originated by dealers. The dealer negotiates the lease, delivers the asset, and then assigns the lease paper to the lessor. The lessor makes title application and notifies the lessee that the lease has been assigned to the lessor to whom lease payments must be made. In contrast, a direct lease refers to an arrangement in which the customer comes to the lessor with the motivation to lease. The lessor refers the customer to a dealer for equipment selection and, after this selection, buys the asset. Subsequently, the dealer makes delivery to the lessee.

Another method of classification is by bearer of risk. By this classification a lease may be either open end or closed end. In an open-end lease, the lessee assumes the risk of damage or loss and the responsibilities of repair and maintenance. The lessee is required to make monthly rental payments plus final payment. By requiring the lessee to guarantee the residual value of the property to the lessor, the lessor is guaranteed its investment in the assets, recovery of its cost of financing, and its profit. The principal difference between a closed-end and open-end lease is the fact that the lessee does not guarantee the residual value of the property under a closed-end arrangement.

Leases may also be categorized as operating or financial leases. The operating lease is a short-term transaction akin to a rental of property. In contrast, the finance lease is long term and can best be compared to a secured term loan. The financial lease is the most appropriate type of lease for commercial banks. This lease may not be cancelled without full payment of all amortized costs to the lessor, so that the bank receives assurance of the return of its funds plus an annual return on funds invested, provided of course that the lessee fulfills all promises. A financial lease is actually the functional equivalent of a loan in that the lease payments are spread over the useful life of the asset. At the end of the lease, the lessee has the option to purchase the asset at its fair market value. Responsibility for taxes, insurance, and maintenance rests with the lessee.

Leases may also be classified either as nonleveraged or leveraged. A nonleveraged lease is an arrangement in which the lessor finances the lease with its own funds. In contrast, with a leveraged lease, the lessor provides only a portion of the required investment for the equipment, with the rest being borrowed from other lenders usually on a non-recourse basis. The lender has recourse only to the asset financed in the case of a default on the lease, in which case the lessor can lose only that equity invested. The originator of a leveraged lease usually invests 20 to 40 percent of the asset cost and must contribute a minimum of 20 percent to qualify as a lease within the rules of the Internal Revenue Service. Leveraged leases are most common on larger capital items such as railroad cars, airplanes, and ships. The mechanics of the leveraged lease are somewhat complicated and usually involve trustees for both lenders and equity participants. The resulting yields are significant in relation to the size of the equity investment, since the lessor still claims all the tax benefits from the entire investment. However, some of these benefits may be passed through to the lessee in the form of lower rental payments. It is interesting to note that the leveraged lease may provide a substantial return to the investor and yet the cash flow to the investor may be negative over the life of the asset. Cash flows are usually positive in the early years of the lease (negative in later years), and the differential time value of money produces a positive time-adjusted rate of return. Calculations of the "true" rate of return on these types of transactions are fairly difficult since conventional calculations of the rate of return when the cash flows alternate in sign over the time horizon of the investment will produce more than one estimate of the true rate of return.

As with the mortgage banking industry there is limited information available on the structure of the leasing industry. The leasing market appears to contain several layers of firms. At the top is a group of firms serving a nationwide market and competing for large corporate accounts. Below these are smaller leasing companies serving local and regional markets and in competition with only a few firms. One factor which heightens competition in the industry is the number of different firms that provide leasing services. These services are offered by banks and bank holding companies, consortiums of banks, pension funds, insurance companies, financial lessors, lease brokers, and captive leasing companies. In addition, some major manufacturing companies have expanded their leasing operations from a merchandising activity into a dual profit center arrangement, with merchandising as one focal point and the investment of funds as another. The volume of annual leases is not known with certainty. Estimates place the annual amount of equipment leases written at over $10 billion and growing at a rate of 10 to 30 percent per year.[2]

Perhaps the most significant development in the leasing industry in recent years has been the entry by banks and bank holding com-

---

[2] Weiss and McGugh [6].

panies. Ownership and leasing of real property (excluding certain well-defined items) is still prohibited to a bank, although not to bank holding companies. However, banking organizations cannot stock inventories of property to satisfy demand. Property may be purchased by banking organizations only after the leasing customer makes an application. The lease arrangement must be, in effect, a credit transaction arranged at the request of the lessee, much as a bank loan is extended in response to a credit application from a customer. Leases prepared by bank holding company subsidiaries must be full-payout leases in which the lessor recovers in full the acquisition cost of the leased property through rentals, salvage value, and tax benefits. The Federal Reserve system seems determined to keep banks and bank holding companies out of the riskier aspects of leasing.

REAL ESTATE INVESTMENT TRUSTS

The real estate investment trust (or REIT) is a financial institution which was created in order to permit many small investors to pool their funds (as in the mutual fund industry) and to invest these funds in commercial real estate. REITs were designed to allow the individual investor who has neither the time nor the knowledge to manage real property to participate in the potential tax advantage and inflation-hedging characteristics associated with income-producing property. The REIT industry is a relatively recent and controversial institution. Created by Congress through the Real Estate Investment Trust Act of 1960, the REITs experienced phenomenal growth in the late 1960s, especially during the tight money period of 1969. In the early and mid-1970s substantial difficulties with loan quality began to develop, many REITs (including some of the largest affiliated with bank holding companies) were forced into bankruptcy, and a number of observers began to question the viability of the industry as an effectively functioning financial intermediary. Moreover, many of the largest REITs were sponsored by major commercial banks, and the financial difficulties of the REITs brought into question the soundness of some of the nation's largest banks.

REITs operate under the Real Estate Investment Trust Act of 1960 which exempts the individual trust from income taxes if it complies with certain provisions of the Internal Revenue Code. As such, the REITs are able as with investment companies which commit funds to stocks and bonds to flow through income to shareholders and thereby act as a conduit. The most important of the provisions required for a REIT to be treated as a conduit are:

1. At least 90 percent of the net income of the trust must be distributed to shareholders.

2. The trust must be a passive investor and cannot manage its own properties. The trust must exist primarily as a conduit for investment capital and must hire property managers on a fee basis.
3. The trust must have at least 100 shareholders, and no group of five individuals or less can own more than 50 percent of the shares.
4. The income that the trust may receive in capital gains from the sale of a particular parcel of property is limited to 30 percent of the gross income of the trust.

As of year-end 1977, the REIT industry had total assets of over $15 billion (see Table 19–2). The two largest financial assets held were commercial mortgages ($3.8 billion) and multifamily mortgages ($2.3 billion). These uses of funds were financed primarily by access to bank credit. Bank term loans and revolving credit provided $6.5 billion, while mortgages provided an additional $2.4 billion. At one time a number of REITs relied heavily upon the commercial paper market for short-term financing. However, the financial problems of the industry effectively precluded the REIT from gaining additional access to this market.

REITs are classified into three basic groups: equity trusts, short-term mortgage trusts, and long-term trusts. REIT equity trusts are engaged primarily in the ownership of real property. The most common form of equity trusts pay off long-term mortgages out of rental or lease income while also passing along part of this income to shareholders. The reduction of debt along with an anticipated inflation-aided increase in property values may potentially give shareholders substantial real estate equity.

Equity trusts

Typical holdings of equity trusts include office buildings, apartment houses and condominiums, and commercial property such as shopping centers. In addition, some trusts have holdings in more diverse properties like college dormitories, motels, indoor tennis centers, and even oil wells. Among the larger and better-known equity trusts are: Real Estate Investment Trust of America, U.S. Realty Investment, and Pennsylvania Real Estate Investment Trust.

One of the key elements in the operation of an equity trust is the use of depreciation as a tax deduction. The following example shows how these depreciations charges may benefit shareholders. Assume that a trust-owned apartment house cost $1 million and yields $125,000 a year in rental income. Operating expenses (maintenance, utilities, taxes) are $40,000 and the mortgage, $30,000 ($7,500 princi-

TABLE 19–2

Assets and liabilities of real estate investment trusts, 1970–1977 ($billions)

	1970	1971	1972	1973	1974	1975	1976	1977
Total assets	$4.8	$7.8	$13.9	$20.2	$21.8	$21.3	$18.7	$15.8
Physical assets	0.9	1.4	2.5	3.2	4.3	7.3	8.9	8.6
Multifamily	0.3	0.4	0.8	1.1	1.4	2.4	3.0	2.8
Nonresidential	0.6	1.0	1.7	2.1	2.9	4.9	5.9	5.7
Financial assets	3.9	6.4	11.4	17.0	17.5	14.0	9.8	7.2
Home mortgages	0.6	0.8	1.2	1.9	1.7	1.4	1.1	0.9
Commercial mortgages	2.0	3.2	5.0	7.5	7.7	7.0	5.2	3.8
Multifamily mortgages	1.3	2.2	4.2	6.6	6.8	4.8	3.1	2.3
Other	—	0.2	1.0	1.0	1.3	0.8	0.5	0.2
Total liabilities	$2.2	$4.1	$8.8	$14.4	$16.6	$17.8	$16.0	$13.0
Mortgages	0.5	0.7	1.2	1.5	1.6	2.0	2.4	2.4
Corporate bonds	0.6	1.0	1.4	1.9	2.1	2.1	1.9	1.8
Bank loans	1.0	1.6	3.0	7.0	11.4	10.8	8.9	6.5
Other	0.1	0.8	3.2	4.0	1.5	2.9	2.8	2.3

Source: Federal Reserve System Flow of Funds Accounts.

pal and $22,500 interest). Subtracting the $70,000 total of expenses and mortgage payments, a cash flow of $55,000 is left that the trust can pass on to its shareholders. Only part of this $55,000 cash flow is considered taxable income. For IRS purposes, the $40,000 operating expenses plus the $22,500 interest are added to the depreciation for the year. Assuming that yearly depreciation is straight line at $55,000, then total expenses on the tax form add up to $112,500. Subtracted from the $125,000 rental income, this leaves a taxable income of $12,500. Shareholders then pay taxes on the $12,500 while actually obtaining the right to a cash flow of $55,000. While the REIT industry has had enormous financial problems, the equity trusts have been least affected.

Short-term mortgage trusts

These trusts do their investing in construction and development loans of less than one year to maturity. While mortgage trusts do not have the benefits of depreciation write-offs, they have another valuable tool to increase income to shareholders—leverage. These trusts make their money on the difference between the cost of borrowed funds and the rate at which they lend out these funds. In periods when yield relationships are unfavorable, the short-term investment trust finds profitable operation quite difficult. Many trusts, especially short-term trusts, can also grow without borrowing by selling new shares at a price higher than book value. For example, assume a trust with $50 million in equity, $6.25 million in earnings, and 5 million shares outstanding with a book value of $10 per share. If these shares are selling in the market at above book value, then a new offering can be made at a price of $12 per share, for example. If 5 million new shares are sold and the $60 million worth of new capital raised is invested to yield 12.5 percent, then earnings per share would rise from $1.25 to $1.38. This method of increasing earnings is referred to as *contradilution* and was one of the favorite techniques used by real estate investment trusts to expand during the period when their stocks were selling at high price-earnings ratios. Moreover, the sale of new stocks increases the equity base and provides the opportunity for additional financial leverage.

Long-term trusts

These long-term mortgage trusts are the most recent type of REIT. Their loans may run for up to 30 years and are often made at rates substantially lower than short-term construction and development loans. The spread between short-and long-term rates reflects the added risk the short-term lender takes that the project may never be completed or that take-out money (long-term funds used to pay off the short-term construction and development debt) might never be obtained by the builder. This differential between short- and long-term rates does not violate the generalization that long term rates are usually higher than short-term rates since risk here obviously is not held constant.

Long-term trusts have little use for conventional forms of leverage, because the spread between the long-term bond rate and the long-term mortgage loan rate is usually quite small. Even though financial leverage works in only a small fashion for these types of organizations, long-term trusts can raise their return by adding extras into the agreement with builders such as *equity kickers*. These agreements can take the form of either an ownership interest in the property (office buildings, shopping center, or apartment house) or a percentage of the rental income above a certain level.

Industry trends

While the REITs are generally organized under the Real Estate Investment Trust Act of 1960, rapid expansion of the industry did not occur until the late 1960s. The breakthrough for REITs came in 1968 and 1969. In that period, a severe credit crunch curtailed almost all sources of funds for mortgage loans. As a result, REITs were able to commit large amounts of funds at attractive rates and the value of their shares of stock moved upward rapidly. During the latter stages of 1969 and 1970, REITs were started by major financial institutions such as the Bank of America, Chase Manhattan Bank, and Connecticut General Life Insurance Company. Approximately 31 public offerings of REITs with assets of $10 million or more occurred during the first nine months of 1971. With increasing competition for available properties and declining interest rates on available investments, the REITs began to have difficulties in maintaining profit margins. Moreover, the stock prices of the REITs declined, making it more difficult to raise additional equity as a base for more financial leverage and setting the stage for financial disaster in the mid-1970s.

It was the 1974–76 period which really exposed the problems of the industry. Profit margins continued to erode. Also, more and more developers were forced into default because of high interest rates and escalating materials costs. Hence, not only were the REITs making fewer loans, but also many existing loans were becoming problems. Many short-term trusts experienced especially large losses. These losses were accentuated by the accrual accounting system whereby many trusts continued to accrue interest on their loans even though no cash interest payment had been made for some time and even though it was highly doubtful if such interest payments would be made in the future. Finally, the cash drain on these REITs became so intense that major default occurred on the debt of the REITs and many of the largest REITs became bankrupt. It remains uncertain what the future of this financial institution will be.

The significant trends in the REIT industry are illustrated by the information provided in Table 19–2. The rapid growth of the industry through the mid-1970s is evident with total assets expanding from $4.8 billion in 1970 to $21.8 billion in 1974. As discussed earlier, most of this expansion was concentrated in multifamily and commercial mortgage lending. Commercial mortgages held by REITs rose from $2.0 billion in 1970 to $7.7 billion in 1974, and holdings of multifamily mortgages expanded from $1.2 billion to $6.8 billion in the same period. Yet what is most vividly revealed by the information in Table 19–2 is the severity of the financial problems which have plagued the industry beginning with the 1974–75 recession. Total assets fell from $21.8 billion in 1974 to $15.8 billion in 1977. More importantly, the mix of assets changed dramatically. Physical assets—property owned by the REITs—rose from $3.2 billion in 1973 to $8.9 billion in 1976. Most of this property acquired by the REITs reflected the foreclosure on defaulted loans.

CONCLUSIONS

This chapter has presented information on three important financial institutions involved in long-term lending. These three are not widely known. Yet they play an important role in the American financial system. Leasing has become important in many parts of the economy in recent years and promises to become even more so. Mortgage banking has evolved into a diversified financial institution involved in all aspects of real estate. Only the REITs face a questionable future. And even if REITs shrink in significance in the future they at least will have provided us with an illustration of how not to manage a financial institution.

QUESTIONS

19–1. Discuss the similarities of mortgage banks, leasing firms, and real estate investment trusts with reference to the long-term commitment of funds, real estate financing, and historical development.

19–2. What is it exactly that a mortgage bank does? Does the mortgage bank generally act as a principal or as an agent in financial transactions?

19–3. From what three sources does a mortgage banking firm generally obtain its income?

19–4. What is leasing and what are its advantages? When is it used? Differentiate between dealer-generated, direct, open-end, closed-end, and financial leases.

19–5. Discuss the significant developments in the leasing industry in recent years.

19–6. What are REITs? Of what significance is the Real Estate Investment Trust Act of 1960?

19–7. REITs are classified into what three basic groups? Give a definition of each group.

19–8. What is contradilution and how is it related to REITs? What are equity kickers?

REFERENCES

1. Anderson, Paul F. "Financial Aspects of Industrial Leasing Decisions." *MSU Business Studies*, Michigan State University, 1977.

2. Colean, M. L. *Mortgage Companies: Their Place in the Financial Structure.* Englewood Cliffs, N.J.: Prentice-Hall, 1962.

3. De Hurzar, William I. *Mortgage Loan Administration.* New York: McGraw-Hill Book Co., 1972.

4. Pease, Robert H., and Kerwood, Lewis O. *Mortgage Banking.* 2d ed. New York: McGraw-Hill Book Co., 1965.

5. Schulkin, Peter A. "Real Estate Investment Trusts: A New Financial Intermediary." *New England Economic Review*, November–December 1970.

6. Weiss, Steven J., and McGugh, Vincent J. "The Equipment Leasing Industry and the Emerging Role of Banking Organizations." *New England Economic Review*, 1973, pp. 3–30.

section

IV

Innovations and reform in the financial system

20

Reform of the financial system

There has been substantial concern in recent years expressed over the ability of the financial system to efficiently provide the funds necessary to allow for full employment of resources and economic growth at stable prices. This concern has been most evident in periods of monetary restraint when the flow of credit to some segments—especially housing and state and local governments—has been curtailed. It has given rise to a series of studies designed to investigate the causes of suspected problems in the financial system and to make recommendations concerning improvements in the entire financial mechanism. The studies have included major efforts by the Commission on Money and Credit, the Hunt Commission, and the discussion principles recently set forth by the House Banking Committee (known as the "Financial Institutions and the National Economy" study) which were designed to provide the basis for complete reform of the financial structure. While none of these recommendations have been adopted in total (and indeed few of their specific recommendations have been incorporated into legislation), their views have shaped the thinking of public policymakers and have contributed to a number of specific changes in legislation. Moreover, it appears highly likely that many of the proposals will become reality at some point as the

433

pressures of technological change and competition seem certain to bring about important shifts in the financial system. It is unlikely, for example, that the nature of the financial system in the year 2000 will at all resemble the system in 1980.

Major proposals for reform of the nation's financial system have been put forward by the Commission on Money and Credit, the Hunt Commission, and the United States Congress through the House Banking Committee. The proposals have centered in the following areas: the functions of specific financial institutions, especially the depository financial institutions, the role of competition in the financial system, the ability of the existing financial structure to channel funds adequately into areas of high social priority (especially housing), and the regulatory structure appropriate for the efficient operation of the financial system. Each of these topics is covered separately below, although naturally they are interrelated in many important respects.

FUNCTIONS OF FINANCIAL INSTITUTIONS

As was pointed out earlier, financial institutions have evolved as specialized units in the economic and financial marketplace. Savings and loan associations as well as mutual savings banks have traditionally served the needs of households—obtaining funds from households by accepting small savings accounts—and dispensing funds to households in the form of first mortgage loans for the purpose of acquiring residential property. Credit unions developed to serve those with some affinity, such as a common source of employment, and provide savings accounts and consumer loans as their primary services. Even commercial banks—perhaps now the most diversified type of financial institution—originally concentrated on serving the needs of business (commerce) through offering demand deposit and commercial loan services.

Considerable concern over the viability of a financial system composed of numerous specialized institutions has been created during periods of rising interest rates and intense credit restraint (especially in 1966, 1969, 1974, and 1979). For example, when interest rates have increased, the role of savings and loan associations in the financial marketplace has been sharply curtailed. Moreover, financial institutions generally borrow short and lend long (and thereby practice maturity intermediation) and are especially affected by the elimination or reversal of the upward-sloping yield curve in periods of high interest rates. As a result, there have been a number of suggestions for broadening the scope of these institutions, particularly savings and loan associations, and (more generally) blurring the distinction between different financial institutions. A brief summary of the major reform proposals bearing on the functions of individual financial institutions follows.

Sources of funds

The sources of funds for individual financial institutions would be broadened considerably under all of these proposals. Savings and loan associations, mutual savings banks, and credit unions would be permitted to offer demand deposits and other forms of third-party payments services. No longer would the commercial bank have a monopoly of demand deposits. However, the right to offer demand deposits would be restricted to a significant degree. The Hunt Commission Report recommended that savings and loan associations be allowed to offer demand deposits only to household accounts and that this institution be prohibited from seeking demand deposit funds from business firms in direct competition with commercial banks. In addition, the discussion principles of the study of "Financial Institutions and the National Economy" (FINE) of the House Banking Committee proposed that credit unions be allowed to offer demand deposit services to the general public only for community credit unions situated in low-income areas. To a considerable extent the pressure of events is already forcing the change as savings and loan associations and mutual savings banks in the New England and a few other states have been authorized to offer Negotiable Order of Withdrawal (NOW) accounts which are basically demand deposits which pay interest, and it seems likely that these accounts or some variant of them will spread.[1] Indeed the growth of NOW accounts raises the likelihood that all depository financial institutions will begin to pay interest on demand deposit accounts.[2]

A particularly important aspect of these recommendations which affects the sources of funds at financial institutions is the proposed elimination of the Regulation Q ceilings on the maximum rates payable on time and savings deposits. These regulations as they affect commercial banks, savings and loan associations, and other financial institutions substantially restrict the ability of these institutions to raise funds in periods of high interest rates and particularly reduce the degree of competition of financial institutions versus open mar-

---

[1] There have been a proliferation of different kinds of third-party payment services including negotiable orders of withdrawal which pay interest, negotiable orders of withdrawal which do not pay interest, and various types of share drafts.

[2] The Federal Reserve, in fact, authorized the automatic transfer of funds from savings to checking accounts effective in November 1978, which in effect allows commercial banks to pay interest on demand deposits.

ket instruments.[3] Regulation Q ceilings were originally adopted following the view that excessively high rates paid for funds by financial institutions in the early 1930s contributed to the large number of failures in that era. It was argued that financial institutions which paid high rates to attract funds would have to invest in high risk assets (securities and loans) in order to earn a sufficiently high return to both pay the interest cost for funds and earn a reasonable rate of profit. However, beginning in the 1960s, Regulation Q was used for a different purpose. In 1966, in a period of intense monetary pressure and rapidly rising interest rates, the Federal Reserve allowed the Regulation Q ceiling to remain below open market interest rates.[4]

As a result, large commercial banks which were heavily dependent on business certificates of deposit for funds found that their sources of funds and hence their lending ability were curtailed by Regulation Q ceilings. In this instance, the Federal Reserve was using Regulation Q as an instrument of general monetary control. As a separate use of the interest rate ceiling, Regulation Q has been used as a device to indirectly encourage the flow of funds into the mortgage market. A differential rate has been established with the maximum rates allowable for thrift institutions set at a higher level (generally one quarter of 1 percentage point) than for commercial banks. Thrift institutions have argued that such a differential is necessary for them to compete effectively against commercial banks since they believe commercial banks have a regulatory edge in that they are the only financial institution generally allowed to offer demand deposits, and the advantage of one-stop shopping would lead the consumer to prefer savings accounts at banks over savings and loan associations at identical rates. In contrast, commercial banks argue that the differential is unfair since savings and loan associations already are allowed greater latitude in tax avoidance than commercial banks.

Regulation Q has come under substantial criticism in recent years. Many argue that there is no evidence to support the argument that failures of financial institutions in the early 1930s were the result of excessive competition for funds and high rates paid for deposits. Moreover, critics argue that the use of Regulation Q as a tool of monetary control is questionable at best. While Regulation Q may affect the ability of one bank to obtain funds and grant credit, it does not influence the total volume of bank reserves. It is, therefore, ques-

---

[3] Such as Treasury bills, commercial paper, banker acceptances, and other money market instruments.

[4] In previous periods of rising interest rates the Fed had accommodated the banks by raising the Q ceiling whenever it appeared that the ceiling would curtail the ability of the banks to raise funds.

tionable whether Regulation Q affects the ability of the entire banking system to provide credit. Moreover, even if Regulation Q ceilings affect the amount of credit in the banking system, it is argued that it does so at the expense of discriminating against a few banking organizations. Finally, it is argued that Regulation Q ceiling differentials do not substantially improve the flow of funds to mortgage-oriented financial institutions. While Regulation Q ceilings do curtail the competition for funds between banks and thrift institutions, they do not influence the ability of unregulated financial markets (such as the Treasury bill market) to compete with thrift institutions for funds. Hence, in periods of monetary restraint and high interest rates, funds flow out of thrift institutions into open market instruments because of the existence of Regulation Q (a process known as disintermediation). The financial markets are amazingly efficient in devising means of avoiding artificial constraints on the flow of funds based simply on risk/return considerations.

Arguments against Regulation Q have been made by each of the major groups proposing reforms of the financial system—the Commission on Money and Credit, the Hunt Commission, and the FINE study of the House Banking Committee. It appears likely that Regulation Q will be eliminated, although it most likely will be phased out gradually and retained only on a standby basis for potential use in periods of financial emergency. Indeed, there has been substantial relaxation of the Q ceilings with the complete elimination of the interest rate ceilings on business CDs ($100,000 and over). Moreover, in 1978, commercial banks and savings and loan associations were allowed to offer six-month savings certificates (money market certificates) of $10,000 smallest denomination with the rate tied to the Treasury bill rate.

These proposals for reform, then, would change dramatically the sources of funds for depository financial institutions. Thrift institutions would become more like banks in their sources of funds and would have much greater latitude for competition with other financial institutions. However, there would still be significant limits on their sources. It appears likely that thrift institutions will continue to specialize in attracting funds from household accounts although they will be able to offer a much wider variety of financial instruments than in the past in seeking these funds.[5]

---

[5] It appears that one goal of these proposals is to turn the savings and loan associations, credit unions, and mutual savings banks into financial institutions which specialize in providing a large variety of financial services to households—that is, into family finance centers. It is not clear though what the impact of this development would be on the commercial banking system since banks have obtained their greatest growth in recent years from shifting from business emphasis (wholesale banking) to consumer services (retail banking).

Uses of funds

Consistent with a shift in sources of funds, proposals for reform of the financial system have concentrated also on changing the types of loans and investments made by the nation's financial institutions, especially the thrift institutions. Again the intent has been to eliminate the narrow specialization by individual financial institutions and allow a diversity of uses of funds both as to the nature of the borrower and as to the maturity of the financial instrument. It has been suggested that the impact of these reforms will be to quickly create thousands of new banks with an unknown impact on the profitability of the individual institution.

The greatest impact of these proposed changes in the uses of funds would be at the thrift institutions. Savings and loan associations, mutual savings banks, and credit unions would be allowed much greater flexibility in their loan portfolio. They would be able to establish revolving lines of credit, to make unsecured consumer loans, to make interim construction loans not related to taking the permanent financing on the property, and to issue credit cards. These institutions would also be allowed to invest in corporate debt obligations such as notes and bonds, commercial paper, and bankers acceptances. In addition, the thrift institutions would be allowed to establish trust departments, a financial function which has to this point been reserved for the commercial banking industry. Indeed, legislative action in 1977 did substantially broaden the power of credit unions.

While most of the proposed changes in the uses of funds have centered on the nonbank thrift institutions, there have been some notable proposals which would affect commercial banks. For example, the Hunt Commission recommended that any restrictions except those which center on the risk of the individual loan be eliminated from bank real estate lending. Currently there are restrictions on several aspects of real estate lending by commercial banks including the maturity and the percentage of total assets made up by mortgage loans; national banks cannot lend mortgage money in excess of 70 percent of their time and savings deposits or 100 percent of capital and unimpaired surplus, whichever is greater. Moreover, amortized real estate loans at national banks have a maximum maturity of 25 years and may not exceed 80 percent of the appraised value of the property.

COMPETITION

Central to all of the various proposals for reform of the financial system is the desire to increase the degree of competition between firms in a given financial sector and among the various financial institution groups. While the body of law and regulation which evolved out of the financial crises of the 1920s and 1930s emphasized reduction of competition and the preservation of stability in the financial system, the current proposals—drawing upon a long period of relatively stable economic conditions as well as the results of a vast body of financial research—emphasize increasing the degree of competition. It would, of course, be expected that the intensified competition would result in a greater number of failures. It is argued that the gains in the form of lower prices for credit and higher prices paid on sources of funds (more efficient financial intermediation) would more than offset any difficulties associated with the failure of individual financial institutions. Moreover, it is argued that the existence of deposit insurance would prevent individual failure from leading to a liquidity crisis and mass failures for the entire financial system.[6]

There are a number of specific proposals designed to increase competition. The discussion principles of the FINE study included recommendations that a federally chartered savings and loan association should be allowed to convert to a national bank charter if it wished, subject only to the constraint that it meet adequate capital and other technical requirements. Similarly, mutual savings banks would be allowed to convert to a national bank or savings and loan association. In addition, mutual savings banks would be able to achieve a federal charter and therefore operate throughout the nation. As pointed out in Chapter 12, mutual savings banks currently are restricted to only a few states since there are no federal charters available and because only a few states have legislation allowing the chartering of this type of financial institution.[7]

Perhaps the most significant proposal regarding competition concerns the chartering of new institutions. At present, the chartering process is involved and expensive. Groups which seek a new charter must not only establish that competent management exists and that adequate capital is being injected into the institution, but also that there is a need for the proposed institution in the community and that the establishment of a new financial institution would not seriously harm existing financial institutions in the market area. These latter restrictions substantially reduce the number of new entrants and

---

[6] For an excellent review of the literature dealing with these issues, see George J. Bentson, "The Optimal Banking Structure," *Journal of Bank Research*, Winter 1973, pp. 220–37.

[7] Similar proposals were made by the Hunt Commission which recommended that federal charters be granted to stock savings and loan associations, mutual savings banks, and mutual commercial banks, and that it be relatively simple for one institution to convert into another type of financial institution.

thereby restrict the degree of competition. The various proposals for reform of the financial system would substantially liberalize the conditions necessary for chartering new financial institutions. Barriers to entry would be reduced considerably and competition would be accentuated. In fact, the discussion principles of the FINE study proposed that a new depository financial institution should be chartered if capital and other technical requirements were met regardless of the economic and financial characteristics of the market area. These proposals would essentially eliminate the regulatory barriers which have restricted the number of individual financial institutions.

The degree of competition under the proposed changes in the financial structure would be increased not only by the establishment of new institutions but also by a marked increase in the market area served by existing institutions through liberalized branching restrictions. All of the studies which have examined the branching question have favored substantial relaxation of the restrictions on branching. The Hunt Commission report advocated statewide branch banking in all 50 states for example. The discussion principles of the FINE study went even further; it supported interstate branching of federally insured depository financial institutions as long as this did not conflict with state law. In those instances where there was a conflict with state law, the FINE study argued for branching in standard metropolitan statistical areas (SMSAs) in which the population exceed 1 million. Naturally, any such branching would be controlled by the regulatory authorities to ensure that it was pro- rather than anticompetitive.

One area in which competition is substantially affected through federal legislation is that of taxation. The federal income tax burden for financial institutions varies widely. For example, the tax burden (i.e., effective rate of taxation) of savings and loan associations and mutual savings banks has traditionally been substantially below the tax burden of commercial banks. Credit unions are completely exempt from the federal income tax. These differentials stem primarily from differences in the amount of tax-free additions to reserves for future loan losses allowed for each type of financial intermediary. However, due to changes in the federal income tax code in 1969, as well as greater investments in municipal bonds by banks, the tax burden of commercial banks has fallen considerably and the tax burden of savings and loan associations and mutual savings banks has increased sharply. In 1960, the effective tax burden for insured commercial banks was 35 percent, while the effective tax burden for savings and loan associations and credit unions was almost zero. By 1975, the effective tax burden for commercial banks was less than 15 percent, while the effective tax burden of savings and loan associations was almost 25 percent.[8]

Clearly equality of competition among financial institutions requires equality of effective tax burden. The Hunt Commission recommended a single tax method for all financial institutions which offer third-party payment services and eventually a single tax method for all financial institutions. Similarly, the FINE study recommended equal tax treatment for banks, savings and loan associations, mutual savings banks, *and* credit unions. However, this objective of horizontal and vertical tax equality is a difficult one to achieve in practice. And perhaps of equal importance is the proposal to establish equal reserve requirements for financial institutions which perform the same functions.

MORTGAGE CREDIT

One area in which there has been serious concern and a number of proposals advanced for reform is the allocation of credit by individual financial institutions. At present, the Federal Reserve controls the total quantity of money and credit, but the allocation of that total quantity of credit into specific sectors depends upon the decision made by the management of each individual financial institution. Presumably, the management of a financial institution makes the allocation decision after evaluating relative rates of return on different commitments of funds and risk consideration as well as on other factors. In an imperfectly competitive market, there is no reason why the allocation of credit by these financial manager should necessarily be efficient, and even in a competitive financial market, this allocation may be different from that desired by those in positions of political authority.

Concern over the allocation of credit has focused upon two separate but interrelated issues. First, is the allocation of funds by private financial intermediaries consistent with national goals in areas such as housing, credit availability for state and local governments, and the provisioning of an adequate supply of credit for minority individuals for personal and business purposes? Second, do cyclical fluctuations in the economy and financial markets bear unevenly on specific sectors such as housing? To a certain extent, reforms such as broadening the sources and uses of funds at individual financial institutions, reducing the degree of specialization of each institution, and the

---

[8] Margaret E. Bedford, "Federal Taxation of Financial Institutions," *Monthly Review*, Federal Reserve Bank of Kansas City, June 1976, pp. 3–15.

elimination of Regulation Q relate to these problems, and especially to the second of these two concerns. Moreover, there has been direct intervention by the federal government into the credit allocation process already to a substantial extent, particularly as it relates to agriculture and housing. For example, the farm credit system through its subsidiaries provides both operating and permanent financial capital to farm organizations at below-market rates of interest. Similarly, the Federal Home Loan Bank System injects funds into the savings and loan associations in periods of monetary restraint in order to allow these institutions to make more loans than the funds available from private sources would allow.

Many of the proposals for reform would inject the federal government more significantly into the credit allocation process. One of the most important of these relates to the availability of mortgage credit for the purpose of acquiring single-family dwellings, a goal deemed to have an important social function. Both the Hunt Commission and the FINE study propose changes which would make mortgage credit more readily available. The proposals contained in the FINE study are the most comprehensive and will be briefly covered here.

The FINE study proposed a number of approaches in order to improve the allocation of credit to the mortgage market. First, there would be a mortgage interest tax credit. Under this proposal any financial institution could obtain a tax credit based upon the volume of mortgages in its portfolio. However, the mortgages eligible for the tax credit would be restricted to those on housing units for low- and moderate-income families. Second, the Federal Home Loan banks would have the authority to lend to any financial institution—not just the savings and loan associations—as long as the funds were used for mortgage loans on construction and occupation of low-income housing units. The Federal Home Loan banks would, in turn, obtain their funds from the capital market—presumably at a lower cost than the individual financial institution could obtain funds—and financial institutions would be required to reflect the lower cost of funds in their mortgage rates. Third, a mortgage reserve credit system would be established. Under this system, the Federal Reserve could provide reserve credit to all financial institutions which provide funds for low- and middle-income housing. These financial institutions would hold reserves at the Federal Reserve and the institutions would receive a credit against these reserves for their low- and middle-income housing loans. Hence, extra funds devoted to these types of loans by any financial institution would free funds (reserves) for other purposes and therefore should make these types of loans more attractive.

THE REGULATORY STRUCTURE

One area in which there have been a large number of proposals for reform is that of the structure of regulation of financial institutions. Currently, there is a great diversity of regulatory agencies, with a specialization of regulation along industry lines: Federal Reserve System (commercial banks) versus Federal Home Loan banks (savings and loan associations) for example. Moreover, there is enormous overlap among the regulatory agencies, particularly in the banking area. For example, the bank regulatory agencies include the Comptroller of the Currency, the Federal Reserve System, the Federal Deposit Insurance Corporation, and the individual banking commissions of the 50 states. Moreover, the United States Department of Justice plays an important role in the approval of mergers and holding company acquisitions under the bank merger and bank holding company acts.

The confusing and confused nature of the regulatory process for financial institutions may perhaps best be illustrated with the banking industry. For example, a commercial bank may be chartered by either the Comptroller of the Currency or the relevant state banking commission. Once a charter is received, the bank may seek to change from state to national charter or vice versa if the regulatory philosphy of one supervisory authority is more agreeable to it. Indeed, many banks have shifted their charters in recent years. In the early 1960s for example, when the Comptroller of the Currency James Saxon was taking a broad interpretation of the functions which commercial banks could perform (such as leasing), there were a large number of shifts from state to national charters. Moreover, there have been frequent shifts from national to state charters in order to escape the relatively high reserve requirements imposed by the Federal Reserve. National banks, of course, must be members of the Federal Reserve, while state banks may choose to be either members or nonmembers. Most banks which have a choice have opted for nonmembership status.

Once a charter is granted, the bank seeks insurance of its deposits from a separate agency—the Federal Deposit Insurance Corporation. Moreover, the bank is then subject to examination by a variety of regulatory agencies. For example, if the bank obtained its charter from the Comptroller of the Currency (a national bank), it may be examined by the Comptroller, by the Federal Reserve System (since the bank must be a member of the Federal Reserve), and by the Federal Deposit Insurance Corporation (since the bank must be an insured bank). Similarly, if the bank received its charter from the state, it could be subject to examination and be required to submit reports to the state bank supervisory authority, the Federal Deposit Insurance Corporation (if it is insured, which 98 percent of all commercial banks are), and the Federal Reserve (if it is a member bank). Moreover, if the shareholders and management of the firm desire to form a holding company, the creation of that holding company and its activities are regulated by the Board of Governors of the Federal Reserve System.

Critics have charged that this overlapping of authority has a number of deficiencies. First, it creates excessive cost and burdens financial institutions with enormous amounts of required reports. Second, it may lead to "competition in laxity" by which the individual regulatory authority concerned with the size of the groups under their control (since many of the agencies are financed by assessments on the institution under their control) relaxes the standards of regulation in order to induce firms to choose their authority. For example, one regulatory authority may be more liberal in granting charters than another, or one regulatory agency may allow its banks to perform certain functions while another may not. Third, it has been charged that the substantial regulatory burden imposed on the Federal Reserve System hinders its ability to properly administer monetary policy. Not only does it divert the Fed's energies away from the difficult task of properly controlling the monetary aggregates and interest rates, but it also divides the Fed's loyalty since the central bank may become concerned with the impact of a particular monetary policy action on the group of banks under its supervision moreso than on its impact on the entire economy.

Proposals for reform of the regulatory structure are numerous. The Hoover Commission in 1949, the Commission on Money and Credit in 1961, and the Hunt Commission in 1971, all advocated substantial changes in the regulatory framework. However, our survey is limited to the FINE study since it is the most recent proposal and since it embodies most of the earlier proposals.

The overlapping jurisdiction of a number of regulatory agencies would be eliminated by the creation of a single agency, the Federal Depository Institutions Commission. This commission would take over the regulatory and supervisory activities of the Comptroller of the Currency, the Federal Reserve System, the Federal Deposit Insurance Corporation, the Federal Home Loan Bank System, and the National Credit Union Administration. The offices of the Comptroller of the Currency and the National Credit Union Administration would be abolished, and all agencies that insure financial institutions would fall under the control of the Federal Depository Institutions Commission. The Federal Reserve Board would have control only of monetary policy and would have no supervisory and examining function. Similarly, the Federal Home Loan Bank System would administer the Federal Home Loan Mortgage Corporation and would also have charge of the federal program to encourage financing of housing for low- and middle-income individuals.

The Federal Depository Institutions Commission would have five members: the deputy attorney general, a commissioner of the Securities and Exchange Commission, the vice chairman of the Federal Reserve Board, and two public interest representatives. One of the public interest representatives would serve as chairman of the commission. It would be responsible for the chartering and supervision of all federally chartered financial instititutions, including financial holding companies. Hence, all federally chartered banks, savings and loan associations, mutual savings banks, and credit unions would be under the direct supervision of the commission. Moreover, the examination and supervision of state-chartered, but federally insured financial institutions would be under the control of the commission unless it chose to delegate this responsibility to the individual states.

The proposed changes in the structure of regulation of individual financial institutions would remove the supervisory functions from the Federal Reserve System and would thereby change the role of the Fed in the financial system to a considerable extent. However, there has also been concern in recent years on the part of many (especially the U.S. Congress) aimed at reducing the degree of independence of the Federal Reserve System and bringing the monetary policy decision-making process more into the public spotlight. The discussion principle of the FINE study would contribute to such a change. The FINE study recommends, first, that the Board of Governors would be reduced in number from seven to five. The president of the United States would continue to appoint members of the board, subject to confirmation by the United States Senate. However, the terms of individual governors would be 10 years rather than 14 years. In addition, while the president would continue to select the board's chairman, the four-year term of the chairman would be concurrent with that of the president. Of substantial significance, the activities of the board would be audited by the General Accounting Office. Currently, the board and the reserve banks are subject to internal audit only and do not have to justify their expenditures to any outside group, either in the legislative or executive branch of the federal government.

Perhaps the most significant changes in the Federal Reserve System would be centered at the 12 reserve banks. Currently, the 12 Federal Reserve banks are "owned" by the member banks, since each member bank holds stock in its regional reserve bank (indeed the law requires that member banks subscribe to reserve bank stock for an amount up to 6 percent of the capital and surplus of the member bank). Moreover, these "owners" are represented on the boards of directors of the regional reserve banks and, in fact, hold a majority position on each board. The board of directors of the Federal Reserve banks then select a president for each reserve bank subject to the agreement of the Federal Reserve Board. As discussed in Chaper 5, the president of each Federal Reserve bank plays a vital role in the monetary policy process through participation on the Federal Open Market Committee.

This present arrangement at the reserve banks has created concern that private interests (specifically banking interests) were becoming too deeply involved in the public business of formulating and implementing monetary policy. The FINE study proposed the following changes to reduce the potential impact of the problem. First, all stock of the reserve banks would be retired. As a result, the reserve bank would be legally as well as in fact a public rather than a quasi-private institution. The board of directors of the regional reserve banks would be eliminated. Reserve bank presidents would be appointed in the same fashion as the members of the Federal Reserve Board—by the president of the United States subject to confirmation by the Senate. Their positions would be for five years and their salaries would be the same as those of the Board of Governors in Washington, D.C.

One of the most important proposed changes concerns the powers of the reserve bank presidents. Currently, the presidents attend each meeting of the Federal Open Market Committee and vote on the policy directive to be issued to the trading desk of the Federal Reserve Bank of New York. Under the proposals of the FINE study, the presidents of the reserve banks would have no vote on any monetary policy questions; that power would be reserved exclusively for the five members of the Board of Governors of the Federal Reserve System. However, the reserve bank presidents would be present during policy-related meetings and would be able to offer advice where desired.

CONCLUSIONS

The financial system has undergone substantial change in the past few decades. The speed of this change is likely to accelerate in the future. Moreover, the direction of change seems reasonably predictable given the consistency of the large numbers of proposals for reform which have been put forth in recent years. The depository financial institutions seem destined to grow more alike and more competitive.

The traditional monopoly of demand deposits by commercial banks is rapidly coming to an end and the payment of interest on demand deposits—either directly or indirectly—has become common. Profit rates at these depository institutions are likely to be under pressure. And the structure of supervision is likely to be quite different and much more centralized. In short, the decade of the 1980s should provide a fascinating case study of new developments for the student of the financial system.

QUESTIONS

20–1. What are some of the basic areas that proposals for reform of the nation's financial system have centered upon?

20–2. What effects would the elimination of Regulation Q have upon the savings and loan association industry?

20–3. What appears to be the general trend of the major financial institutions in this country with regards to specialization and diversification? What new areas of financial services can the various thrift institutions such as savings and loan associations, mutual savings banks, and credit unions be expected to move into in the future?

20–4. What effect would the proposed reforms for financial institutions have upon competition among the different financial institutions?

20–5. What are some of the specific proposals which would affect such things as competition, income tax burden, and allocation of credit by individual financial institutions?

20–6. What is the FINE study? What are some of the recommendations arising out of this study?

20–7. What is means by the term *competition in laxity*? What would be the purpose of the Federal Depository Institution Commission?

REFERENCES

Fraser, Donald R., and Rose, Peter S. "The Hunt Commission Report: Implication for Banking," *Journal of Commercial Bank Lending*, November 1972, pp. 20–27.

Mayne, Lucille S. "The Deposit Reserve Requirement Recommendations of the Commission on Financial Structure and Regulation: An Analysis, and Critique," *Journal of Bank Research*, Spring 1973, pp. 41–51.

Murphy, Neil, and Weiss, Steven J. "Restructuring Federal Regulation of Financial Institutions," *Banker's Magazine*, Winter 1972, pp. 71–77.

Murphy, Neil B., and Mandell, Lewis. "Reforming the Structure and Regulation of Financial Institutions: The Evidence from the State of Maine." *Journal of Bank Research*, Winter 1979, pp. 200–12.

Robinson, Roland I. "The Hunt Commission Report: A Search for Politically Feasible Solutions to the Problem of Financial Structure," *Journal of Finance*, September 1972, pp. 765–77.

U.S. Congress, House Committee on Banking, Currency, and Housing. *Financial Institutions and the Nation's Economy: Discussion Principles.* 94B Congress, 1st Session, November 1975, pp. 1–21.

21

Innovations in the financial institutions' sector

The financial system, no matter how well developed it may be, is constantly in a state of flux. New financial services are continually appearing, while others no longer in demand disappear. One noted economist, Hyman P. Minsky, observed several years ago that changes in financial practice and in financial institutions typically occur as a result of either legislation or evolution.[1] *Legislative* innovations, he argued, usually follow some malfunction—real or imagined—in the financial system, such as occurred in the early 20th century when a series of financial panics led to the creation of the Federal Reserve System. The proposals of the Hunt Commission and the FINE study of the House Banking Subcommittee on Financial Institutions discussed in the previous chapter are examples of a response to apparent problems in the financial system, especially recurring shortages of credit in important sectors of the economy such as the housing market.

Evolutionary changes in the financial system, on the other hand, result from the profit-seeking activities of financial entrepreneurs and are most likely to occur in periods of tight credit when the availability of loanable funds is scarce relative to

---

[1] See Minsky [10].

the demand for them.[2] At these times interest rates are high, threatening to squeeze the profits of financial institutions, but new techniques (innovations) offer the promise of greater profits. Since the supply of loanable funds is regulated by government policy, high and rising interest rates frequently are a reflection of rising demand for financial services. The higher interest rates and greater demand serve as a signal to market professionals to find new techniques in order to use loanable funds more efficiently. An innovation will appear in some aspect of financial market behavior and quickly will be adopted by market professionals who readily seize upon any opportunity to improve their particular institution's relative position. Undergirding these evolutionary changes at all times is the force of *competition* which encourages financial firms to innovate in order to protect the interests of their stockholders.

In addition, Minsky observed, financial innovation also may decrease the liquidity of financial institutions and other businesses and individuals because new financial devices frequently take the place of cash.[3] For example, both bank and nonbank financial institutions during the postwar period have reduced their investments in riskless, highly liquid U.S. government securities and replaced these with a wide variety of higher-yeilding securities issued by businesses and consumers. The result may be to increase the risk of failure on the part of individual institutions. Beyond the level of the individual financial institution, innovation in the financial sector may bring added risk to the entire financial system. The financial difficulties or failure of a single large intermediary or group of intermediaries may send shock waves through the whole system, as happened, for example, when Franklin National Bank of New York collapsed late in 1974. Financial innovation which encourages individual institutions to reduce their liquidity positions in order to increase earnings may increase the likelihood of such failures. Some observers think that the pace of financial innovation is accelerating today and that, partly as a result, investments in the financial markets have become more risky and interest rates and security prices more volatile. There appears to be a trade-off between the benefits of financial innovation, which results in greater competition and more services for the consumer, and the costs of innovation which may include greater risks to the public.

In this chapter we look at some examples of recent financial innovation in the United States. Specifically, we will examine:

1. The movement toward a nationwide system for electronic payments.

---

[2] Ibid., p. 171–72.

[3] Ibid.

2. The development of NOW accounts.
3. The use of variable-rate mortgages in financing purchases of new homes.
4. The spread of bank holding companies into nonbank business ventures.

Each innovation appears to spring from those causes we have just described—competition, high and rising interest rates, financial crises, and the profit motive. The spread of electronic devices for moving funds and speeding payments, for example, seems to be closely related to the desire to reduce the costs associated with handling checks and other paper items and to increase the market share and/or earnings of individual financial institutions. Similarly, variable-rate mortgages have been developed to protect lenders of funds (principally nonbank thrift institutions) against rising interest rates which typically occur in a period of tight credit. Bank holding companies, as indicated in Chapter 7, have developed both because of restrictive legislation against branch banking and also as a device to offer new financial services and thereby compete in new markets. It is notable that large-scale bank holding company diversification into new financial services really began in the tight-money era of the late 1960s. All of the foregoing innovations seem to have implications for the liquidity of individual financial institutions.

ELECTRONIC TRANSFER OF FUNDS

Most services provided by financial institutions require the assembly and analysis of financial information. Among the most important of these services are facilitating payments for goods and services and transferring funds from one account to another—a task which frequently is more economically done by the computer and other automated devices. Automation and the computer have introduced greater efficiency and dispatch in handling financial transactions and lowered the number of potential errors in handling the public's funds. Potentially at least, automation offers the prospect of greater profits for individual financial institutions provided they are able to successfully merge the new technology with established methods.

The pressure to identify new innovations and new technologies is particularly evident today in the field of check processing. The volume of checks written in the United States alone reached an estimated 40 billion in 1980 compared to only 4 billion in 1940, 8 billion in 1953, and 25 billion in 1972. However, the technology used to clear checks has changed comparatively little in recent years. The process is still labor intensive at the level of the individual financial institution, requiring a substantial commitment of employee time, space, and equipment.

A check, of course, is an order to a bank from its customer to pay some other person or institution immediately upon presentation of the check. Until recently, commercial banks had a virtual monopoly in the market for checking account services. No other major financial institution offered an account that could be used to transfer funds on demand to a third party designated by the account holder. Today, as we saw in earlier chapters, mutual savings banks in New England and savings and loan associations and credit unions in several parts of the nation offer accounts with at least limited third-party transfer powers. Moreover, bills have been introduced in the House and Senate in recent years to grant full checking powers to all deposit-type intermediaries throughout the nation. If enacted into law, these proposals presumably would result in a significant expansion in the number of paper items associated with making payments.

As the volume of checks and other cash items has grown during the postwar period, managers of financial institutions and government agencies have been successful in handling the "paper crunch" without the collapse of the payments system. And, while new technologies have been slow in coming, a few new techniques have appeared to facilitate the clearing process. Most notable among these are magnetic ink coding on checks to speed routing and greater standardization of processing equipment. The long-run problem remains, however, and grows daily. At the root of the problem is a fundamental change in the nature of markets for goods and services. Markets have continuously broadened to encompass larger and larger geographic areas, paralleling advances in communications technology and in transportation methods. As a result, payments must be made over greater distances, involving larger and more complicated clearing systems. The potential for significant problems and delays in clearing checks and other cash items has increased.

Electronic transfers of funds (EFTS) through the use of computers is slowly gaining ground in the United States. However, most of the progress to date is at the so-called wholesale level, involving transfers between financial institutions or between a financial institution and a single business firm. For example, a few, relatively large firms today deposit their payrolls directly into the checking accounts of their employees using computer tape. However, the millions of smaller businesses which also must meet regular payrolls generally avoid reliance upon electronic methods to move funds, though this is likely to be less true in future years as the cost of paper transactions continues to climb. At the so-called retail or consumer level, preauthorized withdrawals from checking and savings accounts to pay recurring bills are becoming more popular with the public. However, this device accounts for a relatively minor percentage of consumer payments made each year. Credit cards have replaced checks and currency for certain kinds of purchases, mainly those involving high-priced durable items. But, credit cards also involve the transfer of paper items and there is evidence that consumers who make heavy use of credit cards also make heavy use of their checking accounts.

A major impetus to the adoption of electronic funds transfer techniques is the increasing expense burden of making the payments system work and clearing the millions of checks which pass through it each day. Reliable estimates of the cost of clearing checks have ranged from about $.16 to $.20 per check, though some authorities cite cost figures at least twice that high. If any of these figures is in the right ballpark, the annual cost of clearing and collecting checks in the United States mounts into the billions of dollars. This cost is likely to increase, not only because of increases in the volume of checks, but also due to higher labor and equipment costs. Sheer economic pressures have begun to push the payments system toward greater automation and greater use of computers to transfer funds.

New techniques for handling payments

Responding to cost increases and the growing volume of paper items, several new payments devices are being used or are under development in the United States and in other industrialized nations. These new methods of funds transfer increase both the efficiency and speed of the payments process and should result in lower unit costs of operation. The actual impact on payments costs will be a function of how rapidly new payments innovations are put in place and will depend upon the role competition is permitted to play. Probably the most rapidly developing and, thus far, most successful payments innovation is the *automated clearinghouse* (ACH), designed to electronically transfer data from one financial institution to another. By means of computer tape and transfers by wire, deposits and other financial data may be moved from the accounts of one intermediary to another nearly instantaneously. Thirty-three ACHs already are in place in various parts of the United States. The ACHs are all part of the National Automated Clearinghouse Association (NACHA) which now also includes more than 50 major nonbank corporations across the nation. Savings and loan associations, mutual savings banks, and credit unions are strongly pushing for access to ACHs in regional locations throughout the United States and have gained access to some. Soon, most regions of the United States will have the option of using ACHs or remaining with the old system of funds transfers.

Some day in the not-too-distant future an ACH network will span the continent.

A second important EFT system in use today is the *automated teller machine* (ATM) which will pay customers cash upon presentation of proper identification and also accept deposits. These so-called money machines link the customer with a bank or nonbank thrift institution electronically. ATMs perform some of the financial services available through branch offices but at lower cost. However, the customer normally cannot communicate with more than one financial institution through an ATM. The absence of this transfer capability differentiates ATMs from ACHs which, as we have seen, link several different financial institutions in an electronic network. A key issue affecting the future growth of ATMs is their legal status. Specifically, is an ATM a branch office or merely a limited-service remote facility? As we saw in Chapter 7, the majority of states restrict or prohibit branch banking and branching across state lines violates current federal law. If ATMs are held by the courts to be branch offices then their spread will be limited by current state and federal laws. While the branching question is still being debated in the courts, various consumer groups and federal agencies have urged that ATMs be exempted from branching restrictions.

ATMs, unlike ACHs, are links between the public and financial institutions offering payments services. Another such link is the *point-of sale terminal* (POS), typically housed in retail stores and shopping malls. Activated by plastic card or electronic code, POS terminals permit the customer to pay for goods and services by instantly moving funds from the customer's payments account to a merchant's account via computer. One unfortunate consequence is that the consumer loses the advantage of float—that is, the ability to delay making payments until a check is cleared. As a partial offset, however, the new service is more convenient with considerably less paperwork.

Competitive issues in the spread of EFTS

The spread of EFTS has raised a number of important issues of public policy. One critical question revolves around the ownership of the equipment. Should EFTS equipment be publicly owned? Should it be jointly owned by all participating financial institutions? Or, should individual institutions be allowed to establish competing systems? There is also the issue of *privacy*—the right of consumers to control access to information concerning their personal financial affairs. EFTS presumably would make such information more readily available to anyone with access to computerized files. Added to these issues is the question of *right of access* to electronic payments systems. Which institutions should be allowed to use ACH facilities? Commercial banks only? Nonbank thrifts offering payments services? And, related to that issue, who ought to be responsible for updating EFT equipment and maintaining it?

Among the foregoing issues and questions the problem of *competition* appears to dominate today. It is not clear whether the public would be served better by permitting competition among financial institutions in the development of electronic funds transfer systems or whether these systems are really in the nature of public utilities. In the latter instance, there would be one or only a few systems serving a given area and duplication of facilities would be minimal or nonexistent. Competing systems probably would result in the greatest benefits for the consumer, reducing prices and resulting in a more efficient allocation of available resources. In contrast, if EFTS is treated as a public utility so that only one system is available for public use in a given area, there may be little pressure for innovation and change. The prices of EFT services may exceed competitive levels.

However, if competition in the development of EFTS facilities is encouraged, what will happen to smaller intermediaries who may not be able to afford their own EFT facility? These institutions will undoubtedly be forced to compete more intensively on a service level, offering a better quality and more personalized product to the public as a substitute for convenience and speed in carrying out financial transactions. Some smaller financial institutions undoubtedly will band together to combine available capital and spread the overhead costs of EFTS equipment. Finally, the correspondent banking system probably will be forced to play a more significant role in channeling EFTS services from larger intermediaries to smaller ones much as larger commercial banks today provide portfolio, tax management, and data processing services for smaller banks.

The issue of financial reform discussed in the previous chapter has a direct bearing on EFTS. Credit unions, savings and loan associations, and mutual savings banks, as we saw in earlier chapters, are rapidly developing third-party payments services. They see these services in an EFTS-oriented economy as vital to their own survival. Those financial intermediaries that are part of electronic systems for moving funds will have a clear and definite advantage in attracting deposits from the public. Credit unions and savings banks in some parts of the nation already have gained access to ACHs, either directly or indirectly through a commercial bank. Once the nonbank thrifts become firmly entrenched within the developing EFTS network, competition between bank and nonbank intermediaries will intensify and extend beyond the offering of payments services. Customers once attracted to an intermediary because of its EFT facilities will probably make use of other services (such as instalment loans, savings deposits, and credit cards) offered by the same institution. Of course, all this presupposes that major financial reforms will take place in the near future, permitting bank and nonbank financial institutions to compete more freely with each other across a broad range of services demanded by the public.

Most experts agree that the pricing of financial services will assume greater importance once EFTS becomes commonplace. Funds transfer services will tend to become standardized so that price will become the key factor in differentiating one institution's services from those of another. Price competition, frequently stifled by regulation in the past, may become a potent force, allowing the customer to make direct comparisons among competing systems and, hopefully in the long run, leading to a more efficient allocation of resources. Moreover, distances will shrink as markets for financial services become broader and broader. Local financial institutions wll find themselves in direct, head-to-head competition with more remote financial institutions. The overall level of competition for payments services (and indirectly for most financial services) will rise, hopefully bringing the consumer greater convenience, efficiency, and speed.

NOW ACCOUNTS

The spread of electronic banking will, as we have seen, create a number of economic, legal, and financial problems, not the least of which will be the necessity to more accurately price payments services and to decide which financial intermediaries should be admitted into the payments system. These problems were further complicated in the early 1970s by the sudden appearance of mutual savings banks, savings and loan associations, and credit unions in a field heretofore reserved exclusively for commercial banks—the making of third-party payments, evidenced usually by a check or draft. The most widely known of these new payments devices is the so-called NOW account or negotiable order of withdrawal. NOWs are similar to checking accounts but with two important differences: (1) interest is paid on the average balance in the account; and (2) a NOW is not technically a demand instrument, since payment may be delayed for 30 to 90 days. (This privilege is rarely exercised however.)

The NOW account is among the most important financial innovations of recent years. It brings all depository institutions which choose to offer the service into direct competition with one another and with commercial bank checking accounts, adding significantly to the consumer's range of alternatives in deciding where to keep transactions balances. The NOW is likely to improve the efficiency of the payments process by providing for more explicit pricing of payments services. And, while there have been many innovations in commercial and savings banking in recent years, most have been of relatively meager benefit to consumers. The NOW account, in contrast, is designed specifically to benefit the consumer by combining the essential features of checking accounts and small savings deposits.

NOWs began in Massachusetts in 1970.[4] Consumer Savings Bank of Worcester submitted a plan to the Massachusetts State Banking Commission to begin offering the service. When the commission denied Consumer's request, the savings bank filed suit on grounds that, while such accounts might be denied to commercial banks under federal law, they should not be prohibited to a state-chartered savings bank operating exclusively under Massachusetts law. The Massachusetts Supreme Court agreed in 1972 and Consumer's began offering the new service. Recognizing that New Hampshire law regarding savings banking was nearly identical to that of Massachusetts, the New Hampshire Savings Bank of Concord began offering NOW accounts in September 1972. Soon state-chartered savings banks throughout Massachusetts and New Hampshire were offering NOWs.

Fearful that NOWs might spread nationwide through the action of the state legislatures, local regulatory bodies, and the courts, Congress responded in August 1973 by passing Public Law 93-100 which prohibited NOWs in all states *except* Massachusetts and New Hampshire. These two states were to serve as a "laboratory" for NOWs before the service was permitted in other states.[5] Later, in March 1976, Congress extended authority to issue NOWs to all six New England states—Connecticut, Maine, Massachusetts, New Hampshire, Rhode Island, and Vermont. And, in order to preserve competitive equality for credit unions, share draft powers were extended to all federally chartered credit unions in the nation, subject to approval of the National Credit Union Administration. As we saw in Chapter 13, share drafts are essentially checking accounts which may carry an interest rate (or dividend yield) up to 7 percent.

---

[4] For a discussion of the history and probable effects of NOWs on the behavior of consumers and offering financial institutions, see Rose [14].

[5] It is not surprising that NOWs began in the New England area. In Massachusetts, New Hampshire, and Connecticut total deposits in mutual savings banks are greater than total commercial bank deposits. Nonbank thrift institutions in New England hold nearly 60 percent of all deposits compared to only about 30 percent nationwide. Also, more than 90 percent of the mutual savings banks in Massachusetts are state, rather than federally, regulated and, therefore, do not need federal approval to develop new services.

Proponents of the NOW account contend that it offers several significant advantages for the consumer. First, NOWs are convenient, avoiding the need for two-stop banking—that is, the necessity of having to hold a checking account at a commercial bank and a savings account at a nonbank thrift institution which, legally, can pay slightly higher interest rates than commercial banks. With NOWs both savings and transactions balances can be held at the same institution, perhaps in the same account, reducing the need to transfer funds. Second, NOWs are more "economically efficient" since the consumer is able to combine savings and transactions balances into one account without foregoing interest. Recent research suggests that customers who hold account balances of about $500 to $2,000 and confine their transactions to no more than 10 cash items per month probably would benefit the most from NOWs. Those who hold larger average balances presumably would be better off investing some portion of their account balances in CDs or other higher-yielding savings instruments.

Finally, NOWs appear to be contributing to a significant increase in competition among the deposit-type institutions offering the service. As we noted earlier, NOWs end the virtual monopoly commercial banks have had over the payments process throughout most of the nation's history. Other things equal, NOWs are likely to reduce the excessive allocation of resources toward the payments process which has occurred because commercial banks have been forbidden since 1933 to pay interest on checking accounts. The rapid growth of commercial and savings bank branch offices which has occurred since World War II has been aimed principally to induce the public to hold its accounts with the neighborhood financial institution, even if it means foregoing some rate of return. Until recently, many banks and nonbank thrifts conducted "give away" programs, offering home appliances, food, plants, and trading stamps to induce the customer to open up a new account or add money to an existing account. Such programs increased the customer's *implicit* rate of return from a checking or savings deposit, though no explicit rate of return could be paid in the case of checking accounts and the yield on savings accounts was held below competitive levels because of regulatory ceilings. NOWs increase the explicit return on checking account balances and possibly may slow the rapid growth in branch offices operated by depository institutions.

Critics of NOW accounts cite a number of potential disadvantages from the service. First, the customer may be forced to pay higher loan rates or higher service charges to offset the additional cost of loanable funds raised through NOWs. Since a bank or other intermediary offering NOWs pays interest on transactions balances, this added cost will have to be passed on to the borrower in the form of higher costs for credit. Moreover, the higher cost of NOWs may force financial institutions to reach for higher-yielding loans and investments in order to protect their earnings. This would have several possible adverse effects. First, the supply of funds to the mortgage market could be reduced as savings banks and savings and loan associations attempt to secure higher yields by switching out of mortgages into other investments with a greater rate of return. Thus, the nation's housing goals might be seriously jeopardized. Moreover, the attempt by deposit-type financial intermediaries to reach for higher-yielding loans and investments will expose them to added risk, perhaps reducing public confidence in the banking and financial system. This risk of greater financial instability is likely to be intensified by competitive pressures on individual intermediaries to pay higher and higher rates on NOWs in order to retain their market shares.

Many of the anticipated effects of NOWs are probably short run in nature, while others are likely to be long lasting. For example, as NOWs penetrate new market areas, there will be a period of transition for local financial institutions as they adjust to the new service. During this time commercial and savings bank earnings probably will drop somewhat, costs per deposit dollar are likely to rise, and the growth of assets and deposits at a number of institutions will slow as funds are bid away by more aggressively managed intermediaries. Most of these effects are likely to disappear, once the transition period ends and equilibrium conditions return to the market for loanable funds.

Many analysts argue that the introduction of NOWs also will bring about some permanent changes. For example, NOWs are probably the forerunner of outright interest payments on demand deposits which would blur the distinction between savings and transactions balances. This, in turn, would complicate the conduct of monetary policy since it would alter the character of the nation's money supply and change the behavior of funds flows in response to interest rate fluctuations and other factors. Also, NOWs may lead to significant changes in the composition of assets and liabilities held by thrift institutions. This will occur not only because of the added cost of NOWs and the resulting pressure on earnings, but also because NOWs tend to be longer-term, more interest-sensitive deposits than those normally held for transactions purposes. Finally, as we noted above, NOWs may adversely affect the mortgage market and the pursuit of the nation's housing goals by causing thrifts to alter the mix of their assets away from mortgages in search of higher yields elsewhere.

Research evidence on the impact of NOWs is extremely limited thus far. There is some evidence that NOWs initially resulted in a runoff of private deposits at commercial banks in Massachusetts and New Hampshire equal to about 3 percent of their total deposits. Moreover, one study found that commercial bank earnings in these two states fell about 3 percent in 1974 and by more than twice that percentage in 1975—the first two years the service was authorized under federal law.[6] It is very difficult, however, to determine what proportion of the decline in earnings was due exclusively to NOWs and what was due to other factors.

Whatever the problems of individual financial institutions offering the service, the number of NOW accounts and the total volume of dollars held in NOWs all have risen sharply since the federal government first authorized the service for New England banks. For example, at year-end 1972, NOW balances in the New England states totaled $45.3 million; by May 1978, there were nearly $3.2 billion outstanding held in 1.9 million different accounts. More than 730 New England financial institutions offered the service in the spring of 1978 compared to only 59 at year-end 1972 and 430 at year-end 1975.[7] Substantial future growth of NOW accounts is expected for the New England area. Moreover, the Carter administration has proposed the extension of NOWs to bank and nonbank thrift institutions nationwide. The outlook for passage of such a bill is uncertain at this time, due to the opposition of a number of important lobby groups.

VARIABLE RATE MORTGAGES

The largest segment of the nation's capital market is clearly the *mortgage market,* or market for financial claims against real estate. In September 1978 total mortgage debt outstanding in the United States exceeded $1.1 trillion. By way of comparison the total gross public debt of the federal government at year-end 1978 was $789 billion. It has been estimated that new mortgages written each year absorb approximately one third of all U.S. savings flows. A mortgage, of course, is a lien against the liquidating value of real property and depends for its ultimate value on the market value of the property mortgaged. Most mortgages written (about 60 percent) are used to finance residential properties (i.e., one-to four-family dwellings), followed distantly in total dollar value by commercial, multifamily, and

---

[6] See especially Paulus [12]. Other studies of the effects of NOW accounts on individual financial institutions include Basch [2], Kimball [6] and [7], and Longbrake and Cohen [9].

[7] The data cited here is derived from monthly releases prepared by the Statistical Section, Research Department, Federal Reserve Bank of Boston.

farm mortgages.[8] Approximately three fourths of all mortgages are conventional (or exclusively private) contracts with the remainder insured or guaranteed by agencies (FHA or VA) of the federal government.[9]

As we have seen in earlier chapters, savings and loan associations, mutual savings banks, insurance companies, and commercial banks are all important financial intermediaries in the market for mortgages. Each institution tends to specialize in one portion of the market—conventional or guaranteed, commercial or residential, and so on. Since the 1930s the federal government has been a pervasive influence in this market in order to improve both the quality and liquidity of the mortgage instrument. Mortgages vary greatly in quality, maturity, and size. Moreover, there is considerable diversity among the various states in foreclosure laws, interest rate ceilings, and tax laws applying to real property.

Another serious problem with this market is its great sensitivity to cyclical changes, reflecting both the nature of the mortgage instrument and also fluctuations in the construction industry. In many ways the mortgage market is a "boom and bust" affair. When credit availability tightens up and interest rates rise, commercial banks, mutual savings banks, and savings and loan associations lose their more interest-sensitive deposits (i.e., financial disintermediation occurs) and are forced to cut back on their mortgage commitments to would-be borrowers.[10] At the same time the flow of funds into the market for government-guaranteed mortgages (FHA and VA) tends to dry up because of interest rate ceilings imposed by law. Moreover, because the mortgage is a long-term loan, even small increases in market interest rates lead to substantial changes in total interest costs. Monthly payments on new home mortgages, for example, rise sharply in periods of escalating interest rates, and the demand for new homes is seriously depressed. In contrast, when credit is relatively easy and interest rates are falling, the mortgage market typi-

---

[8] By the third quarter of 1978 mortgages on one- to four-family properties totaled $727.1 billion; commercial mortgages, $208.0 billion; mortgages on multifamily dwellings, $119.4 billion; and farm mortgages, $73.9 billion out of a total of $1.1 trillion for all U.S. mortgages. (*Federal Reserve Bulletin*, January 1979, p. A-41.)

[9] See especially Robinson and Wrightsman [13].

[10] This is particularly serious since commercial banks, mutual savings banks, and savings and loan associations are critically important to the mortgage market, especially in the field of residential mortgages. In the third quarter of 1978, for example, commercial banks held $202.4 billion in mortgages, $119.3 billion of which were residential (one to four family); savings and loans, $420.9 billion in total mortgages with $343.1 billion residential in nature; and mutual savings banks, $93.5 billion in mortgages of which $61.2 billion were devoted to family dwellings.

cally is buoyant. Mortgage lending institutions have ample funds to lend and the demand for new homes improves with the lower interest costs and monthly payments.

The boom and bust character of this market has had profound effects upon the earnings and liquidity of financial intermediaries, especially savings and loan associations, the majority of whose assets are home mortgages. In periods of tight credit and rising interest rates, savings banks lose deposits, cut back on loans, and typically suffer losses in earnings. During periods of easier credit conditions, on the other hand, interest rates fall, loans rise, and savings-bank earnings improve. For example, the late 1960s and early 1970s brought long periods of interest rate increases, threatening the earnings, liquidity, and solvency of many thrift institutions. In response to these conditions, the industry has pressured Congress and the regulatory agencies for revisions in law and regulation to alleviate the problem. One of the most sought-after revisions is permission to make liberal use of so-called *variable-rate mortgages* (VRMs).

What are VRMs? The VRM is a conventional long-term mortgage loan contract which carries an effective interest rate that changes periodically in sympathy with other market rates of interest. Contrary to conventional fixed-rate mortgages (FRMs), then, neither the mortgagor nor the mortgagee know the average rate that will be generated over the life of a variable-rate mortgage at the time the loan is made. Some savings banks, commercial banks, and insurance companies have been using variable-rate instruments for a considerable period of time, particularly in the New England region and in California.[11]

There are several varieties of VRMS in use. The most popular is probably the demand note. A demand note is simply a loan, secured or unsecured, whose principle is payable at the end of a specified period. The maturity of the demand note is usually much shorter than that of the typical mortgage—5 to 10 years instead of 20 to 30 years. Many commercial mortgages are made in the form of demand notes. For home mortgage financing, the demand note is not particularly popular with consumers. Few families can afford to pay off a mortgage loan with a maturity of only five or ten years and must refinance their loans, which entails some risk. Moreover, this instrument leaves the power to change the interest rate purely in the hands of the lender.[12]

---

[11] As of mid-1978 California led the nation with an estimated $11 billion in outstanding debt under variable-rate mortgage plans. Most of these were issued after April 1975 when state-chartered S&Ls were first permitted to offer the service.

[12] The debate over the advantages and disadvantages of VRMs has spawned a number of alternative mortgage plans. One of the most popular is the so-called *graduated*

Another fairly common type of variable-rate mortgage ties the effective interest rate on the loan to an adjustable index, usually a rate frequently quoted in the open market. Examples include the prime bank lending rate, the rate on medium-term U.S. Treasury bonds, the AAA corporate bond rate, or a weighted average rate that savings and loans must pay to borrow funds. Unfortunately, not all of these rates accurately reflect conditions in the nation's mortgage market. A more severe limitation is that mortgage rates, tied to interest rates in the open market, may change so frequently as to wreak havoc with family budgets. If home mortgage rates changed every month, for example, a homeowner would be hard pressed to plan each month's housing expenses with any assurance. Moreover, if rates rose high enough, the homeowner might be forced to sell due to excessive monthly payments. Another variety of VRM is the income-participation loan (sometimes called an "equity kicker") which is common in insurance company mortgages on commercial projects. This is not widely used today by banks and thrift institutions, though a few large mutual savings banks use them for income property (such as apartments or commercial buildings) where equity participation by the lender is desired.

VRMs can work in several different ways. The maturity of the mortgage instrument can be varied as interest rates change while holding the amount of instalment payments constant. Thus, if interest rates rise high enough, a 25-year mortgage might be extended by the lender to a 26-year loan or to even longer maturities. Falling rates, conversely, would lead to a shortening of the mortgage's maturity. An alternative approach is to vary the amount of monthly payments while holding the maturity of the mortgage instrument constant. Higher interest rates, for example, result in higher monthly instalment payments. A third approach would combine these two basic methods.[13]

There are several potential advantages to the *lender* from the use of VRMs. They provide the lender protection against rising interest rates, enabling the intermediary to more adequately adjust its earnings to offset higher costs (principally rates on deposits). Moreover, VRMs grant lenders greater ability to compete for savings in the form of thrift deposits and reduce the risk of illiquidity since VRMs permit

---

payment mortgage, designed to aid younger families in the financing of a new home. Monthly payments start out low and gradually increase over a five- to ten-year period before leveling out. Typically, the interest rate is higher under such a plan than with either VRMs or FRMs and the down payment may be slightly larger.

[13] A large volume of literature has appeared in recent years discussing the variety of VRM plans and their relative advantages and disadvantages. See, for example, Krupnick [8], Candilis [3], Anderson and Hinson [1], Osborn [11], Gambs [4], and Kaufman [5].

revenues to expand as market interest rates rise. Finally, VRMs shift the risks associated with future changes in interest rates from the lender to the borrower, reducing the risk of insolvency for individual financial institutions.

There are some potential disadvantages to lenders of funds from VRMs. If instalment payments are varied and the maturity of mortgage loans held constant, this might lead to cyclical swings in deposits since mortgage borrowers frequently hold deposits with the lending institution. Some forms of VRMs may violate the letter as well as the spirit of truth-in-lending laws and certainly result in more complex, less easily understood mortgage contracts. Finally, weak lenders could be harmed by strong lenders—that is, strong lenders with VRMs would be able to outbid smaller competitors for the public's deposits.

While the principal advantages appear to lie with the lender using VRMS, there are also some advantages for the *borrower* from their use. For example, if high interest rates prevail at the time a new mortgage is created, the borrower is "locked in" under a FRM if rates subsequently fall, but benefits under a VRM loan. Moreover, mortgage money is likely to be more readily available during tight-money periods with VRMs rather than with FRMs. But, the borrower also must shoulder some significant disadvantages from VRMs, especially the fact that the risk of interest rate fluctuations is passed (completely or partially) to the borrower from the lender of mortgage funds. If interest rates rise rapidly and high rates persist for relatively long periods, unmanageable instalment payments or unacceptable long maturities on mortgages or a combination of both may plague borrowers. In addition, if a borrower lives on a fixed income, a sharp decline in the borrower's real income may result when interest rates rise. Finally, VRMs increase the complexity of the mortgage contract and may make it more difficult for borrowers to fully comprehend their rights and obligations.

VRMs provide borrowers and lenders with a new financial instrument to deal with fluctuations in future interest rates.[14] If the long-term revenues of savings and loan associations and other mortgage lenders can be made more flexible with respect to deposit interest rate costs, these institutions will be able to offer competitive rates on thrift deposits and continue to attract funds from savers, even in

---

[14] The indexation of financial instruments to adjust to changes in economic and financial conditions is not unique to the mortgage market. For example, the federal regulatory agencies recently authorized a variable-rate money market certificate for banks whose rate is tied to the coupon equivalent of the yield on U.S. Treasury bills. However, the minimum-size deposit required is $10,000 and there is an interest penalty for early withdrawal. Nevertheless, these money market CDs have helped to stem outflows of deposits when interest rates in the open market rise to very high levels.

tight-money periods. The availability of mortgage funds should increase and the total supply of funds in the mortgage market should be more stable over the course of the business cycle. On the other hand, there is some danger of a decrease in borrower demand for mortgage funds if VRMs become widespread, because some borrowers will not be willing to accept the greater risks associated with the instrument. There is also the danger of mortgage borrowers putting pressure on governments to prevent mortgage rate increases if interest rates rise appreciably, thus eliminating any potential gains from the use of VRMs.

The legal status of VRMs is in a state of flux. By mid-1978 state-chartered financial institutions in 16 states were offering variable rate mortgages. In other states, local laws and regulations present barriers to the development of the new service. As this book was being written, federally chartered thrift institutions were prohibited from offering VRMs, except in California. However, in July 1978 the Federal Home Loan Bank Board (FHLBB) issued for public comment proposed regulations opening up VRMs and other new types of mortgages to federally chartered savings and loans.[15] Recently congressional hearings have been held concerning the merits of VRMs and other new mortgage plans.

As we have tried to show in earlier chapters, many financial intermediaries—especially commercial banks, mutual savings banks, savings and loan associations, and credit unions—face a special problem. They borrow relatively short-term funds (i.e., their liabilities turn over rapidly), but many of the loans they make are long term (i.e., their assets in many cases turn over slowly). Financial innovations such as the VRM offer the potential for bridging the gap between the rapidly rising expenses and slow-growing revenues of these institutions especially in periods of high and rising interest rates.

BANK HOLDING COMPANIES AND THE NONBANK ACTIVITIES OF COMMERCIAL BANKS

As we saw in Chapter 7, a commercial bank can become a holding company by setting up a corporation which holds the stock of the bank. Once formed, the holding company may acquire other subsidiary bank and nonbank corporations if approved by the Federal Reserve Board in Washington, D.C. According to the 1970 amendments to the Bank Holding Company Act, the Board of Governors of

---

[15] Under the FHLBB plan rates on a variable mortgage could rise up to 0.5 of a percentage point in a single year and up to a maximum of 2.5 percentage points during the term of the mortgage. No more than half of the mortgages written by a savings and loan association in a year could carry variable rates however.

the Federal Reserve System may permit bank holding companies to acquire only those nonbank businesses which are classified as "closely related to banking."

As we noted earlier, the growth of bank holding companies has been exceedingly rapid due, in part, to rising costs, restrictions against branch banking, and the desire of banking organizations to take advantage of economies of size. Bank holding companies seek to diversify into nonbank lines of business in order to improve their earnings, reduce risk, and open up new markets. Federal and state restrictions on bank assets, prices, and expansion through branch banking and mergers also have spurred the movement toward non-banking activities. Nonbank subsidiaries of a holding company may engage in activities prohibited to commercial banks and also cross state lines with their offices, something commercial banks are not permitted to do. Through their nonbank subsidiaries holding companies can more fully utilize managerial resources and achieve cost economies from centralized purchasing, investment management, data processing, and other functions which can be coordinated among the company's various divisions.

What nonbank activities have bank holding companies tended to emphasize? Insurance agencies, finance companies, mortgage banking houses, and leasing companies have been the most common nonbank businesses acquired or started *de novo*. According to Section 4(c)(8) of the Bank Holding Company Act, the Federal Reserve Board may allow commercial banks to venture into those activities "so closely related to banking . . . as to be a proper incident thereto." The board must consider whether the acquisition of nonbanking business ventures by bank holding companies can "reasonably be expected to produce benefits to the public . . . that outweigh possible adverse effects."[16] These two requirements are frequently referred to as the "closely related" test and the "public benefits" test. Nonbank acquisitions must yield net benefits to the public in the form of greater convenience, stronger competition, enhanced efficiency, or other benefits. The board may even approve a holding company acquisition which would reduce competition if potential public benefits would result which override any loss of competition.[17]

The provisions of the 1970 amendments to the Bank Holding Company Act were extremely vague. This is especially true of the sections dealing with permissible nonbanking activities. Congress debated the possibility of spelling out in detail (through a so-called laundry list) the kinds of business activities open to bank holding companies. In

---

[16] See Section 4(c)(8), BHCA (70 Stat. 133).

[17] See, in particular, Rose and Fraser [15].

the end, it left that task to the Federal Reserve to accomplish through regulation. This approach gave the Fed great latitude and flexibility, but has resulted in substantial uncertainty about the future expansion of the banking business. The general goals of the law are clear — greater competition within the financial sector and improved efficiency in the use of financial resources — but translating these general objectives into specific permissible business activities has proved to be a formidable task, occupying great amounts of Federal Reserve resources to regulate and supervise holding company activities.

In the spring of 1971 the Federal Reserve Board issued a list of seven permissible nonbanking activities for bank holding companies. These were:

1. Making or acquiring, for its own account or for the account of others, loans and other extensions of credit such as would be made, for example, by a mortgage, finance, credit card, or factoring company.
2. Operating as an industrial bank, Morris Plan bank, or industrial loan company, in the manner authorized by state law so long as the institution does not both accept demand deposits and make commercial loans.
3. Servicing loans and other extensions of credit for any person.
4. Performing or carrying on any one or more of the functions or activities that may be performed or carried on by a trust company (including activities of a fiduciary, agency, or custodian nature), in the manner authorized by state law so long as the institution does not both accept demand deposits and make commercial loans.
5. Acting as investment or financial advisor, including (i) serving as an advisory company for a mortgage or a real estate investment trust and (ii) furnishing economic or financial information.
6. Leasing personal property and equipment, or acting as agent, broker, or advisor in the leasing of such property, where at the inception of the initial lease the expectation is that the effect of the transaction and reasonably anticipated future transactions with the same lessee as to the same property will be to compensate the lessor for not less than the lessor's full investment in the property.
7. Making equity and debt investments in corporations or projects designed primarily to promote community welfare, such as the economic rehabilitation and development of low-income areas.

Approximately two months later the Fed included another new nonbanking activity — bookkeeping and data processing services — on the list of approved activities. Specifically, a bank holding company was allowed to acquire or start *de novo* companies involved in:

(i) providing bookkeeping and data processing services for the internal operations of the holding company and its subsidiaries; and,

      (ii)   storing and processing other banking, financial or related economic data, such as performing payroll, accounts receivable or payable, or billing services.

This addition permits a holding company to process financial data for itself and its customers.

Also in 1971, the board agreed to let bank holding companies act:

as insurance agent or broker in offices at which the holding company or its subsidiaries are otherwise engaged in business (or in an office adjacent thereto) with respect to the following types of insurance:

      (i)   any insurance for the holding company and its subsidiaries;

     (ii)   any insurance that (a) is directly related to an extension of credit by a bank or bank-related firm of the kind described in this regulation, or (b) is directly related to the provision of other financial services by a bank or bank-related firm, or (c) is otherwise sold as a matter of convenience to the purchaser, so long as the premium income from sales within this subclause, or (d) does not constitute a significant portion of the aggregate insurance premium income of the holding company from insurance sold pursuant to this clause (ii); and,

   (iii)   any insurance sold in a community that (a) has a population not exceeding 5,000 or (b) the holding company demonstrates has inadequate insurance agency facilitates.

From time to time the Federal Reserve Board has considered adding other nonbanking business activities to the approved list. Included among these are:

1. Insurance premium funding, or the combined sale of mutual funds and insurance.
2. Underwriting general life insurance.
3. Real estate syndication.
4. Land development.
5. Management consulting.
6. Property management.
7. Operating a savings and loan association.
8. Real estate brokerage.
9. Underwriting credit life, credit accident, and health insurance.
10. Leasing real property.
11. Armored car and courier services.

Initially, the board decided that only the underwriting of credit life, credit accident, and health insurance should be granted to holding companies. However, the Fed insisted that insurance underwriting activities be limited to those "directly related to extension of credit by bank holding company systems."[18] In applying for permission to engage in insurance underwriting, holding companies must demonstrate that positive benefits (such as lower insurance rates or more liberal benefits) would accrue to consumers in the relevant market area served.

About two years later in the fall of 1973 courier services for banking and financial documents were added to the list of permitted nonbank activities, but the Federal Reserve Board declined to allow holding companies to offer armored car services. A far more important addition took place in 1974, when the leasing of real property was approved. The board insisted that any lease agreements made be "the functional equivalent of a loan, whereby, the leasing company recovers its full investment in the property during the initial term of the lease."[19] Real property leases were limited to a term of no more than 40 years. Moreover, holding companies were not permitted to "stock" equipment in anticipation of future customer requests.

From time to time the board adds new activities to the permissible list of nonbank businesses open to U.S. bank holding companies. For example, in 1976, the Fed affirmed that the leasing of automobiles was an approved holding company activity, equivalent to bank lending, despite opposition by the National Automobile Dealers Association. Similarly, in February 1977, the board announced that holding companies would be permitted to sell money orders, traveler's checks, and U.S. savings bonds to the public through their nonbank offices. However, a maximum value of $1,000 was set for sales of money orders, while sales of variable-denominated financial instruments and financial management courses were not approved for holding companies.

Still, it is not at all clear in what direction commercial banks through their holding companies will be permitted to move in future years. Much will depend upon the changing makeup of the Federal Reserve Board and the relative attractiveness of various nonbanking fields. Certainly the banking industry itself will change markedly in the years ahead, offering new financial services and penetrating new markets. The spark of financial innovation which created the bank holding company inevitably will lead to new organizational forms with the power to offer new kinds of services demanded by the public. If the Federal Reserve unduly restricts holding company expansion into nonbanking fields, new methods of banking growth undoubtedly will be found. And, consistent with past history, new regulations will

---

[18] Board of Governors of the Federal Reserve System, press release, December 11, 1972.

[19] Board of Governors of the Federal Reserve System, press release, March 20, 1974.

be needed after a fashion to safeguard the public interest and to ensure the stability of the financial system.

CONCLUDING COMMENTS

In the foregoing sections we have traced the development of some new financial techniques designed to deal with modern financial problems. Innovation in new products and services is one of the hallmarks of a free-market economy since innovation offers the possibility of increased profits and a larger share of the available market. Innovation also involves risk, however, since entrepreneurs can miscalculate the needs and interests of their customers. Not all innovations succeed and many are only modestly rewarding to those willing. to assume the risks.

Indeed, in few other fields of endeavor are the dangers of miscalculation potentially more disastrous than in the financial markets. Stockholders or depositors in a new venture that does not succeed can lose a lifetime of savings. Financial institutions which misappropriate their funds can threaten the financial stability of an entire community and send shock waves throughout the financial system. As in so many other aspects of economic life, there is a trade-off between the benefits of financial innovation and its costs. There must be latitude for financial innovation, but limits also must be imposed for public safety. Public policy in the field of financial regulation must constantly seek a middle ground between competition and safety. Financial innovation in future years, as in the past, must be tempered by public responsibility.

QUESTIONS

21–1. Differentiate between legislative and evolutionary innovations in the financial field. What are the most important causes of each?

21–2. What are the principal reasons an electronic funds transfer system is needed in the United States? What would be the major advantages to the consumer of switching to such a system? major disadvantages?

21–3. Define the following terms:
a. Automated clearinghouses.
b. Automated teller machines.
c. Point-of-sale terminals.
Which ones reach the consumer directly?

21–4. How might electronic funds transfer systems be compared to public utilities? Would the public be better served by permitting competition among financial institutions in developing electronic funds transfer systems? If so, what problems might arise?

21–5. What are NOW accounts? List their potential advantages and disadvantages to the consumer of financial services. What are the probable short-run and long-run effects of NOWs upon the earnings and growth of deposit-type financial intermediaries?

21–6. What is a variable-rate mortgage? What are the possible advantages of a variable-rate mortgage from the viewpoint of the lender and from the viewpoint of the borrower? disadvantages?

21–7. What restrictions are placed upon bank holding companies with regard to nonbanking activities? What are the acceptable nonbanking activities?

21–8. Why have bank holding companies moved into nonbank business activities? What risks are there in this innovation for individual banks? for the public?

REFERENCES

1. Anderson, Paul S., and Hinson, J. Philip. "Variable Rates on Mortgages: Their Impact and Use." *New England Economic Review*, Federal Reserve Bank of Boston, March–April 1970, pp. 3–20.

2. Basch, Donald. "The Diffusion of NOW Accounts in Massachusetts." *New England Economic Review*, Federal Reserve Bank of Boston, November–December 1976, pp. 20–30.

3. Candilis, Wray O. *Variable Rate Mortgage Plans.* Research paper no. 7, Department of Economic Research, American Bankers Association, 1971.

4. Gambs, Carl M. "Variable-Rate Mortgages—Their Potential in the United States." *Journal of Money, Credit, and Banking.* vol. 7, no. 2 (May 1975), pp. 245–51.

5. Kaufman, George G. "The Questionable Benefit of Variable Rate Mortgages." *Quarterly Review of Economics and Business*, Fall 1973, pp. 43–52.

6. Kimball, Ralph C. "Recent Developments in the NOW Account Experiment in New England." *New England Economic Review*, Federal Reserve Bank of Boston, November–December 1976, pp. 3–19.

7. ———. "Impacts of NOW Accounts and Thrift Institution Competition on Selected Small Commercial Banks in Massachusetts and New

Hampshire, 1974–75." *New England Economic Review,* Federal Reserve Bank of Boston, January–February 1977, pp. 22–28.

8. Krupnick, Alan J. "Variable-Rate Mortgages: Boon or Bane?" *Business Review,* Federal Reserve Bank of Philadelphia, September 1972, pp. 16–23.

9. Longbrake, William A., and Cohen, Sandra B. *The NOW Account Experiment.* Federal Deposit Insurance Corporation, working paper no. 74–9, 1974.

10. Minsky, Hyman P. "Central Banking and Money Market Changes." *Quarterly Journal of Economics,* vol. 71, no. 2 (May 1957), pp. 171–87.

11. Osborn, F. M. "Varying the Interest Rate on a Mortgage Contract— How It Works in Britain." *Journal of the Federal Home Loan Bank Board,* April 1970, pp. 17–18, 24–25.

12. Paulus, John D. *Effects of NOW Accounts on Costs and Earnings of Commercial Banks 1974–75.* Board of Governors of the Federal Reserve System, staff study no. 88, 1976.

13. Robinson, Roland I., and Wrightsman, Dwayne. *Financial Markets: The Accumulation and Allocation of Wealth.* New York: McGraw-Hill Book Co., 1974.

14. Rose, Peter S. "The NOW Row." *Canadian Banker and ICB Review,* vol. 85, no. 4 (July–August 1978), pp. 68–71.

15. Rose, Peter S., and Fraser, Donald R. "Bank Holding Company Diversification into Mortgage Banking and Finance Companies." *Banking Law Journal,* vol. 91, no. 10 (November–December 1975), pp. 976–94.

16. Smaistrla, Charles F. "Electronic Funds Transfer and Monetary Policy." *Business Review,* Federal Reserve Bank of Dallas, August 1977.

17. Talley, Samuel H. "Developments in the Bank Holding Company Movement." *Proceedings of a Conference on Bank Structure and Competition,* Federal Reserve Bank of Chicago, 1972.

Index

*This book has been set VIP in 10 and 9 point
Aster, leaded 2 points. Section numbers are 18
point Palatino bold and 60 point Bodoni; chapter numbers are 42 point Weiss Series I. Section
titles are 20 point Palatino bold; chapter titles
are 18 point Palatino. The size of the type page is
27 × 45½ picas.*